VIETNAM
THE NECESSARY WAR

A Reinterpretation of America's Most
Disastrous Military Conflict

MICHAEL LIND

The Free Press

THE FREE PRESS
A Division of Simon & Schuster Inc.
1230 Avenue of the Americas
New York, NY 10020

Designed by Brady P. McNamara

Manufactured in the United States of America

10 9 8 7 6 5 4 3 2 1

Library of Congress Cataloging-in-Publication Data

Lind, Michael, 1962–
Vietnam, the necessary war : a reinterpretation of America's
most disastrous military conflict / Michael Lind.
p.   cm.
Includes bibliographical references and index.
ISBN 0-684-84254-8
1. Vietnamese Conflict, 1961–1975—United States.   2. United States—
Foreign relations—1963–1969.   3. United States—Foreign
relations—1969–1974.   I. Title.
DS558.L565   1999
959.704'3373—dc21   99-28449
                                                                 CIP

Lines from a 1953 poem on the death of Stalin by To Huu quoted with permission from Bui
Tin, *Following Ho Chi Minh: The Memoirs of a North Vietnamese Colonel*, trans. Judy Stowe and
Do Van (Honolulu: University of Hawaii Press, 1995), p. 18. The excerpts from Nguyen Chi
Thien, *Flowers from Hell*, Huynh Sanh Thong, trans. (New Haven: Yale Center for
International and Area Studies, 1985) are reprinted with permission
of the author and the publisher.

No, Americans don't know how to fight. After the Korean War, in particular, they have lost the capability to wage a large-scale war. They are pinning their hopes on the atom bomb and air power. But one cannot win a war with that. One needs infantry, and they don't have much infantry; the infantry they do have is weak. They are fighting little Korea, and already people are weeping in the USA. What will happen if they start a large scale war? Then, perhaps, everyone will weep.

—JOSEPH STALIN TO ZHOU ENLAI, AUGUST 20, 1952

The U.S. has a population of 200 million people, but it cannot stand wars.

—MAO ZEDONG TO PHAM VAN DONG, NOVEMBER 17, 1968

Contents

Preface

Having sought to avoid this outcome, the United States found itself at war.

The place was an impoverished peninsula near a major industrial region, to which the United States was committed by a long-standing military alliance. The enemy was a communist dictator who skillfully manipulated the nationalism of his people in an attempt to unite all members of his ethnic group into a single enlarged state under communist-nationalist rule. The dictator's regime, ignoring an ultimatum by the United States and its allies, persisted in sponsoring a low-intensity war against the inhabitants of a neighboring territory that the communist-nationalists sought to bring under their control.

The terrain, wooded and mountainous, favored the communist-nationalists. Throughout history, the region had been invaded many times, by external powers that had often come to grief. The president of the United States and his advisers, stunned by the number of troops that Pentagon estimates called for, repeatedly shelved plans for sending in ground forces.

Nevertheless, the administration believed that something had to be done. If the United States allowed itself to be humiliated by the communist-nationalist regime, then its military credibility would be seriously undermined. The regional alliance that the United States led might dissolve as the area's countries lost faith in American protection. Across the world, both enemies and allies might interpret American retreat as a sign of military incapacity or lack of political resolve. The reputation of the United States for power and determination, the basis of its rank in the regional and global hierarchy, was at stake.

Reluctantly the president ordered the bombing of the communist-nationalist dictator's homeland, hoping that air power alone would compel the dictator to abandon his campaign of aggression. Although a majority of Americans initially supported the bombing, the president's critics accused him of waging war in violation of the Constitution. A number of leading radical leftist intellectuals and journalists denounced the bombing as an act of immoral American imperialism. "Realists" in the press and academy, dismissing the importance of U.S. military credibility as a factor in world politics, claimed that no vital American interest was at stake in this poor and peripheral region of the world. Some conservatives denounced the limitations on the military effort as proof of the folly of trying to wage a "liberal war."

When bombing initially failed to change the enemy's policy, the pressures on the president to commit ground troops increased. The president, a politician more interested in the mechanics of domestic reform than in foreign policy, pondered his options. To back off at this point would result in devastating humiliation for the United States, with consequences around the world that could not be foreseen but which might well be severe. To escalate the war by introducing ground troops would be to risk a bloody debacle and a political backlash. Every choice presented the possibility of disaster.

THIS IS A description of the situation that confronted President Bill Clinton in the spring of 1999, after the United States and its NATO allies began bombing Serbia with the goal of forcing Yugoslav dictator Slobodan Milosevic to agree to autonomy for the Albanian ethnic majority in the Yugoslav province of Kosovo. It is also a description of the dilemma of President Lyndon Johnson in the spring and summer of 1965, when the failure of U.S. bombing raids against North Vietnam to dissuade Ho Chi Minh's communist dictatorship from its low-level war against South Vietnam had become apparent. In each case, what was at stake for the United States was its credibility as the dominant global military power and the survival of a regional alliance—NATO in the case of the Balkan war, the Southeast Asia Treaty Organization (SEATO) in the case of the conflict in Indochina. (In fact, SEATO *did* dissolve, when the United States abandoned Indochina to communist conquest between 1973 and 1975.)

Both Slobodan Milosevic and Ho Chi Minh were communist dictators who manipulated the nationalism of their subjects—Milosevic in the service of his dream of a Greater Serbia dominating the former Yugoslav federation, Ho in the service of the dream of a united Vietnam dominating all of Indochina. Both Milosevic and Ho promoted their goals by supporting guerrilla terror campaigns in other countries. Milosevic armed, supplied, and directed Serb paramilitary units engaged in mass murder and ethnic cleansing in Bosnia, Kosovo, and other parts of the former Yugoslavia; Ho armed, supplied, and directed Viet Cong guerrillas in South Vietnam, Laos, and Cambodia who waged war against South Vietnamese military and police forces and murdered tens of thousands of South Vietnamese officials and civilians. In both cases, the low-intensity wars launched by the communist-nationalist dictators produced tidal waves of refugees. Hundreds of thousands of non-Serbs were forced from their homes in different parts of the former Yugoslavia by Serbian ethnic cleansing. Nearly a million residents of North Vietnam fled Ho Chi Minh's rule in the 1950s, and following the communist conquest of South Vietnam in the 1970s more than two million others risked their lives in fleeing the country. Of the two communist-nationalist leaders, Milosevic was the less tyrannical; his Serbian regime was far less repressive than the government of Ho Chi Minh. The latter was a strict Stalinist dictatorship that tolerated no political or intellectual dissent and executed more than ten thousand North Vietnamese villagers in cold blood in a few months because they were landlords or prosperous peasants and thus "class enemies," according to Marxist-Leninist dogma.

Despite these similarities, the U.S. wars in the Balkan and Indochinese peninsulas differed in one fundamental respect. The Yugoslav War was not a proxy war among great powers. Although Russia protested the NATO war against the Serbs and supplied some limited assistance to the Milosevic regime, postcommunist Russia, truncated, impoverished, and weak in the aftermath of the Soviet collapse, did not commit itself to defeating American policy in the Balkans. The situation was radically different in the 1960s. The Vietnam War was a proxy war between the United States, the Soviet Union—then growing rapidly in military power, confidence, and prestige—and communist China. Despite their rivalry for leadership of the communist bloc of nations, the Soviets and the Chinese collaborated to support North Vietnam's effort to destroy South Vietnam, to promote communist revolutions in Indochina and, if possible, Thailand, and to humiliate the United States. In the 1990s, Serbia was a third-rate military power lacking great-power patrons. In the 1960s,

North Vietnam was protected from an American invasion, and equipped with state-of-the-art weapons and air defenses, by the Soviet Union and China, the latter of which sent hundreds of thousands of troops to support Ho Chi Minh's war effort between 1965 and 1968. By the late 1970s, the Vietnamese communists, after annexing South Vietnam, occupying Cambodia, and breaking with and defeating China in a border war, possessed the third largest army in the world and ruled the most important satellite region of the Soviet empire outside Eastern Europe. At the time of the Vietnam War, the United States was engaged in a desperate worldwide struggle with two of the three most powerful and murderous totalitarian states in history; in 1999, the United States faced no significant challenge to its global primacy by another great power or coalition.

The American wars in defense of Kosovo and South Vietnam, then, differed chiefly in this respect: More—far more—was at stake in Vietnam.

As A RESULT of the U.S. intervention in the Balkans, the assumption that America's intervention in Vietnam was an aberration, an assumption shared by many critics across the political spectrum, is no longer plausible. Twice in thirty-five years, American armed forces have engaged in massive military intervention in a civil war in a peripheral region in order to demonstrate the credibility of the United States as a military power and an alliance leader. When the Korean War is taken into account, the Vietnam War looks less like an exception and more like one member of a series of similar American limited wars (as of 1999, the Gulf War looks like the exception to the norm established by the Korean, Vietnam, and Yugoslav wars). Whether or not the American intervention in Kosovo ultimately achieves its goals, one thing is certain—the debate about the Vietnam War in the United States will never again be the same.

After the Vietnam War ended in 1975, it took on a second life as a symbol in American politics. For the radical left, the war was a symbol of the depravity of the United States and the evils of "capitalist imperialism." For the neoisolationists and "realists" of the liberal left, the U.S. war in Indochina was a tragic and unnecessary mistake, brought about by American arrogance and an exaggerated fear of the threat posed to U.S. interests by the Soviet Union and communist China. Conservatives, too, had their orthodox view of the conflict. Conservatives joined many military officers in arguing that the United States could have achieved a quick and decisive victory in Indochina, if only the pusillanimous civilian policymakers of the Kennedy and Johnson administrations had not "tied the hands" of the U.S. military and "denied it permission to win."

One point of view has been missing from the debate over the Vietnam War. The political faction known as liberal anticommunists or Cold War liberals, identified with the Truman, Kennedy, and Johnson administrations, ceased to exist as a force in American politics in the 1970s, more as a result of partisan realignment than of the Vietnam War. One group of former Cold War liberal policymakers and thinkers sought to ingratiate themselves with the antiwar leftists and liberals who were ascendant in the Democratic party after 1968. Among these were the late McGeorge Bundy and his brother William (who, as part of his campaign to rehabilitate himself, recently wrote a harsh and unfair book criticizing Nixon's and Kissinger's handling of the war that the Bundys had helped to begin). Former defense secretary Robert McNamara not only recanted his support for the war in his book *In Retrospect* but endured the abuse of functionaries of the Vietnamese dictatorship during a humiliating pilgrimage to Vietnam in 1997. Another group of former Cold War liberals joined forces with anti-Soviet conservatives, maintaining their support for the Cold War while jettisoning their prolabor liberalism in domestic politics. The number of unreconstructed Cold War liberals thus dwindled in the 1970s and 1980s, making it easy for radical leftists, left-liberals, and conservatives, in their discussions of the Vietnam War and U.S. foreign policy in the 1960s, to caricature and vilify Presidents Kennedy and Johnson and their advisers with no fear of rebuttal.

Almost everything written by Americans about the Vietnam War in the past quarter century has conformed to one of the three scripts of radical leftism, anti–Cold War liberalism, or conservatism. Each of these three partisan schools has drawn attention to evidence that appeared to support its preconceptions, while ignoring evidence that contradicted them. These ritualized debates might have continued for another generation or two. But two historic developments have now made it possible to transcend the thirty-year-old debates about the Vietnam War.

The first development is the end of the Cold War and its aftermath, including the global collapse of communism and the realignment of world politics around the United States as the hegemonic military power. Only now is it possible to view the Cold War as a whole and to evaluate the U.S. strategy of global containment that led to the U.S.

wars in defense of South Korea and South Vietnam, as well as the U.S. protectorate over Taiwan—"the three fronts," according to Mao Zedong, where the communist bloc met the American bloc in East Asia.

The second development is the demise of the radical left in North America and Western Europe as a political force (leftism survives only in pockets in the academy and the press). In the 1960s and 1970s, the ascendancy of the radical left in the liberal and social democratic parties of the West—the Democrats in the United States, the British Labor Party, and the German Social Democrats—caused western electorates to turn to conservative, anticommunist parties under the leadership of Ronald Reagan, Margaret Thatcher, and Helmut Kohl. The economic difficulties of Swedish social democracy, coming soon after the collapse of the Soviet Union, have discredited western as well as eastern Marxism and permitted the emergence of a new, more moderate center-left, variously described as "the Third Way" or "the New Center" and symbolized by President Bill Clinton and British prime minister Tony Blair. As recently as the Gulf War, which the overwhelming majority of Democrats in Congress voted against, foreign policy debates in the United States pitted anti-American leftists and isolationist liberals against interventionist conservatives. But the subsequent U.S.-led NATO war in the Balkans, supported by many liberals and opposed by a number of conservatives, has helped to rehabilitate the legitimacy of military intervention for many left-of-center Americans.

These developments in global politics and western politics have made it possible to write this book, which could not have been written in the 1970s or 1980s. In this book, I examine the Vietnam War in light of the end of the Cold War, from a centrist perspective more sympathetic to American Cold War policymakers than that of their critics on the left and the right.

THE UNITED STATES fought the war in Vietnam because of geopolitics, and forfeited the war because of domestic politics. This being the case, I make two major arguments in this book, one about the geopolitics, and one about the American domestic politics, of the Cold War. The argument about geopolitics is that in the circumstances of the Cold War, and particularly in the circumstances of the 1960s, the United States was justified in waging a limited war to defend South Vietnam and its neighbors against the communist bloc. The argument about U.S. domestic politics is that the Vietnam War was not uniquely divisive. Rather, this particular Cold War proxy conflict exposed preexisting regional, ethnic, and racial divisions in American attitudes about foreign policy—divisions familiar from previous American wars in the nineteenth and twentieth centuries.

The two subjects of geopolitics and domestic politics are connected by the issue of the costs, in treasure and blood, of American Cold War policy. In both the Korean and Vietnam wars, the balance of power between interventionists and isolationists in the U.S. Congress and the public at large was held by a "swing vote" sensitive to casualties. In the 1960s and 1970s, the United States could not afford to do too little in Indochina, for fear of a disastrous setback in the Cold War—a struggle that was as much a test of nerve as a test of strength. At the same time, the United States could not afford to do too much in Indochina, for fear of undermining American public support, first for the defense of the Indochina front, and then for U.S. Cold War strategy in general. The choice between global credibility and domestic consensus was forced on American leaders in the late 1960s and early 1970s by the costs of the war in Vietnam—chiefly, the costs in American lives, though the costs in Indochinese lives and the costs to America's global military infrastructure and its financial hegemony were also important factors.

This, then, is the story I have to tell about the Vietnam War. It was necessary for the United States to escalate the war in the mid-1960s in order to defend the credibility of the United States as a superpower, but it was necessary for the United States to forfeit the war after 1968, in order to preserve the American domestic political consensus in favor of the Cold War on other fronts. Indochina was worth a war, but only a limited war—and not the limited war that the United States actually fought.

The argument set forth here differs fundamentally from a new and misguided consensus on the subject of the Vietnam War that has become influential in recent years. That argument holds that it was a mistake to intervene in Indochina at all, but that once the United States had intervened, it should have used unlimited force to quickly win an unqualified victory. The political appeal of this emerging consensus is obvious. While it offers nothing to the radical left, it makes concessions to "realist" left-liberals (who are acknowledged to have been right about U.S. strategy) and to promilitary conservatives (who are acknowledged to have been right about U.S. tactics). As a rhetorical formula that can "heal the wounds of Vietnam," this emergent synthesis has much to recommend it. Unfortunately, as an assessment of the Vietnam War it is wrong, and to the extent that it influences U.S. foreign policy it is dangerous.

In ADDITION to examining the Vietnam War from a post–Cold War perspective, one of the purposes of this book is to set the historical record straight. I address the major myths about Vietnam disseminated by the radical and liberal left at the time of the war and repeated for three decades afterward. When one examines the historical record, one finds that:

- Ho Chi Minh was not a Vietnamese patriot whose Marxism was a superficial veneer; like North Korea's Kim Il Sung and Cambodia's Pol Pot, Ho was both a nationalist and a doctrinaire Marxist-Leninist whose brutal and bankrupt tyranny was modeled on Stalin's Soviet Union and Mao's China.

- Ho was not the only legitimate nationalist leader in Vietnam; he and his subordinates found it necessary to execute, assassinate, imprison, and exile noncommunist nationalist leaders and dissidents in both North and South Vietnam.

- Ho was not a Southeast Asian Tito who might have created a neutral united Vietnam equidistant from Moscow, Beijing, and the United States in the 1940s or 1950s; there were pro-Soviet and pro-Chinese factions among the Vietnamese, but no prowestern faction. The United States did not miss an opportunity to befriend Ho in 1945 or 1950 or 1954 or 1956.

- South Vietnam did not violate international law by refusing to participate in national elections in 1956.

- The murder of South Vietnam's President Diem in the American-approved coup d'état in 1963 did not abort a potential reconciliation of North and South Vietnam.

- The South Vietnamese insurgency was not a spontaneous rebellion against misgovernment; although many noncommunist South Vietnamese took part, the guerrilla war was controlled by Hanoi from the beginning to the end.

- The Vietnamese communists were never serious about a coalition government for either South Vietnam or the country as a whole, except as a transition to communist rule; talk of a coalition government was a propaganda ploy intended to fool western liberals and leftists. (It did.)

- The South Vietnamese regime did not fall in 1975 because it was uniquely corrupt and illegitimate. It fell to Soviet-equipped North Vietnamese tanks only because the United States, which had left troops in South Korea to defend a comparably corrupt and authoritarian dictatorship, had abandoned its allies in South Vietnam.

To a remarkable extent, anti–Vietnam War activists recycled both Marxist and isolationist propaganda from previous American antiwar movements. For example, much of the anti-Diem and pro–Ho Chi Minh propaganda echoed the left's vilification of China's Chiang Kai-shek and South Korea's Syngman Rhee and its idealization of Mao Zedong; only the names of individuals and countries were changed. Various "missed opportunity" myths about U.S.-Vietnam relations were first spread in the context of relations between the United States and communist China in the 1940s. The influence of the generations-old isolationist tradition in the United States is clear in the arguments that Johnson and Nixon were treacherous tyrants whose foreign wars endangered the U.S. Constitution—arguments almost identical to those made against previous wartime presidents, including Polk, Wilson, Roosevelt, and Truman. The ease with which Francis Ford Coppola could turn Joseph Conrad's *Heart of Darkness*, a parable about European imperialism in Africa, into the movie *Apocalypse Now* illustrates the extent to which much anti–Vietnam War literature and art has been generic antiwar propaganda that could be illustrated by imagery from any war in any country in any period.

In the section of this book dealing with domestic politics, I demonstrate the extraordinary continuities between the anti-Vietnam-War movement and other antiwar movements—both earlier ones, like the movements opposing U.S. intervention in World Wars I and II, and subsequent ones, like the nuclear freeze campaign and the opposition to the Gulf War. Most remarkable of all is the continuity in regional attitudes toward U.S. foreign policy. The Democratic party's abandonment of the Cold War liberalism of Truman, Kennedy, and Johnson for the neoisolationism symbolized by George McGovern and Frank Church can be explained almost entirely in terms of the shift in the party's regional base from the promilitary, interventionist South to Greater New England, the region of the United States associated throughout American history with suspicion of the military and hostility to American wars.

LET THERE BE no doubt: There will be "Vietnams" in America's future, defined either as wars in which the goal of the United States is to prove its military credibility to enemies and allies, rather than to defend U.S. territory, or as wars in which the enemy refuses to use tactics that permit the U.S. military to benefit from its advantage in high-tech conventional warfare. The war in Kosovo fits both of these definitions. Preparing for the credibility wars and the unconventional wars of the twenty-first century will require both leaders and publics in the United States and allied countries to understand what the United States did wrong in Vietnam—and, no less important, to acknowledge what the United States did right.

Acknowledgments

I am grateful to Paul Golob, senior editor at The Free Press, for the skill and patience with which he helped me to present a complex argument. I am also indebted to Adam Bellow, former editorial director of The Free Press, for commissioning this project.

I would like to express my appreciation to Ted Halstead, president of the New America Foundation, and Lewis Lapham, editor of *Harper's Magazine*, for their support during the writing of this book. Thomas S. Langston of Tulane University provided valuable criticism. Finally, I would like to thank my agent, Kristine Dahl of International Creative Management.

CHAPTER I

THE INDOCHINA THEATER

The Cold War in Southeast Asia, 1946–89

In the winter of 1950, Moscow was as cold as hell. On the evening of February 14, 1950, in a banquet hall in the Kremlin, three men whose plans would subject Indochina to a half century of warfare, tyranny, and economic stagnation, and inspire political turmoil in the United States and Europe, stood side by side: Joseph Stalin, Mao Zedong, and Ho Chi Minh.

In the 1960s, when the United States committed its own troops to battle in an effort to prevent clients of the Soviet Union and China from conquering Indochina, many opponents of the American intervention claimed that the North Vietnamese leader Ho Chi Minh's communism was superficial, compared to his nationalism. In reality, there *was* an international communist conspiracy, and Ho Chi Minh was a charter member of it. Beginning in the 1920s, Ho, a founding member of the French Communist party, had been an agent of the Communist International (Comintern), a global network of agents and spies controlled with iron discipline by the Soviet dictatorship. In the 1930s, Ho had lived in the USSR, slavishly approving every twist and turn of Stalin's policy; in the 1940s, he had been a member of the Chinese Communist party, then subordinated to Moscow. Ho Chi Minh owed not merely his prominence but his life to his career in the communist network outside of his homeland. Because he had been out of the country for so many years, he had survived when many other Vietnamese nationalists, noncommunist and communist alike, had been imprisoned or executed by the French or by the Japanese during World War II.

From the 1940s until the 1990s, the regime Ho founded would depend on military and economic support from one or both of the two great powers of the communist bloc. With the blessing of Stalin and the critical aid of Chinese arms and advisers, Ho's Vietminh (Vietnamese nationalist) front would drive the French from Indochina in the mid-1950s; with the help of Chinese logistics troops, Soviet and Chinese antiaircraft personnel, and even Soviet fighter pilots, Ho's North Vietnam would withstand American bombing while guiding insurrection in South Vietnam in the mid-1960s; with Soviet and Chinese aid, Soviet arms and Soviet advisers, Ho's heirs in Hanoi in the mid-1970s would conquer South Vietnam and Laos, invade Cambodia, and convert Indochina into the largest Soviet satellite region in the world outside of Eastern Europe.

Ho Chi Minh owed little to Vietnamese tradition, and almost everything to his foreign models, Lenin, Stalin, and Mao. Like Lenin and Stalin, Nguyen Ai Quoc had renamed himself ("Ho Chi Minh" means the Enlightened One, or the Seeker of Enlightenment). Ho would be the center of a cult of personality, just as Lenin, Stalin, and Mao had been. Lenin had Leningrad, and Stalin had Stalingrad; therefore Saigon, after the communist victory, would become Ho Chi Minh City. Ho's grim tomb in Hanoi would be modeled on Lenin's tomb in Moscow. In death, as in life, Ho Chi Minh would be a minor clone of the major communist tyrants. Even the smallest details of Ho's government would be borrowed from the Soviet Union or from Mao's imitation of Soviet examples. In the 1950s, Mao would copy Stalin's war on the Soviet peasantry, and Ho, with help from Chinese communist advisers dispatched by Mao, would similarly terrorize the North Vietnamese population into submission to the new totalitarian ruling class. In the decade that followed, the North Vietnamese communist oligarchy would persecute and purge North Vietnamese intellectuals, following the example of Mao's purges of Chinese intellectuals, itself modeled on Stalin's campaigns against dissident thinkers. The official culture of North Vietnam, and later of united communist Vietnam, would be a crude copy of the official cultures of the Soviet Union, its satrapies in Eastern Europe, and its Chinese offspring and ultimate rival. The Vietnamese communists would model their "reeducation camps" on communist China's *laogai* and the Soviet gulag. Well into the 1980s, visitors to communist Vietnam would see portraits of Ho's role model and mentor displayed on office walls: "X-talin," as the name is transliterated in Vietnamese. Stalin.

Three men could hardly be more unlike in personality than the conniving Stalin, the impulsive, extroverted Mao, and the quiet, stoic Ho, but all were devout adherents of the political religion of Marxism-Leninism, whose prophet, Lenin, looked down on them from a portrait in the Kremlin banquet hall. It was Lenin's sect of Marx's religion, not the foibles of its individual proponents, that would do the greatest harm to the suffering peoples of the Soviet empire, China, North Korea, and Indochina. It was not Stalin's gangsterism or Mao's egomania but Lenin's doctrines that produced the famines that killed millions in the Soviet Union in the 1930s and even more millions in China during the Great Leap Forward in 1958–62. The campaigns of government terror against the hapless villagers of North Vietnam in the mid-1950s and in Cambodia in the mid-1970s were not the results of Ho's or Pol Pot's personal ambitions or personal cruelty; the public denunciation, imprisonment, torture, and execution of "landlords" and "rich peasants" and "middle peasants" formed an integral part of the demented Marxist-Leninist program for atomizing existing societies in order to create a new socialist man. Stalin claimed to be the true heir of Lenin, and he was. As the historian Martin Malia has observed: "Thus the awful truth of the [Soviet] experiment in the integral Marxist project could be realized only by Leninist means, and the Leninist means could reach their socialist objective only by Stalinist methods."[1]

The greatest atrocities of Mao Zedong and Ho Chi Minh lay in the future, on that evening in the winter of 1950. Ho, after traveling to Beijing, had made a pilgrimage to Moscow to ask for Soviet and Chinese help in his effort to expel the French and subject all of Indochina to totalitarian rule. When Mao had arrived in Moscow two months earlier on December 16, 1949, he had been summoned to the Kremlin for an audience with Stalin. The meeting had been tense; Stalin had feared that Mao might prove to be as disloyal as Yugoslavia's Tito, whom Stalin had recently expelled from the communist camp for failure to follow Moscow's orders. For his part, Mao had wanted to replace the Sino-Soviet treaty of 1945, which Stalin had negotiated with the deposed Nationalist dictator Chiang Kai-shek, with a new treaty more favorable to what was now the world's most populous communist country. When Stalin had asked Mao what he wanted, Mao had answered evasively, saying that he wanted to send for his foreign minister, Zhou Enlai—a hint of his interest in a new treaty. Stalin had pressed Mao to begin the negotiations at once: "If we cannot establish what we must complete, why call for Zhou Enlai?" Mao had answered with an unconvincing rationalization—he, Mao, lacked authority to negotiate, because Stalin, as chairman of the Council of Ministers, was of a higher rank.

Stalin, who preferred to be the manipulator rather than the manipulated, had been offended by Mao's evasiveness. Eventually Zhou Enlai had arrived, and the revised treaty, along with secret protocols, had been signed earlier in the day on February 14. At the banquet in honor of his new Chinese allies, Stalin showed that he had not forgotten the incident of December 16. When Ho Chi Minh, seeking a Soviet-Vietnamese treaty comparable to the Sino-Soviet treaty, gathered up the courage to approach the leader of the communist bloc and to ask for "instructions," Stalin made sure that Mao and his interpreters were near enough to hear his reply. In a Georgian accent tinged with sarcasm, Stalin said to the president of the Democratic Republic of Vietnam, "How can you ask for my instructions? I am the chairman of the Council of Ministers, and you are the chairman of the state. Your rank is higher than mine; I have to ask for *your* instructions."[2]

Ho Chi Minh might have expected any number of responses to his petition for a treaty with the Soviet Union. But he could not have foreseen that his solemn request would give one of his heroes, Stalin, an occasion to mock his other patron, Mao.

The Cold War on the Asian Front

The Cold War was the third world war of the twentieth century. It was a contest for global military and diplomatic primacy between the United States and the Soviet Union, which had emerged as the two strongest military powers after World War II. Because the threat of nuclear escalation prevented all-out conventional war between the two superpowers, the Soviet-American contest was fought in the form of arms races, covert action, ideological campaigns, economic embargoes, and proxy wars in peripheral areas. In three of these—Korea, Indochina, and Afghanistan—one of the two superpowers sent hundreds of thousands of its own troops into battle against clients of the other side.

In the third world war, Indochina was the most fought over territory on earth. The region owed this undesirable honor not to its intrinsic importance but to the fact that in other places where the two superpowers confronted one another they were frozen in a stalemate that could not be broken without the risk of general war. The Soviet Union and the United States fought proxy wars in Indochina because they dared not engage in major tests of strength in Central Europe or Northeast Asia (after 1953) or even the Middle East. Indochina was strategic *because* it was peripheral.

Throughout the Cold War, the bloody military struggles in the Indochina theater were shaped indirectly by the tense but bloodless diplomatic struggles in the European theater. By going to war in Korea and simultaneously extending an American military protectorate over Taiwan and French Indochina, the Truman administration signaled its resolve to defend its European allies. American officials swallowed their misgivings about French colonialism and paid for France's effort in its on-going war in Indochina from 1950 until 1954, in the hope of winning French support for the rearmament of Germany. Khrushchev's humiliation of the United States in the Berlin crisis of 1961 persuaded the Kennedy administration that a show of American resolve on the Indochina front was all the more important. In 1968, concern by members of the U.S. foreign policy elite that further escalation in Indochina would endanger America's other commitments, particularly in the European theater, was one of the factors that led the Johnson administration to begin the process of disengagement from the Vietnam War. The Eastern European revolutions of 1989, which led to the collapse of the Soviet Union itself in 1991, deprived communist Vietnam of its superpower protector and ideological model.

Although Indochina was the site of the greatest number of proxy-war battles, the greatest bloodletting in the Cold War—both in absolute numbers of war-related deaths and in intensity of combat—took place on the Korean peninsula between 1950 and 1953. However, among the regions in which proxy wars were fought, Indochina saw the greatest number of peacetime deaths as a result of state action, during the Khmer Rouge's radical campaign of collectivization in the mid-1970s, which was inspired by the Maoist version of Marxism-Leninism and foreshadowed on a smaller scale by the Chinese-influenced North Vietnamese terror of the mid-1950s.

By the time Stalin met with Mao and Ho in Moscow in 1950, the Cold War had been underway for four years. In 1946, Stalin was tightening his grip on the countries in the Soviet sphere of influence in Eastern Europe. Defeated Germany was divided between Soviet and western zones of occupation that eventually became separate states (Austria, too, was partitioned until the mid-1950s). At the same time, Korea was partitioned between Soviet and American zones. Japan was wholly under U.S. administration.

Although many had expected the emergence of a tripolar world centered on Washington, Moscow, and London, World War II had weakened the British empire fatally. In February 1947, the British informed the Truman administration that the United States would have to assume the burden of supporting pro-Western forces in Turkey and Greece, where Stalin was backing communist insurgents. On March 12, Truman announced what became known as the Truman Doctrine: "the policy of the United States to support free people who are resisting attempted subjugation by armed minorities or by outside pressures." In June, the Marshall Plan for the reconstruction of Europe was announced in a speech at Harvard by Secretary of State George Marshall. Stalin, seeing U.S. economic aid as a threat, prevented the Eastern European nations under Soviet control from accepting the offer. The Truman Doctrine received an answer in September 1947. Andrei Zhdanov, acting as a mouthpiece of Stalin, announced that the world was divided into two camps, socialism and imperialism. Noncommunist nationalist movements in colonial and postcolonial regions, which had been courted as allies by the international communist network in the days of the Popular Front, were now included in the imperialist camp. By contrast, Zhdanov hailed the war of Ho Chi Minh's communist-controlled Vietminh against France in Indochina as an example of "a powerful movement for national liberation in the colonies and dependencies."[3]

Stalin ordered communists in Western Europe to launch a wave of strikes. The United States responded with shipments of economic aid. After Stalin's gambit in Western Europe failed, he orchestrated a coup in Czechoslovakia that replaced the elected government with a communist dictatorship controlled by Moscow. The United States launched a covert program to support pro-American parties in Italy's national elections and considered military intervention if a communist-led coalition won power there. Meanwhile, on the periphery of Europe, American advisers helped a dictatorship in Greece battle a communist insurgency supported by the Soviet bloc in the first major proxy war of the Cold War. The Greek insurgency was defeated, in part because Yugoslavia's communist dictator, Tito, afraid of being purged by Stalin, broke away from the Soviet bloc to assume a position of uneasy neutrality between East and West.

Although the primary theater of the early Cold War was Europe, the United States and the Soviet Union were also drawing battle lines in Asia. In February 1948, at a communist-sponsored conference of radical youth in Calcutta, Chinese and Vietnamese communists called for armed struggle against the West and pro-Western governments. Following the Calcutta meeting, a series of communist-inspired rebellions broke out throughout the region. In March, Burmese communists rose in insurrection against the newly independent government; in June, the Malayan communist party took up arms; and in August, the communist-led Hukbalahap insurgents in the Philippines renewed their war against the pro-American Philippine government. In September 1948, Indonesian communists clashed with the Indonesian authorities, following the return from exile in the Soviet Union of Indonesian communist leader Musso, who had announced that his movement would follow the "Gottwald Plan" (a reference to the communist seizure of power in the recent Czechoslovakian coup). The Indonesian communist revolt was put down within a month, but the Burmese, Malayan, and Philippine insurgencies burned on for years.[4]

In Indochina, Ho Chi Minh's Vietminh—a communist-controlled front of nationalist parties—had seized power in August 1945, when the Japanese occupation of French Indochina had come to an end with the Second World War. To conceal his actual purposes, Ho pretended to disband the Indochinese communist party. In the summer of 1946, while Ho traveled to Paris in the hope of persuading the French to peacefully cede power to his regime, his chief deputy, Vo Nguyen Giap, supervised the systematic destruction of all political opposition by imprisoning, exiling, or murdering tens of thousands of noncommunist Vietnamese nationalists and leftists. Following the failure of Ho's negotiations with France, hostilities began at the end of 1946. France dispatched troops in an effort to reimpose French authority over Indochina. Squeezed between French forces and the nationalist China of Chiang Kai-shek (who was by no means hostile to the effort to expel the French from the region), the Vietnamese communists managed to survive until Mao's Communist party, with critical military aid and logistical support provided by the Soviet Union and North Korea, won the

Chinese civil war in 1949. In early 1950, Ho traveled to Moscow to join Mao and Stalin.

"In the Far East," former Red Army journalists General Oleg Sarin and Colonel Lev Dvoretsky have written,

> China, North Korea, and North Vietnam became Stalin's firm allies. In the latter two, Kim Il Sung and Ho Chi Minh were dictators with immense power who strictly toed the Kremlin's line and who in turn were heavily supported with Soviet arms, goods, and services. Stalin gave them both a great deal of thought and attention, constantly mulling over plans for unifying these two countries under the red banner and thus creating new opportunities for spreading Soviet Communism further into Asia. Stalin was in an excellent position to fulfill the rest of his dreams.[5]

Stalin, who may have hoped that a coalition containing communists would come to power in Paris, was careful to keep the appearance of distance between his regime's and Ho's. He instructed Mao to assume responsibility for aiding the Indochinese comrades. The Chinese communist leadership viewed Indochina as one of "three fronts" contested with the American-led "imperialist" bloc; the other two fronts were Korea and Taiwan, where Chiang Kai-shek's Nationalist regime, defeated on the mainland, still survived. Mao, expecting a conflict with the United States over Taiwan, was informed in the spring of 1950 that Stalin had given his North Korean client, Kim Il Sung, permission to reunify the divided Korean peninsula by force, following the failure of an attempt to do so by means of a guerrilla war that had cost around one hundred thousand Korean lives.

With the backing of Stalin and Mao, Kim launched an invasion of South Korea on June 24, 1950. Viewing the crisis as a test of American credibility in the Cold War, the United States, along with Britain and dozens of allies, dispatched troops under the cover of the United Nations to rescue the South Korean regime of Syngman Rhee. With a daring amphibious landing at Inchon in September, General Douglas MacArthur reversed the current of the war in America's favor. Within weeks the Korean communists were being pushed back toward the Chinese frontier on the Yalu River. At Stalin's urging, and against the advice of much of the Chinese communist military leadership, Mao committed China to the war. Chinese forces crossed the Yalu in large numbers in

November. Soviet military personnel were also taking a limited part in the air war, a fact which the U.S. government kept secret as part of its strategy for keeping the proxy war in Korea limited.

The effect of the Korean War was to solidify the U.S. commitment to denying Taiwan and Indochina, the other two fronts in East Asia, to the Sino-Soviet bloc. Truman sent the Seventh Fleet to control the Taiwan Strait, and dispatched a military mission to help the French in Indochina. By 1954 the U.S. was paying for most of the cost of the French effort to defeat Ho Chi Minh. China, too, considered the wars in Korea and Indochina to be part of a single East-West struggle. General Chen Geng, a leading Chinese military officer, helped organize the Vietminh war against the French before leaving in November 1950 to take up a command in Korea.[6]

The Korean War, like the later Vietnam War, caused political turmoil in the United States. During the Korean War, however, the radical opposition to the government came from the right. President Truman, accused by demagogic red-baiters like Wisconsin senator Joseph McCarthy of coddling communist traitors in the government, and vilified for his dismissal of General MacArthur for insubordination, chose not to run again for president. Dwight Eisenhower, elected president in 1952, threatened to use nuclear weapons against North Korea and China. These threats, combined with the death of Stalin on March 4, 1953, were followed by an armistice in Korea in July of that year.

In Indochina, meanwhile, the war was going badly for the French and their American sponsors. The Sino-Soviet bloc used the Korean armistice as an opportunity to launch a worldwide "peace offensive," as part of which Stalin's successors in the Kremlin proposed a five-power conference to discuss international disputes. In order to strengthen its negotiating position, the Vietminh, with Chinese arms and advice, began a siege of French troops at the strategically important village of Dien Bien Phu. Alarmed by the prospect of the fall of the French outpost, U.S. Secretary of State John Foster Dulles threatened American intervention and called for "united action" by the western democracies. The U.S. Congress, however, was unwilling to support an American war in Indochina so soon after the loss of 56,000 American soldiers in Korea. The Vietminh took Dien Bien Phu on May 7, 1954, the day before the discussion of Indochina at Geneva was scheduled to begin.

The United States, determined to deny Indochina to Ho's Soviet-

and Chinese-backed communists, received little support from France, whose government was eager to achieve a face-saving exit from the region. Britain, which had its own client-states in the region, such as Malaya (itself facing a communist insurgency), played the role of mediator between the United States and the Soviet Union. Under pressure from the Soviet Union and China, which wanted a breathing spell after the Korean proxy war, the reluctant Vietnamese communists were compelled to accept the division of French Indochina into three states—Vietnam, Laos and Cambodia—and the partition of Vietnam at the Seventeenth Parallel between communist and noncommunist zones. The Geneva accords provided for nationwide elections, but because the accords were denounced by the South Vietnamese government and not signed by the United States this provision was a dead letter from the beginning. During a period of voluntary repatriation under international auspices in 1954–55, ten times as many Vietnamese, many of them Catholics afraid of communist persecution, fled from North to South Vietnam as moved in the other direction.

Between Two Wars

By the mid-1950s, the correlation of forces in world politics had shifted in favor of the United States, thanks to the rapid buildup of the U.S. military during the Korean War and the economic reconstruction of western Europe and Japan. The communist insurgencies in Burma, the Philippines, and Malaya had been defeated or were in decline.

In North Vietnam, Ho Chi Minh's regime followed the advice of Mao's government and concentrated on consolidating its rule rather than on sponsoring revolution in South Vietnam. China showered North Vietnam with military aid, which between 1956 and 1963 amounted to 270,000 guns, 200 million bullets, more than 10,000 pieces of artillery along with more than 2 million artillery shells, 15,000 wire transmitters, 28 ships, 15 planes, and more than 1,000 trucks.[7] The Chinese communist military advisers who had helped their Vietnamese allies defeat the French were now replaced by Chinese communist political advisers who guided a Vietnamese collectivization campaign modeled on the previous "land reforms" in China and the Soviet Union. At least ten thousand rural Vietnamese were singled out for denunciation as class enemies and executed after rigged trials organized by Vietnamese communists with the help of Chinese communist advisers. When North Vietnamese peasants finally rebelled against this state terrorism, Ho Chi Minh used his military to crush them. The Maoist rural terror in North Vietnam was followed in due course by a purge of North Vietnamese intellectuals modeled on an earlier purge in communist China.

While Ho was terrorizing the North Vietnamese population into docility, Ngo Dinh Diem was using force and fraud to cobble together a state in the southern half of Vietnam. Diem was a respected upper-class nationalist who had been untainted by collaboration with the French colonialists or the Japanese occupiers of his homeland. Ho had asked Diem to serve in the initial Vietminh coalition government, but after Diem refused to be a token figure in a communist-dominated regime, Ho's government had executed one of Diem's brothers. Diem ousted the French-installed Emperor Bao Dai and made himself president of the government of Vietnam in a rigged plebiscite. In consolidating his dictatorship, Diem had the help of American advisers, including Colonel Edward G. Lansdale and Major Lucien Conein, both celebrated American covert action experts. In the latter half of the 1950s, Diem waged a savage war on the remnants of the communist-dominated Vietminh in the south and also on the Cao Dai, Hoa Hoa, and Binh Xuyen, paramilitary religious "sects" that resembled mafias. Like many Third World rulers, Diem solidified his power by nepotism, favoritism for his Catholic coreligionists, bribery, and a brutality which alienated many South Vietnamese, although it was less severe than the Stalinist reign of terror in North Vietnam.

BY THE LATE 1950s, the initiative in global politics was passing from the United States to the Soviet Union. President Eisenhower failed to devise a plausible military strategy for waging the Cold War. His policy of "massive retaliation" was dismissed as a bluff by Mao and other communist bloc leaders, even before the buildup of the Soviet nuclear arsenal had created a balance of terror between the blocs. Eisenhower also relied ever more on covert action as an instrument of U.S. foreign policy. By the time he left office, a consensus had emerged among national security intellectuals and military dissidents that the conditions of the Cold War required "flexible response," an ability to use American military force effectively in the spectrum of conflict between threats of nuclear war and covert action.

While the United States drifted under Eisenhower, the rise to power of Nikita Khrushchev provided the Soviet empire with a dynamic and flamboyant leader. In 1956, Khrushchev took advantage of the abortive British, French, and Israeli seizure of the Suez Canal from Egypt to invade Hungary; the launching of Sputnik in the same year began the space race and gave the world the impression that the Soviet Union was a dynamic technological power. The dissolution of the European empires in Asia, Africa, and the Middle East created dozens of new, unstable states for whose allegiance the United States and the Soviet Union competed. In this competition, the antiracist rhetoric of the Soviet Union, and the absence of a history of Russian colonialism outside of Eurasia, gave Moscow an advantage at a time when white resistance to the civil rights movement showed the world the evil side of American society.

In Southeast Asia, conflict between the two blocs heated up again at the end of the 1950s. In Laos, an undeclared proxy war was fought by royalist forces backed by the United States and the communist Pathet Lao, supported by the North Vietnamese military, with Soviet and Chinese encouragement. Meanwhile, Hanoi authorized a South Vietnamese communist insurgency against Diem's regime. In May 1959, Hanoi formed Group 559, charged with infiltrating troops and weapons into South Vietnam through the Ho Chi Minh Trail in Laos and Cambodia, and Group 759, in charge of infiltration by sea. (Similar infiltration of South Korea was repeatedly attempted, without significant success, by the North Korean regime.) Between 1959 and 1961 the number of South Vietnamese officials who were assassinated rose from twelve hundred to four thousand per year. As the South Vietnamese insurgency grew more powerful, the United States equipped Diem's military and provided several hundred advisers, who trained the South Vietnamese military in often inapplicable conventional war tactics. In a July 8, 1959, guerrilla raid on a South Vietnamese army headquarters in Bien-hoa near Saigon, along with several Vietnamese the first American soldiers to die in Indochina were killed.

On January 6, 1961, two weeks before John F. Kennedy's inauguration as president of the United States, Khrushchev published a speech calling for Soviet support for "wars of national liberation" as an alternative to world-threatening nuclear war. Kennedy gave his aides copies of the speech, exhorting them to "read, learn, and inwardly digest." Kennedy was warned by Eisenhower that the low-level proxy war in Laos between factions backed by the United States and their rivals, dependent on the North Vietnamese, was approaching a crisis point. On March 9, Kennedy reviewed detailed plans for the introduction of U.S. forces into Laos.

The world's attention was diverted from Indochina to the Caribbean on April 12, 1961, when American-backed Cuban exiles invaded Cuba at the Bay of Pigs. The invasion, designed during the Eisenhower administration and approved by Kennedy, failed to provoke a popular uprising against the pro-Soviet dictator Fidel Castro. In the summer of 1961, Kennedy and Khrushchev engaged in a confrontation over Berlin. By acquiescing in the construction of the Berlin Wall, whose purpose was to prevent the citizens of communist East Germany from fleeing to the West, the United States suffered a humiliating defeat.

In the aftermath of the humiliations in Cuba and Germany, the Kennedy administration felt compelled to demonstrate U.S. resolve in the Indochina theater of the Cold War. In the fall of 1961, Kennedy rejected the advice of the U.S. military that any American intervention would have to be massive, and settled for the "neutralization" of Laos in negotiations at Geneva—a compromise that failed to end the proxy war. This latest retreat by the Kennedy administration made it all the more necessary to defend South Vietnam.

Alarmed by a report about the South Vietnamese situation by Edward Lansdale, in May 1961 Kennedy sent Vice President Lyndon Johnson on a fact-finding mission to South Vietnam. Diem rejected the offer of U.S. troops, asking instead for U.S. funds for an expansion of his military and for additional U.S. advisers. In October 1961, General Maxwell Taylor, chairman of the Joint Chiefs of Staff, visited South Vietnam and suggested that the United States send troops. Kennedy rejected Taylor's advice, but established the Military Assistance Command, Vietnam (MACV) and drastically increased the number of U.S. military advisers in South Vietnam.

Within the communist bloc, the growing rift between Khrushchev's Soviet Union and Mao's China was creating a new hazard for the United States and its allies. The two communist giants competed to demonstrate their leadership of worldwide antiwesternism by striving to outdo one another in support of North Vietnam. Denouncing those who advised caution in confronting the United States as "revisionist," Mao sent high-ranking emissaries to Hanoi in spring 1962 to discuss Sino-Vietnamese cooperation in the event of a war with the United States.[8]

At the same time, the Hanoi-controlled Viet Cong guerrillas in South Vietnam continued to make progress, appealing to popular discontent while assassinating enormous numbers of government officials and supporters of the regime. The Diem government's pacification program backfired, when the uprooting of as much as a quarter of the rural population created new hatred of the regime. On February 22, 1962, two South Vietnamese pilots attempted to assassinate Diem by bombing the presidential palace. Shortly afterward the limited military competence of the Diem regime was exposed in a botched raid by South Vietnamese troops and their American advisers against Viet Cong in the village of Ap Bac.

On May 8, 1962, in the city of Hue, several people were killed when a Catholic deputy province chief sent troops to prevent Buddhists from flying their flags in commemoration of the Buddha's birthday. On June 11, Buddhists arranged in advance for the western media to cover the self-immolation of a Buddhist monk. The horrific photos contributed to the demonization of Diem in the United States. (Needless to say, western journalists were not present to record protests and the far more severe government repression in North Vietnam.)

In the summer of 1962, Ho Chi Minh led a delegation to Beijing, and succeeded in winning a Chinese offer to equip 230 new North Vietnamese battalions. The following spring Chinese delegations to Hanoi promised that China would come to the aid of North Vietnam if the United States attacked and assured the North Vietnamese rulers that they could "definitely count on China as the strategic rear."[9]

In Washington, the Kennedy administration was divided between those who urged cooperation with South Vietnamese generals plotting to depose President Diem, whose unpopularity and incompetence was hampering the war against the communist insurgency, and others opposed to such a move. Following the triumph of the pro-coup faction in Washington, on November 1, 1963, Diem was deposed by mutinous generals, who then murdered him and his brother Ngo Dinh Nhu after offering them safe conduct out of the country. The assassinations in Saigon were followed in a few weeks by the murder of President Kennedy in Dallas, Texas, by Lee Harvey Oswald, a former defector to the Soviet Union who idolized Castro. At the time of Kennedy's death, the United States was spending $500 million per year on South Vietnam; there were fifteen thousand American advisers in the country, and fifty American soldiers had been killed.

Kennedy's successor, Lyndon Johnson, had opposed the overthrow of Diem. He was vindicated in the aftermath of the South Vietnamese coup, when a series of ephemeral governments formed and dissolved as South Vietnamese military officers competed for power. The political chaos gave the Hanoi-controlled insurgents the opportunity to make major gains. Before the coup against Diem, the Viet Cong had controlled less than 30 percent of the territory of South Vietnam; by March 1964, they controlled between 40 and 45 percent.[10]

The desperate situation in South Vietnam was matched by turmoil throughout Southeast Asia. Beginning in 1962, the Indonesian dictator Sukarno had aligned himself with Mao and the Indonesian Communist party, the third largest in the world. Having seized the formerly Dutch western part of New Guinea in 1962, Sukarno initiated a guerrilla war against Malaysia. To help the Malaysians fight Sukarno's forces and their Malaysian allies, the British dispatched elite Special Air Services (SAS) units. Nearby in Cambodia, Prince Norodom Sihanouk, expecting a communist victory in South Vietnam, permitted the Viet Cong and North Vietnamese regulars to use Cambodian territory to infiltrate South Vietnam. In early 1964 Sihanouk secretly agreed to let China use the Cambodian seaport of Sihanoukville to ship military supplies to the Viet Cong. Sihanouk had ordered mob attacks against the United States and British embassies already, and when Thailand's dictator, Marshal Sarit, died shortly after the murders of Diem and Kennedy, Sihanouk made a radio broadcast in which he celebrated the deaths of all three.[11]

In these circumstances, the Johnson administration decided to increase its own secret raids against North Vietnam. Most of the South Vietnamese commandos who were infiltrated into North Vietnam were killed or captured. U.S. and Thai pilots also began bombing North Vietnamese and allied Pathet Lao troops in Laos in Royal Lao Air Force planes. In addition, the United States began maritime intelligence patrols along the North Vietnamese coast. A U.S.-sponsored South Vietnamese raid on two North Vietnamese islands on July 31 was followed by a clash on August 3 in the Gulf of Tonkin between an American naval vessel, the *Madox*, and North Vietnamese torpedo boats. On August 4, radar operators on another ship, the *C. Turner Joy*, claimed to have sighted torpedoes. The Johnson administration, claiming that American ships had been the targets of unprovoked attacks, used the Tonkin Gulf incidents as an occasion for congressional passage of the Southeast Asia

Resolution, a conditional declaration of war modeled on the Formosa and Middle East Resolutions passed during the Eisenhower years. "The challenge that we face in South-East Asia today is the same challenge that we faced with courage and that we have met with strength in Greece and Turkey, in Berlin and Korea, in Lebanon and Cuba," Johnson told the American public in a televised address that put the crisis in Indochina in its Cold War context. On August 7, 1964, the Southeast Asia Resolution was passed in the House by 416-0 and in the Senate by 98-2.

China's response was to denounce the United States, publicly state its support for North Vietnam, and mobilize more than twenty million Chinese in anti-American demonstrations. Beginning in mid-August, the Chinese air force moved units to the Sino-Vietnamese border. China began the construction of two new airports in the border region. China already had promised to send troops if the United States invaded North Vietnam.[12]

As 1965 began, the situation in South Vietnam continued to worsen. On February 7, while National Security Adviser McGeorge Bundy was in Saigon, the Viet Cong killed eight American advisers in an attack on a South Vietnamese army base at Pleiku. In Operation Flaming Dart, forty-nine U.S. navy fighter-bombers attacked a North Vietnamese military installation at Dong Hoi. The Viet Cong responded by killing twenty-three U.S. soldiers when they blew up a hotel in Qui Nhon.

Johnson and his advisers hoped that air strikes against North Vietnam would convince Hanoi to end its support for the South Vietnamese insurgency, so that the deployment of U.S. ground forces would not be necessary. Operation Rolling Thunder, a bombing campaign against the north that began on March 2, 1965, failed to achieve this result. On March 8, two Marine battalions arrived to protect the U.S. base at Da Nang. A few weeks later, Johnson overruled the objections of General Maxwell Taylor, then the U.S. ambassador in Saigon, and sent two more battalions and eighteen thousand logistical troops. U.S. soldiers began to engage in search-and-destroy missions. Meanwhile, in April 1965, Johnson dispatched twenty-eight thousand troops to the Dominican Republic to ensure that a civil war there did not provide the Soviet Union and its satellite Cuba with an opportunity to create a new outpost in the Caribbean.

After a pause on May 13 failed to inspire Hanoi to negotiate, the bombing resumed. Urgent requests by General William Westmoreland in South Vietnam forced the White House to make tough decisions. Undersecretary of State George Ball, who warned of the difficulties of fighting against guerrillas, was a longtime critic of U.S. Cold War commitments throughout Asia. Most of the advisers whom Johnson had inherited from Kennedy, including Bundy and Defense Secretary Robert McNamara, were unwilling to abandon America's Indochinese allies to the communist bloc without a fight.

More than Vietnam was at stake. Much or all of Southeast Asia appeared to be on the verge of incorporation into a radical, antiwestern bloc led by China and Indonesia. With Mao's encouragement, Sukarno, who had adopted the slogan "Crush America," had withdrawn Indonesia from the United Nations and announced the formation of a rival body, the Conference of the New Emerging Forces. Speaking in 1965 of a "Djakarta–Phnom Penh–Hanoi–Peking–P'yongyang axis," Sukarno predicted that China would "strike a blow against the American troops in Vietnam from the north while Indonesia would strike from the south."[13] The prospect of communist takeovers in Indochina that would link Mao's China to a possibly communist Indonesia was regarded with dread by the United States and Britain and by their allies in the region, like Malaysia, Singapore, Thailand, and Australia. Even more important than the possibility of "falling dominoes" was America's credibility as a superpower with worldwide military commitments to weak and endangered allies and client-states. The United States had been humiliated already by the Soviet bloc in Berlin, Cuba, and Laos; yet another retreat threatened both to encourage the Soviet Union and China and to demoralize America's allies. With good reason, Sukarno had declared 1965 to be "the year of living dangerously."

On July 28, after an internal debate about options in the Indochina theater, the Johnson administration announced the dispatch of 125,000 more troops to South Vietnam. In the context of the Cold War struggle for Southeast Asia, the deployment was far from excessive. As late as 1964, Britain, a power of the second rank, had more soldiers east of Suez than in Europe as part of NATO forces. To defend Malaysia against subversion by Indonesia, Britain had dispatched 30,000 troops. In 1964, Britain had 54,000 troops in Southeast Asia—more than the United States had in South Vietnam at the time.[14] Sukarno's border war with Malaysia had led to the deployment of eighty ships from the British Commonwealth.[15]

Escalation

U.S. ground forces began to engage in significant combat with Viet Cong units in the late summer and autumn of 1965. As U.S. troops poured into South Vietnam, the political turmoil in Saigon came to an end. A coup brought to power two military officers, Nguyen Cao Ky and Nguyen Van Thieu, who would rule South Vietnam for the next decade, until its demise.

Beginning on Christmas Day 1965, the Johnson administration suspended the bombing of North Vietnam for thirty-seven days. The United States had already flown fifty-five thousand sorties against targets in North Vietnam. The debate within the administration and the U.S. military over strategy and tactics had been won by those emphasizing a conventional war approach, rather than by advocates of a strategy emphasizing "pacification" or counterinsurgency. The U.S. forces in Indochina were joined by contingents from America's regional allies, including South Korea, Australia, New Zealand, and the Philippines.

In Indonesia, the two-million-member Communist party, evidently with the encouragement of Sukarno and Mao, launched a coup against anticommunist military leaders. A countercoup by the military turned into a massacre in which somewhere between dozens and hundreds of thousands were butchered. Sukarno was stripped of power and replaced by Suharto, a general who ruled Indonesia until 1998. Under Suharto, Indonesia broke its ties with China and assumed a policy of neutrality tilted toward the United States. Mao's dream of a counter-UN and a Beijing-Jakarta axis had been thwarted. Now he turned inward, launching the Cultural Revolution, an extreme Stalin-style purge that reduced China to conditions resembling those of civil war. The year of living dangerously had been an *annus horribilis* for Beijing.

The United States, China, and the Soviet Union were now engaged in the greatest proxy conflict in the Cold War since the Korean War. While the United States fought to prevent being humiliated as a protector of weak states, China and the Soviet Union competed with one another for prestige in the communist bloc and the developing world.

Between 1965 and 1968, China provided massive support for North Vietnam. In addition to supplying Hanoi with military equipment and civilian goods, Mao's government dispatched antiaircraft artillery troops to the northern part of North Vietnam. Even more important, at Hanoi's request China sent engineering troops to repair and expand the North Vietnamese railway system so that it would not be disabled by American bombing. The Chinese troops also freed North Vietnamese regulars to journey into Laos and keep supplies moving down the Ho Chi Minh Trail. Between June 1965 and the end of 1969, the Chinese logistics troops built 20 new railway stations, 39 new bridges, 14 tunnels, and 117 kilometers of new rail lines and repaired 362 kilometers of existing rail lines. In all, China sent 327,000 troops to North Vietnam. As the historian Chen Jian has observed, "although Beijing's support may have fallen short of Hanoi's expectations, without the support, the history, even the outcome, of the Vietnam War might have been different."[16]

In October and November 1966, the number two official in Ho Chi Minh's regime, Le Duan, conferred with Chinese leaders in Beijing. Zhou Enlai urged the Vietnamese to continue the war at least until 1968. Six months later, still worried that North Vietnam would negotiate with the United States, Chinese officials insisted that Vo Nguyen Giap and Pham Van Dong give them a "solemn promise" that they would not end the war.[17]

To continue the war, however, the North Vietnamese needed arms and equipment that China could not supply. Dong and Giap led another delegation to Moscow in April 1967. Despite misgivings, the Soviets chose to resupply the North Vietnamese, for fear that a refusal would lead to an increase in Chinese influence on Hanoi.[18] Indeed, the Soviet Union already had surpassed China as the largest supplier of military aid to North Vietnam. Between 1964 and 1974, aid to North Vietnam amounted to 50 percent of the Soviet Union's aid to communist satellite regimes (the rest was divided chiefly between Cuba and North Korea).[19]

As many as three thousand Soviet advisers took part in the Vietnam War between 1965 and 1968.[20] They instructed North Vietnamese soldiers in the use of Soviet-supplied equipment, manned the ground-based antiaircraft system, and participated in combat actions against the Americans and South Vietnamese.[21] The Soviet government carefully concealed the extent of Soviet involvement in Indochina, forbidding Soviet personnel and their families to discuss the destination of their units. Soldiers heading for Vietnam wore civilian clothes and, on arrival, donned Vietnamese uniforms. (During the Korean War, Soviet pilots and other military "volunteers" had worn Chinese or Korean uniforms.) "The Americans knew only too well that Vietnamese planes of Soviet design were often flown by Soviet pilots," former Soviet colonel Alexei Vinogradov has written.[22] During the Vietnam War, as earlier during the Korean War, the U.S. government kept the degree of Soviet military participation secret in order that public pressure would not make it difficult to keep this proxy war limited.

The war between Israel and its neighbors that erupted on June 5, 1967, increased U.S.-Soviet tensions still further. At a mini summit in Glassboro, New Jersey, on June 23, 1967, Soviet premier Aleksei Kosygin passed along Hanoi's offer to return to the negotiating table if the bombing were stopped (several U.S. diplomatic initiatives, labeled "Mayflower," "Marigold," and "Sunflower" had already failed). Through the Soviets Johnson replied that the United States would consider stopping the bombing, but would resume it if talks failed.

By the autumn of 1967, public support for the Vietnam War in the United States was reaching dangerously low levels. The small antiwar movement, led by radical leftists and pacifists, had failed to convince the American public that the war was immoral; indeed, the anti-American rhetoric of many antiwar activists was creating a backlash from which conservative politicians would profit for decades. Instead, support for the war had declined as a function of rising casualties at roughly the same rate that it had dwindled during the Korean War. Facing declining public support, and challenged by the left wing of the Democratic party, President Johnson in a speech in San Antonio on September 27, 1967, retreated from his earlier insistence that he would stop the bombing only in return for negotiations and from his demand that North Vietnam cease its infiltration of South Vietnam.

But Hanoi already was planning an offensive and uprising in the south. The plan went against China's preference for a long-term, low-level guerrilla war, but the North Vietnamese succeeded in winning supplementary military aid and a declaration of support from Moscow. Historian Ilya V. Gaiduk writes that "for the first time since the start of full-scale Soviet assistance to Hanoi, [a communiqué] even specified what kind of military assistance was being provided. . . . Such an open declaration of all-out support was unprecedented for Moscow in its relations with allies and proxies."[23]

On January 30, 1968, during the lunar new year, Tet, the Viet Cong launched a wave of assaults and raids throughout South Vietnam, attacking the presidential palace and the headquarters of the South Vietnamese general staff in Saigon itself. The U.S. forces and their South Vietnamese allies rallied and decimated the insurgents. In the city of Hue, the communists were defeated only after three weeks of devastating violence. After the fall of Hue, the bodies of almost three thousand South Vietnamese civilians, tortured and executed by the Viet Cong, were found in mass graves.

The failure of the Tet offensive was a devastating military setback for the communists. Nevertheless, the Tet offensive was perceived as a defeat for the United States. One reason was the sensationalism of western journalists, who gave the American public a misleading impression of the power and popularity of the Viet Cong. But a more important reason was the fact that General Westmoreland's optimistic reports from South Vietnam had been discredited. The war was winnable—but it was far from being won at a cost acceptable to the American public.

Forfeiting Indochina

The Tet offensive produced political turmoil in the United States. Senator Eugene McCarthy, a critic of the war, almost defeated President Johnson in a Democratic presidential primary on March 12 in New Hampshire. Also in March 1968, Clark Clifford, long skeptical about the war, replaced Robert McNamara as Secretary of Defense, and General Westmoreland was reassigned as Army chief of staff. On March 31, after being advised by the "Wise Men"—a group of elder statesmen including former Secretary of State Dean Acheson—that the war had to be wound down, Johnson stated that he would not run for reelection and announced a bombing pause. On May 10, peace talks began in Paris. In the fall, American voters—weary of the war, but disgusted with the anti-Americanism of antiwar radicals like those who provoked a police riot at the 1968 Democratic Convention in Chicago—elected Richard Nixon to the presidency. (The Soviet leadership, fearing this outcome, had advised the North Vietnamese that it was in their interest to help Hubert Humphrey's election by making it appear that peace was near.)[24]

On assuming office, Nixon began his arduous search for "peace with honor" in Indochina. His strategy combined military pressure on Hanoi with efforts to encourage Moscow and Beijing to distance themselves from their client.

Two months after entering the White House, Nixon ordered the bombing of communist sanctuaries in Cambodia. Prince Sihanouk approved, on the condition that it be secret and that the populous areas of Cambodia would not be affected. In 1970, Sihanouk was overthrown, and the new, pro-American regime of General Lon Nol ordered the North Vietnamese occupiers to leave the country. Nixon took advantage of this opportunity by ordering a two-month American incursion into Cambodia to search for the headquarters of the communist effort in South Vietnam and to spread the North Vietnamese army thin. The North Vietnamese responded by occupying much of Cambodia and by helping Pol Pot's Khmer Rouge fight the forces of Lon Nol.

Nixon's bombing campaign in Cambodia and South Vietnam covered the withdrawal of U.S. troops and the "Vietnamization" of the war. By the end of 1970, 280,000 U.S. troops had gone; there were only 140,000 left at the end of 1971. Morale declined among U.S. soldiers, none of whom wanted to be the last casualty. At the same time, Vietnamization was proven to be of dubious value in February 1971, when the South Vietnamese army failed in an effort to cut off the Ho Chi Minh Trail in Laos.

Congress, which had hesitated to challenge presidents Johnson and Nixon while troops were in the field, became bolder in legislating restrictions as troop totals diminished. On January 12, 1971, Congress repealed the Southeast Asia Resolution; on the same day President Nixon signed the Cooper-Church Amendment, which banned the use of U.S. ground forces in Cambodia. A growing number of moderate "owls," alarmed by the costs of the Vietnam War both to other U.S. military commitments and to the economy, joined antiwar "doves" in favoring a rapid American extrication from Indochina.

The Nixon administration tried to balance Vietnamization with an attempt to exploit divisions among Hanoi's patrons in Moscow and Beijing. The Soviet invasion of Czechoslovakia in 1968, which had produced hardly any response by the West, was interpreted by Mao as a reassertion of Moscow's authority throughout the communist bloc. In September 1971, following several years of Sino-Soviet war scares, Mao's designated heir, Lin Piao, died in a mysterious jet crash as he attempted to flee to the Soviet Union after allegedly conspiring with the Chinese military to overthrow Mao.

These developments made possible Nixon's dramatic opening to China and trip to Beijing in February 1972. The Sino-American rapprochement, however, did not inspire China to end its support for North

Vietnam. Nixon's courtship of the Soviet leadership also failed to produce results in the Indochina theater. Indeed, in October 1971, the Soviet Union, fearing Sino-American collusion, sent Nikolai Podgorny to Hanoi, where he proposed an alliance of the Soviet Union and North Vietnam against China. In the spring of 1972, Moscow increased its military aid, sending T-54 tanks and long-range artillery among other arms to North Vietnam via the port of Haiphong. A few months later, Soviet arms deliveries reached their second highest point during the war (the earlier peak was in 1967).[25]

Thus encouraged and armed by Moscow, North Vietnam launched its Easter offensive, capturing the South Vietnamese provincial capital of Quang Tri and menacing other key regions. Nixon thwarted the invasion by means of Operation Linebacker, the first U.S. bombing campaign against North Vietnam since Johnson had suspended bombing in 1968. Nixon's adroit diplomacy had ensured that China's response would be muted and that a summit between Nixon and Soviet leader Leonid Brezhnev would proceed.

In October 1972, National Security Adviser Henry Kissinger and Le Duc Tho, leader of the North Vietnamese delegation at the Paris peace talks, reached a preliminary agreement. Although Kissinger had announced that peace was at hand, President Thieu in Saigon balked, and the North Vietnamese suspended the talks. Nixon unleashed eleven days of intense bombing of North Vietnam, which brought the North Vietnamese back to the table, but permitted Nixon's leftist and liberal opponents in the American press and Congress to portray him as a war criminal. On January 27, 1973, the peace agreement ending the war was signed in Paris.

On March 29, 1973, the last American units left Vietnam. In the second American proxy war in Asia during the Cold War, the United States had lost roughly as many soldiers (fifty-eight thousand) as had died in Korea (fifty-six thousand). But the United States had left tens of thousands of troops to guard South Korea from the communist North. In contrast, the United States abandoned its weak South Vietnamese ally to defend itself.

What Nixon called "peace with honor" turned out to be neither peaceful nor honorable. The Paris accords were a thinly disguised capitulation to Hanoi. North Vietnamese regulars were allowed to remain in the sections of South Vietnam that they controlled. First weakened and then driven out of office by the Watergate scandal, Nixon was unable to fulfill his secret pledges to President Thieu that the United States would rescue the regime by using airpower if necessary.

While the Democratic majority in the U.S. Congress refused to provide the levels of aid requested by the Nixon and Ford administrations, the Soviet Union increased its aid to North Vietnam, supplying its proxies with superior weapons, including modern battle tanks and anitaircraft guns. Toward the end of 1974, Hanoi began an attack intended to prepare the way for a final offensive. To Hanoi's surprise, resistance rapidly crumbled, and, while President Thieu and other southern leaders ingloriously fled the country, the North Vietnamese army quickly overran the South. On April 17, 1975, the Khmer Rouge, beneficiaries of the North Vietnamese army's battle against the Cambodian military, came to power in Cambodia. Two weeks later, on April 30, Saigon fell to the North Vietnamese military, as American personnel and desperate South Vietnamese took part in a panicked evacuation. South Vietnam, outmanned and outgunned, had fallen, not to a popular uprising, but to one of the largest and most experienced armies in the world, equipped by the two most powerful totalitarian states since Nazi Germany.

America in Retreat

The brutal *Anschluss* of South Vietnam was followed quickly by a totalitarian *Gleichshaltung* (coordination) of all aspects of political, cultural, and social life. Hundreds of thousands of South Vietnamese were rounded up and thrown in "reeducation camps"; an unknown number were summarily executed. The southern members of the National Liberation Front found themselves shoved aside by communist functionaries from the north, who took over the villas and estates of the Saigon elite and set themselves up as a corrupt and despotic new ruling class.

In Germany, China, Cuba, and other countries where communists came to power, thousands of citizens had voted with their feet by fleeing as refugees. The East German state had to wall itself in to prevent its own subjects from fleeing. In the 1950s, almost a million Vietnamese had fled Ho Chi Minh's repressive rule for the relative freedom of South Vietnam. Now, as Ho's successors consolidated their control over the entire nation, one of the most massive human exoduses in the late twentieth century began. By the mid-1990s, more than 750,000 Vietnamese had fled to the U.S., and more than a million lived in other western countries. Great numbers also escaped to China and other countries in the region. None of the wars of Indochina produced as many refugees abroad as did peace under communist rule. An even greater disaster occurred in Cambodia, where the Khmer Rouge, inspired by Mao's ultra-leftist version of Marxism-Leninism, carried out a brutal collectivization campaign in which between an eighth and a quarter of the Cambodian population was executed or starved to death.

The victory of their Vietnamese proxies and the humiliation and paralysis of the United States in foreign policy that followed the fall of Saigon emboldened the Soviet leadership in its campaign for influence in Asia, Africa, the Middle East, and Latin America. Having inherited the former French empire in Indochina, the Soviet Union now picked up the pieces of the former Portuguese empire in Africa. By the end of the Carter administration the Soviet Union had dispatched roughly fifty thousand military advisers to Third World countries. In the 1960s, the only states outside of Eastern Europe and China with Marxist-Leninist "vanguard parties" had been Mongolia, North Vietnam, North Korea, and Cuba. By the 1980s, these regimes were joined by pro-Soviet Leninist governments in Afghanistan, Angola, Ethiopia, Mozambique, Southern Yemen, Benin, and Congo-Brazzaville, along with loosely affiliated regimes in Zaire, Guinea-Bissau, Cape Verde, and Madagascar. In expanding their influence in the Third World, the Soviets relied on auxiliaries from their empire. The East German State Security Service helped pro-Soviet regimes such as Angola, Ethiopia, Libya, Mozambique, Zambia, and Southern Yemen to establish internal security systems.[26] Cuban personnel trained the praetorian guards of dictators and internal security officers in a number of Third World countries, including Angola, Nicaragua, and Ethiopia.[27] Meanwhile, the Soviet military buildup that had begun after the Cuban missile crisis continued unabated. In the 1960s and 1970s, critics claimed that the CIA, which estimated that 12 to 16 percent of the Gross Domestic Product (GDP) of the Soviet Union was devoted to the military, exaggerated the scale of the Soviet buildup. After the Cold War it was learned that the CIA had *underestimated* Soviet military spending, which was as high as 25 percent of Soviet GDP.[28]

By the mid-1970s, the U.S. position in the world had declined dramatically. The weakness of the United States, evident in its abandonment of Indochina, was further illustrated in October 1973, when all of

America's European allies except for Portugal refused to allow the United States to use their airfields to resupply Israel during the Arab-Israeli War. The Bretton Woods system of fixed exchange rates was abandoned by the Nixon administration, which took the United States off the gold standard. The OPEC oil embargo, carried out without fear of U.S. punishment, harmed the economies of the United States and other industrial democracies. The Helsinki treaties ratified the legitimacy of the Eastern European empire that Stalin had created and that had been maintained only by Soviet invasions in 1953, 1956, and 1968. A pro-Soviet majority formed in the General Assembly of the United Nations.

The Carter administration was divided among a minority of anti-Soviet hardliners, such as National Security adviser Zbigniew Brzezinski, and a majority of anti–Cold War liberals, such as Secretary of State Cyrus Vance, who shrugged off Soviet imperialism by means of Cuban proxies in the Third World and resigned in protest when President Carter used force in a failed effort to rescue the American hostages in Iran. Carter's UN ambassador, Andrew Young, even described Moscow's Cuban auxiliaries in Africa as a "stabilizing influence." Former president Lyndon Johnson, who died of a heart attack in 1973, did not live to see his worst nightmares come true: the United States in retreat around the world before an advancing Soviet empire, the near collapse of the NATO alliance over doubts about U.S. credibility, and a proxy war between the United States and clients of the Soviet Union and Cuba in Nicaragua, a Soviet satellite on the North American mainland.

While the Soviet Union expanded its power and influence around the world in the aftermath of the fall of Saigon, in Indochina the situation was in flux. China, having lost influence over the Vietnamese, sponsored the Khmer Rouge in their border conflicts with Vietnam. After a brief deterioration in relations, the Soviet-Vietnamese alliance was revitalized in meetings in Moscow in May and June of 1977. In early 1978, Giap traveled secretly to Laos, where he asked General G. Pavlovsky, the commander of Soviet ground forces in Indochina, what Vietnam should do about Cambodia. Pavlovsky suggested that Hanoi should "do a Czechoslovakia."[29] In August 1978, the Soviets began to supply Vietnam with equipment to be used in an invasion of Cambodia, and increased the number of Soviet advisers in Indochina from two thousand to thirty-five hundred. On November 3, 1978, Hanoi signed a twenty-five-year Treaty of Friendship and Cooperation with the Soviet Union. With Soviet support thus assured, Vietnam invaded Cambodia on December 15, 1978, and captured Phnom Penh less than a month later. The Khmer Rouge fled to the Thai border, where they and other groups battling the Vietnamese occupiers received support from China, the United States, and Thailand. On February 17, 1979, China invaded the northern border provinces of Vietnam and suffered heavy losses before withdrawing its troops after sixteen days. The Sino-Vietnamese conflict and the Vietnamese occupation of Cambodia inspired the most massive escalation of Soviet military aid yet. At its peak, it exceeded the level of Soviet aid provided to North Vietnam during its war with the United States. In addition to modernizing the Vietnamese air force and navy, Moscow provided Soviet personnel and logistics support for Vietnam's occupation of Cambodia. Vietnamese operations in Cambodia depended on Soviet pilots, and hundreds of Soviet soldiers and civilians unloaded Soviet bloc supplies at Vietnamese ports.[30] In return for enabling Vietnamese communist domination of all of Indochina, the Soviets were granted access to Vietnamese military facilities. The Soviet base at Cam Ranh Bay became the largest and most important Soviet military installation outside of Eastern Europe.

By the mid-1980s, the Soviet-subsidized Vietnamese army, with more than a million regulars and two million additional paramilitary soldiers, was the third largest military force in the world, after the Chinese People's Liberation Army and the Soviet armed forces.[31] The Vietnamese people paid a terrible price for the militarism of their totalitarian rulers. By the late 1970s, the socialist agricultural system of Vietnam was on the verge of collapse. Despite minor market-oriented reforms in 1979 and 1980, only massive Soviet aid prevented Vietnam from sinking into famine like two other Soviet client states: Mengistu's Marxist-Leninist Ethiopia in the 1980s and North Korea in the 1990s.

The Second Cold War

In Afghanistan, a 1978 coup that brought a pro-Soviet regime to power was followed by a civil war and a Soviet invasion on December 27, 1979. The Soviet bloc was now at the height of its global power. While the Soviet Union was engaged in its first full-scale war outside of its Eastern European empire since 1945, its Vietnamese satraps were conquering Indochina and its Cuban proxies were fighting in Africa and encouraging insurgencies in Central America and the alignment of the Sandinista dictatorship in Nicaragua with the Soviet bloc.

The invasion of Afghanistan, together with the crushing of the anticommunist labor movement Solidarity by a martial law regime in Poland in 1981, helped to solidify anti-Soviet sentiment in the West. Anticommunist conservatives came to power in the major countries of the Atlantic Community—Margaret Thatcher in Britain (1979), Ronald Reagan in the United States (1981), and Helmut Kohl in West Germany (1983). In the face of mass opposition by leftists in their countries, the western leaders, including France's socialist president François Mitterrand, deployed NATO missiles to counteract the intimidating threat of Soviet intermediate-range missiles. Under Reagan, the United States abandoned the détente of the Nixon-Kissinger era and Carter's policy of vacillation and appeasement, returning to something like the Truman-Kennedy-Johnson policy of militant global containment of the Soviet Union. Reagan's military buildup, support for anticommunist insurgents in Afghanistan, Nicaragua, Angola, and elsewhere, and uncompromising ideological war (which included his much derided but accurate description of the Soviet Union as an "evil empire"), succeeded in taxing the Soviet system to a point at which the Soviet leaders had to choose between retreat and bankruptcy. The policy of retreat chosen by Soviet leader Mikhail Gorbachev in the 1980s was not enough to prevent the economic collapse of the Soviet Union.

In 1989, pressured by Moscow, Hanoi announced its withdrawal from Cambodia. Horrified by the democratic revolutions sweeping Eastern Europe, the aging Stalinists in Hanoi cracked down on dissent in their own country. Vietnam, called the "Asian Cuba" by China in recognition of its dependence on Moscow, found itself cast adrift when the Soviet Union disintegrated in 1991. Marxist-Leninist rulers continued to hold power in Vietnam as well as in China, North Korea, Laos, and Cuba. But communism, as a fighting faith, was moribund. And the third world war was over at last.

Winners and Losers in Vietnam

Who won and who lost in the Vietnam War?

The only complete losers were the officials of South Vietnam, whose state was erased from the map. The North Vietnamese communists won, but at the cost of bankruptcy and isolation when their sponsor the Soviet Union collapsed.

The Vietnamese people as a whole were losers. The loss of around two million Vietnamese on both sides, and the devastation of much of the landscape, was followed by extension of the brutal and irrational Stalinist system of North Vietnam throughout the entire country in 1975. All Vietnamese suffered from the communist victory—those who stayed, and the nearly two million who fled. The Laotian people suffered similarly. The greatest agony befell the Cambodian people, who endured mass murder and large-scale starvation under the rule of the Cambodian communists.

Among the major powers that intervened in Indochina during the Cold War, France, China, and the United States were all losers. France sacrificed nearly one hundred thousand troops and still lost its Southeast Asian empire, upon which its claim to great power status after World War II was partly based. China discovered too late that by helping Hanoi it had created an ally for the hated Soviet Union on its border.

For its part, the United States suffered a devastating defeat. In the zero-sum reputational game of the bipolar world order, Washington's defeat was Moscow's gain. At the same time, the cost in American dead and wounded temporarily destroyed the domestic consensus in favor of the Cold War. The United States negotiated an unfavorable armistice with the Soviet empire and gave up the policy of global containment for the better part of a decade, returning to a militant anti-Soviet policy only in the late 1970s. The Vietnam War, then, was the second greatest defeat suffered by the United States in the Cold War. (The greatest defeat of American Cold War policy, though not of arms, was the victory of the Soviet-sponsored Chinese communists in 1949—a victory without which neither the Korean nor the Indochinese wars would have taken place in the form in which they did, if they had taken place at all.)

It is often said that the United States, an arrogant superpower, was defeated by the heroic efforts of a small, weak nation in Asia. It is not true. The deterrent provided by the Soviet Union and China—particularly the threat that China would intervene with combat troops, as it had in Korea—prevented the United States from invading or engaging in all-out war against North Vietnam. And the Soviet and Chinese military-industrial complexes kept the North Vietnamese effort going until its successful conclusion in 1975, after which even higher levels of Soviet aid made possible Vietnam's empire in Laos and Cambodia. Hanoi's success was inconceivable without the support of two of the three most powerful and murderous totalitarian states in history.

The Vietnam War inaugurated the era of the greatest Soviet successes in the Cold War. If the impositions of communist regimes by the Red Army and Soviet agents in Eastern Europe are not counted as genuine revolutions, then the greatest triumphs of the Soviet Union in sponsoring Marxist-Leninist regimes around the world came in the 1970s, when the United States, bloodied in Indochina, temporarily abandoned the containment strategy and began retreating into isolationism. By supporting Stalin's disciple, Ho Chi Minh, and his successors in a proxy war, the Soviet leaders, at a relatively small cost to themselves, regained world revolutionary leadership from Mao's China, pinned down China on its southern border, and humiliated and temporarily paralyzed the United States.

The only clear winner of the Vietnam War, then, was the Soviet Union.

CHAPTER 2

WHY INDOCHINA MATTERED

American Credibility and the Cold War

The Vietnam War, like the Korean War, the Afghan War, the Greek Civil War, the Taiwan crises, and a number of other conflicts, was at one and the same time a civil war and proxy battle in the Cold War. During the Cold War, Indochina mattered—and it mattered to the Soviet Union and China as well as to the United States.

Examining the Vietnam War in its Cold War context does not necessarily justify it. Indeed, some argue that while it was necessary for the United States to wage the Cold War, success in the Cold War did not require the Unites States to establish or defend a protectorate over most of Indochina. This is the claim that was made by a number of American "realists" at the time of the Vietnam conflict and in the succeeding decades. Realism, or realpolitik, is the theory of international relations that emphasizes the primacy and legitimacy of power struggles in world politics. Several of the most prominent American realist thinkers—diplomat George Kennan, journalist Walter Lippmann, and scholar Hans Morgenthau, among others—criticized the Vietnam War in particular, and in some cases the Cold War as a whole, as an unnecessary or disproportionate response to the threats posed by Soviet expansionism and communist Chinese revolutionary radicalism. Within the U.S. government in the 1960s, Senator William Fulbright, chairman of the Senate Foreign Relations Committee, and Undersecretary of State George Ball, one of the Democratic party's most influential foreign policy experts, also used the language of realism to criticize what they considered to be an overly ambitious U.S. grand strategy.

The realist critique of the Vietnam War remains very popular today. It permits aging veterans of the sixties left, embarrassed by their former support for Ho Chi Minh's vicious dictatorship and their denunciations of American presidents as war criminals or their avoidance of the draft, to claim that they were right to oppose the war, even if their rationale was mistaken. The realist critique permits former Maoists turned Metternichs to declare that the Vietnam War, even if it was not an immoral atrocity, was a strategic mistake. The realist critique of the Vietnam War also serves the purposes of many contemporary advocates of an assertive U.S. foreign policy: for them to say that the Vietnam War resulted from strategic folly denies a debating point to opponents who claim that a contemporary intervention that they favor threatens to become "another Vietnam." Finally, the fact that some of the policymakers who played a role in the war, like former Secretary of State Robert McNamara, have claimed that it was a mistake from the beginning has appeared to strengthen the realist critique (even though other policymakers, such as former national security adviser Walt Rostow, continue to argue that the war made sense in terms of U.S. strategy).

In light of all this, it is important to recall that there was, and is, a realist case in favor of the Vietnam War, as well as one against it. If some American realists such as Lippmann, Kennan, and Morgenthau doubted the importance of America's commitment to denying Indochina to the communist bloc, others, such as Walt and Eugene Rostow, Samuel P. Huntington, and John P. Roche, were convinced of the significance of that commitment. The fact that the United States was defeated in Vietnam does not necessarily discredit the strategic logic that inspired the U.S. commitment to South Vietnam, Laos, and Cambodia and their Southeast Asian neighbors. The failure of American policy in Indochina may have resulted from inappropriate military tactics, or the characteristics of the North Vietnamese and South Vietnamese societies and governments, or the support provided Hanoi by the Soviet Union and China, or the peculiarities of American political culture—or some combinations of all of these factors. The case that Indochina was worth a limited American war of some kind, particularly in the circumstances of the Cold War in the 1960s, is compelling in light of what we now know about the pattern and result of the Cold War as a whole.

Why Were We in Vietnam?

Contemporary critics of the Johnson administration spoke of its "credibility gap" in connection with the Vietnam War. In addition to having exaggerated the progress of the United States and its South Vietnamese allies in the war, Johnson and his aides were accused of a failure to clearly explain the goal of the war to the American public and the world. Typical of this line of criticism is a comment in 1968 by William R. Corson, a former marine colonel in Vietnam, in his critique of the war, *The Betrayal:* "The emergence of the credibility gap came from the ill-fated attempts of Secretary [of State Dean] Rusk to justify the war successively as, first, a defense of Vietnamese freedom, then a defense of our national interest, and finally the defense of the world from the yellow peril."[1]

Indeed, Johnson and officials of his administration provided several rationales for the escalation of the U.S. effort in Vietnam. Johnson cited "the deepening shadow of China. The rulers in Hanoi are urged on by Peking." On another occasion he stressed the need to thwart guerrilla warfare as an instrument of communist expansion: "Our strength imposes on us an obligation to assure that this type of aggression does not succeed." Secretary of State Dean Rusk stressed the potential effects of a defeat of U.S. policy in Southeast Asia on America's global alliance system, including "our guarantees to Berlin."[2]

From today's perspective, the Johnson administration does not appear to have been more inconsistent or disinguous in describing the aims of U.S. foreign policy than other U.S. wartime administrations. During World War II, the Roosevelt administration sometimes justified the U.S. effort in terms of the security of the United States and at other times claimed that the defeat of the Axis powers would help promote a utopian world characterized by the "Four Freedoms." In the run-up to the Gulf War, the Bush administration provided a number of rationales, including the atrocities committed by Saddam Hussein's regime (some of which were exaggerated) and the importance of Middle Eastern oil for American jobs. President Clinton and members of his administration explained the U.S.-led NATO war against Serbia in terms of a number of different rationales: the moral imperative of preventing or reversing the ethnic cleansing of Albanians in Kosovo by the Serbs, the need to demonstrate the military credibility of NATO and the United States, the economic importance of a stable Europe, and the danger that the conflict would expand and draw in Greece and Turkey. Government officials addressing different audiences on different occasions for different purposes may emphasize different goals of foreign policy. The apparent inconsistencies that result are not necessarily evidence of official duplicity or official confusion. Nor does the fact that some official goals were misguided or overemphasized mean that others were not sound.

What is more, the notion of the "credibility gap" ignores the possibility that in escalating the Vietnam War the Johnson administration had several purposes, not just one. By successfully defending South Vietnam against subversion from North Vietnam, a client of the Soviet Union and China, the United States could deter the Soviets, reassure its allies, discourage the adoption of the Chinese and Vietnamese model of revolutionary "people's war" by antiwestern insurgents in developing countries, and encourage the economic development and liberalization of South Vietnam as well as of South Korea and Taiwan, all at the same time.

While the U.S. intervention in Vietnam served a number of complementary purposes, there was a hierarchy among U.S. goals. The administrations of Kennedy, Johnson, and Nixon may not have made that hierarchy as clear as intellectuals would like. Nevertheless, in hindsight it is possible to identify the place assigned to different goals in the hierarchy of purposes by these three presidents and their aides. The chief purpose of the United States in Vietnam was to demonstrate America's credibility as a military power and a reliable ally to its enemies and its allies around the world. The danger was that if the United States were perceived to be lacking in military capacity, political resolve, or both, the Soviet Union and/or China and their proxies would act more aggressively, while U.S. allies, including important industrial democracies such as West Germany and Japan, would be inclined to appease the communist great powers. It was in this global geopolitical context that preventing "falling dominoes"—whether in Southeast Asia proper, or in Third World countries far from Vietnam—was important. Least important of all the U.S. purposes in intervening in Vietnam was promoting liberty, democracy, and prosperity in South Vietnam itself. The defeat of the attempted takeover of South Vietnam by North Vietnam was a necessary, but not sufficient, condition for the evolution of the authoritarian government of South Vietnam toward liberalism and democracy. But America's political goals in South Vietnam were appropriately incidental and subordinate to America's goals in Southeast Asian power politics, which, in turn, were incidental and subordinate to America's global strategy in the third world war.

Regional Dominoes and Global Waves

One of the myths about the Vietnam War is the claim that the chief rationale for U.S. intervention was the "domino theory." This derived its name from a metaphor used by President Eisenhower to explain U.S. concern about the consequences of communist takeovers in Indochina: "You have a row of dominoes set up, you knock over the first one, and what will happen to the last one is the certainty that it will go over very quickly. So you could have a beginning of a disintegration that would have the most profound influences."[3] The danger that the "loss" of Indochina would lead to a "loss" of Southeast Asia in its entirety to the American bloc ("the free world") was stressed at different times by U.S. policymakers, usually in rhetoric intended for the general public. "The security of all Southeast Asia will be endangered if Laos loses its neutral independence," President Kennedy told the American public in a televised press conference on March 23, 1961.[4] President Johnson, in his characteristically hyperbolic style, claimed that if the communists were not stopped in Vietnam the United States might have to fight them in Waikiki.

But this "regional" version of the domino effect was not the only interpretation of the metaphor. Examining the statements and actions of American statesmen and commentators during the Vietnam era reveals that it is necessary to untangle three conceptions bound up in the idea of the domino effect. At different times the domino effect was used to mean a *regional domino effect*, a *global revolutionary wave effect* or a *global bandwagon effect*. It was feared that the loss of South Vietnam to Hanoi-sponsored communist insurgents would lead to communist takeovers in neighboring countries in Indochina or Southeast Asia, or to copycat communist or antiwestern revolutions in other areas of the developing world, or to bandwagoning with or appeasement of the Soviet Union or communist China by U.S. allies and neutrals unsure of the reliability of U.S. security guarantees. In the worst case, all of three of these domino effects might occur. The fall of South Vietnam and a few neighboring countries might, at one and the same time, inspire imitative revolutions elsewhere in Asia, Africa, and Latin America, and frighten U.S. allies into appeasing Moscow and/or Beijing. Once the issue has been clarified in this way, it becomes obvious that to dismiss the concerns of U.S. policymakers about the prospective loss of Indochina to the communist bloc, it is not enough to prove that their fears of the regional domino effect in Southeast Asia were exaggerated. Even if they were mistaken about the extent of the regional domino effect, they might have been right about the dangers of the other two domino effects—the revolutionary wave effect and the bandwagon effect. As it happened, the fall of only three regional dominoes in Indochina *did* trigger a worldwide revolutionary wave and an even more dangerous trend of pro-Soviet bandwagoning in world politics.

One of the central claims of opponents of the Vietnam War was the assertion that American policymakers tragically mistook spontaneous nationalist movements in Vietnam, Laos, and Cambodia as evidence of the existence of an international communist conspiracy. "Where communism takes root in Asia," George McTurnan Kahin and John W. Lewis wrote in their influential book *The United States in Vietnam*, "its strength arises, not through subversion directed from China or Russia, but because of locally generated social, economic, and political factors."[5] A look at a map of Asia in 1989 is enough to refute this argument. Every successful communist insurgency in Asia took place in a country bordering on one or more countries under communist rule, beginning with China, where Mao's communists received massive Soviet aid across the Sino-Soviet border. Communist insurgencies were defeated in countries such as the Philippines and Malaya that lacked any borders with a Marxist-Leninist regime. When the Cold War ended, not one communist movement had succeeded in an Asian country without a communist neighbor—not one.

The regional domino effect in Asia, then, was real. The broader domino theory, however, was discredited. While South Vietnam, Laos, and Cambodia were incorporated into the communist bloc (itself divided by the Sino-Soviet rivalry), Thailand, Indonesia, and other important Southeast Asian states were not. Some defenders of the U.S. effort have acknowledged this outcome by offering a modified version of the domino theory. Former Johnson administration National Security Adviser Walt Rostow has argued that the U.S. intervention, although ultimately unsuccessful in Indochina, averted a wider regional domino effect because it bought time for the noncommunist regimes of the Association of Southeast Asian Nations (ASEAN) to consolidate their power and to engage in successful economic growth.[6] After he left office, Rostow's predecessor as National Security Adviser, McGeorge Bundy, expressed the similar opinion that the U.S. effort in Southeast Asia, though initially justified, had been "excessive" after 1965, when "a new anti-communist government took power in Indonesia and destroyed the [Indonesian] communist party."[7]

The revolutionary wave effect produced by the fall of Saigon in 1975 was far more significant than the regional domino effect in Southeast Asia proper. The political scientist Mark N. Katz has identified a "Marxist-Leninist revolutionary wave" that peaked in the 1960s and 1970s, along with an "Arab nationalist revolutionary wave" in the 1950s and 1960s and an "Islamic revolutionary wave" that began with the Iranian Revolution. Samuel P. Huntington has identified a "democratic wave" that began with the defeat of the Soviet bloc in the Cold War. While the Arab nationalist and Islamic revolutionary waves were limited to Arab or Muslim countries, the Marxist-Leninist and democratic waves were global phenomena. According to Katz, the Marxist-Leninist revolutionary wave

> originated in the early 1970s, when the American crisis of confidence, caused by its unsuccessful military intervention in Indochina, was reaching the crescendo that would lead to the complete American withdrawal in early 1973, as well as the "Vietnam syndrome," which made it politically impossible for the U.S. government to undertake large-scale military intervention anywhere in the Third World until the 1991 Gulf War.[8]

The Marxist-Leninist revolutionary wave associated with the Vietnam War saw "affiliate Marxist-Leninist revolutions" come to power outside of Indochina in the Congo (1964, 1968), Benin (1972), Ethiopia and Guinea-Bissau (1974), Madagascar, Cape Verde, Mozambique, and Angola (1975), Afghanistan (1978), and Grenada and Nicaragua (1979). All of these revolutions were inspired in part by the example of the successful struggle of the Indochinese communists against the United States. Along with Cuban communists who worked to export revolution on behalf of the Soviet bloc in Africa and the Middle East, the Vietnamese communists exported their successful revolution by invading and occupying Laos and Cambodia. If dominoes such as Thailand and Indonesia did not fall, other dominoes far from Southeast Asia, such as Nicaragua and Angola and Ethiopia, did—and they fell to a revolutionary wave emanating, in part, from Indochina.

The communist victory in South Vietnam, then, was followed by a minor regional domino effect and a major global revolutionary wave effect. And yet the most powerful argument for U.S. intervention in Vietnam came from a third variant of the domino theory. What was primarily at stake in Vietnam for the United States was its global reputation as a military superpower and as a reliable ally—its credibility—not the alliance memberships or constitutions of Thailand, Indonesia, and a handful of other nations, nor even the affiliation of Marxist-Leninist regimes in Nicaragua and Ethiopia with Moscow. The primary danger facing the United States was the likelihood that, if the Soviet Union and/or China helped a proxy state annihilate an American protectorate, the Soviet Union and China would be dangerously emboldened, while weak American allies and neutrals around the world would be frightened into appeasing one or the other of the two communist great powers. By stressing the regional domino theory or a possible revolutionary wave effect instead of the defense of America's global credibility, successive U.S. presidential administrations confused the public, undermined their own case, and provided hostages in the form of weak arguments to critics of U.S. Cold War strategy. This is a tragedy, because the commitment to defend America's client states in Indochina, along with U.S. commitments to South Korea and Taiwan, was justified by the need to demonstrate American credibility both to America's enemies and to American allies and neutrals.

The Cold War: Sieges and Duels

Credibility, in power politics, is a country's reputation for military capability combined with the political resolve to use it in order to promote its goals. The concern of statesmen with the reputation of their states for military ability and resolve is as old as interstate politics. The Athenian leader Pericles, in a debate at the beginning of the Peloponnesian War, told the Athenians why they should resist the demands of their enemy, Sparta:

They order us to raise the siege of Potidaea, to let Aegina be independent, to revoke the Megara decree; and they conclude with an ultimatum warning us to leave the Hellenes independent. I hope that you will none of you think that we shall be going to war for a trifle if we refuse to revoke the Megara decree, which appears in the front of their complaints, and the revocation of which is to save us from war, or let any feeling of self-reproach linger in your minds, as if you went to war for slight cause. Why, this trifle contains the whole seal and trial of your resolution. If you give way, you will instantly have to meet some greater demand, as having been frightened into obedience in the first instance; while a firm refusal will make them clearly understand that they must treat you more as equals. Make your decision therefore at once, either to submit before you are harmed, or if we are to go to war, as I for one think we ought, to do so without caring whether the ostensible cause be great or small, resolved against making concessions or consenting to a precarious tenure of our possessions.[9]

The natural concern of U.S. leaders with credibility was heightened into something like an obsession by the peculiar dynamics of the Cold War—a world war fought by means of sieges and duels. Unlike World Wars I and II, the third global conflict of the twentieth century took the form of a half-century siege on the European front and duels or proxy wars in a number of other theaters. The forward deployment of U.S. troops in Central Europe, Japan, and South Korea following the Korean War, together with U.S. efforts to maintain conventional and nuclear superiority, made up the siege aspect of the Cold War. In the long run, the superior military-industrial capability of the United States and its affluent allies was bound to wear down the military-industrial base of the Soviet empire, as long as two conditions were met. The first condition for western success in the Cold War was alliance unity; the alliance of the United States, West Germany, Japan, Britain, France, and the other major democracies could not be split by a Soviet diplomatic strategy of divide-and-rule. Meeting this condition required periodic reaffirmations of alliance unity, like the deployment of the Euromissiles by NATO in the early 1980s in response to Soviet intimidation. In addition, the American bloc was required to match and surpass the Soviet imperium in the arms race. Because the goal was to spend the Soviet Union into bankruptcy, not merely to defend the western allies against an implausible threat of invasion, the American bloc could not accumulate a sufficiency of nuclear missiles and other weapons and then quit. The arms race was an auction that had to be continued until one side dropped out.

The military-industrial siege of the Soviet empire took far longer than early Cold War leaders such as Truman and Eisenhower and their advisers had expected. In the 1950s, Eisenhower hoped that U.S. troops might be withdrawn from Europe in the next decade. Instead, the siege lasted almost half a century. While manning the siegeworks in Europe and northeast Asia, the United States also had to demonstrate its determination by threatening war, or, if the threat failed, by waging limited war, with the Soviet Union and/or China and their proxies in regions on the periphery of the main theaters of Cold War competition. Sometimes the United States had to fight where it was challenged by its enemies, not where it would have preferred to fight. Because perceived power is power (except in times of war, when actual power is tested), the danger that a strategic retreat will be misinterpreted as evidence of a loss of will or capability is quite real. To refuse to duel is to lose the duel.

Thus defined, credibility became the central strategic concern of the United States in the Cold War. Henry Kissinger described the American interest in Indochina in terms of U.S. credibility in global power politics: "With respect to Indo-China, we are not equating the intrinsic importance of each part of the world, and we are not saying that every part of the world is strategically as important to the United States as any other part of the world . . . [The question of aid to allies in Indochina] is a fundamental question of how we are viewed by all other people."[10] John Foster Dulles made a similar point in calling on the United States to protect the anticommunist remnant of the Chinese Nationalist regime on Taiwan in spring 1950: "If we do not act, it will be everywhere interpreted that we are making another retreat because we dare not risk war."[11]

Who was the intended audience for American displays of credibility? Makers and defenders of U.S. Cold War strategy reasoned that the United States had to deter its enemies and reassure its allies at the same time. In a speech at Johns Hopkins University on April 7, 1965, President Johnson invoked these two reasons for demonstrations of credibility in the context of the war in Indochina. First, he cited the need to reassure America's allies: "Around the globe, from Berlin to Thailand, are people whose well-being rests, in part, on the belief that they can count on us if they are attacked. To leave Vietnam to its fate would shake the confidence of all these people in the value of America's commitment, the value of America's word." Second, President Johnson sought to discourage America's enemies: "The central lesson of our time is that the appetite of aggression is never satisfied. To withdraw from one battlefield means only to prepare for the next. We must say in Southeast Asia, as we did in Europe, in the words of the Bible: 'Hitherto shalt thou come, but no further.'"

Using less orotund language, Johnson adviser John McNaughton, in a memo of March 25, 1965, emphasized American credibility in listing the aims of U.S. policy in Indochina:

70%:—To avoid a humiliating defeat (to our reputation as a guarantor)

20%:—To keep South Vietnam (and the adjacent territory) from Chinese hands

10%:—To permit the people of South Vietnam to enjoy a better, freer way of life[12]

Credibility as Deterrence: The Lesson of Munich

The deterrence rationale for demonstrations of credibility was illustrated by the so-called lesson of Munich. The appeasement of Hitler by the British and French at Munich in 1938, it was argued, only encouraged the Nazi dictator by convincing him that the western democracies were weak and indecisive. Applied to Vietnam, the lesson of Munich suggested that if the United States sacrificed Indochina to the communist bloc, then the communist bloc—whether led by the Soviet Union or Maoist China—would grow bolder in its attempt to subvert and intimidate the noncommunist world (not just Southeast Asia). Critics of the Vietnam War claimed that U.S. policymakers were misled by historical analogies. For example, James C. Thomson writes: "Highly dubious analogies from our experience elsewhere—the 'Munich' sellout and 'containment' from Europe, the Malayan insurgency and the Korean War from Asia—[were] imported in order to justify our actions."[13] Similarly, Robert Cohen writes that Secretary of State Dean Rusk was guilty of "mistakenly casting Ho Chi Minh as Hitler, misreading a civil war as a war of foreign aggression, and responding to the regional power of Vietnam as if it represented some Axis-style global threat."[14]

No analogy is perfect. But in light of what is now known about the perceptions and motives of America's communist enemies in the Cold War, it appears that U.S. policymakers invoked historical analogies in an intelligent manner.

According to Yuen Foong Khong in his book *Analogies at War: Korea, Munich, Dien Bien Phu, and the Vietnam Decisions of 1962* (1992), the conflict in Vietnam in the 1960s was most frequently compared by top U.S. officials in speeches and briefings "to the following five historical cases: the Korean War, the fascist aggression of the 1930s, the Greek crisis of 1947, the Malaya insurrection of 1948–1960, and the Berlin crises." These are exactly the analogies that one would expect well-informed policymakers to use. Indeed, the sophistication of U.S. officials is revealed by the fact that in 1961, when the conflict was almost a pure insurgency, South Vietnam was compared most frequently to Malaya, Greece, and the Philippines, whereas comparisons to Korea became more frequent in the debates of 1964–65, when the infiltration of North Vietnamese regulars and the incidence of large-scale battles with Viet Cong units in the south were increasing. Khong criticizes the policymakers of the Kennedy and Johnson administrations for neglecting the analogy favored by antiwar leftists and liberals who claimed that Ho Chi Minh could have been an "Asian Tito." In retrospect it is clear that the analogy between North Vietnam and North Korea was more accurate than a comparison of North Vietnam with Yugoslavia. There is no evidence that Yugoslav-style neutrality was ever considered by the North Vietnamese communist elite, and the severe Stalinist tyranny of North Vietnam resembled that of North Korea, not Yugoslavia's moderate authoritarianism. Ho Chi Minh was not an Asian Tito; he was a Southeast Asian Kim Il Sung.[15]

The lesson of Munich, applied to the Cold War in Indochina, did *not* rest on a parallel between Ho Chi Minh's North Vietnam and Hitler's Germany. The implicit comparison was not between Nazi Germany and North Vietnam, but between Nazi Germany and North Vietnam's great-power sponsors—the Soviet Union, and China, when it aspired, in the mid-sixties, to lead a worldwide antiwestern movement. Ho Chi Minh was not compared to Hitler but to Hitler's allies and clients Franco and Mussolini, whose successes in Spain and Ethiopia in the 1930s were important psychological and geopolitical victories for the fascist bloc. Nor did the comparison of the Soviet Union or China with Nazi Germany go beyond the fact that all three were totalitarian states bent on revising the international order in their own favor. As Secretary of State Rusk put it, using the metaphor of the United States as the world's policeman:

> There are those who object to analogics—that Mao Tse-tung is not a Hitler, that Ho Chi Minh is not a Mussolini. Of course no one supposes they are. But one robber may be named John Doe, another robber may be named Richard Doe—there may be infinite differences between the two, but what they have in common, namely robbery, is what sends them both to prison.[16]

The lesson of Munich provides the answer to the argument that the rivalry between the Soviet Union and China in the 1960s rendered the U.S. policy of containing the communist bloc obsolete. In the early and mid-sixties, the Kennedy-Johnson administration viewed Mao's antiwestern radicalism as a greater threat in Southeast Asia than the more moderate policy of the Soviet Union. By the second half of the 1960s, however, the Soviet Union had replaced China as the primary sponsor of North Vietnam—a role it would play until the end of the Cold War. Even if Vietnam had been nothing but a proxy war between the United States and China, the American defense of Indochina would have been justified by the logic of containing the Soviet Union in the world as a whole. Indeed, it might have been more damaging to America's reputation to be defeated in a proxy war by a military power of the second rank such as China than by the rival superpower. In the zero-sum game of the Cold War, the Soviet Union benefited when it humiliated the United States; it also benefited when China or OPEC or Iran humiliated the United States. This kind of reasoning does not depend on conditions like those of the Cold War, and it is valid for lesser powers as well as for superpowers. Countries that take a hard line toward weak enemies may be sending a signal to both strong enemies and weak allies. In the late 1930s, Oliver Harvey, a British Foreign Office official, wrote in his diary: "We were weak with Franco, and as a direct consequence Japan is now bullying us. If we are weak again with Japan, we shall have Hitler and Mussolini beating us up. And, above all, if we are weak in helping China, who is fighting our battle, we shall find our own little allies ratting on us. Why shouldn't they?"[17]

The fear of American policymakers that communist bloc leaders, underestimating U.S. military capability and resolve, would be tempted to engage in a more assertive strategy, was vindicated repeatedly during the Cold War. In the late 1940s, Stalin was skeptical about the prospects for Kim Il Sung's success in the Korean peninsula. He remarked that the Americans would refuse to be driven out of Korea for fear of losing "their reputation as a great power." After the United States failed to intervene to prevent a communist victory in China in 1949, however, Stalin and Mao, according to political scientist Douglas J. Macdonald, "generalized from the particular U.S. failure in China and assumed that the United States would not react in the rest of the region." Stalin therefore authorized Kim Il Sung to launch his invasion of South Korea; the result was the Korean War. Macdonald concludes: "The flat declarations of analysts such as Ted Hopf that there exists 'no evidence' that decision-makers 'infer an opponent's irresoluteness and weakness from encounters in the periphery' are incorrect in the Asian case in the early Cold War."[18]

Even the massive and unexpected U.S. effort in Korea was not enough to refute Stalin's perceptions of American weakness. "America cannot defeat little Korea," Stalin remarked to Zhou Enlai on August 20, 1952, in the middle of the war. "Americans are merchants . . . Germans conquered France in 20 days. It's been already two years, and America has still not subdued little Korea." Warming to his theme, Stalin mocked both the military capability and the collective resolve of the United States:

> No, Americans don't know how to fight. After the Korean War, in particular, they have lost the capability to wage a large-scale war. They are pinning their hopes on the atom bomb and air power. But one cannot win a war with that. One needs infantry, and they don't have much infantry; the infantry they do have is weak. They are fighting little Korea, and already people are weeping in the USA. What will happen if they start a large-scale war? Then, perhaps, everyone will weep.[19]

It is instructive to compare Stalin's analysis of American capability and will with a similar analysis of U.S. capability and will in a telegram that Joachim von Ribbentrop, foreign minister of National Socialist Germany, sent from Berlin to Tokyo on August 25, 1941. In an effort to persuade Hitler's Japanese allies to disregard the prospect of American intervention in World War II and to proceed to attack Singapore and other outposts of the British empire in the region, Ribbentrop argued that the threat of American intervention in Southeast Asia was not credible:

> The fact that the United States has reacted to Japan's occupation of Indochina only with economic sanction, . . . the fact that the Roosevelt-Churchill meeting produced only words, and the fact that the United States has made the hopeless and almost desperate attempt to keep Japan out by means of insincere negotiations are clear signs of weakness on the part of the United States, proving that it will not risk any serious military action against Japan. This is no news to the military expert, for he has long known that the army and the air force of the United States are not yet ready and that its navy is still inferior to the Japanese navy. Moreover, a large majority of the American people are opposed to war.[20]

Both Stalin and Ribbentrop, as experienced foreign policymakers, measured American credibility by assessing the military capability and the domestic consensus of the United States—in exactly the same order. First, U.S. military capability: "One needs infantry, and they don't have much infantry; the infantry they do have is weak" (Stalin); "[T]he army and the air force of the United States are not yet ready and . . . its navy is still inferior to the Japanese navy" (Ribbentrop). The second factor that they considered was the will of the American people: "[A]lready people are weeping in the USA" (Stalin); "Moreover, a large majority of the American people are opposed to war" (Ribbentrop).

Defined narrowly as the importance of signaling adversaries of one's resolve, the lesson of Munich can find support from episodes in the Cold War involving Mao as well as Stalin. One is the Taiwan Straits crisis of 1958. In July 1958, while the United States was diverted by its intervention in Lebanon, Mao saw an opportunity to test American credibility in East Asia on one of what he called the "three fronts" (Taiwan, Korea, and Indochina). On August 23, 1958, coastal units of the Chinese military began to bombard Jinmen (Quemoy Island), controlled by the Nationalist government of Taiwan. The Eisenhower administration responded to this probe with proof that it was willing to live up to its obligations as Taiwan's superpower protector. Eisenhower sent the U.S.

navy to the straits of Taiwan, while the United States and Chinese negotiated in Warsaw. The crisis ended on October 6, when a message
drafted by Mao calling for peaceful resolution of the division of China
was sent to Taiwan.

Earlier, on August 25, 1958, in the midst of the Sino-American confrontation over Taiwan, Mao explained the reason for the attacks to
members of his Politburo: "In fact, our bombardment of Jinmen with
30,000–50,000 shells *was a probe*. . . . The main purpose of our bombardment was not to reconnoiter Jiang's defenses on these islands, but *to
probe the attitude of the Americans in Washington, testing their determination*."[21]

Apart from the mistaken impression of U.S. military weakness and
political irresolution that led Stalin to authorize the Korean War, perhaps the most remarkable confirmation of the validity of the lesson of
Munich during the Cold War is found in the context of the Vietnam
War itself. Newly opened Chinese archives make it clear that the Chinese and North Vietnamese escalated the Hanoi-controlled campaign
against the Saigon regime in the early 1960s in part because *neither Mao
nor Ho and his government believed the United States would go to war*.

On August 13, 1964, following the Tonkin Gulf incidents, Mao told
North Vietnam's Le Duan that "it seems that the Americans do not want to
fight a war, you do not want to fight a war, and we do not necessarily want
to fight a war" and therefore "there will be no war." In a meeting with another North Vietnamese delegation on October 5, 1964, Mao repeated his
prediction, based on his assessment of America's military capability:

> It is impossible for the United States to send many troops to South
> Vietnam. The Americans altogether have 18 army divisions. They
> have to keep half of these divisions, i.e., nine of them, at home, and
> can send abroad the other nine divisions. Among these divisions, half
> are in Europe, and half are in the Asia-Pacific region. And they have
> stationed more divisions in Asia [than elsewhere in the region],
> namely, three divisions. One [is] in South Korea, one in Hawaii, and
> the third one in [original not clear]. They also placed fewer than one
> division of marine corps in Okinawa in Japan.[22]

The significance of these conversations can hardly be exaggerated.
We now know that the nightmare of American strategists had come true

in the summer and fall of 1964. The lesson of Munich is based on a danger that a country's enemies will act assertively because they have *underestimated* the nation's actual military power and will. Chinese encouragement of North Vietnam's escalation of its war on South Vietnam was based on a classic Munich-type underestimation of American power and will—an underestimation that the Johnson administration reluctantly corrected, by escalating the American military effort in Vietnam.

Years later, Mao admitted being stunned by the fact that the United States had actually gone to war to preserve South Vietnam. "I never thought that they would attack North Vietnam," he told Pham Van Dong on November 17, 1968. "But my prediction was wrong when they bombed the North."[23] Like Stalin, who was shocked when Harry Truman went to war over South Korea, and like Saddam Hussein, who did not expect George Bush to go to war over Kuwait, Mao had underestimated the determination of America's leaders. The new archival evidence thus confirms the prudence of Johnson, who told his aide Bill Moyers that if the United States did not act to defend South Vietnam "'they'll think we're yellow and don't mean what we say.' 'Who?' 'The Chinese. The fellas in the Kremlin. They'll be taking the measure of us.'"[24]

Once the Vietnam War was underway on a large scale, Mao continued to evaluate the American threat in terms of the calculus of military capability and political resolve. Again and again, in conversations with his North Vietnamese allies and others, Mao stressed two points—American military forces were overextended, weakening U.S. credibility; and domestic divisions in American society weakened U.S. resolve. "You call it a special war, a limited war, but for the U.S., they concentrate all their forces on it," Mao reminded Pham Van Dong in the November 17, 1968, conversation noted above. "At present their allies in Europe are complaining a lot, saying that [the U.S.] reduces the number of its troops [in Europe] and withdraws its experienced troops and good equipment [from Europe], not to mention the troops withdrawn from South Korea and Hawaii." What is more, according to Mao, "The US has a population of 200 million people, but it cannot stand wars."[25] Like Stalin during the Korean War, Mao argued that the American public would not tolerate many casualties. "The Americans do not have enough manpower to distribute in the world, since already they have been overextended," Mao told Le Duan on May 11, 1970. "Therefore, when their people were killed their hearts were broken. *The death of several dozens of thousand is a huge matter for them.*"[26]

Newly released archival evidence, then, makes it clear that communist leaders like Stalin and Mao, on numerous occasions, really did interpret American restraint as evidence of American military incapacity or lack of political resolve—exactly as leaders of the Axis alliance had done a generation earlier. As the lesson of Munich predicted, the forfeiture of Indochina by the United States between 1968 and 1975 encouraged Soviet leaders to engage in more assertive and reckless imperialism throughout the world, with a greatly reduced fear of confrontation with the United States. "Inspired by its gains and by the decline of U.S. prestige resulting from Vietnam and domestic upheaval, the Soviet leadership adopted a more aggressive and rigid foreign policy, particularly in the third world," writes Russian historian Ilya Gaiduk in *The Soviet Union and Vietnam* (1996).[27] Basing his conclusions on formerly secret Soviet archives, Gaiduk concludes: "The lessons of Vietnam had a diametrically opposite effect in Moscow" than in the United States. Other experts on Soviet foreign policy agree. According to William Curti Wohlforth, "What can be discerned in the speeches of Brezhnev and other Politburo members in the years between 1972 and 1979 is a cautious expectation about two processes: the tendency for certain 'non-aligned' nationalist Third World regimes to align themselves with Soviet positions in world affairs . . . and the increase in the number of 'revolutionary' Third World states, the so-called countries of socialist orientation." The Soviet elite viewed the victories of their clients in Indochina as the first of a series of successes, which included the rise to power of pro-Soviet regimes in Angola, Mozambique, Guinea-Bissau, Ethiopia, Nicaragua, and Afghanistan. Wohlforth writes: "The key event that sparked optimism about the competition for influence in the Third World was the war in Vietnam."[28]

American leaders had feared that a U.S. abandonment of Indochina would convince America's communist-bloc adversaries of America's military inability or political unwillingness to fight limited proxy wars in the Third World, and thus encourage them to be bolder and more assertive elsewhere, perhaps to the point of risking a direct superpower confrontation. All of these consequences followed the U.S. forfeiture of Vietnam. While China aligned itself with the United States, America's major adversary, the Soviet Union, grew ever bolder in its imperialism—ferrying Cuban mercenaries to fight in proxy wars in Angola and Ethiopia, sending its own troops into Afghanistan. The result, by the early 1980s, was a crisis in superpower relations more intense than any since the Cuban missile crisis—a confrontation so dangerous that much of the educated public in Europe and North America believed that nuclear war was imminent. President Johnson had argued that "we learned from Hitler at Munich that success only feeds the appetite of aggression. The battle would be renewed in one country and then another country, bringing with it perhaps even larger and crueler conflict, as we have learned from the lessons of history."[29] Following the U.S. retreat from Indochina, the battle was indeed renewed as Johnson and his advisers had feared "in one country and then another country"—Angola, Ethiopia, Nicaragua, Afghanistan. And these proxy wars, in turn, led to an "even larger and crueler conflict"—the expensive and perilous Second Cold War of the late 1970s and early 1980s.

Credibility as Reassurance: The Bandwagon Effect

The major rationale for demonstrations of American credibility during the Cold War, then, was their effect in deterring America's enemies. At the same time, Cold War policymakers in the U.S. government believed that displays of American credibility were necessary to reassure U.S. allies and neutrals that otherwise might be intimidated into appeasing the Soviet Union or China.

In the jargon of international relations theory, "balancing" refers to the tendency of states to team up to stop any single state from dominating an international system, while "bandwagoning" (from the phrase "get on the bandwagon") is a metaphor describing the tendency of states to appease a potentially dominant great military power. Another phrase for the bandwagon effect, used by the historian John Lewis Gaddis, is the "psychological domino effect."[30] If the dominoes of the regional domino effect were countries in Southeast Asia bordering the communist regimes of China and North Vietnam, and the dominoes of the revolutionary wave effect were unstable countries threatened by communist insurgencies far from Southeast Asia, such as Nicaragua and Angola and Ethiopia and Afghanistan, then the dominoes of the bandwagon theory were American dependencies such as Japan and West Germany that might respond to perceived American weakness and unreliability by appeasing the Soviet empire or China.

So-called "minimal realists" believe that in most systems of competitive states balancing behavior is more common than bandwagoning behavior. According to minimal realism, any state that seeks to accumulate too much power will more or less automatically provoke a balancing coalition of other states seeking to check the expansion of its influence. It follows that a great power can lose many peripheral struggles with little or no danger to its reputation as a great power. Indeed, a rational great power will impose limits on its own expansion, even reduce its own power and influence, in order to avoid provoking other countries (a strategy comparable to giving away much of one's money in the hope of ensuring that one will not be robbed).

During the Cold War, the assumptions of minimal realism led prominent American realist thinkers such as diplomat and scholar George Kennan and journalist Walter Lippmann to argue that the United States greatly exaggerated the Soviet threat to American interests. The Kennan-Lippmann school favored a modest American foreign policy of "finite containment" that would have limited U.S. security guarantees to a few key countries and regions—Western Europe, Japan, and perhaps oil-producing states in the Middle East. If the United States did less, other countries could be counted upon to do more to balance Moscow. The political scientist Stephen Walt justified finite containment by alleging that "balancing behavior predominates in international politics."[31]

The proponents of what has been called "maximal realism" take an entirely different view of the underlying trends of world politics. The two schools share an emphasis on the primacy of power and interest in competitive state systems. But maximal realists are more likely to recognize that state systems are the exceptions, not the rule, in history. When systems of multiple great powers do appear, they are usually absorbed, after a few centuries or even a few generations, into "universal empires"—that is, imperial entities that incorporate most or all of the peoples and territories of a particular region, or perhaps, in the future, the planet as a whole.

Maximal realists also stress the extent to which the world of interstate politics is organized as a hierarchy of power and function. According to the political scientist William Curti Wohlforth, "The hierarchical understanding of the balance of power . . . [by contrast with the balance-of-power model of minimal realism] highlights a different set of laws and regularities in world politics: concentrated, hegemonic distributions rather than equilibria; the possibility of translating power into political preeminence; a greater tendency to bandwagon; and an eternal struggle among the leading states for control of the system."[32] That there is a system for the leading states to control results from the tendency of the hierarchy of power to be accompanied by a vertical division of labor among states. The state at the top of the international pecking order, the empire or hegemon, specializes in providing military security to weaker states, or in using its military power for extortion (the difference may be blurred in some cases). If it is an economic powerhouse as well as a military great power, the top-ranking state may also control international finance and investment, as Britain did in the nineteenth century and as the United States did in the twentieth. Assured of protection by the powerful countries, weaker states may cut back on their defense spending and concentrate on a particular niche in the hierarchical system—for example, by becoming sites for specialized functions in the international economy (offshore tax havens or oil-producing sheikdoms, for example), or by exporting mercenaries for use by the great powers (as the early modern Swiss cantons and German duchies and Castro's communist Cuba have all done).

Maximal realists, then, believe that it is not only possible but likely that a single superpower or great-power alliance will dominate the hierarchical, specialized global system. Once a country that specializes in coercion accumulates a sufficient surplus of intimidating military power, many, perhaps most, of the other countries in the world will bandwagon with it rather than militarize their own societies or unite with other weak countries in order to challenge the dominant power. In this view, world politics is like the politics of a pack of dogs. The top dog could easily be defeated by a combination of weaker dogs. But the majority of the pack, accustomed to their subordinate places in the hierarchy, will defer individually to the top dog. The top dog need only defeat his most credible challenger for the entire pack to fall into line. By the same token, the top dog need be defeated by only one powerful challenger, in only one or a few fights observed by the rest, in order to be deserted by the entire pack, whose members will bandwagon with the new top dog.

The bandwagon effect emphasized by maximal realism provides the answer to the question: In what way could the humiliation of the United States in the Vietnam War or a similar conflict have caused the United States to lose the Cold War—or at least brought American defeat in the Cold War much closer?

In the mind of the western public, the idea of defeat in the Cold War was associated with nuclear armaggedon. But the defeat of the United States in the global struggle might have resulted from America's backing down in confrontations involving Berlin, or Korea, or Taiwan, or Indochina, or Cuba, or similar contested areas charged with significance by the superpower rivalry. After the first major defeat or retreat, or perhaps the second or third or fourth in a row, confidence in America's military capability, or its determination to use it, would have collapsed. At that point, something akin to a panic in the stock market would have ensued. In a remarkably short period of time—a few years, perhaps even a few months—the worldwide American alliance system would have unraveled, as European, Asian, Middle Eastern, African, and Latin American states hurriedly made deals with Moscow. Thanks to runaway bandwagoning, the United States would have found itself marginalized in a world now aligned around the Soviet Union (there having been no other military power with global reach and global ambitions at the time). The Soviets might not have had to fire a shot in anger. There need not have been any additional communist revolutions. The same elites might even have remained in power in the same capitals around the world. Indeed, America's alliances such as NATO and the U.S.-Japan alliance might have lasted formally for a few more years, though moribund. But Moscow would have displaced Washington at the apex of the global military hierarchy, and everybody would have known it.

The bandwagon effect is the reason why it was a mistake to argue that the Soviet empire was bound to collapse of overextension. Power in the international arena is relative, not absolute. If the Soviet Union had managed, by means of military intimidation, to divide the alliance of the United States, Western Europe, and Japan, or to frighten the United States into isolationism and appeasement, then it might have achieved and maintained a position as the world's leading military power in relative terms even while it reduced its expenditures on the military. In the same way, the abatement of the Soviet challenge permitted the United States to become relatively more powerful in world politics in the 1990s, even as it slashed its defense spending and overseas troop deployments.

Having frightened the weak and divided industrial democracies into bandwagoning with it, a Soviet Union that had won the Cold War by intimidation would have had little trouble keeping its empire intact. In 1967, the leading minimal realist thinker George Kennan wrote that "one must not be too frightened of those who aspire to world domination" because of "the continued and undiminished relevance in the modern world of Gibbon's assertion that 'there is nothing more contrary to nature than the attempt to hold in obedience distant provinces.'"[33] In fact, conquest can be profitable, if the costs of repressing the conquered are outweighed by the additions to the resource base of the conqueror. In *Does Conquest Pay? The Exploitation of Occupied Industrial Societies* (1996), the political scientist Peter Liberman demonstrates that the economic benefit to the Soviet Union of its control of Eastern Europe from 1945–89 far outweighed the relatively low costs of repressing the Eastern Europeans in 1953 (East Germany), 1956 (Hungary), 1968 (Czechoslovakia), and 1981 (Poland). Without the resources of Eastern Europe, the Soviet empire might have been bankrupted sooner by the military competition with the West; and without the ability to divert western military spending to meet threats in Asia, the Middle East, and Latin America, Moscow might have faced a much greater western military challenge in its core region. In the case of Cuba, the Soviet Union gained a strategically valuable ally and a supply of mercenaries it could use in Africa. The victory of Moscow's Vietnamese clients gave the declining Soviet regime a boost in prestige and morale for much of a decade.

Kennan himself admitted the legitimacy of concerns about bandwagoning in world politics and the possibility of Soviet primacy as a result of intimidation rather than of war. In the late 1940s, Kennan summed up the idea of the bandwagon effect with characteristic eloquence:

> One of the vital facts to be borne in mind about the international communist movement in the parts of Europe which are not yet under Soviet military and police control is the pronounced "bandwagon" character which that movement bears. By that I mean the fact that a given proportion of the adherents to the movement are drawn to it by no ideological enthusiasm . . . but primarily by the belief that it is the coming thing, the movement of the future . . . and that those who hope to survive—let alone thrive—in the coming days will be those who had the foresight to climb on the bandwagon when it was still the movement of the future.[34]

In the 1970s, arguing against U.S. Cold War policy from his later, self-described "isolationist" perspective, Kennan was honest enough to admit that a Soviet strategy of winning global primacy by intimidation short of war made sense, from Moscow's perspective: "Certainly, if all this could be achieved bloodlessly, without upsetting repercussions at home and increased responsibilities for the Soviet Union, the leadership of that country would no doubt be pleased—but only within limits [!]—to see such things as abandonment of the Western position in Berlin, a clear Soviet military ascendancy all the way from the Atlantic to the Chinese Frontier, and heightened Soviet prestige the world over."[35]

The Cold War, then, was most likely to end with a rapid and more or less bloodless global diplomatic realignment in favor of the superpower that was perceived to be the most militarily powerful and the most politically determined. We know that this is how the Cold War would have ended if the United States had lost, because this is how the Cold War ended when the Soviet Union lost.

The Bandwagon Effect in the Cold War: The Test of History

In 1961, Soviet premier Nikita Khrushchev described the strategic nightmare of Soviet policymakers, a nightmare in which the failure of the Soviet Union to vindicate its credibility in a largely symbolic crisis at a largely symbolic flashpoint would lead to greater American pressure, the dissolution of Soviet alliances, and, ultimately, the overthrow of communism:

> The question of access to West Berlin and the whole question of the peace treaty is for [the Western powers] only a pretext. If we abandoned our intention of concluding a peace treaty, they would take this as a strategic breakthrough and would in no time broaden the range of their demands. They would demand the abolition of the socialist system in the German Democratic Republic. . . . And if the Western powers achieved all this, they would come forward with their principal demand—that the socialist system be abolished in all the countries of the socialist camp.[36]

Khrushchev's nightmare bore a remarkable resemblance to what actually happened to the Soviet bloc under his successor Mikhail Gorbachev.

Throughout the Cold War, Moscow was as worried as Washington about the threat posed to its bloc by runaway bandwagoning. Fear of the bandwagon effect led the Soviet leadership to believe—perhaps correctly—that the overthrow of communism in Afghanistan would endanger Moscow's control over its Central Asian republics and weaken its overall credibility in the communist bloc and the world. The Soviets thwarted that threat by invading Afghanistan in 1979. However, Gorbachev's decision not to invade Eastern Europe in order to prop up communist rule there set in motion a chain of events that led to the disintegration not only of the external empire but of the USSR itself. Given what happened in 1989–91, it seems quite likely that the Soviet empire in Europe, and perhaps the Soviet Union itself, might have unraveled in 1953, or 1956, or 1968, had the Soviets not promptly and ruthlessly crushed East Germany, Hungary, and Czechoslovakia.

The evidence for the importance of the bandwagon effect in world politics is not limited to the single case of the dissolution of the Soviet empire. The larger history of the Cold War supports it as well. The bandwagon theory predicts that weak states around the world would have been most likely to bandwagon with the Soviet Union as its power relative to the United States grew—and that they would have been likely to distance themselves from the Soviet Union as its relative power declined. This is exactly the pattern that an examination of the historical record reveals. In the mid-1950s and the late 1980s, when the Soviet Union was relatively weak, the Soviets had few allies. In the mid-seventies, when Soviet military power reached its peak relative to that of the United States, the Soviet alliance system attained its greatest extent. This pattern contradicts the predictions of balance-of-power theory—but it accords perfectly with the predictions of bandwagoning theory. So does the fact that the United States had the greatest number of allies at the beginning of the Cold War (when the Soviet Union was still devastated by World War II) and at the end of the Cold War (when the Soviet Union's former satellites as well as former allies and neutrals were deserting Moscow to seek the favor of Washington).

The General Assembly of the United Nations provides yet a third test of the theory of the bandwagon effect. When American military power was at its relative peak in the early 1950s, Third World states tilted toward the United States. As Soviet power rose, more became neutral; finally, when Soviet military might peaked in the 1970s, there was a dramatic pro-Soviet tilt in the United Nations General Assembly. "The United States was seen to be reeling back in compounded defeat, incapable of retaliation, unwilling even to contemplate retaliation," former U.S. ambassador to the UN Daniel Patrick Moynihan recalled. According to Moynihan, in the mid-1970s "U.N. assemblies were almost wholly given over to assaults on Western positions by combined Communist and Third World blocs."[37] The fact that the Soviet–Third World bloc was based on the perception, by weak states, of American decline and the rise of Soviet power, rather than on some other factor, like postcolonial radicalism or the appeal of the Soviet model, is clear from the astonishing reversal of Third World attitudes toward the United States in the United Nations that followed the demise of the Soviet Union—a reversal of foreign policy orientation by many of the same elites that had been pro-Soviet only a few years before.

Even proponents of minimal realism concede that weak states tend to bandwagon with threatening great powers rather than attempt to balance them. Stephen M. Walt writes that "in general, the weaker the state, the more likely it is to bandwagon rather than balance."[38] If West Germany and Japan, despite their wealth, are considered to have been weak states during the Cold War, in which the only military superpowers were the United States and the Soviet Union, then minimal realist theory itself would predict that the West Germans and Japanese would be tempted to accommodate the Soviet Union if they believed they could not rely on the United States to protect not only their territories but their regional and world-order interests.

The fact that West German and Japanese leaders often complained that the Vietnam War was diverting resources and attention from their own defense merely demonstrates the degree of their anxiety about the Soviet threat and the shallowness of their confidence in American credibility. In the case of West Germany, the record demonstrates that the tendency to appease the Soviet Union flowed or ebbed more or less in sync with perceptions of U.S. credibility. When the Kennedy administration backed down during the Berlin crisis of August 1961, Chancellor Konrad Adenauer's hardline policy of requiring reunification of Germany as a precondition for German détente with the Soviet bloc collapsed. "I said later that in August 1961 a curtain was drawn aside to reveal an empty stage," wrote the German Social Democratic leader Willy Brandt in 1976. "[East German dictator Walter] Ulbricht had been allowed to take a swipe at the Western superpower, and the United States merely winced with annoyance. My political deliberations that followed were substantially influenced by this day's experience, and it was against this background that my so-called Ostpolitik—the beginning of dé-tente—took shape."[39] Convinced that the weakness and vacillation of their American protector made a West German policy of confrontation impossible, the West Germans hoped that the liberalization of the Soviet bloc might lead to German reunification. Even this cautious hope was crushed when the Soviet bloc invaded Czechoslovakia in 1968 to restore Soviet authority in Eastern Europe, including East Germany. The *Ostpolitik* (eastern policy) pursued by West Germany after 1968 was a policy of appeasement based on the disillusioned West German leadership's recognition of Soviet determination, and the absence of American re-solve. It is no coincidence that West Germany and the other Western European states legitimated the Soviet empire in Eastern Europe by rati-fying the Helsinki Accords at the very moment in the 1970s when Soviet military power reached its peak. West German foreign minister Egon Bahr candidly justified the German policy of détente with the Soviet bloc by describing it as a response to German doubts about the validity of the American alliance commitment: "Would America answer with nu-clear missiles if the Russians took Hamburg? The answer [was] no. So détente was our only option."[40] Although the immediate reason for Ger-man anxiety was the achievement by the Soviets of nuclear parity with the United States in the 1970s, the context included the withdrawal of the United States from Indochina, followed by President Carter's tenta-tive plans to pull U.S. troops not only out of South Korea but out of Western Europe itself. The history of West German foreign policy dur-ing the Cold War, then, is a powerful exhibit in the case for the central-ity of the bandwagon effect. The political scientist John Orme writes: "The catalysts of this evolution of German policy, as the record clearly shows, were two brutal but powerfully persuasive uses of force by Moscow—the construction of the Wall in Berlin and the destruction of liberty in Prague"—two Soviet shows of power and resolve to which the United States responded all too weakly.[41]

Similarly, during the Cold War there was a genuine possibility that Japan would distance itself from the United States if its conservative and pro-American leadership feared that Washington could no longer pro-tect Japan or its regional and global interests. The Japanese elite was not averse to using the threat of Japanese neutralism or defection from the American-led Free World bloc in hope of extorting concessions from its imperial protector. In 1966, in response to American efforts to help Texas Instruments break into the protected Japanese market, the leading Japanese business daily warned that "American failure to 'understand' Japanese treatment of Texas Instruments and similar foreign direct investment cases might endanger Japan's support for U.S. security policies."[42] At the peak of the so-called Second Cold War in 1982, the director general of the Trade Policy Bureau of the Ministry of International Trade and Industry warned that American pressure on Japan to open its market might force Japan to join the communist bloc.[43] These threats may not have been credible, but the fact that they were made at all is significant.

The Bandwagon Effect After the Cold War—and Before

When the Soviet empire fell in the late 1980s, the intellectual empire of minimal realist theory fell with it. For decades, American minimal realists in the academy and the press had scoffed at maximal realists who had claimed that the loss of military reputation by a superpower could cause an abrupt disintegration of its informal empire. Most minimal realists envisioned the gradual decline of both the United States and the Soviet Union, accompanied by the emergence of new superpowers—a remilitarized Japan, a United Europe, China. The "solvency school" realists and "world-order liberals" of the 1970s and 1980s never imagined that the Soviet empire would rapidly implode, following a few symbolic defeats by the West in Afghanistan and Europe. Nor did they imagine that Cold War bipolarity would give way abruptly to the unipolarity of a world order dominated by the United States. Such dramatic bandwagoning was not supposed to occur in a balance-of-power world.

Nevertheless, bandwagoning happened. And it happened twice.

The dynamics of Middle Eastern power politics in the aftermath of the U.S.-led coalition's victory over Saddam Hussein's Iraq in 1991 recapitulated, in miniature, the dynamics of world politics that followed the American bloc's victory over the Soviet empire. As soon as it became apparent that there would be only one superpower where lately there had been two, Third World regimes that formerly had been neutral or pro-Soviet strove to improve their relations with the United States. Thus, with an undignified haste, every regime in the Middle East (with the exception of defeated Iraq, Libya, and Iran, then in a phase of its internal Shia revolution) discovered that it wanted to be on good terms with the United States, once the United States had displayed its willingness to go to war to become and remain the military hegemon of the Persian Gulf.

If balance-of-power theory had been right, none of this should have occurred. The decline of the Soviet Union should have led the countries of the world to team up in order to cut American power down to size. Needless to say, no global anti-American coalition formed. On the contrary, most countries appeased the now unchecked United States. In the Middle East following the Gulf War, as in the world following the Cold War, no anti-American alliance materialized. The fact that the enterprise of expelling the United States from the region was undertaken by stateless terrorists based in a few marginal countries like Afghanistan and Sudan underlines the point.

Long before the end of the Cold War and the Gulf War, an earlier example of the importance of the bandwagoning dynamic in world politics was provided by the remarkable success of Hitler's Germany in the 1930s and early 1940s. Never has a great power come so close to world domination by taking advantage of a classic case of the bandwagon effect. At the beginning of the 1930s, Germany was a disarmed pariah state. At the end of the decade, even before the Nazi-Soviet alliance launched a general war, Germany dominated continental Europe. Hitler had used force and intimidation successfully to discourage or break up anti-German alliances. The stronger the Third Reich grew and the more threatening it became, the less willing its frightened neighbors were to confront it and the more willing they were to appease it. Instead of forming a coalition to contain Germany in the middle of the 1930s, Britain, France, and the Soviet Union competed to appease the aggressive and expansionist Nazi regime. Indeed, the Soviet Union sought to protect itself by entering into an alliance with Hitler in 1939. Hitler hoped to intimidate Britain into entering a similar alliance, which would permit him to conquer the Soviet Union and prepare for a final global struggle between Berlin and Washington that he believed would occur in the late twentieth century. If Britain had appeased Germany or had gone down to defeat before the United States entered World War II, Hitler would have succeeded in using coercive diplomacy and a series of small wars (along with a Korea/Vietnam-style proxy war in Spain) to bandwagon his way to global hegemony by the early 1940s.

Once the German and Japanese empires had been shattered in World War II, and the postwar weakness of Britain had become evident, the United States probably would have become the global hegemon by the late 1940s—if not for the Soviet challenge. The fact that few countries objected to the proposal that the United Nations be located either in New York or San Francisco speaks volumes. If the Soviet Union had been content with the status of a regional Eurasian power after 1945, the kind of unipolar world centered on Washington that emerged in the 1990s might have evolved by the 1950s, as a result of a pro-American global bandwagon effect.

The replacement of the bipolar world order of the Cold War by a unipolar world order in the 1990s came as no surprise to maximal realists, who believe that power tends to be concentrated in a single alliance or state—in this case, the United States. If the world should become more decentralized in time as a result of the diffusion of wealth and military power to countries other than the United States, this will not prove that the balance-of-power model of minimal realism was correct after all. Balance-of-power theory is not to be confused with "the law of uneven growth" of national economies, or alterations in relative shares of world population resulting from different fertility rates. For balance-of-power theory to be correct, it is not enough that China and India should become relatively more important, and the United States relatively less important, as a result of unequal rates of growth in productivity or population. For balance-of-power theory to be vindicated, the United States must be consciously cut down to size by a coalition of other great powers that have united for that specific purpose. There are no signs of this happening at present.

"A Small Country on the Edge of Nowhere"

It is possible to argue that even if the Soviet Union and China considered the fate of Indochina to be important, the United States could have ceded the region to one or both of the communist great powers with little or no damage to its foreign policy. During the Cold War, minimal realists such as George Ball, George Kennan, and Walter Lippmann advocated a strategy of finite containment limited to the North Atlantic and North Pacific as an alternative to the policy of global containment that the United

States actually pursued. Ball wrote that U.S. strategy should focus on "the principal Atlantic nations." The only area of the non-European world of any importance, apart from Japan, was the Middle East, because of its oil reserves. The Vietnam War (and presumably the Korean War) was based on the mistaken equation of a commitment "in the jungles and rice paddies of a small country on the edge of nowhere with our most important treaty commitments to defend our Western allies in the heart of Europe—the center of world power and hence the center of danger."[44] Like other minimal realists, Ball saw little reason for the United States to oppose Soviet imperial gains anywhere outside of an imaginary border that encircled North America, Western Europe, and the Middle East. Even the nearby nations of the Caribbean and Central America should be "free to create their own versions of chaos."[45] George Kennan advocated an even greater degree of American retrenchment. In *The Cloud of Danger* (1977), Kennan suggested that the Europeans were imagining the Soviet threat: "In this respect, we have to treat our European friends as a species of psychiatric patient with hallucinations".[46] In an interview with George Urban in *Encounter* in September 1976, Kennan described himself as an "isolationist."[47] The difficulties involved in drawing a line around commitments have been noted by Edward Luttwak, in a critique of George Kennan's strategic views: "If the necessity of an immediate circle of allies is recognized, as it is in Mr. Kennan's minimalist formula, the logic of collective security, the regional concerns of each primary ally, and the maintenance of a global balance of power will certainly require a further and wider sphere of secondary involvement."[48]

Even if the maximal realist premises that underpinned U.S. grand strategy during the Cold War were sound, the application of that strategy in Indochina (or for that matter Korea or Taiwan) might have been mistaken. It might be argued that the "three fronts" of Korea, Taiwan, and Indochina were not as important in Cold War power politics as American presidents from Truman to Nixon believed. The question of whether a given country or region is strategic or not can be approached by means of a simple question: Do the great powers of a given era consider it worth fighting for?

The importance that U.S. policymakers placed upon Indochina antedated the Cold War. Shortly before Pearl Harbor, Secretary of War Henry Stimson suggested to President Roosevelt that "an attack without further warning" against the Japanese empire might be in America's interest if Japan moved toward Thailand.[49] On December 6, 1941, FDR drafted a personal message to the Japanese emperor, warning about the consequences of Japanese expansion in Indochina.[50] Even in advance of Pearl Harbor, then, the Roosevelt administration considered mainland Southeast Asia to be so important to America's overall Asian and global strategy that it had to be kept out of the control of the hostile Axis bloc.

What is more, between 1946 and 1989, every major military power of the Cold War era—the United States, China, France, the Soviet Union, and the British Commonwealth—sent at least some troops into combat in Indochina or nearby countries in Southeast Asia. If Indochina was a peripheral region of no strategic importance in world politics, it is curious that this fact escaped the attention of policymakers in Washington, Moscow, Beijing, Paris, and London.

If Indochina *was* a key strategic region during the Cold War for which the two superpowers were willing to fight, directly or indirectly, why was it of strategic importance? The answer has less to do with sea-lanes than with symbolism. The symbolic significance of Indochina in the global rivalry for world primacy between the American bloc and the communist bloc, and in the simultaneous competition within the communist bloc between the Soviet Union and China, arose from the fact that the Cold War was an ideological war as well as a power struggle.

The interaction between ideology and power in the Cold War was misunderstood by two groups: conservative anticommunists and minimal realists. Anticommunist conservatives were mistaken when they interpreted the Cold War as a battle between communism and "western civilization." The Cold War began in 1946, not in 1917. Soviet efforts to spread communism in the world by means of subversion and proxy wars such as the Spanish Civil War during the years between the Bolshevik coup d'état in 1917 and World War II were miserable failures. The status of the Soviet Union as one of two military superpowers—the result of Germany's suicide in World War II—was the necessary condition for the political and military successes of Marxism-Leninism beyond the USSR and Outer Mongolia, beginning with the Soviet-assisted Chinese communist victory in 1949. What is more, the Cold War ended with the collapse of the Soviet Union's ability and determination to challenge American global predominance, even though Marxist-Leninist regimes survived in China, North Korea, Indochina, and Cuba.

If the anticommunist right exaggerated the ideological dimension of the Cold War, minimal realists tended to ignore that dimension altogether. The American academic Stephen Walt claimed in 1989 that "as the history of international communism reveals (e.g. the quarrels between Stalin and Tito, Khrushchev and Mao, and the fratricidal conflict between Kampuchea, Vietnam, and China), Marxist ideology has been a relatively weak motive for alignment."[51] Many realists in the Cold War era, such as George Kennan, were in the habit of using "Soviet" and "Russian" interchangeably, as though the Soviet Union were tsarist Russia beneath superficial Marxist-Leninist trappings.

More sophisticated maximal realists took Marxism-Leninism seriously as a militant secular religion. Dean Acheson, reflecting on the late 1940s and early 1950s, wrote that "the threat to Western Europe seemed to me singularly like that which Islam had posed several centuries before, with its combination of ideological zeal and fighting power."[52] In the 1950s, the British political scientist Martin Wight made the same comparison: "The Jacobins of the French Revolution, and the Communists (on a parallel with Islam), divided the world into Dar-al-Islam and Dar-al-Harb"—that is, the "Abode of Peace" and the "Abode of War."[53] Bertrand Russell (who became a bitter critic of the Cold War in his old age) had written as early as 1921: "Bolshevism combines the characteristics of the French Revolution with those of the rise of Islam. . . . Among religions, Bolshevism is to be reckoned with Mohammedanism rather than with Christianity and Buddhism. Christianity and Buddhism are primarily personal religions, with mystical doctrines and a love of contemplation. Mohammedanism and Bolshevism are practical, social, unspiritual, concerned to win the empire of this world."[54] In this connection, it is worth noting that the term "cold war"—*guerra fría*—was first used in the thirteenth century in connection with the low-level border war in Spain between the rival religious civilizations of Latin Christendom and Islam.

The dismissal of the ideological factor in the foreign policies of communist states was clearly an error. In the aftermath of World War II, a noncommunist Russian regime might have sought a Russian sphere of influence in Eastern Europe, but would not have imposed a totalitarian social order on Poland, Czechoslovakia, or other countries. Had Chiang Kai-shek's Nationalist government survived, the foreign policy of China in the 1950s and 1960s would have been radically different from that of Mao. Although Mao's successors began to think like Bismarck or Metternich, Mao himself thought like Lenin or Robespierre or Khomeini. In the cases of both the Chinese communist revolution and the Iranian Shia Muslim revolution, it took a full generation for the revolutionary regimes to show signs of moderation and to consider rapprochement with the United States and other western states. (The final flare-up of Maoist radicalism came in the 1970s in Cambodia, where Pol Pot tried to create a version of what he had seen in China during the Cultural Revolution a decade earlier.)

Even the relatively moderate Soviet leader Nikita Khrushchev emphasized that Moscow's support for communist revolutionaries in Asia was inspired not by the "national interest" of "Russia" but by the Soviet regime's ideology: "No real Communist would have tried to dissuade Kim Il-Sung from his compelling desire to liberate South Korea from Syngman Rhee and from reactionary American influence. To have done so would have contradicted the Communist view of the world."[55] The Soviet Union was not only a superpower but the headquarters of the global religion of Marxism-Leninism, with zealous adherents in dozens of countries who looked to Moscow not only for military and economic support but for ideological guidance. Mao and his colleagues also viewed support for foreign communists as a test of their commitment to Marxism-Leninism. Zhou Enlai told North Vietnamese leaders in 1971, "Not to support the revolution of the Vietnamese people is like betraying the revolution."[56] This viewpoint can be compared instructively with a recent description of Shiite Iran's foreign policy: "Because Iran sometimes portrays itself as a guardian of Shiites worldwide, experts in the region said today that it may feel under pressure to respond with military force if it can be proven that the Shiites [in Afghanistan] were attacked for reasons of religious faith."[57]

The global alliance that the United States led in the Cold War was far more diverse than the communist bloc; it included liberal democracies, military dictatorships, and Muslim theocracies that shared little more than a common fear of Soviet power and influence. To the disappointment of Americans who wanted the United States to crusade for a "global democratic revolution," U.S. policymakers properly limited the goal of American grand strategy to the negative one of preventing hostile great powers from winning military hegemony over Europe, Asia, or the Eurasian supercontinent as a whole. The democratic wave of the 1990s was a byproduct of America's Cold War victory, not the goal of America's

Cold War strategy. U.S. foreign policy had to be narrowly anticommunist because a pro-democratic foreign policy would have prevented the United States from having many allies outside of Western Europe, where most of the world's outnumbered democracies were found during the Cold War.

Symbolic Frontiers

The important ideological dimension of the Cold War gave struggles in certain countries a significance in addition to that which they would have possessed merely by being objects of great-power competition. The regions outside of the North Atlantic/Japanese core of the Cold War American bloc that were most important in terms of ideological symbolism were Korea, Taiwan, and Indochina. Like Germany, these areas were partitioned between the communist bloc and the American bloc. Unlike West Germany, which was an industrial "core," and like West Berlin, neither South Korea nor Taiwan nor Indochina were of any intrinsic strategic value to the United States. Indeed, in the 1940s the U.S. government had considered sacrificing all three of these difficult-to-defend areas to the communist alliance. When North Korea invaded South Korea in 1950, however, the Truman administration sent the Seventh Fleet to prevent the Chinese communists from capturing Taiwan, and threw America's weight behind the effort of the French to deny Indochina to Ho Chi Minh's Soviet- and Chinese-sponsored communists. The end of the Korean War restored the "tripwire" bisecting Korea at the Thirty-eighth Parallel. The withdrawal of the French from Indochina resulted in another frontier between the communist bloc and the Free World bloc along the Seventeenth Parallel, separating North Vietnam from noncommunist South Vietnam, Laos, and Cambodia. Yet a third invisible tripwire separated Taiwan from communist mainland China.

The location of these tripwires was thus the result of a number of contingent events, the most important of which was the Chinese communist victory in 1949. Had the history of the late 1940s and early 1950s taken another turn, there might have been no divided countries in East Asia—while there might have been tripwires running between the communist and prowestern sections of a divided Austria, or a divided Greece, or a divided Italy, or a divided Yugoslavia. Major proxy conflicts such as the Korean and Vietnam wars might have been fought between the rival blocs in areas far from Korea and Vietnam, and today's anti–Cold War historians might be writing that the United States "lost its innocence" or "overcommitted itself" in the "Italian debacle" of the 1940s or the "Balkan tragedy" of the 1950s. But as it happened, Korea, Taiwan, and Indochina were what Mao called the "three fronts" in Asia—the three places where the communist bloc had a border with the anticommunist alliance. These three regions were not contested because they were important. *They were important because they were contested.*

A proxy war could not be fought over West Germany or West Berlin without risking the involvement of the United States and the Soviet Union in a general war. The deadlock on the primary front of the Cold War, Europe, meant that the major tests of strength and willpower had to take place along the second front in Asia—in particular, in the Asian countries in which the metaphorical border between the so-called free world and the communist world was an actual frontier. It was this logic, the reputational logic of power politics, combined with the symbolic logic of ideological politics, that was responsible for most of the crises in the Cold War—not the territorial logic of old-fashioned geopolitics.

The United States went to the verge of war with the Soviet Union over West Berlin. Why? The Soviet Union engaged in its biggest airlift since World War II to resupply North Vietnamese and communist Laotian troops during the Laos crisis of the early 1960s. Why? The United States rolled back a conventional invasion of South Korea, and intervened to thwart an insurgency reinforced by an invasion in South Vietnam. Why? The Soviet Union and China supported the wars waged by North Korea and North Vietnam, deterred American escalation by threats, and even sent their own troops to take part in combat. Why? The Soviet Union went to war in Afghanistan to prop up a communist regime, while the United States and China armed its enemies. Why? Most if not all of these actions make little sense in terms of archaic geopolitical conceptions of "spheres of influence" and "vital interests." But all of these campaigns on both sides are perfectly understandable in light of the duelist's logic of power politics and the crusader's logic of ideological war. In essence, these struggles were battles of nerve along the symbolic border between the two Cold War blocs—a symbolic border that ran through the city of Berlin and down the middle of the Taiwan Strait and bisected the national territories of Korea and Vietnam.

South Korea, Taiwan, and South Vietnam were as important to the informal American Cold War empire as, say, Puerto Rico and Guam and Hawaii had been to the American maritime empire of 1898–1941. It should be remembered that the U.S. participation in World War II began with Japan's attack on Hawaii and America's other Pacific territories—territories that were as remote and unfamiliar to most Americans in 1941 as South Korea was in 1950 and South Vietnam was in 1965. To describe the Korean and Vietnam wars, along with the confrontations over Taiwan, as mere contests for influence in the Third World is therefore inaccurate and misleading. South Vietnam, South Korea, and Taiwan were not just three developing countries among dozens. They were frontline states in a world war and they were U.S. protectorates.

The connection between the U.S. defense of Taiwan and the U.S. defense of Indochina was taken for granted by China's Zhou Enlai, who told Vietnamese officials in Beijing on May 16, 1965, "Because [the Americans] do not want to withdraw from Taiwan, it also means that they do not want to withdraw from South Vietnam. The people in Taiwan have not risen up as in South Vietnam. We have to render self-criticism to our shortcomings not to lead them to rise up."[58] Like Taiwan, South Korea was linked to South Vietnam in the same strategic chain. Many realist critics of the Vietnam War have sought to draw a distinction between Korea, a "vital interest" of the United States, and Indochina, which, it is alleged, was never a vital interest, despite the "tragic" belief of American policymakers to the contrary. Some of the realists who, in the 1960s and 1970s, contrasted "strategic" Korea with "insignificant" Vietnam had expressed quite different opinions during the Korean War. During the Vietnam War, George Kennan declared: "There are some [places], such as Korea and Cuba, that are of strategic importance in the sense that they affect the interest of this country and other great powers in an intimate and sensitive way. There are others . . . [that] are of minor significance from the standpoint of the world balance of power. The two must not be equated."[59] However, Kennan had not always been so impressed by Korea's intrinsic strategic significance. On August 21, 1950, a month before the American landing at Inchon reversed North Korea's conquest of South Korea, Kennan, then in the State Department's Policy Planning Unit, wrote a memorandum recommending that the United States abandon the entire Korean peninsula to the Soviet bloc:

It is beyond our capabilities to keep Korea permanently out of the Soviet orbit. The Koreans cannot really maintain their own independence in the face of both Russian and Japanese pressures. From the standpoint of our own interests it is preferable that Japan should dominate Korea than that Russia should do so. But Japan at the moment is too weak to compete. . . . *A period of Russian domination, while undesirable, is preferable to continued [American] involvement in that unhappy area*, as long as the means chosen to assert Soviet influence are not, as was the case with those resorted to in June of this year, ones calculated to throw panic and terror into other Asian peoples and thus to achieve for the Kremlin important successes, going far beyond the Korean area.[60]

Not one of the histories that mentions Kennan's opposition to the Vietnam War points out that, at the beginning of the Korean War, Kennan had advised the Truman administration to abandon South Korea to the Soviet bloc. George Ball's reaction to the invasion of South Korea by North Korea was similar. Ball's first instinct was to oppose American intervention on the grounds that "an American intervention would not only jeopardize the . . . Schuman Plan [for Franco-German economic cooperation], it would create serious problems for European unity."[61] The fact that both George Ball and George Kennan had wanted the United States to cede South Korea to Stalin and his allies in 1950 casts an interesting light on their willingness to see the United States abandon South Vietnam, Laos, and Cambodia a little more than a decade later.

The Factor of Timing

The timing of the large-scale U.S. intervention in Indochina is another factor that American realists of the two rival schools would assess in different ways. Minimal realists have argued that the Soviet threat—narrowly defined as the threat of actual invasion of Western Europe or Japan—peaked in the late 1940s, when a still powerful Red Army menaced a ruined Western Europe and a defeated Japan. Once the Western European and Japanese economies had recovered, behind a wall of American military forces, the danger had passed. According to this view, by the 1970s—perhaps even by the 1960s—America's Cold War strategy was obsolete.

The logic of maximal realism leads to a quite different conclusion. The danger was not that the Soviets would overrun and physically occupy Western Europe or Japan, but rather that the Western Europeans and Japanese, left to fend for themselves, would have been frightened by Moscow's military buildup and displays of belligerence into appeasing the Soviet Union (this was called "Finlandization," after the way that Finland purchased its internal sovereignty after 1945 by appeasing the Soviet Union in foreign policy). Maximal realists are not as impressed as minimal realists by the postwar growth of the Western European and Japanese economies. GDP by itself does not translate into military power. Civilian, consumerist societies such as those of Western Europe and Japan (and North America) might opt for appeasing a relatively poor but militaristic empire such as the Soviet bloc rather than shift spending from consumption to defense. The western alliance easily might have spent the Soviet Union into bankruptcy a generation before 1989; this did not happen because of the constraints imposed by public opinion in the liberal democracies. (The leaders of the Soviet bloc were far less restricted by the preferences of those whom they ruled.)

Maximal realism suggests that the greatest danger of Soviet global predominance came not in the late 1940s but in the 1960s and 1970s. At that time, Soviet military power was greatest relative to that of the United States, increasing the danger that weak states, including rich but militarily weak countries such as those of Western Europe and Japan, might be intimidated into effective neutrality or bandwagoning with Moscow. The danger of appeasement was increased further by the success of the Soviet Union in breaking out of the circle of containment and sponsoring new client states and revolutionary movements in Asia, Africa, the Middle East, and the Americas.

In the view of maximal realists, the geopolitical significance of the Sino-Soviet split should not be exaggerated. Arthur M. Schlesinger, Jr., stating the opinion of many minimal realist critics of U.S. Cold War strategy, has written that American leaders made the mistake in the 1960s of seeing "communism as a relatively unified world movement directed from a single center."[62] In fact, after a period of only a few years in the mid-sixties in which China fought the Soviet Union for leadership of the communist bloc and Third World antiwestern movements, Moscow resumed its role as the only significant patron and sponsor of communist insurgencies and governments throughout the world—and exercised that role from the late 1960s until the late 1980s. Apart from China, the communist regimes that broke with the Soviet Union, such as Yugoslavia and Albania, were of negligible weight in the scale of world politics.

If the maximal realist analysis of the Cold War is correct, then, the 1960s were a truly perilous time for the United States and its alliance system. In the mid-sixties, the United States was in retreat on all fronts. Khrushchev had humiliated the United States and intimidated its European allies, by approving the construction of the Berlin Wall. The Cuban missile crisis, which apologists for the Kennedy administration have pretended was a U.S. victory, resulted in the final defeat of the United States to keep Cuba, the most strategically important country in the Caribbean, from becoming a Soviet satellite. The U.S. policy of preserving noncommunist regimes in South Vietnam, Laos, and Cambodia—key links in America's Indochina-Taiwan-Korea perimeter on the Asian front of the third world war—was on the verge of failure. According to William Bundy, assistant secretary of state for Southeast Asia: "The decision to compromise in Laos made it essential to convey by word and deed that the United States would stand firm in South Vietnam and in the rest of Southeast Asia."[63] In these circumstances, it was reasonable for the Johnson administration to decide that the escalation of the U.S. commitment to South Vietnam was the lesser of two evils, compared to abandonment of the entire region either to Chinese or Soviet domination. It is worth noting that Britain sent fifty thousand troops to defend its clients in Malaysia against a communist insurgency sponsored by Indonesia in the early 1960s. Were South Vietnam, Laos, and Cambodia really worth a smaller U.S. commitment than Malaysia alone was worth to Britain, in the circumstances of 1965?

The fall of Indochina in 1975 resulted in a geopolitical catastrophe for the United States—a worldwide Marxist-Leninist revolutionary wave, and discernible bandwagoning with the Soviet Union by frightened American allies and neutrals in the mid-1970s. As grave as these global consequences were, they might have been far greater had the United States abandoned Indochina without a fight in the mid-1960s, instead of fighting and then withdrawing in the early 1970s. In 1965, Mao was trying to renew the communist revolution at home and export it throughout Southeast Asia and the world; in 1975, Mao's last revolutionary spasm was a decade behind, and China was a de facto ally of the United States against the Soviet Union. In Southeast Asia, the bloody

Indonesian coup had eliminated any possibility of a communist revolution in the region's largest nation, while the U.S. effort in Vietnam had bought time for the noncommunist countries of the area to achieve a degree of political stability and rapid economic growth.

As late as March 1971, Le Duan told Zhou Enlai, "The Thai government is very much afraid of the Thai Communist Party's armed forces. It knows that weapons to the TCP armed forces are transported via Vietnam and Laos. It also knows that China has a road that runs to the Sino-Lao border. Therefore, [Thailand] faces the threat of the war expanding all over Southeast Asia." Le Duan continued: "We want to smash the US-Japan alliance as well as the alliance between the US, Japan, and the regional bourgeois class. We have to establish a world front that will be built first by some core countries and later enlarged to include African and Latin American countries." Le Duan proposed a "conference of the world peoples" in China to "further isolate the US, weaken the US-Japan alliance and shake the Southeast Asian bourgeois class, thus contributing to the defeat of the US global strategy."[64] One can only imagine what might have happened in Southeast Asia and elsewhere in the developing world, if in 1965 communists with these attitudes had come to power in Indochina, destabilizing neighboring countries by sending millions of refugees fleeing across borders and sponsoring communist insurrection in Thailand, at a time when the antiwestern Sukarno was still in power and Mao was presiding over the Cultural Revolution. As late as May 1970, Mao told Le Duan, "In my opinion, *Stalin is alive again.* The main tendency in the world today is revolution, including the whole world."[65]

It might be argued that the best time to have "ceded" Indochina to the communist bloc was 1954, rather than 1965. But again, in the context of the global Cold War power struggle, such a "cession" would not have served either the interests of the United States or the global anticommunist alliance that it led. It would have made no sense for the United States, having lost fifty-six thousand lives to prevent the Sino-Soviet bloc from incorporating the entire Korean peninsula, to have permitted the same enemy alliance to take over the contested Indochina peninsula. For an equivalent one must imagine President George Bush, after having ousted Iraq from Kuwait, allowing Iraq to conquer a handful of other Persian Gulf emirates in compensation.

The idea that the United States could simply cede whole continents and subcontinents to the Soviet or Chinese communists and their clients, without a devastating loss in prestige, shows a failure to understand the nature of the Cold War. This was not some eighteenth-century competition between European dynasts, who could settle their differences amicably by carving up countries and exchanging territories. This was a world war, a hegemonic war, in which the future governance of the international system was at stake, and in which the great powers opposing the United States and its allies were the moral equivalents of Nazi Germany.

Even in the absence of hegemonic struggles, great military powers are usually reluctant to cede territories to their adversaries. The danger that the voluntary cession of territory by one power or bloc to another will be interpreted, not as evidence of prudence, but rather as evidence of military weakness or lack of political resolve, is very real. Ralph Hawtrey observes:

> Prestige is not entirely a matter of calculation, but partly of indirect inference. In a diplomatic conflict the country which yields is likely to suffer in prestige because the fact of yielding is taken by the rest of the world to be evidence of conscious weakness. The visible components of power do not tell the whole story, and no one can judge better of the invisible components than the authorities governing the country itself. If they show want of confidence, people infer that there is some hidden source of weakness.

Hawtrey concludes:

> A decline of prestige is therefore an injury to be dreaded. But in the last resort prestige means reputation for strength in war, and doubts on the subject can only be set at rest by war itself.[66]

Believing that Korea was a vital interest and Indochina a peripheral interest may help Americans feel better about the American success in Korea and failure in Indochina. Nevertheless, it remains an after-the-fact rationalization. It is clear from the historical record that the United States went to war in Korea for exactly the same reason that it later went to war in Indochina: to preserve U.S. military and diplomatic credibility in the global Cold War.

On April 29, 1947, the Joint Chiefs of Staff declared that the major reason for U.S. involvement in Korea was the fact that "this is the one country in which we alone have for almost two years carried out ideological warfare in direct contact with our opponents, so that to lose this battle would be gravely detrimental to U.S. prestige, and therefore security, throughout the world."[67] In his memoirs, Harry Truman noted his agreement with the military that the Korean peninsula was of little or no intrinsic military value to the United States. Truman interpreted the Soviet-sponsored North Korean invasion as "a repetition on a larger scale of what had happened in Berlin. The Reds were probing for weaknesses in our armor."[68] (It is striking that both the Korean and Vietnam wars followed Soviet-American confrontations over divided Berlin.) The political scientist and historian Robert A. Pape says flatly that the U.S. intervention in the Korean war "was driven by reputational rather than strategic concerns."[69]

Although the circumstances of the Cold War magnified the importance of demonstrations of U.S. credibility in crises involving Berlin, South Korea, Taiwan, Cuba, and South Vietnam, the need for the United States to prove its credibility did not end when the Soviet challenge to American global hegemony collapsed. The Gulf War was justified not merely by the need for unrestricted access to Persian Gulf oil or the danger that Iraq would develop weapons of mass destruction, but also by the need for the United States to demonstrate to its allies and clients in Europe and East Asia that it was able and willing to go to war to protect the key resource on which the industrial nations depended.

Credibility was even more important as a factor in the decision of the United States to go to war alongside its NATO allies against Yugoslavia in the spring of 1999. The columnist George Will observed that "NATO went to war to defend two things—Kosovars and its own credibility."[70] In addition to arguing that NATO intervention was needed to punish, if not prevent, Serbian atrocities in Kosovo, the Clinton administration claimed that the United States and NATO could not afford to lose face by backing down in their confrontation with the regime of Slobodan Milosevic. Secretary of State Madeleine K. Albright told the Senate Foreign Relations Committee that "Belgrade's actions constitute a critical test of NATO, whose strength and credibility have defended freedom and ensured our security for five decades."[71] Testifying before a House subcommittee on April 21, 1999, Secretary of Defense William Cohen declared, "Well, I'm . . . not the secretary [of Defense] who's going to give up the importance of our word. You asked the question, what's our word worth? A lot. To the extent that the United States doesn't stand behind its word, then I think that sends a signal that will invite more complications."[72]

A number of members of Congress and former U.S. government officials, some of them critics of NATO tactics in the war, agreed about the importance of preserving military credibility. Senator Joseph Lieberman of Connecticut argued that defeating Serbia was "important to our security and to NATO's credibility."[73] According to former National Security Adviser Zbigniew Brzezinski, "It is no exaggeration to say that NATO's failure to prevail would mean both the end of NATO as a credible alliance and the undermining of America's global leadership."[74] Former Secretary of State Henry Kissinger agreed that "NATO cannot survive" if it retreated from its confrontation with Milosevic. According to Kissinger, the use of NATO ground troops "will have to be considered to maintain NATO credibility."[75] Senator John McCain of Arizona stated:

> It seems to me obvious on the face of it that after two separate American presidents warned Milosevic that the United States would not tolerate Serb aggression against Kosovo, and after President Clinton twice delivered ultimatums to Milosevic to come to terms or else, that the failure to make good on those threats would devastate our credibility everywhere. And by that I don't mean President Clinton's credibility or Secretary Albright's credibility or any other individual's credibility. I mean our credibility—America's credibility.

McCain, a former Air Force pilot and prisoner of war during the Vietnam War, provided an eloquent and concise summary of the logic of military credibility in international affairs:

> Friend and foe alike perceive a gap between a great power's rhetoric and its actions as weakness. Our enemies, of course, will soon test our resolve in other ways to determine how far they can exploit our debility. Our friends will seek new arrangements to compensate for what they perceive as our unreliability. Thus, whether we had a strategic interest in the Balkans or not we acquired one the moment we threatened force. Credibility is a strategic asset of the highest order, and well worth fighting to maintain.[76]

In hindsight, America's Cold War trip-wire strategy with respect to the three fronts in Asia was all of a piece. Once the trip wires had been laid down by the Truman and Eisenhower administrations, the imperatives of America's sensible and ultimately vindicated Cold War strategy of global containment required the United States to wage limited wars if necessary to prevent Taiwan, South Korea, and South Vietnam, along with Laos and Cambodia, from being incorporated by invasion or subversion into the communist bloc. The only surprising thing about the Cold War in Asia is the fact that it ended without an American war for Taiwan in addition to the American wars for South Korea and South Vietnam.

CHAPTER 3

INFLEXIBLE RESPONSE

The U.S. Military and the Vietnam War

The U.S. Cold War strategy of global containment of the communist bloc made it practically inevitable that the United States would engage in some major attempt to prevent communist takeovers in South Vietnam, Laos, and Cambodia in the mid-1960s. The trip-wire strategy required the United States to go to war, if necessary, to prevent South Korea, Taiwan, or Indochina from being incorporated into the communist bloc by means of either invasion or subversion. The strategic significance of these three areas in Asia, like that of West Berlin, was almost entirely symbolic. By defending these three fronts, the United States demonstrated its credibility as a military superpower both to its communist enemies and to allies, clients, and neutrals. The strategic rationale for U.S. intervention was essentially the same in both the Korean and Vietnam wars.

Although the American interest in saving the noncommunist regimes of Indochina was genuine, it was also limited in scope. To prevent paying terrible costs in terms of its reputation as an alliance leader and military protector, the United States could not afford to do too little in Indochina; at the same time, because of the need to prevent the erosion and collapse of American public support for the Cold War, the United States could not do too much. This may seem obvious, but the conclusion that it leads to is not. *For the United States to achieve a partial success in its Indochina policy, it was not necessary for the United States to win the Vietnam War.* Denying Indochina to the communist bloc was the preferred outcome; but if the cost of doing so was too high, then losing Indochina also should have been acceptable, on the condition that the loss could be managed in a way that preserved both America's external credibility and its domestic consensus.

The United States failed to devise a military strategy that fulfilled both of these geopolitical and domestic political requirements. The strategy adopted by the U.S. military in Vietnam between 1965 and 1973 succeeded insofar as it prevented communist victories throughout Indochina—but it failed insofar as it reduced the support of the U.S. public for both the Vietnam War and the Cold War as a whole. The result of the decline in U.S. public support for the Cold War, in turn, was the erosion of America's global credibility, as the United States, paralyzed by the post-Vietnam isolationist backlash, failed to respond to ever bolder Soviet challenges around the world. What might have been a regional setback became a global rout for the United States that was not reversed until the Second Cold War of the 1980s.

Diminishing Returns

In the end, Indochina was not worth the limited war that the United States fought; but that does not mean that it was not worth *any* limited American war. The fact that the denial of Indochina to the communist bloc was not worth fifty-eight thousand American lives does not mean that it was not worth some substantial figure less than fifty-eight thousand (if one rejects the false morality of pacifism, then such grim calculations are unavoidable). A war to defend a great power's military credibility might be compared to an art auction, which is, among other things, a competition among the rich for prestige. The fact that one stops bidding for a painting when its price reaches $9000 does not mean that the painting was worthless all along; it merely means that one has reached the limit imposed by one's budget. The painting might well have been worth the expenditure of $8,800.

Even if one is outbid at an auction, one may have achieved the primary purpose of impressing observers with the fact that one is rich. A country that forfeits a war may nevertheless have preserved its reputation for military power and political resolution if it has exacted a high price from the enemy before it withdraws. In power politics, defeat is often preferable to retreat. If the United States was doomed to leave Indochina, it was best to be thrown out. As Johnson administration aide John McNaughton put it, the United States had to be "sensitive to how, as well as whether, the area is lost."[1]

Once this logic is understood, it becomes clear that the United States did not have a simple choice between winning and losing in Indochina. Rather, the United States had four options. It could win well, lose well, win badly, or lose badly. Winning well and losing well meant vindicating U.S. global military prestige and preserving the domestic Cold War consensus at the same time. Winning badly or losing badly meant damaging U.S. military credibility, or destroying public consensus in favor of the Cold War, or both.

The United States would have lost badly if it had simply "bugged out" of Indochina in 1965, as George Ball and others recommended. The domestic Cold War consensus might have been preserved, but America's credibility abroad would have suffered a catastrophic blow (particularly when it was revealed that the United States had been partly responsible for the 1963 coup against South Vietnam's President Diem). Ceding Indochina to the communist bloc without a fight would have been equivalent to abandoning South Korea to conquest by North Korea, or Taiwan to a mainland Chinese invasion. Something like the disastrous partial pro-Soviet realignment in world politics that occurred in the 1970s almost certainly would have taken place, but on a far greater scale, as panicked American allies and neutrals hastily appeased Moscow and perhaps Beijing as well.

The United States won badly in the Tet Offensive of 1968, which technically was a victory for the United States and South Vietnam and a defeat for the Viet Cong and North Vietnam. But the excessive costs of winning badly by means of an ill-conceived attrition strategy in South Vietnam made a U.S. withdrawal as a result of domestic pressure inevitable. Winning badly preserved America's credibility as a military protector of weak allies—but at the cost of undermining the Cold War consensus in the United States itself.

The alternatives to losing badly by retreating from Indochina without a fight and winning badly by piling up American and Vietnamese casualties too quickly were winning well or losing well. To win well or to lose well in Indochina, the United States had to keep the costs of its involvement limited. The chief cost to be controlled was the toll in American lives. Although George Ball, in arguing against the escalation of the war in the summer of 1965, was wrong to dismiss the strategic importance of Indochina and Southeast Asia, he was right to remind his fellow policy-makers of the correlation between rising battle deaths and growing public disaffection during the Korean War. On the evidence of the wars in Korea and Vietnam, the United States could afford to lose only around 15,000–20,000 soldiers in a superpower proxy war before the majority of the public turned against it. In both Korea and Vietnam, the United States ended up spending nearly sixty thousand lives. Even though South Korea survived, the cost of the Korean War made the U.S. public and the U.S. military excessively wary of further military interventions for a decade. The Vietnam War, a failure rather than a stalemate like the Korean War, had the same effect. What this suggests is that the Vietnam War should have been waged in such a way that, whether it was won or lost, the American public would continue to support similar small wars elsewhere on behalf of the global containment strategy that required occasional duels as well as enduring sieges. For the United States to have won at too high a cost in Vietnam might have been as great a political disaster as losing.

From the beginning, then, Washington should have imposed an informal limit on the number of American lives it was willing to spend on behalf of America's real but limited interest in a noncommunist Indochina. The number should have been a ceiling, not a goal. The argument set forth here is not that the United States should have provoked conflict or raked up casualties as evidence of its good faith. To send troops to their deaths purely for the purpose of reputation, in a war that could not be won by any plausible means, would be murder. Rather, the argument is that even a well-thought-out and realistic effort to rescue America's Indochinese allies should have been called off, once a critical level of American casualties had been reached. The loss of a few hundred soldiers in Vietnam may have been too small a sacrifice to preserve American credibility; the loss of fifty-eight thousand made preserving the American Cold War consensus impossible.*

---

*The fact that the U.S. public supported the war for two and a half years, until battle deaths passed fifteen thousand, may suggest what a reasonable informal ceiling for U.S. losses should have been. It is interesting to note that the Soviet government, evidently in response to some degree of unofficial public pressure, withdrew its forces from Afghanistan after losing around fifteen thousand soldiers.

All of this provides a better understanding of the difficult challenge that faced the Johnson administration. By 1968 the calculus would change, but in 1965 the balance between credibility abroad and consensus at home favored the escalation of the U.S. effort in Indochina. Domestic support for U.S. intervention was still high, while America's military and diplomatic reputation had been endangered by a series of a humiliations, particularly the Berlin and Cuba crises. The question was not whether to escalate—that was practically a foregone conclusion—but rather how to escalate. To use a metaphor employed by Johnson aide John McNaughton, the United States had to prove to its allies around the world that it was a "good doctor" by making a good-faith effort to save the patient before giving up.

The Praetorian Critique

Even before the Soviet-provided tanks rolled into Saigon in 1975, many members of the U.S. military and their allies on the political right had perfected an explanation for the failure of the United States in Vietnam. Indochina had been lost because civilian policymakers had not permitted the military to win. The claim that the Johnson administration had overlooked or rejected sound military strategies for winning the Vietnam War at a cost acceptable to U.S. public opinion provided the theme for retrospective books by the two top military commanders during the first three years of the war—General William C. Westmoreland of the Military Advisory Command–Vietnam (MACV) and Admiral U. S. Grant Sharp, commander in chief–Pacific (CINCPAC).[2] The most impressive and influential statement of this thesis was provided by Colonel Harry Summers of the U.S. Army in *On Strategy: A Critical Analysis of the Vietnam War* (1981).[3] In the 1990s, this argument was restated by one of the heroes of the Gulf War, Captain H. R. McMaster, in his book *Dereliction of Duty: Lyndon Johnson, Robert McNamara, the Joint Chiefs of Staff, and the Lies that Led to Vietnam* (1997).

In 1976, Westmoreland, noting a concern among his fellow officers that "the military served as the scapegoat of the war in Vietnam," argued that "[t]he military quite clearly did the job that the nation asked and expected of it, and I am convinced that history will reflect more favorably upon the performance of the military than upon that of the politicians and policy makers."[4] In an introduction to Sharp's *Strategy for Defeat* (1978), Hanson W. Baldwin claimed that it is "clear that the blame for the lost war rests, not upon the men in uniform, but upon the civilian policy makers in Washington—those who evolved and developed the policies of gradualism, flexible response, off-again-on-again bombing, negotiated victory, and, ultimately, one-arm-behind-the-back restraint, and scuttle-and-run."[5] In 1981, President Ronald Reagan repeated this myth: "Several years [ago], we brought home a group of American fighting men who obeyed their country's call and fought as bravely and well as any Americans in our history. They came home without a victory not because they had been defeated but because they had been denied permission to win."[6] Eliot A. Cohen, one of America's leading civilian defense experts, observed in 1998 that "Vietnam has become the defense establishment's morality play, a cautionary tale of civilian meddling, military timidity, and ensuing—but unnecessary—disasters. From it both statesmen and generals have derived lessons about how to direct and fight wars, lessons accepted virtually without question by the younger generation of politicians and soldiers for whom Vietnam represents nothing more than a vague memory of childhood television."[7] Not all military and civilian defense experts agree with this analysis, but it is so influential within the ranks of the military that it can be called the "praetorian critique" of the Vietnam War. As early as 1968, Marine Colonel William R. Corson complained that "an American version of the German 'stab in the back' myth is being actively promoted by the hawks on Vietnam."[8] In 1980, 92 percent of the Vietnam veterans polled by the Veterans Administration agreed with the statement: "The trouble in Vietnam was that our troops were asked to fight a war which our political leaders in Washington would not let them win."[9] The praetorian critique has hardened into an orthodoxy shared not only by most of America's soldiers and veterans but by conservative Republican politicians who would like to blame the outcome of the Vietnam War on Lyndon Johnson, a liberal Democrat, or on Richard Nixon, a Republican but not a Goldwater-Reagan conservative.

The praetorian critique faults the Kennedy and Johnson administrations for alleged failures on the Indochina front and the home front. On the Indochina front, Kennedy and Johnson should not have allowed an unrealistic fear of Chinese intervention to prevent them from invading North Vietnam or at least cutting it off from its Chinese and Soviet sponsors by measures such as mining North Vietnamese ports. Instead of an invasion or massive, unrestricted bombing of the North, the Johnson administration engaged in bombing campaigns that were limited and ineffectual. The praetorian critique also holds that Kennedy and Johnson and their advisers exaggerated the importance of the insurgency in South Vietnam. Properly defined, the threat in South Vietnam was not an insurgency but infiltration of North Vietnamese regulars via the Ho Chi Minh Trail in Laos and Cambodia and, ultimately, a conventional invasion from the North. According to most versions of the praetorian critique, the United States made a terrible mistake by not cutting off the Ho Chi Minh Trail in the early stages of the war.

In analyzing policy on the home front, the praetorian critique holds that the Johnson administration made a serious error in deciding not to mobilize the reserves or ask Congress for a formal declaration of war. (Ironically, many military and conservative critics of the Johnson administration agree with the liberal and radical left that the Southeast Asia Resolution, a conditional declaration of war, did not meet constitutional standards.) The failure to rally the public behind the war, according to adherents of the praetorian school, gave the Vietnamese communists and the antiwar left in the United States that parroted the communist line an unnecessary advantage in debate. Many members of the praetorian school, both military and civilian, have argued that in the Gulf War President Bush avoided the mistakes of President Johnson. Unlike Johnson, it is said, Bush went to Congress and rallied the public in advance. Backed by overwhelming public support, Bush then unleashed massive U.S. military power against Iraq. What is more, the Bush administration, unlike the Johnson administration, did not micromanage military decisions—or so it is said. The alleged result was a war as brief, decisive, and popular as the Vietnam War had been protracted, stalemated, and ultimately unpopular. (In reality, of course, Bush waged a limited war for a limited goal, which left Saddam Hussein in power in Iraq and still capable of threatening his neighbors; and Congress authorized the Gulf War by only a few votes, while the Southeast Asia Resolution passed with near unanimity.)

Not everyone who subscribes to the praetorian critique of U.S. strategy in the Vietnam War makes all of the points listed here. To his credit, Colonel Harry Summers criticizes those who have blamed civilian policymakers for their interference: "Such criticism is off the mark. Our problem was not so much political interference as it was the lack of a coherent military strategy—a lack for which our military leaders share a large burden of responsibility."[10] Still, the praetorian theory of the Vietnam War is the new orthodoxy in the Pentagon, the Republican Party, and in conservative intellectual circles. Thanks to the majority status of the Republican party and the deference that civilian policymakers today are expected to show to top military officials, the praetorian critique is likely to inform America's military strategy in the early years of the twenty-first century. Unfortunately, the lessons of Vietnam that the U.S. military establishment and its political allies have learned are the wrong lessons. Widespread acceptance of the erroneous praetorian critique of the Vietnam War will make it more, not less, likely that the military will repeat the mistakes of that war.

In this chapter I examine the flaws of the standard praetorian critique of the war in Vietnam. In doing so, I rely heavily on the work of scholars who have also been soldiers, such as Colonel Andrew Krepinevich, as well as that of civilian participants in what Henry Cabot Lodge called "the other war" of counterinsurgency in Vietnam, such as the late Robert W. Komer and former Director of Central Intelligence William Colby. The retrospective debate over strategy in Vietnam is not one between military and civilian thinkers; it is just as much a debate within the military over appropriate responses to different kinds of war.

Operational Checkmate: China and the Invasion Alternative

Like any other war, the Vietnam War must be analyzed in terms of three levels of conflict: the strategic, the operational, and the tactical. At the strategic level, the anti-American alliance of convenience between the estranged Soviet Union and China between 1959 and 1975 provided North Vietnam with indispensable material and diplomatic support. At the operational (theater) level, the threat of direct confrontation between the United States and China or the Soviet Union effectively deterred the United States from pursuing certain military approaches, including the invasion or isolation of North Vietnam. The successful policy of deterrence by the communist great powers forced the United States to limit the geographic scope and intensity of its operations in the Indochina theater. As a result, at the tactical level the United States was faced, in the first few years of its large-scale intervention, with a mixed war that was primarily though not entirely an externally-directed local insurgency in South Vietnam.

Curiously, military and conservative critics have had little to say about the strategic level of the Vietnam War, although it is obvious that North Vietnam's policy might have been frustrated had the United States persuaded the Soviet Union or China or both to cut Hanoi off. (Nixon tried to alter the strategic variables by diplomacy, with only limited success.) Instead, many members of the praetorian school argue that the United States failed at the operational level, by taking seriously the threat of Chinese or Soviet intervention. "Why were we not permitted to win?" Admiral Sharp asked in 1978. "In my view, it was partly because political and diplomatic circles in Washington were disproportionately concerned with the possibility of Communist Chinese and Soviet intervention." Sharp wrote dismissively of "the apparent specter of the mythical 'hordes' of Chinese coming down from the north, or a supposed 'confrontation' with the Soviet Union."[11] Sharp's skepticism was shared by Westmoreland in 1976: "Influencing many of the major decisions was an almost paranoid fear of nuclear confrontation with the Soviet Union and a corresponding anxiety over active participation by Chinese Communist troops. On those matters the President's advisers took undue counsel of their fears."[12] In his influential *Summons of the Trumpet* (1978), General Dave R. Palmer wrote, "The Johnson administration had already barricaded the one sure route to victory—to take the strategic offensive against the source of the war. Memories of Mao Tse-tung's reaction when North Korea was overrun by United Nations troops in 1950 haunted the White House. America's fear of war with Red China protected North Vietnam from invasion more surely than any instrument of war Hanoi could have fielded."[13] Harry Summers agreed that the United States was foolish to allow fears of Chinese intervention to deter an invasion of North Vietnam. According to Summers, "Whether the Soviets or the Chinese ever intended intervention is a matter of conjecture." He faults the United States for allowing itself "to be bluffed by China throughout most of the war."[14]

Until recently, the lack of detailed information about the Sino-Vietnamese relationship in the 1960s made it impossible for historians to judge whether the Johnson administration had been realistic in its fears of possible Chinese intervention or whether, as critics claimed, those fears had been exaggerated. In the 1990s, however, new archival evidence from China and Vietnam made it clear that the Johnson administration's fears were justified. The possibility that Mao would have sent combat troops to fight the United States in Vietnam had been quite real.

It is now known that in late 1964 and early 1965, China clarified its commitment to North Vietnam. If the United States did not merely bomb North Vietnam but invaded it, China would send combat troops, as it had during the Korean War. Through various means, including diplomatic messages via other nations, Mao's government, hoping to deter the United States, sent signals of its determination to intervene if necessary to Washington. The same message was given to Hanoi. "We will go to Vietnam if Vietnam is in need, as we did in Korea," Zhou Enlai assured members of the South Vietnamese communist National Liberation Front (NLF) in May 1965.[15] The importance that Mao placed on the Vietnam War can be gauged from a Chinese Communist party Central Committee document of April 12, 1965, which declared that the top priority for the Chinese government was supporting North Vietnam against the United States. Also in April 1965, the North Vietnamese communist leaders Giap and Le Duan secretly visited Beijing with a request for the dispatch of Chinese pilots to fight the American air force. Although the Chinese turned down that request, they agreed to Le Duan's request for Chinese engineering troops that would build or repair railways, roads, and bridges, freeing North Vietnamese regulars to infiltrate South Vietnam. This meeting was followed up in May-June 1965 by a secret meeting in China between Ho Chi Minh and Mao. As a result of these clandestine discussions, the Chinese and North Vietnamese worked out plans for various contingencies. If the United States limited itself to bombing the North and fighting in the South, the Vietnamese communists would fight on their own, with China providing military, material, and diplomatic support. If the United States invaded North Vietnam, however, China would enter the war.[16]

"If the actions recommended by [Colonel Harry] Summers had been taken by Washington in Vietnam, there would have been a real danger of a Sino-American war with dire consequences for the world," writes historian Qiang Zhai in an analysis of the new documentary evidence. "In retrospect, it appears that Johnson had drawn the correct lesson from the Korean War and had been prudent in his approach to the Vietnam conflict."[17]

Like the Truman and Eisenhower administrations during the Korean

War, the Johnson administration minimized what it knew about Chinese and Soviet involvement in Vietnam. Hindsight suggests that this was a public relations blunder, because it permitted critics on the left as well as military and conservative critics to argue that the government exaggerated the roles of the communist great powers in Indochina. "You will ask why in relation to Hanoi the Chinese and Russians did better," John Kenneth Galbraith wrote in the *New York Times* on July 12, 1975, after the Soviet-equipped North Vietnamese army invaded and conquered South Vietnam. "One answer is that they were wiser: No Chinese or Russian troops were sent; no great body of advisers debouched. . . . They were not thrown out because they were not there." Galbraith did not know what he was talking about. The Chinese and Russian troops *had* been there, and, in the case of the Chinese, in great numbers. According to the Chinese government's own calculations, between 1965 and 1973 320,000 People's Liberation Army soldiers, not disguised but wearing Chinese uniforms, were assigned to North Vietnam. The greatest number of Chinese soldiers present in North Vietnam at any one time was 170,000.[18] To put the figure of 170,000 into perspective, it should be recalled that the number of troops that the United States had in Indochina at the height of its involvement in 1968 was roughly 543,000. In short, at the height of the Vietnam War the Chinese uniformed military forces in North Vietnam had almost one-third of the maximum manpower of the U.S. forces in the South. By the time the last Chinese troops left Vietnam in August 1973, 1,100 are alleged to have been killed and 4,200 wounded.[19]

In May 1966, activists in Students for a Democratic Society (SDS), a radical leftist campus group, passed out a "counterexam" at nine hundred sites where the Selective Service was testing students. Among the questions on "The National Vietnam Examination," written by SDS leaders Todd Gitlin and Mike Locker, was this one: "The war in South Vietnam is supposed to be part of our policy to contain Communist Chinese aggression. How many Communist Chinese troops are actively engaged in combat in Vietnam? (A) None (B) 1,000 (C) 50,000 (D) 100,000 (E) 500,000." The answer, according to Gittlin and Locker, was (A) None.[20] The SDS propagandists hedged their bets by using the phrase "actively engaged in combat." After all, most U.S. troops in South Vietnam were not "actively engaged in combat"; rather, they were involved in logistics operations in support of the American and South Vietnamese war effort. The best answer to the question asked by SDS, then, was 100,000 (though 200,000 would have been a more accurate round number). The Chinese logistics troops in North Vietnam freed North Vietnamese regulars to fight in the south, as the following conversation in Hunan, China, on May 16, 1965, between Mao and Ho Chi Minh makes clear:

President Ho: First of all, we need China to help us build 6 roads from the border areas. These roads run south through our rear. And in the future they will be connected to the front. At present, we have 30 thousand people building these roads. *If China helps us, those people will be sent to the South.* At the same time we have to help Lao comrades to build roads from Samneua to Xiengkhoang and then from Xiengkhoang to Lower Laos, and to the South of Vietnam.

Mao Zedong: Because we will fight large-scale battles in the future, it will be good if we also build roads to Thailand. . . .

President Ho: If Chairman Mao agrees that China will help us, *we will send our people to the South.*

Mao Zedong: We accept your order. We will do it. There is no problem.[21]

While tensions arose between the Chinese troops and the North Vietnamese, Hanoi was pleased to receive the help. On April 13, 1966, in Beijing, Le Duan assured the Chinese communist leaders Zhou Enlai, Deng Xiaoping, and Kang Sheng:

Concerning China's assistance to Vietnam, we are very clear and we don't have any concern about it. Now, there are more than a hundred thousand Chinese military men in Vietnam, but we think that whenever there is something serious happening, there should be more than 500,000 needed. . . . We think that as a fraternal socialist country, you can do that, you can help us like this.[22]

Far from being negligible, the Chinese military intervention in the Vietnam War was the single most massive and sustained effort of the Chinese armed forces outside of China's borders since the Korean War.

On September 23, 1968, in a conversation with North Vietnamese premier Pham Van Dong in Beijing, Mao commented on the remarkable fact that the United States, afraid of provoking a greater crisis, had not publicized the use of China as North Vietnam's strategic reserve and the assignment to North Vietnam of hundreds of thousands of Chinese troops:

> *Mao Zedong:* Why have the Americans not made a fuss about the fact that more than 100,000 Chinese troops help you building railways, roads and airports although they knew about it?
>
> *Pham Van Dong:* Of course, they are afraid.
>
> *Mao Zedong:* They should have made a fuss about it. Also, their estimate of the number of Chinese troops in Vietnam is less than their real number.[23]

The Soviets were in Vietnam, too. The Russian historian Ilya Gaiduk has observed, "Although the Democratic Republic of Vietnam was supported throughout the war by its powerful allies, the USSR and the People's Republic of China, these supporters have virtually escaped the attention of historians of the conflict in Indochina." In his 1996 book *The Soviet Union and the Vietnam War*, Gaiduk shows how the Soviet Union competed with Mao's China for leadership of the communist bloc and Third World radical movements—by, among other things, replacing China in the mid-1960s as the chief military sponsor of North Vietnam. In a 1970 memo to Moscow, the Soviet embassy in Hanoi wrote: "It is not excluded that Indochina may become for us a key to all Southeast Asia."[24]

In *Alien Wars: The Soviet Union's Aggressions Against the World, 1919 to 1989* (1996), two former Red Army officers, General Oleg Sarin, a former editor of the Soviet military newspaper *Red Star*, and Colonel Lev Dvoretsky, who served in the Red Army from 1948 until 1982, matter-of-factly treat the Soviet role in the Vietnam War as one of a number of Soviet "aggressions" along with the West Berlin blockade, the Korean War, the invasions of Afghanistan, Hungary, and Czechoslovakia, and the Cuban missile crisis. In Vietnam, the two Red Army journalists write, the Soviets "not only were enlarging and strengthening the overall socialist group of countries, but were doing so in Asia, a long-desired objective. Additionally, successes in the Vietnamese jungle were a boost to the reputation of Soviet arms. . . . Vietnam, like Korea, apart from political considerations, presented an obvious opportunity to be a kind of proving ground for the Soviet military-industrial complex."[25]

The Vietnam War, then, was a proxy war between the United States, the Soviet Union, and China—and sometimes more than that. According to Sarin and Dvoretsky, "Although the truth about the Vietnam War was being carefully concealed, the fact of Soviet military participation in this region was becoming more and more widely known. . . . It became apparent . . . that Soviet pilots were participating actively in flights of the Vietnamese Air Force in countering American raids into North Vietnam."[26] Soviet antiaircraft teams on the ground in Indochina downed dozens of U.S. planes during the Vietnam War. On March 30, 1968, when a Soviet Dvina antiaircraft complex near Hanoi shot down a USAF F-111, Soviet Minister of Defense Andrei Grechko considered the event important enough to merit a direct phone call to General Secretary Leonid Brezhnev.[27] For its part, the Chinese government has admitted that it provided North Vietnam with antiaircraft teams that shot down U.S. planes. Beijing claims that these antiaircraft teams suffered four thousand wounded and more than one thousand dead as a result of conflict with American and South Vietnamese forces.[28]

In Indochina, as in Korea, American soldiers and their allies, often without realizing it, were engaged in direct combat with Soviet and Chinese troops. On occasion the soldiers of Brezhnev and Mao were killing Americans in Vietnam. The decision of the Johnson administration not to invade North Vietnam, then, was based on a correct evaluation of the threat of direct Chinese military intervention, as well as on a well-informed fear of provoking a Soviet-American confrontation. The argument of the praetorian school that Johnson could have brought the war to a quick end by invading North Vietnam has been completely discredited.

The Air War Against North Vietnam

In *A Soldier Reports* (1976), General Westmoreland writes that "the war still might have been ended within a few years, except for the ill-considered policy of graduated response against North Vietnam. Bomb a little bit, stop it a while to give the enemy a chance to cry uncle, then bomb a little bit more but never enough to really hurt. That was no way to win."[29] According to Admiral Sharp, the United States should have "hit the enemy where it hurt—in the heartland of North Vietnam" before Hanoi's Soviet and Chinese patrons constructed powerful air defenses. In addition, Sharp argues that the United States should have cut off Soviet and Chinese supplies by mining North Vietnamese harbors and using air power to destroy overland supply routes from China. Sharp denounced "those civilian, political decision-makers who chose out of flagrant arrogance or naïve wishful thinking to ignore the sound, time-vindicated principles of military strategy in their direction of the Vietnam air war."[30] Admiral Thomas H. Moorer, chairman of the Joint Chiefs of Staff during the latter part of the Vietnam War, claimed in 1987 that without restrictions on bombing "we could have polished those clowns off in six months."[31]

The Joint Chiefs of Staff, supported by Secretary of State Dean Rusk, advocated a rapid bombing campaign to destroy key industrial targets in North Vietnam. This option was defeated by the option preferred by Secretary of Defense Robert McNamara: gradual escalation of bombing. Operation Rolling Thunder, the air war against North Vietnam waged by the United States from 1965 to 1968, failed—but not because of excessive restrictions on bombing.

Operation Rolling Thunder had two purposes: to break the will of the Hanoi regime, and to cripple the ability of North Vietnam to intervene in the South by destroying North Vietnamese industrial capability and by interdicting the flow of recruits and supplies into South Vietnam. The U.S. air war failed to accomplish either objective. The United States did not break the will of the North Vietnamese dictatorship, and the damage done to North Vietnamese industry and supply lines did not significantly affect the conflict in South Vietnam. The Hanoi regime proved to be more determined and callous in inflicting suffering on its own population than the Johnson administration had expected. Interdiction failed, because of the limited importance of material support from North Vietnam for the Hanoi-directed insurgency in South Vietnam before 1968.

The problem with using air power to destroy North Vietnam's industrial base was that the actual industrial base of North Vietnam was the Soviet Union and its Warsaw Pact satellites and China. The communist great powers funneled supplies to the Vietnamese communists overland through China, through North Vietnamese ports, and also through the Cambodian port of Sihanoukville. The claim that mining North Vietnamese harbors such as Haiphong could have isolated North Vietnam and brought the war to a quick conclusion has crumbled in response to new revelations from the other side. "At present, Haiphong port has not been blockaded," Zhou Enlai observed in a conversation with Pham Van Dong in Beijing on April 10, 1967:

> Therefore, the use of China's ports has not been considered yet. The Soviet Union once said that the US would not attack Soviet ships. Of course, in case Hai Phong port is blockaded, and there are no other ports accessible in Vietnam, foreign shipments to Vietnam will have to be transported through China's ports. We have an agreement for this contingency. But as far as the utility of China's ports for Soviet aid to Vietnam is concerned, we will consider the factual situation and circumstances and then negotiate another agreement. The Soviets want to have access to China's ports not only for shipments of aid to Vietnam but for other ulterior motives as well.[32]

The Chinese archives make it clear that if the United States, early in the war, had blockaded North Vietnamese ports and cut off the flow of Soviet supplies through the Cambodian port of Sihanoukville, Soviet bloc supplies would have continued to flow into North Vietnam through Chinese ports as well as by rail from the Soviet Union, as long as Beijing had been certain that Moscow was not taking advantage of the limited Sino-Soviet effort on behalf of Hanoi.

The rail lines from China converged at two bridges in North Vietnam, the Paul Doumer bridge in Hanoi and the Than Hoa bridge. Destroying these two bridges would have crippled the ability of North Vietnam to resupply the southern insurgency (although, insofar as the insurgency depended chiefly on local supplies and recruits in the early years, the insurgency itself would not necessarily have been thwarted). If the United States had possessed the technology it had during the Gulf War, taking out these two bridges would have been relatively easy. Unfortunately, the technology of the time was not up to the task. Both bridges survived so many U.S. air attacks that the U.S. military abandoned strikes against the Doumer Bridge altogether in 1967. Only in 1972, using newly developed "smart" bombs, were U.S. aircraft able to cripple both bridges until the United States left Vietnam. Even if the United States had possessed such technology sooner, however, it might have been irrelevant inasmuch as the Viet Cong before 1968 were capable of waging guerrilla war without supplies from North Vietnam, China, and the Soviet Union.

Nor is there any merit to the argument that a "sharp knock" instead of gradual bombing would have changed the outcome of the war. One careful study notes that a twelve-week bombing campaign from August to October 1967 "closely approximates the air chiefs' plans. There is no evidence that executing the sharp knock in 1965, instead of 1967, would have produced better results."[33] Another myth repeated by military and conservative critics of the conduct of the war holds that pauses in bombing imposed by the Johnson administration over the objections of the military allowed the North to resupply the southern insurgency. The pauses were too few, however, to have had the effect attributed to them; during Operation Rolling Thunder, bombing was halted eight times for a total of 60 days out of 1,337 days, and of those 60 days, 37 were part of a single bombing pause that began in Christmas 1965.

The claim that the success of Nixon's Linebacker II bombing campaign forced Hanoi to resume negotiations in 1972 is based on a failure to understand the different situations that the Johnson and Nixon administrations confronted. Between 1968 and 1972, Hanoi had abandoned its emphasis on guerrilla war in favor of a conventional war strategy that was extremely vulnerable to air bombardment. What is more, one of the major factors that had made Johnson cautious in his war against North Vietnam, the possibility of large-scale Chinese intervention in combat, had diminished in importance after 1968, as the Sino-Soviet rift had deepened, as Hanoi's increasing identification with Moscow had estranged many of its leaders from Beijing, and as the United States and China began a rapprochement. "Both Rolling Thunder and Linebacker demolished military-related targets in North Vietnam," Robert A. Pape writes. "Yet one failed while the other succeeded." The difference was that the war between 1965 and 1968 was primarily an insurgency: "During the Johnson years, air attacks could not affect the guerrilla war and so had no effect on Hanoi's behavior. During the Nixon years, the destruction of military targets did affect Hanoi's behavior because the North had adopted a conventional invasion strategy that air power could effectively derail."[34]

It is also a mistake to believe that the success of U.S. air power in the Gulf War and the Kosovo War meant that the United States could have used similar means to achieve a similar result in Indochina. "Not to denigrate what we accomplished against Hussein, but Hussein was no military strategist," former Secretary of the Navy James Webb pointed out following the Gulf War. "If Ho Chi Minh had put sixty percent of his army in one spot where there were not any trees, we would have blown them away in forty days too."[35]

In 1999, industrialized Serbia was far more vulnerable to air power than agrarian North Vietnam had been in the 1960s. And Serbia lacked effective defenses against NATO bombing; not one NATO pilot was killed or even captured.

Finally, there is no merit to the claim that President Johnson "tied the hands of the military." After the early phase of the bombing, Johnson did not personally supervise the details of the war—something that was all but impossible in any event. Instead, following the advice of his military and civilian advisers, President Johnson set overall policy goals and left implementation to the military. In the words of historian John Prados, "He behaved intelligently as a strategic commander."[36]

"Bomb, bomb, bomb," Johnson is reported to have complained in a meeting with military strategists. "That's all you know. Well, I want to know why there's nothing else. You generals have all been educated at the taxpayers' expense, and you're not giving me any ideas and solutions for this damn little piss-ant country. Now, I don't need ten generals to come in here ten times and tell me to bomb."[37] As early as December 30, 1964, in a cable to Ambassador Maxwell Taylor in Saigon, Johnson complained: "Every time I get a military recommendation, it seems to me that it calls for a large-scale bombing. I have never felt that this war will be won from the air, and it seems to me that what is much more needed and would be more effective is a larger and stronger use of Rangers and Special Forces and marines or other appropriate military strength on the ground and on the scene."[38] Johnson's skepticism about the military's panacea of bombing was justified. Before the conflict evolved into a conventional North Vietnamese invasion in the aftermath of the Tet Offensive in 1968, it was not possible to win the war in Vietnam by "unleashing" U.S. air power. Indeed, a case can be made that the Johnson administration engaged in too much bombing, not too little. Contrary to what critics of the war claimed at the time, Operation Rolling Thunder, for all its inevitable brutality, was more discriminating than U.S. bombing cam-

paigns in Korea and World War II had been. Even so, the proportion between the civilian suffering caused in North Vietnam and the limited military
results made it easier for pacifists and procommunist leftists and liberals in
the West to portray the United States as a monstrous empire engaged in
Nazi-like technological genocide. The air war against North Vietnam between 1965 and 1968 turned into a political disaster that might have been
avoided by an even more narrowly tailored bombing campaign.

What Kind of War?

Other versions of the praetorian critique rule hold that what was needed
was not an invasion of North Vietnam but an early attack on the Ho
Chi Minh Trail in Laos and Cambodia. The Johnson administration
ruled out plans for such an incursion because the United States simply
did not have enough troops to wage General Westmoreland's war of attrition in South Vietnam and to cut off the Ho Chi Minh Trail at the
same time. It has been estimated that a static defense in depth from the
demilitarized zone across the Laotian panhandle would have required
six American divisions, with two more divisions serving as a strategic reserve; at the height of the war in 1968, the United States had only
eleven divisions in Indochina.[39] Perhaps the bulk of U.S. forces could
have been used to cut off the Ho Chi Minh Trail, leaving the war in
South Vietnam to Saigon's soldiers. But the inability of the South Vietnamese government to make progress against both Viet Cong guerrillas
and mainforce units was what had prompted U.S. military intervention
in the first place.

This is not to say that an incursion into Laos and Cambodia would
not have been necessary at some point in the war. Indeed, a Korean-
style stalemate in Indochina might have required the United States and
its allies to create and garrison a Vietnam-to-Thailand demilitarized
zone. The only question is the timing of such an incursion. That question, in turn, must be answered by an analysis of the nature of the war
in the South.

The character of the war in Vietnam changed radically between 1959
and 1975. The war began as a low-level guerrilla insurgency, developed
by the mid-1960s into an insurgency with conventional war elements,
and, finally, after the Tet Offensive, evolved into a conventional war with

a partisan guerrilla dimension. The evolution of the war was captured well by Lewis R. Ward, a retired lieutenant colonel in the U.S. Army Reserve, in a 1989 issue of *Military Review:*

> For purposes of analysis, despite the risk of oversimplification, we can look at the Vietnam War as two separate but interlinked conflicts—as both an insurgency and an invasion. . . . The two conflicts had one manager, the politburo in Hanoi, which merged and coordinated both conflicts very effectively into one war. The insurgency preceded the invasion. The invasion forces initially supported the insurgency and then took over. The insurgency and the invasion became interdependent after the United States entered the war with U.S. forces. Neither could have succeeded alone as long as the United States supported South Vietnam. Together they were sufficiently effective in time to force the U.S. government into withdrawing its forces from Vietnam and reducing military, political, and economic support to Vietnam.[40]

Eliot A. Cohen expressed a similar nuanced understanding of the nature of the Vietnam War when he wrote in 1984 that

> in 1965, American troops engaged a Vietnamese enemy predominantly organized and equipped for guerrilla warfare; in 1972, it helped fight a much more conventionally organized foe; and in 1975, its hapless South Vietnamese ally succumbed to a thoroughly conventional invasion, spearheaded by armored columns. These forces were sustained by a Soviet logistical and naval apparatus far greater than that of the 1950s and 1960s, and one comparable (if yet inferior) to that deployed by the United States.[41]

Although the war dragged on until 1975, the crucial years were those between 1965 and 1968, when American public support for the U.S. commitment to Indochina had eroded past the point of no return. Until the Tet Offensive in 1968, the communists primarily followed an insurgent guerrilla war strategy. In almost all engagements, small units of Viet Cong confronted U.S. and South Vietnamese forces. From 1965 to 1967, attacks by battalion-sized Viet Cong units diminished from 9.7 per month to 1.3 per month. By 1967, Viet Cong units the size of companies or smaller were responsible for more than 96 percent of all engagements.[42] In the same period, the estimated 245,000 Viet Cong guerrillas greatly outnumbered the estimated 55,000 North Vietnamese troops in the South.[43] The dependence of the Viet Cong on supplies from the North was limited, given their ability to use terror and persuasion to obtain food and supplies from villages in South Vietnam.

According to Ward, "Victory in the Vietnam War would have required the United States to have two strategies: a strategy to enable the South Vietnamese to defeat the Viet Cong insurgency and a strategy that would enable the American forces to stop the North Vietnamese infiltration and invasion of South Vietnam." Ward observes that "U.S. 'search and destroy' tactics were not effective because they involved too much searching in relation to the number of NVA [North Vietnamese Army] units found that could be destroyed. The NVA took the tactical initiative only to maintain the morale of their supporters and to wear down American patience over time in a protracted war."[44] Ward argues that the United States should have shifted to a primarily conventional strategy only in mid-1968, when the Viet Cong had been so decimated that the United States could "turn over to South Vietnam the struggle against the Viet Cong insurgency." The U.S. military would then have been free to mine and blockade North Vietnam's harbors and to cut the Ho Chi Minh Trail "by placing U.S. troops across Laos and into North Vietnam just north of the demilitarized zone."[45]

Flawed Tactics

This understanding of how the Vietnam War changed its nature over time lends support to critics of General Westmoreland's strategy. Working within the constraints imposed by the Johnson administration, which included no invasion of North Vietnam and no major incursion into Laos and Cambodia, Westmoreland and his staff devised a plan in which the South Vietnamese military and police forces were primarily responsible for pacifying the populated regions of South Vietnam, while U.S. forces concentrated on a war of attrition against Viet Cong insurgents and North Vietnamese infiltrees in South Vietnam. "In effect we are fighting a war of attrition," Westmoreland explained in a speech at the Waldorf-Astoria hotel in New York City in 1967. "The only alternative is a war of annihilation." Similarly, Westmoreland told President Johnson, "In the final analysis, we are fighting a war of attrition in Southeast Asia."[46] Progress in Westmoreland's war of attrition was measured, not by territory permanently retaken by the Saigon government, but by the controversial "body count" or count of Viet Cong guerrillas and North Vietnamese soldiers killed by United States and South Vietnamese forces.

"The U.S. continues to concentrate the bulk of . . . resources and military might on controlling the terrain and looking for massed enemy formations," Carl Bernard, a former province senior adviser, wrote in 1969. "The VC continues to concentrate its talents on controlling the people. Each succeeds."[47] Advocates of a "pacification" or "population security" strategy have claimed that before 1968 the major task was cutting off the flow of recruits and supplies to the Viet Cong from the populated coastal areas and using a combination of military and police work to dismantle the secret communist political infrastructure in South Vietnam. In *The Army and Vietnam* (1986), Andrew F. Krepinevich, Jr., a former United States Army colonel, argues that the United States and the South Vietnamese military should have deployed small units along the densely populated South Vietnamese coastal plain to patrol villages on foot by day and to prevent Viet Cong movement in and out of villages at night.[48] Among other things, a pacification strategy, proponents argue, would have permitted a far more discriminating and less expensive approach to the use of firepower, while reducing American losses. If the United States lacked the manpower to cordon off the entire populous coastal region at first, then pacification could have proceeded in "ink-blot" fashion, with an ever growing area of South Vietnam freed from insurgency. If the Viet Cong, forced into the wilderness, attempted large-scale attacks, they would have been vulnerable to United States conventional forces. If Hanoi had decided to launch a conventional invasion, then its forces and infrastructure would have been vulnerable to U.S. air power, as they were during the Easter offensive in 1972.

At the time, the importance of pacification was recognized, within the U.S. military, chiefly by the Marine Corps, who had considerable success with their Combined Action Patrols (CAP) in patroling Vietnamese villages and assisting South Vietnamese government counterinsurgency efforts. Unlike the other services, the Marines possessed an institutional memory of the early-twentieth-century "Banana Wars" waged by the United States in the Caribbean and Central America. "I was reminded of my early days as a young officer, learning the fundamentals of my profession from men who had fought Sandino in Nicaragua or Charlemagne in Haiti," Marine Corps General Lewis W. Walt, reflecting on the Vietnam War, wrote in 1970. "The Caribbean campaigns had many lessons applicable to Vietnam forty or fifty years later." Most of the United States military wanted to fight the war using conventional combat techniques. "But the war in Vietnam is not a simple one in which we seek only to find, fix and destroy another uniformed force." Unfortunately, according to Walt, "These seemed new ideas to this generation [of American soldiers], with Dachau and Belsen, Hamburg and Coventry, Nagasaki and Hiroshima, Seoul and Pyongyang fresh in the history books."[49] Walt and other marines were rewarded for their insight with criticism from General Westmoreland, who thought that they should stop patroling villages (as pacification theory required) and get out into the jungle to chase guerrillas.

Looking back at the United States military effort in Vietnam, former director of central intelligence William Colby, who had assisted the South Vietnamese government with pacification efforts, was puzzled: "The American dismissal of the French experience in Indochina and Algeria, of the British in Malaya, and of the plain warnings of Mao Tsetung, Khrushchev and Ho Chi Minh and his lieutenants that Vietnam would be a different kind of war than the Americans contemplated on the North German plain or experienced in Korea, is difficult to understand." After all, Colby pointed out, the United States military had prior experience in "the pacification of such disparate hostile forces as American Indian tribes, Aguinaldo's guerrillas in the Philippines, and Sandino in Nicaragua."[50] But that had been the prior experience chiefly of the marines. The collective memory of the army and air forces, the services that dominated the Pentagon, was shaped by the experience of using firepower to pulverize the conventional forces and infrastructure of Germans, Japanese, North Koreans, and Chinese.[51]

Advocates of the pacification strategy do not claim that pacification should have been the sole task of the United States military before 1968 (after 1968 they recognize that the war was primarily conventional). Robert W. Komer, Johnson's "counterinsurgency czar" and a strong advocate of pacification, wrote that "thwarting the VC/NVA 'main forces' had become indispensable to creating a climate in which pacification could get started again. After 1964 it was essential to fight both main-force and village wars."[52] Nor do advocates of an emphasis on pacification argue that the Vietnam War could have been won by counterinsurgency alone. Rather, the point of pacification would have been to force Hanoi to choose between waging a conventional Korean-type war (in which the United States had a comparative advantage) or abandoning its attempt to conquer South Vietnam.

The suggestion that a greater emphasis on pacification rather than on attrition in the mid-1960s might have altered the outcome of the Vietnam War has been criticized on several grounds. Harry Summers approvingly quotes former State Department officer Norman Hannah: "In South Vietnam we responded mainly to Hanoi's simulated insurgency rather than to its real but controlled aggression, as a bull charges the toreador's cape, not the toreador."[53] But between 1965 and 1968, the Hanoi-controlled Viet Cong insurgency in the South was not the cape but the toreador. Summers writes that the United States "had substituted the negative aim of counterinsurgency for the positive aim of isolation of the battlefield."[54] But the goal of a counterinsurgency strategy was to isolate the battlefield—not from the Ho Chi Minh Trail, but from the South Vietnamese population. The insurgency would have withered if United States and South Vietnamese forces had cut off the recruits and supplies flowing to the Viet Cong from the villages in South Vietnam's densely populated coastal rim.

The claim that pacification could not have succeeded in Vietnam because American-sponsored pacification programs everywhere were failures has been made by the political scientist D. Michael Shafer.[55] In instances in which United States -backed counterinsurgency efforts appear to have succeeded, as in Greece and the Philippines, Shafer argues that the victories were due to factors other than pacification. As James Wirtz skeptically observes, Shafer "then leaves it up to the reader to explain the fantastic coincidence that led [Philippine leader Ramon Magsaysay] to conceive independently policies that were the same as those advocated by his American advisers."[56] The claim that insurgencies are almost impossible to defeat is the opposite of the truth. Most of the communist or leftist insurgencies during the Cold War, including those in Greece, the Philippines, Malaya, Guatemala, Salvador, and Peru, were defeated by embattled governments, sometimes, as in Guatemala, at enormous cost in innocent life.

In the alternative, some have argued that the pacification effort in

South Vietnam was doomed from the beginning because the Saigon regime was illegitimate from the beginning, or perhaps after the assassination of Diem, who had possessed some legitimacy as a nationalist leader. The presence of an insurgency in the South rather than the North, however, may indicate merely that the North Vietnamese communists were more brutal than the South Vietnamese authoritarians. The flight of almost two million refugees from communist rule after unification in 1975, and the exodus of almost a million from communist North Vietnam in the mid-1950s, casts doubt on the claim that the Vietnamese population was overwhelmingly in support of Ho Chi Minh and his successors. The evidence suggests that most Vietnamese watched fearfully as two armed minorities, each supported by outside great powers—the Hanoi regime and the Saigon regime—battled for control of territories and populations. On the basis of his experience with Marine Corps CAPs in Vietnam, Colonel William R. Corson in 1968 wrote: "The peasant in Vietnam cares as little about the ideology of the VC as he does about the ideology of the GVN. This fact in itself provides the [South Vietnamese government] with as great an opportunity to build up popular non-ideological support as the VC, and nonideological support is essential for victory."[57]

To the extent that the outcome depended on the skillful use of coercion, the United States was capable of helping the Saigon regime, by providing both advice and troops. Building a just, popular, liberal, and democratic society in South Vietnam was beyond the abilities of the United States. Helping South Vietnamese authorities defeat the Viet Cong by separating the insurgents from the densely populated regions and dismantling their secret networks, and using American military power to defeat attempted North Vietnamese invasions of South Vietnam, *was* within American power. This was the argument of a school of counterinsurgency theorists led by two RAND analysts, Nathan Leites and Charles Wolf, Jr. They criticized the "hearts-and-minds" school of counterinsurgency theorists who had influenced the Kennedy and Johnson administrations for overemphasizing social and economic reform as a cure for insurgent warfare. "Evil governments may quell virtuous rebellions, and virtuous governments may lose to evil rebellions."[58]

The key variable was American public opinion. Would the United States have supported a long-term, low-level war of pacification in South Vietnam? Richard A. Hunt, a former Army captain in Vietnam, argues that a pacification-based strategy "would most likely have taken too long and would in any case have exhausted the patience of the American people, inevitably eroding political support in the United States."[59] But American public support for the Korean and Vietnam wars declined at approximately the same rate as a function of casualties—not as a function of time. It is reasonable to believe that there would have been more public support for a longer American effort with fewer American deaths. As long as the war was predominantly an insurgency, the pacification strategy promised lower levels of United States casualties. Marine Combined Action Patrols and "strike teams" or United States mobile guerrilla forces suffered fewer casualties, while achieving a higher rate of contact with the enemy, than did conventional army maneuver battalions.[60]

What is more, a strategy emphasizing pacification in the early years of the Vietnam War would have required fewer United States troops in South Vietnam and would have relied less on expensive, high-tech equipment that needed to be prepositioned and maintained. At the end of 1968, by the most generous estimate, only around 200,000 of the 536,000 American soldiers in South Vietnam served in combat positions.[61] The logistical requirements of United States forces would have been greatly reduced by a strategy that compelled American soldiers to live in small units among villagers, rather than in bases with amenities like those stateside. According to historian Russell F. Weigley, "the effort to maintain an approximation of the American standard of living in the Army and even in the combat zones diverted an excessive amount of manpower away from the essential combat units of the Army."[62] The friction produced by using American troops to provide population security could hardly have been worse than that produced by the concentrations of troops that the attrition and bombing strategies required.

If pacification had succeeded, the result might not have been peace, but a wider war—a United States incursion into Cambodia and Laos to cut off the Ho Chi Minh Trail, a conventional invasion by the North. Eventually the "crossover point" in American public opinion might have been reached, albeit in different circumstances, and perhaps at a later date. But as Robert W. Komer put it in 1973 in his reflections on pacification in Vietnam:

> At the least, its even half-hearted execution would probably have resulted in less militarization and Americanization of the conflict, and

in a greatly reduced toll in human life and resources as well as tragic side effects. And it is the very contrast between this enormous toll and the ambiguous results achieved that has fed U.S. disillusionment with the war. Hence the very way in which we have fought the Vietnam War may have been what has foreclosed the "long-haul, low-cost" pacification strategy which in hindsight offered perhaps the best hope of achieving U.S. aims.[63]

A mixed strategy that emphasized pacification in the first years of the Vietnam War may or may not have offered the United States and its South Vietnamese allies the best opportunity to win well. One thing seems clear: An initial emphasis on pacification would have offered the best opportunity to lose well.

A Military Failure

In hindsight, the record of the Kennedy and Johnson administrations compares favorably with that of the Pentagon. The constraints imposed on theater operations by the Johnson administration did not cause the war to be lost—and those constraints may well have averted a second Sino-American war in little more than a decade. The argument that Kennedy and Johnson were wrong to ask the U.S. military to wage a difficult and ambiguous war of counterinsurgency in a peripheral country is unpersuasive. The Cold War was going to be fought under difficult conditions in places like Vietnam, or it was going to be forfeited by the United States.

The U.S. military succeeded in the "siege" aspect of the Cold War by amassing nuclear bombs and missiles, putting first-rate conventional armies in Germany, Japan, and South Korea and deploying surface and submarine fleets. But the U.S. military neglected the kind of forces that were most useful in the equally important duels of the Cold War—expeditionary forces for prolonged low-intensity conflicts in the Third World, such as the Vietnam War. Writing in 1961, one British expert observed that whereas Britain had "combat forces" for use in Third World contingencies, the United States had only "deterrent forces."[64] Although the situations were only partly comparable, the success of the British in waging an effective war of counterinsurgency against the

Sukarno regime along the Indonesian/Malaysian border in the 1960s shows that other great military powers in the Cold War era were able to master the art of pacification.

In hindsight, the theory of flexible response championed in various forms by the Kennedy and Johnson administration's civilian and military thinkers offered an intelligent contrast to the mainstream military's all-or-nothing orthodoxy. In his 1962 address to the graduating class at West Point, President Kennedy called on the military to adapt to the need to fight low-intensity proxy wars:

> Korea has not been the only battleground since the end of the Second World War. Men have fought and died in Malaya, in Greece, in the Philippines, in Algeria and Cuba, and Cyprus and almost continuously on the Indo-China peninsula. No nuclear weapons have been fired. No massive nuclear retaliation has been considered appropriate. This is another type of war, new in its intensity, ancient in its origin—war by guerrillas, subversives, insurgents, assassins, war by ambush instead of by combat; by infiltration, instead of aggression, seeking victory by eroding and exhausting the enemy instead of engaging him. It requires in those situations where we must counter it . . . a whole new kind of strategy, a wholly different kind of force, and therefore a new and wholly different kind of military training.[65]

Unfortunately, the military's response to pressure from the Kennedy and Johnson administrations to master the complexities of counterinsurgency was to dismiss it as a fad. General Lyman L. Lemnitzer, chairman of the Joint Chiefs of Staff in 1960–61, thought that the Kennedy administration was "oversold" on unconventional warfare. General George Decker, army chief of staff in 1960–62, claimed that "any good soldier can handle guerrillas." Even General Maxwell Taylor, who as chairman of the Joint Chiefs of Staff from 1961–64 championed flexible response, claimed that "Any well-trained organization can shift the tempo to that which might be required in this kind of situation."[66] John A. Nagl, a U.S. Army captain and professor at West Point, suggests that "it was the organizational culture of the British army that allowed it to learn counterinsurgency principles effectively during the Malayan emergency, whereas the organizational culture of the U.S. Army blocked organizational learning during—and after—the Vietnam War."[67] During the conflict in

Indochina, one anonymous U.S. army officer was quoted as saying, "I'm not going to destroy the traditions and doctrine of the United States Army just to win this lousy war."[68]

The institutional bias of the U.S. military was on display in other Cold War crises. During the Cuban missile crisis, the all too predictable recommendation of the Joint Chiefs was to engage in air attack against Cuba followed by invasion and occupation as the "lowest-risk course of action." President Kennedy rejected their advice in favor of a blockade, which, together with a secret deal with the Soviets to remove U.S. missiles from Turkey, ended the confrontation. During the crisis in Laos in 1961, the Joint Chiefs told Kennedy that no fewer than sixty thousand troops should be deployed. General Lemnitzer and General Decker told the president that he should not take any action in Laos unless he was willing to use nuclear weapons to "guarantee victory."[69] Earlier in 1954, when the United States was considering military intervention in Indochina on the side of the French and their Vietnamese allies, Secretary of State Dulles was alarmed by the recommendation of the Joint Chiefs of Staff, which he summarized in a memo as the argument "that United States power should be directed against the source of the peril which was, at least in the first instance, China, and that in this connection atomic weapons should be used."[70] During the Vietnam War, Lyndon Johnson confided to Canadian prime minister Lester Pearson that General Curtis LeMay, the former head of the Strategic Air Command, as well as other hawks in the military, had encouraged him to bomb Beijing.[71]

Throughout the Cold War, the U.S. military prepared to fight Field Marshal Rommel and Admiral Yamamato, when it should have been preparing itself in addition to fight opponents like Nicaragua's Sandino and Haiti's Charlemagne. Under the "the buck stops here" principle, President Johnson must be held ultimately responsible for the disaster in Vietnam between 1965 and 1968. On the other hand, it is not the responsibility of civilian politicians in a democracy to instruct military professionals in the rudiments of their art. An argument in extenuation of the failures in Vietnam of Presidents Kennedy and Johnson and Nixon appears more plausible when one considers the impressive string of military failures in the last quarter of the twentieth century under a succession of very different presidents: Desert One in Iran; the bombing of the U.S. marines barracks in Beirut; the bungled invasion of Grenada; the botched invasion of Panama; the debacle in Somalia. If not for the Kosovo War, which failed to prevent the expulsion of most Albanian Kosovars, and the Gulf War, which left Saddam in power, despite a later renewal of the air war under President Clinton, the U.S. military would have little to show since the Korean War except for a string of disasters or botched successes—all of which, the Pentagon's apologists would have us believe, represent failures of presidential conception and direction rather than of military implementation. Generals Colin Powell and Norman Schwarzkopf won the Gulf War, but Admiral Sharp and General Westmoreland did not lose the Vietnam War. The point is not to impugn the integrity of America's soldiers as individuals, but to wonder how the military leadership can ever be held accountable if an alibi for military failures can always be had by blaming civilian political leaders.

Indeed, a case can be made that President Johnson deferred too much to the military, not too little. Remembering the controversy that surrounded Harry Truman's firing of General Douglas MacArthur, who became a martyr in the eyes of conservatives in Congress and the country, Johnson as commander-in-chief was careful to show support for the military commander in Vietnam. "General, I have a lot riding on you," Johnson told Westmoreland. "I hope you don't pull a MacArthur on me."[72] Johnson kicked Westmoreland upstairs by promoting him in 1968. A case can be made that he should have replaced him long before.

In 1976 General Westmoreland wrote: "I am convinced that history will reflect more favorably upon the performance of the military than upon that of the politicians and policy makers."[73] In retrospect, many of the options favored by civilian policymakers in the Johnson administration, including the attempt to influence Hanoi by means of limited bombing and Defense Secretary Robert McNamara's technocratic enthusiasm for an electronic barrier across the Ho Chi Minh Trail, deserve the criticism that they have received. In the final analysis, however, the American public's support for a sound grand strategy of global military containment of the communist bloc by means of flexible response collapsed for most of the 1970s because the U.S. military in Vietnam was too inflexible in its response to the enemy's tactics.

Chapter 4

THE FALL OF WASHINGTON

The Domestic Politics of the Vietnam War

Saigon fell to Soviet-supplied North Vietnamese tanks in 1975. But Washington, D.C., had already fallen metaphorically several years before. For roughly a decade, between the Tet offensive in 1968 and the Soviet invasion of Afghanistan in 1979, the United States abandoned the global containment policy that it had followed since the Truman administration in favor of several makeshift strategies that disguised the reality of American retreat and demoralization—Nixon's "détente," Carter's "human rights" policy. The chief cause of the U.S. retreat in the 1970s was the collapse of public support for military intervention abroad that was caused by the costs of the Vietnam War.

By 1968, the high number of U.S. casualties had eroded U.S. public support for the American effort in Indochina. The challenge to Richard Nixon, who took office in 1969, was to reduce the U.S. involvement in Indochina in a manner that preserved domestic support for the Cold War in other theaters. Unfortunately Nixon, emphasizing U.S. geopolitical credibility too much and paying too little attention to the endangered domestic political consensus in favor of the Cold War, inadvertently helped to provoke a neoisolationist backlash by pursuing a prolonged strategy of extrication that added twenty-four thousand more American dead to the total killed in the Johnson years. Joined by alarmed "owls," or moderate interventionists, the antimilitary, antiinterventionist "doves" in the U.S. Congress, emulating the progressive isolationists who had opposed Franklin Roosevelt's foreign policy in the 1930s, sought to strip the presidency of its foreign policy prerogatives and imposed embargoes on U.S.

overt or covert aid to American allies and clients fighting the Soviet bloc in Indochina, Africa, and Central America. The Soviet Union took advantage of the post-Vietnam isolationism of the United States by engaging in a campaign of bold empire-building in the Third World that was reversed only by the costly and dangerous Second Cold War waged by the United States and its allies in the 1980s.

U.S. public opinion, then, was a key factor both in the disastrous outcome in Vietnam and the successful outcome of the Cold War. In the words of Leslie H. Gelb and Richard Betts, "American public opinion was the essential domino."[1] Although this is widely recognized, most discussions of the U.S. political debate over the Vietnam War treat that debate as though it took place in a social and cultural vacuum. The opposing sides are usually identified in terms of "left" and "right," categories of dubious utility derived from the politics of nineteenth-century Europe. In reality, ideological labels such as "liberal" and "conservative," as well as partisan labels such as "Democrat" and "Republican," were less useful in predicting the views of any given American about the Vietnam War in particular and the Cold War in general than ethnicity, race, religion, and regional background. The Vietnam War was disproportionately opposed by blacks and Jews and by white Protestants in New England and regions such as the upper Midwest, the northern prairie, and the Pacific Northwest. White southerners disproportionately supported the war. White Catholics also tended to support the war, but this group was complex and divided.

What accounts for these ethnic and regional divisions? Unlike the case in World Wars I and II, there was no substantial Indochinese-American population comparable to German and Japanese Americans. Nor do economic or class interests appear to have influenced American attitudes. The hypothesis that these divisions were rooted in cultural traditions is confirmed by the fact that the division of the public into pro- and anti-war groups long antedated, and survived, the Vietnam War.

Ethnicity and the Vietnam War

Black Americans have been far more likely than white Americans to oppose U.S. foreign wars as long as data on the subject has been gathered. Black American leaders, identifying American expansionism with slavery and racism, denounced the Mexican War and the Spanish-American War, agitated for the termination of the U.S. occupation of Haiti that began in 1915 to preempt German influence, and took a special interest in the conditions of blacks and mulattos in the American-ruled Panama Canal zone. In the twentieth century, black liberals tended to identify with noncommunist anticolonial movements in Africa, Asia, and Latin America; Gandhi's India provided a model for Martin Luther King, Jr. Black radicals such as W. E. B. DuBois and Paul Robeson, by contrast, were more likely to identify with Marxism-Leninism in the Soviet Union and the Third World.[2]

Many black American soldiers supported the U.S. effort in Indochina. Black Americans, who had received no Medals of Honor in World War I or World War II, received 20 of the 237 awarded during the Vietnam War. General Colin Powell, who would go on to command the U.S. military as chairman of the Joint Chiefs of Staff during the Persian Gulf War, won 11 medals in Vietnam, including a Bronze Star and a Purple Heart.[3] At the same time, a substantial part of the black American population was deeply suspicious of the U.S. military, which for most of its history had been segregated and dominated by racist southerners. During World War II, the future black civil rights leader Bayard Rustin refused to be drafted, arguing against "the moral error that racism (American) can overcome racism (Fascist)."[4] Nation of Islam leader Elijah Muhammad and several fellow black nationalists were sentenced to prison during World War II for advocating draft evasion, as was Nation of Islam member Muhammad Ali for refusing to be drafted during the Vietnam War.[5]

If black American antiwar sentiments reflected a history of alienation from a racist society, the opposition of many American Jews to U.S. military interventions abroad reflected the powerful traditions of communist and noncommunist socialism that many Jewish immigrants in the early twentieth century brought with them from the former tsarist empire in Russia and Eastern Europe. Most American Jews in the twentieth century became mainstream liberals. Even so, the dwindling number of radicals in the Jewish community contributed far out of proportion to their numbers to the Communist Party USA as well as to its allies and rivals on the American left, which in the nineteenth century had been dominated by German and Scandinavian immigrants. Although only a small minority of American Jews were communists, by the 1930s a majority of

American communists were Jews.[6] A generation later, many leading anti-communist intellectuals during the Cold War were Jewish-American ex-communists who had broken with the Moscow-controlled party. The division of the American Jewish left among procommunist, anticommunist, and anti-anticommunist factions gave its internecine disputes a kaleidoscopic complexity.

"No one has failed to notice that in the American student movement of the 1960s, students with a Jewish background played a distinctive role," Paul Berman has observed.[7] A nationwide survey by the American Council of Education in 1966–67 revealed that the best single predictor of campus protests was a high proportion of Jewish students.[8] Apart from Jews, few American students in the sixties were radical. At the height of the antiwar movement in 1970, only 11 percent of American college students identified themselves as "radical or far left."[9] The political scientist John E. Mueller speculates that campus leftism had less to do with the supposed innate qualities of intellectuals as a "new class" or "adversary culture" than with the ethnic heritage of Jewish intellectuals:

> Outside of a few sections in a few cities, the only easily identifiable places that Jews are found in striking disproportion are the colleges and universities of the land—and very particularly the better ones. Thus the liberalism of those associated with the better universities may not derive from anything endemic in the university situation. Rather, it may stem from the influence of a major subpopulation in the university community inclined toward liberalism and war opposition regardless of its association with the college.[10]

The presence of a substantial radical minority in the American Jewish population accounts for its divergence from the national norm in its attitudes toward the Vietnam War. In 1964, Jews were twice as likely as Protestants and Catholics to favor pulling out of Vietnam altogether—and about half as likely as Protestants and Catholics to agree with the statement "Take a Stronger Stand Even If It Means Invading North Vietnam." In 1970, when a majority of Protestants and Catholics favored fighting while negotiating or escalating the war, half of the Jewish respondents surveyed favored an immediate pullout.[11] "The only large population group not represented among the combat deaths [in Vietnam] in proportion to their U.S. demographics were those who designated themselves Jewish," B. G. Burkett and Glenna Whitley write in *Stolen Valor* (1998), their study of myths and facts about Vietnam veterans. Although Jews accounted for 2.5 percent of the U.S. population, Jewish men accounted for only 0.46 percent of the war-related deaths in the Vietnam War. The evident explanation for this discrepancy is the use of college deferments by the higher than average proportion of Jewish men in college to avoid military service.[12]

While Jews were overrepresented on the anti–Cold War left in the United States, Catholic politicians and thinkers were disproportionately represented among the leaders of American anticommunism. The American Catholic community is composed of many different ethnic groups who arrived in different eras. Nevertheless, some generalizations are possible. American Catholic opposition to Marxism-Leninism was catalyzed by the anticlerical atrocities of the Bolshevik Revolution.[13] In the 1930s, many American Catholics sympathized with Franco's Spain, which portrayed itself as a defender of Christian civilization against communism. After World War II, Catholic anticommunism in the United States was strengthened by the Soviet repression of the church in its Eastern European empire. According to historian Michael Kazin, "Catholic organizations constituted the largest and best financed—as well as most uncompromising—battalion in the anti-Communist movement."[14] Despite the prominence of Catholic anticommunist Republicans and conservatives such as Senator Joseph McCarthy and William F. Buckley, Jr., most American Catholics during the Cold War retained their allegiance to the Democratic party, in which they had historically been the allies of white southern Protestants. The Irish-American Catholics who dominated the U.S. labor movement, such as George Meany of the AFL-CIO, sought to purge the ranks of organized labor of Moscow-controlled communists, and enthusiastically supported the anticommunist foreign policy of the New Deal/Cold War liberals. However, beginning with the campaigns of George Wallace and Richard Nixon for the presidency in 1968, many working-class Catholic "hardhats" broke with the Democratic party to support Republican presidential candidates, rejecting the increasingly dovish foreign policy views of the Catholic hierarchy and Catholic pacifists such as Dorothy Day and the Berrigan Brothers.

It is worth noting that the only American group that was overrepresented in the U.S. armed forces during the Vietnam War was Catholics.

THE FALL OF WASHINGTON

Although Catholics accounted for only around 24 percent of the population, about 30 percent of the American soldiers who were killed in Vietnam were Catholic.[15]

Regionalism and American Wars, 1798–1945

While Jewish and Catholic attitudes toward communism and the Cold War were influenced by Old World immigrant traditions, the foreign policy attitudes of old-stock white Protestant Americans tended to be correlated with their regional origins.

Regions in the United States are notoriously difficult to define. The best guide, perhaps, is provided by speech regions. Most linguists identify four regional dialects of American English—northern, midland, highland southern, and coastal southern. The Greater New England or northern speech region, according to historian David Hackett Fischer, includes "New England, upstate New York, northern Ohio and Indiana, much of Michigan and Wisconsin, the northern plains, and the Pacific North West, together with islands of urban speech at Denver, Salt Lake City and San Francisco."[16] Since the late 1700s, this area has been the heartland of opposition to foreign wars and the U.S. military establishment. Prowar, promilitary attitudes have been strongest in the areas identified with the coastal southern speech region (the Tidewater South) and, to a lesser degree, in the Highland South from West Virginia through Tennessee to Texas.

The pattern of Greater New England opposition to foreign war, and the opposite tendency of the South, especially the Tidewater South, to be strongly interventionist, manifested itself in the earliest years of the American Union. In the War of 1812, the war hawks tended to be southerners such as Henry Clay of Kentucky and John C. Calhoun of South Carolina. The vote on the war followed sectional lines, not partisan lines. In the House, the Federalist Party—with thirty-one representatives from the northern and midatlantic states and only nine southerners (all from the Highland South)—voted unanimously against the war. The southerners who controlled the Republican party were solidly in favor of the war. Of the twenty-two Republicans who voted against the war, eighteen came from the northern and midatlantic states.[17]

This pattern reemerged in subsequent conflicts. Southerners generally favored the western expansion of the United States at the expense of Indian nations and Spain/Mexico; northerners disproportionately opposed it. In the 1830s, the most extreme American pacifists broke away from the American Peace Society and formed their own organization, which foreswore the use of force even in self-defense. Its name tells the story: the New England Non-Resistance League.

Another example of the extreme antimilitarism of New Englanders is provided by Charles Sumner (1811–74), the powerful Massachusetts senator who was chairman of the Senate Foreign Relations Committee between 1861 and 1871. Sumner's first major public speech was an 1845 Fourth of July oration in Boston, in which he horrified the veterans in the audience by blaming war on arms manufacturers, calling West Point a "seminary of idleness and vice," and describing soldiers as "wild beasts" who rejoice "in blood." His speech culminated in the declaration: "In our age there can be no peace that is not honorable; there can be no war that is not dishonorable."[18] True to his pacifist principles, Sumner refused to fight back when he was caned on the floor of the House in 1856 by South Carolina congressman Preston S. Brooks, in retaliation for Sumner's verbal assault on Brooks's cousin, South Carolina Senator Andrew P. Butler.

For New Englanders such as Sumner, the Mexican War (1846–48) was a national disgrace. Boston, the capital of the antiwar movement during the War of 1812, was the center of opposition to the Mexican War. The Boston-based American Peace Society charged the U.S. government with aggression against a "poor, feeble, distracted country." Both the Democrats and their opponents, the Whigs, were divided along regional lines. In February 1847, just before the U.S. victory at Buena Vista, Thomas Corwin, a Whig senator from Ohio, encouraged the Mexican enemy to welcome American soldiers "to hospitable graves." When the Kentucky abolitionist Cassius M. Clay gave up the editorship of an antislavery newspaper to join the other Kentucky volunteers, other abolitionists prayed that he would be the "first to perish" in Mexico.[19] The Boston Brahmin Henry David Thoreau refused to pay taxes, claiming that to do so would make him an accomplice in an unjust war. Jailed, he wrote his classic essay *Civil Disobedience*, which inspired later generations of mostly northern antiwar activists in the United States.

In general the South was as enthusiastic about the Mexican War as the North was hostile. Many leading southern military officers, including Robert E. Lee, became members of the Aztec Club, an organization of veterans of the Mexican War. Indeed, from the beginning of the republic, the U.S. military had been dominated by southerners. "The South gave military professionalism its only significant support in the pre–Civil War years," Samuel P. Huntington has written. "A 'Southern military tradition' existed in a way in which there was never a New England, Middle Western, or Rocky Mountain military tradition." Huntington points out that in the U.S. Army of 1837, three of the four active generals, six of the thirteen colonels of the line, and ten of the twenty-two highest ranking officers were not only from the South but from one state: Virginia.[20]

The pattern of southern support for foreign wars was broken during the Spanish-American War when—for the first and only time in U.S. history—intervention abroad was the project of northeastern elites. "As a political theory," historian Richard Franklin Bensel notes, "imperialism rationalized the interests of the northern industrial core, their agrarian allies, and the Republican party"—at the time a northeastern/midwestern coalition.[21] Many former Confederates opposed the war out of bitterness toward the federal government. Even though the Spanish-American War was a northern enterprise, it was opposed vehemently from within the north itself. David Hackett Fischer writes: "Anti-imperialism was a regional movement, centered in New England."[22] Once again Boston became the center of an antiwar movement.

After the outbreak of World War I in Europe, congressional voting on preparedness legislation between 1915 and 1917 revealed the by now familiar pattern. In terms of geography, the antiinterventionists were concentrated in New England and northern states settled by New Englanders, with a few allies among populists in the Highland South. The myth of "conservative isolationism" to the contrary, most of the World War I–era isolationists were to the left of center in their political views: progressive Republican followers of Wisconsin Senator Robert La Follette and southern and western populists of the William Jennings Bryan school. In the Senate, the most consistent opponents of preparedness and intervention in World War I were all from the western section of Greater New England: Robert La Follette (R.-Wisconsin), George W. Norris (R.-Nebraska), Asle J. Gronna (R.-North Dakota), and Harry Lane (D.-Oregon).[23] In the House, as in the Senate, all but one of the representatives with 100 percent antipreparedness and antiintervention voting records were from the same region: William J. Cary (R.-Wisconsin),

Henry Allen Cooper (R.-Wisconsin), Charles Davis (R.-Wisconsin), Henry Helgesen (R.-North Dakota), John M. Nelson (R.-Wisconsin), and William H. Stafford (R.-Wisconsin). Remarkably, five of the ten most consistent congressional opponents of U.S. involvement in World War I came from the same state in Greater New England: Wisconsin.

The South was overwhelmingly in favor of U.S. participation in this European war, as it had been in favor of U.S. involvement in the Napoleonic Wars in 1798 and again in 1812. Two-thirds of the southern members of the Senate, and four-fifths of the southern members of the House, voted in favor of every one of Woodrow Wilson's wartime policies.[24] The exceptions tended to be found in the Highland South. Among the Highland southern allies of the Yankee isolationists in the years preceding World War I was Senator Thomas P. Gore of Oklahoma, whose Gore Resolution prohibited travel by U.S. citizens on armed merchant vessels. Gore, the grandfather of novelist Gore Vidal and a distant relative of Tennessee senator Albert Gore, Sr., and his son, Vice President Al Gore, belonged to the populist wing of the Democratic party and shared his antiinterventionism with the leader of that faction, Woodrow Wilson's secretary of state, William Jennings Bryan.

Between World War I and World War II, the leaders of isolationism in Congress were William E. Borah (R.-Idaho), Hiram Johnson (R.-California), George Norris (R.-Nebraska), and Robert La Follette, Sr. (R.-Wisconsin). These individuals, often described as "Midwestern conservative isolationists" were in reality Greater New England progressives, usually to the left of center in domestic policy. North Dakota Senator Gerald P. Nye, elected in 1925, became an important progressive antiinterventionist. In 1934–35, Nye chaired the Nye Committee, which investigated allegations that the munitions industry and international finance had drawn the United States into World War I. According to historian Thomas N. Guinsberg, Nye, along with Arthur Vandenberg (R.-Michigan) and a Missouri Democrat, Bennett Champ Clark, "collaborated in staging a most effective pre-emptive attack that took the leadership of foreign policy away from the White House."[25] The "pre-emptive attack" took the form of neutrality laws similar to those of the years preceding World War I—and also similar to legislation passed by the northern-dominated Democrats in Congress during their later attack on presidential foreign policy prerogatives in the 1970s and 1980s.

As war with Hitler and his Axis allies appeared imminent, the American political elite was divided along regional rather than partisan or ideological lines. One historian describes the regional basis of opposition to U.S. intervention in World War II: "If members of the House of Representatives at all reflect their constituency, one can point to a substantial cadre of anti-interventionist sentiment, based in particular in the Old Northwest and Great Plains states, but extending as well to the Border states, Pacific coast, rural Northeast, and even sections of northern cities."[26] Southern Democrats such as Senators Harry Byrd and Carter Glass of Virginia supported FDR's military policy, even though they bitterly opposed his liberalism in domestic matters. As war with the Axis approached, Alabama congressman Luther Patrick joked that "they had to start selective service to keep our boys from filling up the army" as volunteers.[27] The isolationist America First Committee was least successful in the South.[28]

At the same time, many northerners, both Democrats and Progressive Republicans such as Wisconsin senator Robert La Follette, Jr., endorsed the New Deal while opposing FDR's military measures. In exactly the same way many northern Democrats and liberal Republicans later supported the civil rights and welfare programs of Harry Truman and Lyndon Johnson while opposing their anti-Soviet foreign policies. The New Dealer Rexford Tugwell pointed out that the prairie and Pacific West supported FDR's progressive domestic policy but not his interventionist foreign policy, while the South supported an interventionist foreign policy but not a progressive domestic policy.[29] In a vote to discharge a war referendum law from committee in 1941, 100 percent of the representatives from Wisconsin, the Dakotas, and Kansas supported the measure, as did all but one from Minnesota and Nebraska; only 17 percent of southern congressmen favored the antiwar measure.[30] In August 1941, a few months before Pearl Harbor, interventionist southern Democrats provided the votes without which the extension of the draft law would have gone down to defeat.[31] In the fall came the vote on the revision of the neutrality act, which FDR signed into law on November 17, 1941. Seven southern states cast all of their votes in favor of revising neutrality to permit the United States to aid Britain in its struggle with Hitler. Four Greater New England states—Iowa, North Dakota, South Dakota, and Idaho—cast all of their votes against the measure.[32] It is no exaggeration to say that southern interventionist congressmen, by providing Franklin D. Roosevelt with a narrow margin of victory on preparedness measures, played a key role in defeating Nazi Germany.

The Regional Division over the Cold War

The pattern of northern isolationism and southern interventionism continued into the Cold War. Ohio's senator Robert A. Taft voted against both the Marshall Plan and NATO. The legacy of Greater New England isolationism explains the curious fact that William Langer, a progressive Republican senator from North Dakota, opposed the censure of Wisconsin senator Joseph McCarthy—and the fact that McCarthy was admired by Robert La Follette's son Philip. Although McCarthy's demagogy is usually attributed to his Irish Catholic background, his hatred and suspicion of U.S. national security agencies resonated with many left-of-center progressive isolationists in Wisconsin and surrounding states. Indeed, it is no accident that the same region produced both Wisconsin senator Joseph McCarthy, determined to expose alleged communist subversion of American national security agencies in the 1950s, and Idaho senator Frank Church, determined to expose the immorality of the CIA in the 1970s. Both McCarthy and Church must be placed in the context of two centuries of Greater New England opposition to standing armies and the national security state. Nor is it an accident that it was the Wisconsinian McCarthy's attack on the Virginia-bred General George Marshall and the largely southern U.S. Army that finally led to his downfall at the hands of the southern-dominated U.S. Congress.

The regional continuities in American foreign policy during the Cold War are clear in spite of the political realignment of 1964–94, in which the two parties exchanged their constituencies. As the right-wing Goldwater movement, based in the South and the West, became more powerful in the GOP, growing numbers of progressive and liberal Republicans from New England and Yankee states such as Ohio, Michigan, Wisconsin, the Dakotas, and Oregon joined the Democratic party. At the same time, blacks deserted the party of Lincoln and joined their traditional northern Protestant and Jewish white allies in the Democratic coalition. Meanwhile, white southerners and, more slowly, northern white Catholics moved into the Republican party. By the early 1970s, the Greater New England Protestant-black-Jewish alliance was predominant in the national Democratic party. In 1972, leading northern Catholic Democrats such as Mayor Richard Daley of Chicago and Massachusetts congressman Tip O'Neill were denied seats at the Democratic national convention that nominated George McGovern. Following the congressional election of 1974, conservative and moderate southern Democratic committee chairmen were purged by mostly northern left-liberal reformers. (In 1955–56, two-thirds of the Democratic chairmen of House committees had been southerners.)

The reason for the collapse of Cold War liberalism in the Democratic party was not the Vietnam War, but rather the transformation in the Democratic party's base. Even if there had been no Vietnam War, the Democratic party probably would have become more isolationist in the 1960s and 1970s as its demographic base moved northward. Lyndon Johnson, a product of the old southern/northern Catholic New Deal coalition, found himself presiding over a party increasingly identified with antimilitary northern Protestants and Jews. Lady Bird Johnson marveled in 1967 at the way that the Republicans supported the Cold War while the Democrats were abandoning it: "Lyndon and I watched senator John Tower for the Republicans and senator Joe Clark for the Democrats on television—the *Today* show—talking about Vietnam. What a twist of fate it is to see the Administration—indeed us—being explained, backed—yes, even defended—by John Tower, while that red-hot Democrat Joe Clark slashes at the administration's policy with rancor and emotion."[33] What escaped the First Lady's attention was the fact that the difference was less partisan than regional: Tower was from Texas, Clark from Pennsylvania. (Senator George Aiken, famous for saying that the United States should declare victory and get out of Vietnam, was from Vermont.)

In taking over the Democratic party, left-liberals and radical activists—many of whom came from progressive Republican or Marxist backgrounds—delegitimated the older elements in the party by demonizing them. America's soldiers, far more likely to be southerners than northerners, were "baby-killers" and "Nazis"; northeastern police, far more likely to be Irish-American, Polish-American, or Italian-American Catholics than Yankee or German- or Scandinavian-American Protestants, Jews, or blacks, were denounced as "pigs" and "fascists." Pro–Cold War labor leaders, disproportionately Irish Catholic, were "labor fascists." In the 1960s and 1970s the institutions in which the northern Protestant/Jewish left-liberal alliance was overrepresented—the press, universities, and the federal courts—were identified by the media and Hollywood with liberty and justice, while the institutions that the southern white/northern Catholic New Deal Democrats dominated—the urban political machines, the U.S. military, the police, the U.S. Congress, and the state legislatures—were vilified as tyrannical and corrupt. The battles within the Democratic party during the Vietnam era were only superficially about ideology. They were really about regional subculture, ethnicity, and race. Similarly, the divisions within the Republican party over Vietnam and the Cold War followed the geographic fault lines familiar in earlier American wars. Northern Republicans tended to be more dovish than southern Democrats. At a 1965 Republican governors' conference, the only two governors who refused to sign a resolution of support for the war were two politicians from the Greater New England antiinterventionist belt—George Romney of Michigan and Mark Hatfield, then governor of Oregon.[34] In spring 1967, three Republican senators from Greater New England—Jacob Javitz of New York, Charles Percy of Illinois, and Margaret Chase Smith of Maine—met to promote a more dovish line for the GOP. Mark Hatfield, elected senator, began calling for the Republican party to be the "peace party" in 1968.[35] The drift of Greater New England Republicans into the Democratic party was symbolized by the conversion of senator Floyd Haskell of Colorado, an antiwar Republican.[36]

The contrast between northern antiinterventionism and southern interventionism can be illustrated by a comparison of Idaho senator Frank Church and Representative Mendel Rivers of Charleston, South Carolina, who was chair of the House Armed Services Committee from 1965 to 1970. Church, a harsh critic of U.S. Cold War policy and national security agencies such as the CIA, took part in a photo opportunity in 1966 in which he held up a photo of his hero and predecessor in the Senate from Idaho: the interwar isolationist Republican senator William Borah.[37] Rivers, reflecting the tradition of South Carolina "fire-eaters" in the nineteenth century, summed up his attitude toward the Vietnam War thus: "Words are fruitless, diplomatic notes are useless. There can be only one answer for America: retaliation, retaliation, retaliation, retaliation! They say, 'Quit the bombing.' I say, 'Bomb!'"[38]

With only five exceptions, every one of the fifteen members of Congress whose denunciations of President Nixon's Linebacker II bombing campaign against North Vietnam were quoted in the prestige press came from a state in the Greater New England isolationist belt. Not one southern or southwestern senator was found among the vocal opponents of the Christmas bombing.[39]

The northern Democrats in Congress in the 1970s, turning against the interventionist Cold War policy that the disproportionately southern and Catholic Cold War liberals had supported, revived techniques used by the isolationist northern Republicans of the 1930s, such as banning U.S. military aid to factions in countries such as Angola and Nicaragua, and attempting to strip the presidency of foreign policy powers. The leader of the movement in favor of a War Powers Act was a Democrat from historically antiinterventionist Wisconsin, Clement J. Zablocki.

The domestic divisions over U.S. foreign policy in the 1980s, Peter Trubowitz writes, "were sectional, not ideological. . . . While Cold War internationalism continued to strike a responsive chord in the South, it had lost much of its appeal in the Northeast." (As we have seen, the Cold War never had much appeal in the Northeast, except in regions with large numbers of anticommunist Catholics.) According to Trubowitz, "Most of the so-called doves were liberal Democrats and Republicans" from the Northeast, while by contrast "[t]he hawks were a group made up of conservative Democrats from the South and Republicans from the West."[40]

The Greater New England antiinterventionist bloc coalesced once more in the 1980s behind the nuclear freeze movement, which won the endorsement of 446 New England town meetings. The sponsors of the first resolution in favor of the nuclear freeze in Congress came from Massachusetts (Senator Edward Kennedy and Representative Edward J. Markey) and Oregon (Senator Mark Hatfield). Three out of four voters in Massachusetts supported the nuclear freeze; Cambridge, Massachusetts, and Ashland, Oregon, among other cities in the New England–to–Oregon isolationist belt, declared themselves "nuclear-free zones."[41]

Meanwhile, white southern Democrats rallied behind Ronald Reagan's militant Cold War policy. Southern whites who favored higher defense spending were 52 percent Democratic to 34 percent Republican in 1980; just four years later, they were 49 percent Republican to 38 percent Democratic. Seventy-nine percent of southern whites who voted for Reagan believed that defense spending should be increased beyond Reagan's buildup—the largest peacetime buildup in U.S. history.

By the 1990s, the Tidewater South was the most solid Republican region, and Greater New England the bastion of the Democrats. Between the 1960s and 1994, enough southerners left the Democratic party to give the Republican party a majority in both houses of Congress and a near lock on the White House from 1968 to 1992. The regional polarization of the two parties was reflected in the congressional vote authorizing President Bush to wage war on Iraq. A majority of Democrats voted against the war; most of the dissenting Democrats whose alliance with the Republican minority permitted the declaration of war to pass were southerners.

The familiar regional division in attitudes toward war manifested itself yet again in the controversy over the NATO war against Serbia in the spring of 1999. On April 28, the House of Representatives voted on several proposed endorsements of the war. For the most part, the vote reflected partisanship: the Republican majority, which had voted to impeach Clinton, voted against approving Clinton's Balkan policy, whereas a majority of Democrats voted to endorse their party's leader. However, the deviations from the partisan norm were instructive. Respresentatives from Greater New England states such as Wisconsin, Minnesota, Washington, Oregon, Illinois, and Ohio were overrepresented among the Democrats who broke with their party to vote against the president's military policy. The only Texas Democrat who did so was Lloyd Doggett, whose constituency reflected the liberalism of Austin, a major college town. Just as significant was the regional identity of the Republicans who voted in favor of formally authorizing the Balkan war. Approximately half of these were from southern or southwestern states. The state of Virginia alone provided one-fifth of the Republicans who broke with their party to vote for an authorization of war. Even more significant, perhaps, is the fact that a different proposed resolution in which Congress on behalf of the U.S. government formally would have declared war on Yugoslavia was supported by only two members of the House, one from Texas (Republican representative Joe Barton) and one from Mississippi (Democratic representative Gene Taylor).[42]

War and Regional Culture

The historical record could not be more clear. There is a centuries-old northern antiinterventionist, antimilitary culture in the United States, centered in New England and the regions of the Great Lakes, Midwest, Upper Plains, and Pacific Northwest settled by New Englanders. In the twentieth century, as European Catholic immigrants diluted the influence of old-stock Yankee Protestants in New England itself, the epicenter of this political culture shifted westward to the Middle West and Far West. For generations, the isolationists of Greater New England have battled the promilitary interventionists of the Tidewater South. The populists of the Highland South have often been divided over foreign policy, as they were divided in their loyalties during the Civil War and the American Revolution. The pedigree of Yankee isolationism runs from the New England Federalists through the northern Whigs and northern Democrats who opposed the Mexican War to the New England antiimperialists of the late nineteenth century, the liberal Republican antiinterventionists of the first half of the twentieth century, and the anti–Cold War northern liberal Democrats of the second half. Today's promilitary interventionist Republicans, for their part, are the political heirs of the promilitary interventionist Roosevelt and Wilson Democrats as well as of the expansionist Democrats of the early nineteenth century and their predecessors, the Jeffersonian Republicans who favored the War of 1812.

What accounts for this remarkably persistent pattern of North-South disagreement about the necessity and legitimacy of U.S. military intervention abroad? Traditional accounts of U.S. interventionism and isolationism have explained these phenomena in terms of the ties between immigrant groups and Old World countries. This explanation has some validity in the case of the opposition of German-Americans and anti-British Irish-Americans to U.S. intervention in World Wars I and II. But political scientists such as Samuel Lubell who attributed interwar American isolationism chiefly to the influence of German- and Irish-American voters were mistaken.[43] Isolationist sentiment in the period from 1914–41 was strong in many northern states in which the German and Irish populations were negligible.

Quasi-Marxist economic determinist explanations are no more convincing. In *Defining the National Interest* (1998), the political scientist Peter Trubowitz attributes the persisting sectional divisions between the interventionist South and the antiinterventionist North to different regional economic strategies. In light of the South's enthusiasm for other American wars, it is not necessary to explain the southern hostility to Hitler and his allies, as Trubowitz does, in terms of a southern strategy of defending overseas markets for cotton exports.[44] The agrarian explanation of Greater New England isolationism is no more convincing. The historian Paul Michael Rogin speculates that the opposition to the Vietnam War of South Dakota Senators Quentin Burdick and George Mc-Govern "owes something to the radical agrarian heritage."[45] Agrarianism cannot be invoked to explain both the antiinterventionism of the North and the interventionism of the South.

The real reason for the persistence of sectionalism in U.S. foreign policy can be found in the ethnoregional theory of American politics, which has been developed by the historians David Hackett Fischer, Daniel Elazar, D. W. Meinig, Kevin Phillips, and others. The ethnoregional theory holds that in the United States powerful ethnic and regional subcultures are more important and enduring than political parties or ideologies. The labels "Democrat" and "Republican" differ in their meaning from generation to generation; regional subcultures such as those of New England and the Tidewater South change far more slowly.

The greatest insight of ethnoregional theorists is that immigrants in the United States do not assimilate to a uniform American national culture; rather, they assimilate to one of a small number of preexisting regional cultures. The historian Wilbur Zelinsky has defined a thesis he calls the Doctrine of Effective First Settlement that holds: "Whenever an empty territory undergoes settlement, or an earlier population is dislodged by invaders, the specific characteristics of the first group able to affect a viable, self-perpetuating society are of crucial significance for the later social and cultural geography of the area, no matter how tiny the initial band of settlers may have been." According to Zelinsky, "[I]n terms of lasting impact, the activities of a few hundred, or even a few score, initial colonizers can mean much more for the cultural geography of a place than the contributions of tens of thousands of new immigrants a few generations later."[46] Another historian, John Porter, has used the term "charter group" for "the first ethnic group to come into a previously unoccupied territory," and says that this group, "as the effective possessor, has the most to say."[47]

Historians differ on the question of how many of these enduring regional cultures there are in the United States. Most agree on three: a Yankee culture that spread westward overland from New England; a Quaker culture originating in Pennsylvania; and a Cavalier culture originating in the coastal South. Most, but not all, identify a fourth regional culture, that of the Scots-Irish Highland South from Appalachia to the Ozarks and Texas. In his magisterial *Albion's Seed: Four British Folkways in America* (1989), David Hackett Fischer argues persuasively that these four "hearth cultures" originated in different regions of early modern Britain and were transplanted to North America by four waves of immigrants. In the first wave (1629–40), Puritans from the eastern counties of England settled New England. The second wave (1642–75) brought anti-Puritan, royalist Cavaliers from the south of England to Virginia. Quakers from the North Midlands of England colonized Pennsylvania and the Delaware Valley after emigrating during the third wave (1675–1715). The fourth and final major Anglo-American migration, which lasted from 1717 to 1775, transplanted so-called Scots-Irish from northern England, lowland Scotland, and the north of Ireland (Ulster).

In addition to having distinctive folkways and dialects of English, these four groups of British-American immigrants had their own unique variants of a common individualistic and liberal British political culture. Fischer describes the New England Puritan ideal as "ordered freedom," the Quaker ideal as "reciprocal freedom," the Scots-Irish ideal as "natural freedom," and the coastal southern ideal as "hegemonic freedom" (deference to traditional elites). Another historian, Daniel J. Elazar, calls the New England tradition the "moralistic" culture, the midatlantic tradition the "individualistic" culture, and the coastal southern tradition the "traditional" culture. Elazar does not identify the Scots-Irish Highland South as a separate cultural region, an error that leads him to treat it unconvincingly as a hybrid of the moralist and traditional subcultures.

These British-American regional cultures have been overlaid and altered by waves of European and, more recently, Latin American and Asian immigration. The concentration of European Catholic immigrants in the industrial belt more or less effaced the older midatlantic Quaker region. By 1955, New England itself had ceased to be Yankee; thanks to European immigration, fewer than 30 percent of the inhabitants of Connecticut had ancestors who had lived in New England for more than two generations.[48] The Yankee tradition therefore lived on chiefly in the Great Lakes region, the upper prairie, and the Pacific Northwest. Along with the Scots-Irish Highland South and the Anglo-American Tidewater South, the western section of Greater New England has been little affected by large-scale immigration, other than that of German- and Scandinavian-Americans whose cultures have tended to reinforce Yankee norms. These three regions show greater continuities in attitudes toward foreign policy than do areas such as the industrial belt or California and the Southwest, where populations have been churned by massive immigration and relocation. Contrary to popular belief, regional cultures have proven to be far more stable than the ethnic cultures of immigrant groups, which usually fade away after a generation or two.

The ethnoregional theory provides the answer to the mystery of American sectional differences with respect to war. Regional disagreements about war are part of a larger pattern of regional disagreement about the legitimacy of all forms of violence. "Historians of Southern mores are agreed that violence as an aspect of Southern life clearly distinguished the region from the rest of the country," writes historian Bertram Wyatt-Brown.[49] Of the southerner, Alexis de Tocqueville observed that "the energy which his [northern] neighbor devotes to gain turns with him to a passionate love of field sports and military exercises; he delights in violent bodily exertion, he is familiar with the use of arms, and is accustomed from a very early age to expose his life in single combat."[50] Southern states lead the nation not only in military academies but in homicide rates and death penalty laws and in low penalties for domestic violence. Northern states have the lowest homicide rates and the greatest number of statutes requiring a citizen to retreat before attacking an assailant or intruder in his home.[51]

These regional differences reflect the difference in moral systems between the post–Calvinist Puritanism of Greater New England, which shuns violence as a means for resolving disputes, and the cultures of honor of the Scots-Irish Highland South and the Anglo-American Tidewater South. The two southern cultures are quite different, but compared to Greater New Englanders, both Highland and Tidewater southerners look with greater approval on violent retaliation for insults. But southerners are not indiscriminately violent. The difference between northern and southern homicide rates is accounted for almost entirely by the violent responses of southerners to personal offenses: arguments, insults to women, lovers' quarrels, and disputes within the family. The researchers Richard E. Nisbet and Dov Cohen discovered that, at the same university, white southern students were more likely to respond aggressively than white northern students to the same set of insults and provocations. The same researchers have pointed out the similarities between the culture of honor of white southerners and that of inner-city black Americans, most of whom are descendants of southern migrants.[52]

In addition to different attitudes toward violence, both collective and personal, Greater New Englanders and southerners have inherited different conceptions of the character of the United States. The idea of American messianism or exceptionalism, of a special American destiny in the world, is a northern idea. It is a secularized version of the Calvinist utopia of the perfect Puritan commonwealth, safe in the New World from the corrupting influences of the Old. The power of this utopian tradition, in both its Protestant and secular forms, explains why almost every wave of social and moral reform in American history has emanated from New England or areas settled by New Englanders such as California: abolitionism, prohibition, animal rights, pacifism, suffragism, and, most recently, the antismoking campaign. By contrast, the Tidewater southern gentry and the Highland southern yeomen have viewed North America in terms of cheap land and quick wealth. For southerners, British North America is a "new England," different in scale but not in kind from the old England; for the Puritans and their cultural descendants, North America is, or should be, a New Jerusalem.

The fundamental incompatibility of the mentalities of the rival American regions was captured by Henry Adams: "The Pilgrims of Plymouth, the Puritans of Boston, the Quakers of Pennsylvania, all avowed a moral purpose, and began by making institutions that consciously reflected a moral idea. No such character belonged to the colonization of 1800. From Lake Erie to Florida, in long, unbroken line, pioneers were at work, cutting into the forest with the energy of so many beavers, and with no more moral purpose than the beavers they drove away. The civilization they carried with them was rarely illumined by an idea."[53] Of the mostly southern Jeffersonian Republicans this quintessential Yankee intellectual, the descendant of two scholarly Massachusetts presidents, wrote: "I am at times almost sorry that I undertook to write their history, for they appear like mere grasshoppers kicking and gesticulating on the middle of the Mississippi River. There is no possibility of reconciling their theories with their acts."[54] To southerners, even intellectual and progressive southerners, the notion that a government or an entire society should be organized according to a theory or idea, rather than on the basis of tradition and custom, is the ultimate in New England folly.

The ethnoregional theory also clears up a minor historical mystery. For much of the twentieth century, American historians (most of them northerners) struggled to understand why the South had been so ardently in favor of war with Britain in 1812. Surely, they thought, the claim that America's "national honor" had been insulted by British practices such as the impressment (kidnapping and conscription) of American sailors had to be a pretext for other motives. Some historians speculated that economic motives, not maritime grievances, were the "real" reason for the War of 1812. In recent decades, however, a number of historians have argued that national honor as a motive for the War of 1812 must be taken seriously.[55] Unlike New England Puritans, Pennsylvania Quakers and Germanic Protestants, southerners based their way of life on the violent defense of honor—personal honor, family honor, communal honor, and national honor.

David Hackett Fischer notes that the only time the Federalist party, based in New England, gained the support of Tidewater southerners and Highland southerners was during the "quasi-war" with France in 1798–99. This suggests that southerners were motivated by cultural attitudes rather than by strategy during the Napoleonic Wars. Southerners were just as enthusiastic about fighting France and helping Britain in 1798–99 as they were about fighting Britain and helping France in 1812–14. There was a world war on, and southerners wanted a fight; choosing whom to fight was a secondary matter. "The war fever of '98 marked the beginning of a consistent pattern in American military history," Fischer writes. "From the quasi-war with France to the Vietnam War, the two southern cultures strongly supported every American war no matter what it was about or who it was against. Southern ideas of honor and the warrior ethic combined to create regional war fevers of great intensity in 1798, 1812, 1846, 1861, 1898, 1917, 1941, 1950 and 1965."[56]

The ethnoregional theory explains another curious fact of American political life—the tendency for the most outspoken "doves" to be found in the U.S. Senate, rather than in the House of Representatives. For example, two senators from Idaho—the progressive Republican William Borah and the liberal Democrat Frank Church—symbolize the traditional hostility of left-of-center antiinterventionists to national security agencies and foreign wars. The underpopulated states of New England and the Yankee-settled northern tier and Rocky Mountain states have disproportionate clout in the U.S. Senate, thanks to the provision that allots Senate seats on the basis of statehood rather than population. Throughout American history, the House has usually been more hawkish than the Senate because the nation as a whole has been more hawkish than the overrepresented inhabitants of Greater New England.

The Cold War and the Intellectuals

Like all attempts to generalize about political behavior, the ethnoregional theory of American politics is subject to many qualifications. It predicts the behavior of large groups of voters and the politicians who respond to them better than the views or actions of individuals or small groups. But though it should not be pressed too far, the ethnoregional theory is strikingly successful in explaining the pattern of opposition and support for the Vietnam War among intellectuals as well as in partisan politics.

The regional and ethnic divisions within the American intellectual community in the Vietnam years mirrored the partisan divisions between the two national parties and within each party. The overrepresentation of northern Protestants and Jews in the media and prestige universities meant that the centers of institutional power in the intellectual world tended to be identified with the antimilitary, antiinterventionist left wing of the Democratic party. In his 1987 book *The Last Intellectuals*, Russell Jacoby quoted Charles Kadushin's list: "In 1970 the ten leading intellectuals were Daniel Bell, Noam Chomsky, John Kenneth Galbraith, Irving Howe, Dwight McDonald, Mary McCarthy, Norman Mailer, Robert Silvers, Susan Sontag, and 'tying' at tenth place, Lionel Trilling and Edmund Wilson."[57] If this sample is a guide, the typical American "public intellectual" of the sixties era was a literary critic of northeastern birth, Jewish or northern Protestant ancestry, and socialist or social democratic politics. That the leftism of many Jewish and northern Protestant intellectuals reflected their ethnic political heritages, rather than their status as "intellectuals," is proven by the existence, throughout the same period, of an impressive Catholic and southern conservative anticommunist intelligentsia, of which William F. Buckley, Jr., was the impresario. Despite the fact that they have had far more influence on late-twentieth-century American politics, Catholic and southern intellectuals are seldom included among lists of major American thinkers, for the simple reason that the lists tend to be drawn up by the liberal and leftist Democrats who dominate the prestige press and the elite academy.

The fact that much of the "intellectual" opposition to the Vietnam War had more to do with ancestry than with geopolitical strategy is clear in the case of two celebrated antiwar intellectuals, the poets Allen Ginsberg and Robert Lowell. Like many antiwar leftists, Ginsberg was a "red-diaper baby," the son of a Russian Jewish immigrant who belonged to the Moscow-controlled Communist party USA. In the poem "Returning North of Vortex" (1967), this child of a Stalinist family wrote: "Let the Viet Cong win over the American Army! . . . And if it were my wish, we'd lose & our will/be broken/& our armies scattered."[58] Ginsberg's fellow Beat, the novelist Jack Kerouac, supported the Vietnam War—perhaps because he came from a working-class Catholic background.

The refusal of the poet Robert Lowell to attend a White House gathering of artists in 1965 on the grounds that he could "only follow our present foreign policy with the greatest dismay and distrust" was published on the front page of the *New York Times*. The editor of the *New York Review of Books*, Robert Silvers, lined up a number of prominent intellectuals, most of them leftist literati, to endorse Lowell's position in a telegram to President Johnson, which was also published in the *New York Times*. Lowell's letter to President Johnson echoed a letter that he had sent to President Roosevelt in 1945 grandly announcing that he would be a conscientious objector in World War II. Writing as one northeastern patrician to another, Lowell told FDR: "You will understand how painful such a decision is for an American whose family traditions, like your own, have always found fulfilment in maintaining, through responsible participation in both the civil and military services, our country's freedom and honor. I have the honor, Sir, to inscribe myself, with sincerest loyalty and respect, your fellow-citizen, Robert Traill Spence Lowell, Jr."[59] The *New York Times* printed that letter to FDR on its front page because the then obscure author was a Lowell. In opposing World War II and the Vietnam War, Lowell was living up to the tradition of his New England dynasty. His distant relative, the famous poet James Russell Lowell, during the Mexican War had written antiwar poetry in folksy New England dialect.

Writing in 1975, Daniel Patrick Moynihan, a sociologist before he became a public servant, noted the conflict between the American "officer corps, with its Protestant, rural, antiurban complexion," and leading American "intellectuals, who were not Protestant and not rural."[60] The validity of Moynihan's observation was unwittingly illustrated by Mary McCarthy, a member of the northeastern leftist *New York Review* circle, who began a 1967 report from South Vietnam with the admission: "I confess that when I went to Vietnam early last February I was looking for material damaging to the American interest." McCarthy complained that "the majority of the Americans I met in the field in Vietnam were WASPs from Southern California; most of the others were from the rural South." (Those *bêtes noires* of the northeastern left, Richard Nixon and Lyndon Johnson, were, respectively, from southern California and the rural South). McCarthy complained, "As we drove into downtown Saigon, I had the fresh shock of being in what looked like an American city, a very shoddy West Coast one."[61] McCarthy praised New England Yankee abolitionism as "the nearest thing to a resistance movement the Republic has ever had."[62]

If the U.S. Cold War left had an intellectual center of gravity outside of New York City and Cambridge, Massachusetts, it was Madison, Wisconsin. This is where the far-left anti–Cold War "Wisconsin School" of American historical scholarship was born, and where the influential radical journals *The Progressive* and *Studies on the Left* were founded. The Progressive tradition associated with the University of Wisconsin at Madison had attracted leftist members of the Russian/Eastern European Jewish diaspora in the United States. "I am struck by the lack of Wisconsin born people [at Madison] and the massive preponderance of New York Jews," one member of SDS at the University of Wisconsin wrote in the 1960s.[63] The synthesis of Greater New England Yankee progressive isolationism and immigrant Jewish Marxism was symbolized by the fact that the two leading members of the Wisconsin School in the 1960s were William Appleman Williams, an Iowa native who beneath his Marxist veneer was essentially an old-fashioned La Follette Progressive, and the Marxist radical Harvey Goldberg, the grandson of a Russian rabbi.

The University of Dallas symbolized the rival southern/Catholic intellectual tradition during the Cold War. This Catholic school in Texas, as far to the right as the University of Wisconsin at Madison was to the left, included southern conservative intellectuals such as M. E. Bradford as well as Catholic thinkers such as Frederick Wilhelmsen on its faculty. Willmoore Kendall, a populist conservative from Oklahoma, joined its faculty after Yale University paid him to relinquish his tenure rights in order to get him off campus. Kendall's disciple, William F. Buckley, Jr., the Catholic son of a Texas oil man, was a living symbol of the confluence of the Catholic and southern conservative traditions.

During the 1970s and 1980s, a growing number of Jewish intellectuals, many of them former radicals or liberals, joined the conservative intelligentsia (there had always been a few). The philosopher with the greatest influence on the American right was the German Jewish émigré Leo Strauss, whose defense of ancient wisdom against modern thought appealed to Americans in the Catholic and southern conservative traditions.

While most of the prestigious intellectuals of the 1960s opposed the Vietnam War, a number of leading American writers and thinkers supported the U.S. effort. The black writers Ralph Ellison and Albert Murray refused to join Martin Luther King, Jr., and black radicals in opposing the war. Ex-leftists such as John Steinbeck, John Dos Passos, and James T. Farrell supported the U.S. effort in Vietnam because of their opposition to communism. The novelist John Updike no doubt spoke for most of the prowar intellectuals when he wrote in 1966: "I do not believe that the Vietcong and Ho Chi Minh have a moral edge over us, nor do I believe that great powers can always avoid using their power."[64]

Nixon in Perspective

The ethnoregional theory of American politics makes it possible to put the presidency of Richard Nixon into perspective. After 1968, the capture of the Democratic party by a neoisolationist left-liberal coalition based on Greater New England Protestants, Jews, and blacks meant that the continued prosecution of the Cold War depended on an alliance (in foreign policy, if not in domestic policy) between largely southern and Catholic anticommunist Democrats and conservative Republicans. The election of a Democrat to the White House in either 1968 or 1972 probably would have resulted in geopolitical disaster or domestic political catastrophe or both. If the Democratic president had sided with the ascendant left-liberal isolationist wing of his party, the result would have been a policy of appeasement of the Soviet Union ending, perhaps, in panicky rearmament, as happened during the Carter administration of 1977–81. If a Rooseveltian Democratic president had insisted on carrying out Truman-style containment of the Soviet empire, then, in a recapitulation of the experience of Lyndon Johnson, he would have found himself attacked by most of his own party and supported chiefly by Republicans. After 1968, Republican presidents were more likely than Democratic presidents to carry out the containment strategy of Truman, Kennedy, and Johnson.

This was apparent at the time to America's enemies in the Cold War.

"I was sure that [General Secretary Leonid] Brezhnev and [Premier Andrei] Kosygin had been no more anxious for me to win in 1968 than Krushchev had been in 1960," Richard Nixon wrote in his memoirs. " . . . In fact, I suspected that the Soviets might have counselled the North Vietnamese to offer to begin the Paris talks in the hope that the bombing halt would tip the balance to Humphrey in the election—and if that was their strategy, it had almost worked."[65] Nixon's suspicions have since been confirmed by declassified Soviet records. In the fall of 1968, Brezhnev and Kosygin told North Vietnamese premier Pham Van Dong that it was in North Vietnam's interest to assist the election of the Democratic candidate Hubert Humphrey to the U.S. presidency by making it appear that peace was near.[66] To pressure the North Vietnamese even more, Boris Ponomarev, the secretary of the central committee and chief of the international department, proposed sending Hanoi an assessment of the adverse consequences of a Nixon victory.[67] Truong Van Thu, a member of the Viet Cong who became a high-ranking officer after 1975, wrote later that one "of 1968's major events was less encouraging. On November 7, Richard Nixon was elected president. As far as we were concerned, there was no question that Nixon would prove an obdurate opponent, who would bend every muscle to achieve a military resolution."[68]

The claim that Robert Kennedy, if he had not been assassinated and had won the Democratic nomination and the presidency in 1968, might have extricated the United States from Indochina at a minimal cost to America's reputation abroad and with minimal turmoil at home does not withstand analysis. The centerpiece of Kennedy's Vietnam strategy in 1968 was the call for a "coalition government" in South Vietnam. The North Vietnamese after 1975 admitted what intelligent observers knew all along—the proposal for a coalition government in the South was merely a ruse to facilitate Hanoi's takeover of South Vietnam. In a then secret conversation with Zhou Enlai in Beijing on September 17, 1970, Pham Van Dong admitted that the Vietnamese communist proposals combining the withdrawal of U.S. troops with a coalition government were merely ploys: "But the reason we focus on them is that we want further to corner Nixon by influencing public opinion in the US and the rest of the world. These points are also aimed at supporting the military and political struggles in the South. *We do not have any illusion that they will bring about any results.*"[69] A few months earlier, on July 7, 1970, Mao had reminded Kaysone Phomvihane, the General Secretary of the Laotian Communist party: "The purpose of organizing a coalition government is to destroy the coalition government." When Phomvihane replied, "That is correct," Mao repeated himself: "A permanent coalition government? There is no reason to believe in it."[70]

If Kennedy sincerely believed Vietnamese communist propaganda about a coalition government, then he was too naïve to be commander-in-chief. If, as seems more likely, Kennedy did not believe his own campaign rhetoric about a coalition government in South Vietnam, then he cynically and deliberately lied to the American electorate, and did so in a manner that undermined the bargaining ability of the United States and its South Vietnamese client state. In contrast, Richard Nixon, during his presidential campaign, was appropriately reticent about his "secret plan" for dealing with the situation in Indochina.

If Kennedy had been elected in 1968, he would have been forced to make choices certain to alienate one or another segment of the Democratic party and the American public. If he had leaned too far to the left, the result might have been the defection of anticommunist Democrats to the Republican party in 1972. If John F. Kennedy's indirect role in the assassination of Diem had been revealed, then the Republican party could have claimed that one Kennedy brother had thrown South Vietnam into chaos by encouraging the overthrow, followed by the murder of an American ally, after which another Kennedy abandoned the country and its neighbors Laos and Cambodia to communist conquest. On the other hand, if Kennedy had sought to appeal to centrist voters by pursuing a Nixon-like policy of honorable retreat, then he would have been denounced by his disillusioned and bitter supporters on the left.

This discussion would not be complete without mention of the troubling questions raised by post–Cold War revelations about Robert Kennedy's clandestine dealings with the Soviet leadership in the 1960s. In researching their 1997 study of the Cuban missile crisis, *"One Hell of a Gamble"*, historians Aleksandr Fursenko and Timothy Naftali made an astonishing discovery in the Soviet archives. In 1963–64, then attorney general Robert Kennedy allegedly sent family friends William Walton and Charles Bartlett to meet with aides of Soviet premier Nikita Khrushchev without the knowledge of President Lyndon Johnson and other U.S. government officials. Kennedy's emissaries, according to the Soviet archives made accessible to Fursenko and Naftali, told the Soviet leadership:

The Kennedy clan considered the selection of Johnson a dreadful mistake. "He is a clever timeserver," Walton explained, who would be "incapable of realizing Kennedy's unfinished plans." Walton relayed his own and Robert Kennedy's fear that Johnson's close ties to big business would bring many more of its representatives into the administration. This was certainly not designed to please Khruschchev. Surprisingly, Walton believed that the one hope for U.S.-Soviet relations was the former automobile executive Robert McNamara, who would probably remain in the cabinet as secretary of defense. Walton described McNamara as "completely sharing the views of President Kennedy on matters of war and peace." For the sake of good relations between Moscow and Washington, Walton assured Bolshakov, it was even more important that McNamara stay put than that Secretary of State Dean Rusk remain.

Walton's purpose was clear in his discussions of Robert Kennedy's political future. He said that Kennedy intended to stay on as attorney general through the end of 1964. He would then run for the governorship of Massachusetts to build up his political capital for an eventual run for the presidency. Walton, and presumably Kennedy, wanted Khrushchev to know that only RFK could implement John Kennedy's vision and that the cooling that might occur in U.S.-Soviet relations because of Johnson would not last forever. He added that he was surprised to hear some Russians say that Bobby was more reactionary in his views on the Soviet Union than his brother. "This is untrue," asserted Walton. "If Robert differed from Jack, it was only in that he is a harder man; but as for his views, Robert agreed completely with his brother, and, more important, actively sought to bring John F. Kennedy's ideas to fruition."[71]

"Inexplicably, associates of the Kennedy family continued to send information to Moscow that undercut the new president and increased Khrushchev's fears about the shift in U.S. politics," write the historians. In January 1964, Charles Bartlett, a former Kennedy confidante, approached a KGB source in New York. The message he relayed to the Soviet leadership was that "the new president would never equal Kennedy in terms of the consistency and sincerity of his thinking on relations with the USSR." According to Fursenko and Naftali, "Bartlett continued the litany of criticisms of Johnson by the Kennedys."[72]

If the Soviet archives are accurate, and if the statements made by Walton and Bartlett were authorized by him, then Robert Kennedy was guilty of acts of insurbordination and political treachery with few if any parallels in American history. A sitting attorney general, by channels chosen to avoid drawing the attention of the president whom he served and other officials of the U.S. government, was denigrating the newly inaugurated president behind his back—and, worse, was urging America's Soviet enemies to stand firm until he, Robert Kennedy, could become president in 1968 and pursue a policy more to Moscow's liking. Richard Nixon's secret dealings with the South Vietnamese government in the election of 1968, and his later conniving with the Greek military dictatorship, were petty misdemeanors by comparison; those regimes were allies, not rivals. (The claims of Robert Dallek and other presidential historians that Lyndon Johnson's fears of sabotage by the Kennedy circle were "paranoid" must be reevaluated, in light of the revelations from Moscow.)[73]

The fact that Moscow and Hanoi did their best to promote a Humphrey victory in 1968, and no doubt would have welcomed a second President Kennedy, thanks to Robert Kennedy's secret communications in 1963–64, must make even former Humphrey and Kennedy supporters think differently about their candidates. Richard Nixon's disgrace and downfall in the Watergate scandal has made it difficult for a generation of Americans to view his presidency with the objectivity that historical analysis requires. The effort nevertheless must be made. Nixon was a corrupt politician, but hardly the Hitlerian figure portrayed by his contemporary enemies on the liberal and radical left. He was elected twice by the American people—the second time, in a landslide—not because of his criminality or his personal biases, but because his foreign policy and domestic policy appealed to a broad majority of Americans that included many Democrats as well as Republicans. In terms of U.S. foreign policy, Richard Nixon was far from the best imaginable U.S. president in 1968 and 1972. Unfortunately, given the alternatives, he was the best available president.

How Nixon Turned a Regional Retreat into a Global Defeat

By 1968, the costs of the war in Vietnam—costs magnified by the misguided attempt to defeat an insurgency using conventional war tactics and technology—had reduced public support for an open-ended U.S.

commitment to Indochina to dangerously low levels. In addition, the costs were beginning to endanger public support for other Cold War commitments.

What the United States needed in 1969 was a Charles de Gaulle. The American de Gaulle would have pulled U.S. troops out of Indochina quickly, to ensure that the American death toll did not greatly exceed that reached between 1965 and 1968. By doing so he might have preserved public support for defending Indochina from communist takeovers by means of airpower; and if that failed, the American de Gaulle could have capitalized on the inevitable horrors that would have followed communist victories in order to discredit the American radical left and to rally the American people behind a renewed anti-Soviet crusade in other theaters of the Cold War. China might have become a de facto ally, but the morally questionable Sino-American alliance would have been downplayed. Instead of rehabilitating the murderous Mao, the American de Gaulle would have flown to Berlin and shaken his fist before the Berlin Wall—after having presided over a moving ceremony for the American and Indochinese heroes of the failed Indochina campaign.

Instead of an American de Gaulle, the United States got Richard Nixon. Nixon's stubborn determination to preserve American military credibility abroad long after the danger point in American public opinion had been reached was a mistake, not a crime. Even George Kennan, who believed that the United States commitment to Indochina had been an error, told the Senate Foreign Relations Committee in 1966 that United States credibility would be endangered by an outright forfeiture of the war: "A precipitate and disorderly withdrawal could represent in present circumstances a disservice to our own interests, and even to world peace, greater than any that might have been involved by our failure to engage ourselves in the first place."[74] Unfortunately, in foreign policy one is judged by results, not intentions. Nixon's plan for peace with honor in Indochina combined triangular diplomacy with China and the Soviet Union, at the level of grand strategy, with a tactical plan based on the use of American airpower to help America's Indochinese allies once U.S. ground forces had been withdrawn. The strategy failed, and the tactic probably would not have worked.

Nixon's dramatic opening to China marked the beginning of an informal Sino-American alliance against the Soviet Union that would last until the end of the Cold War. Nevertheless, Mao's regime continued to compete with Moscow for influence in Indochina by supplying the anti-American forces until the bitter end in 1975. Nor did Nixon's divide-and-rule strategy toward the two communist giants succeed in reducing Soviet material or diplomatic support for North Vietnam. The Soviets were not willing to allow Soviet-American tensions over Vietnam to disrupt their negotiations over other issues, such as ratifying the status quo in Europe and limiting the arms race (to the advantage of the Soviet Union, which had a comparative advantage in conventional military forces in Eastern Europe). But neither did the Soviets see fit to reduce the stream of supplies to North Vietnam, or to make a serious effort to pressure Hanoi into ending the war. Moscow was able to have it both ways. It could engage in global détente (defined as American acceptance of the equality of the Soviet empire as a military and diplomatic superpower) even as it helped Hanoi bleed the United States in Southeast Asia.

In addition to failing to separate Hanoi from its Soviet and Chinese patrons, the Nixon-Kissinger policy gravely weakened the ability of the United States to wage the ideological war that was an essential component of the containment strategy. Even if he had received more in return, Nixon's dining and drinking and sailing with the totalitarian rulers of the Soviet empire and the Chinese dictatorship tended to undermine the claim that there was a moral difference between the two sides in the Cold War. Kissinger's allusions to nineteenth-century European Realpolitik had a similar effect.

Nixon's policy toward the Soviet Union and China, then, conceded too much in the ideological war, while producing few benefits in the Vietnam War. Nixon's tactics were as flawed as his strategy. Nixon hoped that airpower alone would be sufficient to ensure the survival of South Vietnam, once U.S. combat troops had been completely withdrawn. The Watergate scandal and the crisis that ended in Nixon's resignation and his replacement by the unelected Gerald Ford made a dead letter of Nixon's secret written assurances to South Vietnam's president Thieu that the United States would respond with air strikes to North Vietnamese violations of the Paris peace accords. Even without the congressional cutoff of U.S. military involvement in Indochina, it seems unlikely that any endgame that did not lead to an indefinite Korean-style commitment of U.S. forces to Indochina probably would have doomed South Vietnam along with Laos and Cambodia.

Nixon's Vietnam policy, then, was a resounding failure in every way.

Worst of all, in pursuing an unworkable plan, Nixon added an additional twenty-four thousand to the American death toll in the Vietnam War. After all of those additional sacrifices, the United States abandoned Indochina anyway. The difference between allowing Indochina to fall in 1970 and allowing it to fall in 1975 may have been the difference between the loss of public support for one Cold War intervention and a public backlash against the Cold War as a whole.

Public opinion polls track the meltdown of the Cold War consensus as a result of the Vietnam War. The public never agreed that the antiwar movement had been right. In a 1970 Gallup poll, the unfavorable rating for South Vietnam (13 percent) was much lower than the unfavorable ratings for Students for a Democratic Society (42 percent) and the Viet Cong (69 percent). After the police riot that leftist agitators provoked during the 1968 Democratic convention in Chicago, the American public overwhelmingly sided with the police against the protestors.[75] A statement by an old Boston Irish politician summed up the attitude of many if not most Americans at the time: "My people want to end the war, and shoot the draft-dodgers." The claim that young people overwhelmingly opposed the war is false. Indeed, according to a Gallup poll taken as late as May 1970, the number of those who thought that the government should "withdraw all troops from Vietnam immediately" increased with age, while remaining a minority: 21–29 year olds (23 percent) and 30–49 year olds (22 percent) were less likely to agree with the statement than respondents over 50 (25 percent).[76] The chief result of the antiwar movement was to elect Nixon to the presidency and to inspire the public to distrust the ability of the neoisolationist Democratic party to conduct foreign affairs. Most white baby boomers became Republicans.

The American public turned against the Vietnam War not because it was persuaded by the radical and liberal left that it was unjust, but out of sensitivity to its rising costs. According to polling data, there was higher public support for the Vietnam War than there had been for the Korean War when comparable numbers of casualties had been reached.[77] In both Asian proxy wars support declined as body counts rose. In 1965, only 25 percent of the American public thought that it was a mistake to send troops to Vietnam. The number rose to 31 percent in November 1966 and to 46 percent in October 1967. By June 1968, more than 50 percent agreed that dispatching troops to Indochina had been a mistake.[78] In the next few years, opposition to the Vietnam War metastasized into opposition to Cold War interventions anywhere. According to one poll, in 1975 a majority of Americans surveyed opposed sending U.S. troops to defend any ally from invasion—with the sole exception of Canada.[79]

Note that a quarter of the U.S. public was opposed to the Vietnam War from the beginning. For support for the war to collapse under 50 percent, no more than a quarter of the public—the "owls," as distinguished from the hawks and doves—needed to move into opposition. To prosecute the Cold War, a president had to put together, or preserve, an alliance of owls and hawks that marginalized the doves in Congress. This meant reassuring the owls, who were far more sensitive than largely southern hawks to the costs of U.S. military engagements and far less likely to support a U.S. military campaign to the bitter end. An able tactician in foreign affairs, Nixon failed at this essential domestic political task.

The chain of causation is clear: The cost in American lives of Nixon's prolonged withdrawal from Indochina caused many formerly supportive moderate cold warriors to join left-liberals and leftists in a new isolationist majority in Congress. This new voting bloc did not eliminate or reduce America's existing military commitments to NATO, Japan, and South Korea, but it did, inconsistently, seek to ban new U.S. efforts to prevent the expansion of Soviet bloc influence in countries such as Angola and Ethiopia and Nicaragua and El Salvador. The congressionally imposed limits on U.S. foreign policy in turn inspired the Soviets to act more boldly than they might otherwise have done. Increasing Soviet adventurism, culminating in the invasion of Afghanistan, then produced a backlash against the Soviets in the West, discrediting mid-seventies isolationism and rehabilitating Cold War interventionism in the second half of the Carter administration and in Reagan's first term.

One of the ironies of the Vietnam era is that the moderate cold warriors who broke with Nixon in order to unite with the doves in voting against Nixon's Vietnam policy may have laid the groundwork for rebuilding public support for the successful policies of the United States in the Second Cold War of the 1980s. The leading example is Washington senator Henry M. "Scoop" Jackson, an anticommunist liberal Democrat in the Roosevelt-Truman-Johnson tradition who declared that he was "neither a hawk nor a dove" but a "wise owl." By the early 1970s, Jackson, a former supporter of the Vietnam War, believed that the United States should withdraw rapidly from Indochina. His nuanced understanding of the issues at stake is shown by the fact that he voted for the

Cooper-Church Amendment, which prohibited widening the war, and yet opposed the McGovern-Hatfield Amendment, which would have reduced U.S. leverage in negotiations by imposing an arbitrary deadline for U.S. withdrawal.[80] This was strategic thinking of a high order.

In the final analysis, it may have been the owls like Jackson who stopped the Vietnam-induced hemorrhaging of public support for the Cold War, saved the American commitments to Western Europe, Japan and South Korea from being revoked by isolationists in Congress, and made it possible for President Reagan to wage the Second Cold War in the 1980s. By temporarily teaming up with the doves for tactical reasons, the owls managed to prevent the doves from doing more harm. The owls saw to it that the War Powers Act was passed only in a watered-down form. And while collaborating with the doves to prevent new American commitments, the owls managed to thwart the dovish attempt to reduce existing U.S. commitments to allies outside of Indochina.[81]

The owls were much more Machiavellian than Nixon the hawk. But then owls as well as hawks are birds of prey—and it is owls, not hawks, that have a reputation for being wise.

CHAPTER 5

DISINFORMATION

Vietnam and the Folklore of the Antiwar Movement

Between the beginning and the end of the Vietnam War, the Democratic party repudiated the foreign policy of global military containment that Harry Truman had bequeathed to John F. Kennedy and Lyndon Johnson. The Democrats, who had been more interventionist than the Republicans in the 1950s, turned toward isolationism in the 1970s and 1980s under leaders such as George McGovern and Jimmy Carter. At the same time, many Cold War liberal Democrats joined forces with Republican conservatives to revive containment in the aftermath of the Vietnam disaster and détente. In the Second Cold War of the 1980s, the anti-Soviet strategy of the Truman-to-Johnson Cold War liberals was applied with successful results by a former New Deal Democrat and labor leader who had voted four times for Franklin Roosevelt: Ronald Reagan.

It is often claimed that the Vietnam debacle destroyed widespread support among Democrats for an anti-Soviet foreign policy. However, as I demonstrated in the previous chapter, the real cause of the neoisolationism of the Democratic party between the late 1960s and the present was the transformation of the party's ethnoregional base. As white southerners and white northern Catholics filtered out of the Democratic party into the Republican party, the core constituencies of the Democratic party became Greater New England Protestants, Jews, and blacks. For generations, all three of these subcultures had been disproportionately likely to oppose American wars and coercive diplomacy—the Greater New Englanders because of a secularized New England Puritan and

Teutonic progressive opposition to all things military, Jewish leftists and liberals because of the residues of Eastern European immigrant socialist traditions, and blacks because of their historic alienation from American society.

For the most part, the academics, journalists, editors, and producers who opposed the Vietnam War came from the core constituencies of the post-sixties Democratic party. As a result, the consensus story that the liberal left told about the Vietnam War in particular and the Cold War in general combined themes from both the northern Protestant progressive tradition and the radical leftist mythology. Earlier in the twentieth century, leftists and their progressive allies had argued that foolish and indiscriminate anticommunism had caused the United States to "miss an opportunity" to be friendly with Lenin, Stalin, Mao, and Castro; the same argument was made in the 1960s and 1970s in the case of North Vietnam's Ho Chi Minh. Presidents Johnson and Nixon were accused of waging unconstitutional presidential wars and tricking the electorate into voting for them as peace candidates—crimes of which Presidents Roosevelt and Truman earlier had been accused by antiinterventionist progressives. The claim that Woodrow Wilson's foreign policy was turning the United States into a garrison state, recycled by progressive and radical leftist opponents of Roosevelt, Truman, and Eisenhower, was revived yet again by opponents of the Vietnam War. In fact, the only original contribution that the anti–Vietnam War movement added to the inherited progressive/leftist antiwar script was the absurd claim that the Nixon administration was to blame for the Stalinist-Maoist class genocide committed by the Cambodian communists after they came to power in the wake of the U.S. abandonment of Indochina; this was the equivalent of blaming the executions and mass famine in the Ukraine that accompanied Stalin's collectivization of agriculture in the Soviet Union in the 1930s on the anti-Bolshevik policy of Woodrow Wilson following World War I.

With its elements disseminated by leftist journals such as *The Nation*, the *New York Review of Books*, and *Ramparts*, as well as by countless polemical and academic books, this synthesis of progressive and leftist myths became the conventional wisdom about the Vietnam War for several decades following the conflict. Today it is at once possible and necessary for a new generation of both centrist liberals and conservatives to disentangle fact from fiction about the Vietnam War.

The Myth of Missed Opportunities

The notion that the United States had missed an opportunity to be on good terms with this or that Marxist-Leninist tyrant was one of the familiar folklore motifs in the composite mythology of the American left from 1917 to 1989. All of the later missed opportunity fables were modeled on the original myth of America's failure to befriend the Soviet Union in the years following World War I. As the tale went, the United States missed a chance for a constructive relationship with Lenin and his fellow Bolsheviks when President Wilson sent U.S. troops to Siberia in a misguided effort to help the White Russian armies defeat the communists. In fact, the chief task of the U.S. contingent in the Russian Far East was to protect the territorial integrity of Russia against a possible threat from Japan, at the time a nominal U.S. ally. This was understood by Lenin, who in May 1918 told the Central Executive Committee that "an inevitable conflict will arise between Japan and America for the supremacy of the Pacific and its coasts. The conflicting interests of the two imperialistic countries, now screened by an alliance against Germany, check the movement of Japanese imperialism against Russia."[1]

Throughout the 1960s and early 1970s, the missed opportunity theme was recycled by apologists for the Chinese communists such as the American historian Barbara Tuchman. In a widely praised book entitled *The March of Folly: From Troy to Vietnam* (1985), Tuchman argued that the United States should have appeased both Mao Zedong and Ho Chi Minh. In an essay in *Foreign Affairs* entitled "If Mao Had Come to Washington in 1945," Tuchman criticized Franklin Roosevelt for not listening to admirers of the Chinese communists such as U.S. diplomat John Stewart Service and for failing to side with the admirable Mao against the evil Chiang Kai-shek. "Yet we repeat the pattern in Vietnam," Tuchman complained, by not taking the side of the Stalinists of Hanoi.[2] Of the China that she visited in the summer of 1972, a nation still recovering from the unnatural deaths of as many as thirty million people in the Great Leap Forward a decade earlier, Tuchman wrote: "In a country where misery and want were the foundation of the social structure, famine was periodic, death from starvation common, disease pervasive, thievery normal, and graft and corruption taken for granted, the elimination of these conditions in Communist China is so striking that negative aspects of the new rule fade in relative importance."

On March 7, 1975, thirty-eight members of the U.S. House of Representatives wrote President Ford an angry letter, complaining that even the limited aid that the United States was providing the embattled non-communist regimes of Indochina was too much: "As the distinguished historian Barbara Tuchman wrote about the similar efforts of the United States to resurrect the Chiang Kai-shek regime: 'In the end China went its own way as if the Americans had never come.' In the same sense, Cambodia and South Vietnam will go their own ways; and at this point the American people have stated clearly that they have no interest in postponing this process."[3] Taught by Mao's admirer Barbara Tuchman, these antiwar members of Congress hoped to avoid missing an opportunity to befriend the Khmer Rouge.

The Myth of the Asia Hands

Closely related to the myth of the missed opportunity in China was the claim that the McCarthy-era purge of "Asia hands" in the State Department that followed the Soviet-assisted Chinese communist victory in 1949 deprived the U.S. government of Asia experts who were wise enough to realize that it was folly to oppose Mao Zedong and Ho Chi Minh. In *The Best and the Brightest* (1972), David Halberstam disseminated the argument that the United States had missed an opportunity to befriend Mao Zedong:

> If the decay and erosion of Chiang's forces were a historical force, so too was the rise of the new China. Produced in reaction to all the political sickness around it, it reflected a new and harsh attempt to harness the resources of that huge and unharnessed land. The Communists were rising from the ashes of the old China, and they were in stark contrast to what had existed before. They were powerfully motivated, almost prim and puritan in their attitudes to the world, their view of corruption. On the mainland itself a brilliant group of young State Department officers were reporting the events with great insight.[4]

Despite Halberstam's claim of inevitability (reinforced by geological metaphors like "decay" and "erosion"), there was nothing inevitable about the takeover of the world's most populous nation by communist dependents of Stalin. The victory of Mao's communists over Chiang Kai-shek's Nationalists in 1949 was the result of a number of factors: the weakening of the Nationalist regime by the war with Japan, Chiang's military blunders, the decision of the Truman administration to cut its losses in China—and, perhaps most important of all, the massive military aid and logistical support provided by the Soviet Union.[5] Far from being a rational attempt to "harness the resources" of China, Chinese communism, like its Soviet model, was a lunatic creed that produced mass starvation and ecological devastation. Moreover, the "prim and puritan" Chinese communists, like other Marxist-Leninist nomenklaturas, on seizing power quickly turned into a corrupt, quasi-hereditary mafia.

Halberstam praises John Paton Davies and John Stewart Service as "the most distinguished" American foreign service officers; "they were the best of an era, and the Foreign Service does not produce that many men of rare excellence." According to Halberstam, "The young American Foreign Service officers warned that we had to come to terms with the failure of Chiang's order. It was a story which would repeat itself in Vietnam."[6] In 1979, Halberstam, in an effort to excuse the many errors of fact committed by the group of journalists in Saigon to which he had belonged, claimed that "their political reporting was limited by the absence of serious skilled Asia experts in the American embassy. The McCarthy era had taken care of that."[7]

The leading Asia hands were not communist agents, as demagogues such as McCarthy claimed, but there is no doubt that a number of them were gullible dupes of Chinese communist propaganda. John Stewart Service, reporting from communist-controlled Yenan on September 8, 1944, declared that Mao's communists were the Chinese equivalent of the British Labour Party: "[T]he Communist Party becomes a party seeking orderly democratic growth toward socialism, as is being attempted for instance, in a country like England, rather than a party fomenting immediate and violent revolution. . . . [T]he Communist political program is simply democracy. This is much more American than Soviet in form and spirit." Another one of Halberstam's heroes, the diplomat John Paton Davies, in a report from Yenan on November 7, 1944, entitled "How Red Are the Chinese Communists?" described them as "backsliders" who "lust after the strange gods of class compromise and party coalition, rather shamefacedly worship the golden calf of foreign investments and yearn to be considered respectable by worldly standards."[8] Historian Michael Sheng observes: "In light of various reports written by American officers in China, such as John Service and John Davies, Mao had good reasons to believe that his policy of enlisting the Americans to curb [Chiang] was rather successful. On 13 July 1943, Mao told Peng Dehuai that 'our propaganda campaign has got positive result.'"[9] (In 1972, ten years after the end of the Great Leap Forward, in which as many as thirty million Chinese may have starved because of communist policy, Halberstam wrote approvingly in *The Best and the Brightest* that "Davies insisted that American policy makers had to get out of the habit of looking at communism as a moral issue.")[10]

The illusions about Asian Marxism-Leninism of the leading Asia hands in the U.S. diplomatic corps were shared by many naïve liberals in the United States. "They could more appropriately call themselves the Chinese democrats," *The New Republic* said of Mao's communists on March 13, 1944. In the same year Maxwell S. Stuart, an editor of *The Nation*, compared the Chinese Stalinists "to the grass-roots populist movements that have figured in American history." The *New York Times*, on November 1, 1944, declared that the Chinese communists—who were in near daily radio communication with Stalin, and who had already set up the first *laogai* or concentration camps in the territory they controlled—"are in fact peasant agrarians."[11]

Later, the record of many of America's leading academic East Asia experts in understanding and evaluating Asian communism was equally appalling. Harvard's John K. Fairbank, the most influential student of China in the United States, described the reign of Mao, who is now known to have executed or starved more of his subjects than any tyrant in history, as "one of the best things that has ever happened to China." "I was committed to viewing 'communism' as bad in America but good in China, which I was convinced was true," Fairbank wrote.[12] Warren I. Cohen, often described as the "dean" of Asian studies in the United States, suggested that the Truman administration missed an opportunity to befriend Mao's regime—a claim that recent research has demolished.[13] Cohen criticized American foreign policymakers for refusing to believe that many countries would be better off under communist rule: "In the mid-1960s, some liberals shed their universalism and recognized the irrelevance of liberal democracy and a Eurocentric peace system for much of Asia and Africa. They concluded, as more radical thinkers had long before, that anti-Communism was senseless when Communism might be the best alternative offered a people."[14] Today it is the "liberals" and "radical thinkers" praised by Cohen who believed that Marxist-Leninist totalitarianism was "the best alternative" for "much of Asia and Africa" who look foolish—not American liberal anticommunists such as the target of Cohen's criticism, Secretary of State Dean Rusk.

By the 1960s and 1970s, the academic study of Asia in the United States was warped by a McCarthyism of the left. American experts on Asia who were too critical of communism risked being ostracized by their colleagues.[15] From today's vantage point, it is clear that many of the procommunist Asia hands and their admirers and allies in the American academy and press displayed "clientitis"—the syndrome that affects foreign policy experts who come to identify emotionally with a faction in the nation they study. "Too great familiarity can hinder just observation," the political scientist Martin Wight once observed, "and not only does involvement lead to distorted knowledge, but noninvolvement is almost a necessary ingredient of clear knowledge. To judge correctly, one must remain an outsider, although a well-informed one." Wight quoted Lord Palmerston: "When I wish to be misinformed about a country I ask the man who has lived there thirty years."[16]

The Myth of the Missed Opportunity in Vietnam

During the Vietnam War, the western left recycled the myth of the missed opportunity yet again by substituting Ho Chi Minh for Mao Zedong and Vietnamese communism for Chinese communism. Just as the United States was alleged to have missed an opportunity to befriend Mao, so it was said to have missed a chance to befriend Ho. The fact that the United States cooperated with Ho Chi Minh during World War II was taken as evidence of Ho's unrequited desire for a good relationship with the United States. Those who made this argument usually ignored the fact that Ho's patrons Stalin and Mao had been allies of the United States during World War II as well. Further evidence for the alleged missed opportunity was found in Ho's quotation from the U.S. Declaration of Independence in the speech in which he announced the formation of an independent Vietnam in 1945. The fact that all Marxist-Leninist dictatorships had formal constitutions that were as liberal and democratic as those of the United States and its democratic allies should have been sufficient to cast doubt on this assertion.

The agents of the American Office of Strategic Services (OSS) in Indochina during World War II who were convinced of Ho's admiration for the United States were as gullible as many of the American foreign service officers, presidential emissaries, and journalists who met with Mao during the Second World War.[17] Both Mao and Ho pretended to be pro-American, as long as they believed that they could win U.S. support, or at least ensure American neutrality in their struggle with noncommunist nationalists in their countries. Both were just as quick to denounce the United States as the leader of global imperialism and reaction, when it served their purposes and the strategy of the transnational communist bloc. While there were pro-Soviet and pro-Chinese factions in the Vietnamese communist oligarchy, it appears that there was never a pro-American faction. In time, the Vietnamese communist archives will almost certainly demonstrate that the claim that Ho was interested in genuine neutrality between the blocs, like that of Tito's Yugoslavia, was an illusion of the western left.

To a remarkable degree, the vilification by the anti–Vietnam War movement of the noncommunist dictators of Indochina such as South Vietnam's president Ngo Dinh Diem and Lon Nol in Cambodia recapitulated the vilification of China's Chiang Kai-shek by American leftists and fellow-traveling liberals in the 1940s. One historian writes: "The image of a corrupt, oppressive, and moribund regime, headed by a chauvinistic ruler resistant to American advice, was an important factor in the unwillingness to use American forces in postwar China."[18] Even the term used by Vietnamese communists to vilify Diem, *My-Diem* (America-Diem), was a translation of the Chinese communist epithet *Mei-Chiang* (America-Chiang). In addition to echoing the left's earlier denunciations of Chiang Kai-shek, the vilification of Diem by American liberals in the early 1960s recycled criticisms of the South Korean dictator, Syngman Rhee, in the previous decade. "Liberals," Frank Gibney wrote in 1945 in *Harper's* magazine, ". . . make Rhee the incarnation of this country's failure to insure 'real democracy' thoughout the non-Communist world, the man who mocks the honest peace-making of the United Nations, whose 'authoritarian' tactics do more damage to the cause of the United States than reinforcements to the Russian air force."[19]

The Myth of the All-Vietnamese Election

One of the central claims of the critics of the Vietnam War was the argument that the entire conflict could have been avoided, if only the United States had pressured South Vietnam into permitting all-Vietnamese elections in 1956—elections which Ho Chi Minh's communists would have won. The Geneva Conference of 1954 had made provisions for such nationwide elections. But with the support of the United States, the anticommunist nationalist Ngo Dinh Diem expelled the first provisional ruler, the French-installed Emperor Bao Dai, made himself president and dictator, and refused to agree to nationwide elections. Thus, it is said, both Diem's regime and the United States "violated" the Geneva agreements.

Contrary to the mythology of the anti–Vietnam War movement, none of the major parties in the Vietnam War—North Vietnam, South Vietnam, Laos, Cambodia, or the United States—endorsed the Geneva Agreements. The State of Vietnam (South Vietnam) became formally independent of France on July 21, 1954. By the time of the Geneva conference, the State of Vietnam had been recognized by more than thirty countries and a number of UN agencies, and had been endorsed for membership in the United Nations by the General Assembly. Thus South Vietnam took part in the Geneva negotiations as a sovereign state, not as a French colony. (If the de facto dependence of South Vietnam on France and the United States is thought to detract from its de jure sovereignty, then by the same standard North Vietnam must be treated as a de facto colony of China and the Soviet Union.)

The South Vietnamese government used its sovereign authority to denounce French negotiations at Geneva purporting to bind South Vietnam, and rejected the provision for national elections: "[T]he Government of the State of Vietnam . . . solemnly protests against the manner in which the armistice has been concluded and against the conditions of that armistice." Indeed, July 20, 1955, the anniversary of the Geneva Agreements, was observed as a "day of shame" in South Vietnam. In 1956, when the Soviet Union and China sought to bring about national elections by convening a second Geneva conference, Britain responded—correctly, as a matter of international law—that South Vietnam was not obligated to hold elections.[20] For its part, the United States merely "took notice" of the agreements, and promised to "seek to achieve unity through free elections, supervised by the United Nations to ensure that they are conducted fairly." The State Department later pointed out that the complete absence of political freedom in North Vietnam and the monopolization of power by the Communist party made "impossible any free and meaningful expression of popular will."[21] Even if South Vietnam had been a democracy rather than a dictatorship, the outcome of a national plebiscite would have been a victory for the communists, for the simple reason that communist North Vietnam had more inhabitants than noncommunist South Vietnam. Critics of the U.S. effort in Vietnam have frequently misquoted Eisenhower to the effect that Ho would have won any national elections. What Eisenhower really said, in *Mandate for Change* (1963), was that "had elections been held as of the time of the fighting [in 1954], possibly 80 per cent of the population would have voted for the Communist Ho Chi Minh as their leader rather than Chief of State Bao Dai." There is no evidence to support the contention that a majority of South Vietnamese in the mid-1950s or 1960s wanted Stalinist rule, notwithstanding the presence of a large communist minority in the South.

Not even the most ardent defenders of Ho Chi Minh ever suggested that there would have been a *second* round of free national elections in Vietnam if the communists won the first. In the first national elections held after the communist conquest of South Vietnam, on April 25, 1976, 99 percent of the voters voted for communist candidates. As the Viet Cong's former minister of justice observed: "They hadn't much choice. The penalty for not voting was confiscation of the abstainer's ration card, without which he and his family could not buy anything to eat."[22]

Although there were no free elections in either North or South Vietnam during the 1950s, many Vietnamese did get a chance to vote with their feet. The Geneva agreements provided that during a three-hundred-day period "any civilians residing in a district controlled by one party who wish to go and live in the zone assigned to the other party shall be permitted and helped to do so by the authorities in the district." Roughly ten times as many Vietnamese—almost a million—moved South from the North as migrated in the opposite direction. The western left tried to blame this flight from communism exclusively on psychological warfare operations by the CIA intended to persuade Vietnamese Catholics to regroup in the South, controlled by their fellow Catholic Diem. That propaganda played at best a minor role is suggested by the record of mass flight from other communist dictatorships such as the Soviet Union, China, North Korea, Laos, Cambodia, Cuba, and East Germany (from which three million of a population of eighteen million fled before the remaining population was walled in). The exodus was repeated on a larger scale in the years following the communist unification of Vietnam in 1975, when one and a half to two million Vietnamese nationals fled their homeland. The post-Geneva exodus might have been far greater than it was. According to the Canadian members of the international peacekeeping mission, many Vietnamese were prevented from departing the North during the resettlement period. One Canadian observed that "soldiers, political cadres and local militias were frequently stationed in the houses of the Catholic population with instructions to prevent them from leaving their homes in order to contact the teams."[23]

In the final analysis, it is a mistake to treat the partition of Indochina in abstract legal terms that ignore the realities of Cold War power politics. The division of Vietnam between communist and noncommunist states was no different in kind from the partition of Germany, China, and Korea. Other countries might have been partitioned in a similar manner. If the Soviets had not decided to withdraw from Austria, that country might have been divided into East and West Austria. Italy is another country that escaped partition during the Cold War. In 1948, George Kennan, then in the State Department's Policy Planning Staff, worried that communists might win forthcoming national elections in Italy. He suggested that the Italian government outlaw the Communist party:

> This would admittedly result in much violence and probably a military division of Italy; but we are getting close to the deadline and I think it might well be preferable to a bloodless election victory, unopposed by ourselves, which would give the Communists the entire peninsula at one coup and send waves of panic to all surrounding areas.[24]

It is only necessary to substitute "Vietnam" for "Italy" to have an explanation of the strategic logic that inspired U.S. policymakers to oppose the unification of Vietnam under communist rule not only by means of war but by means of an election.

The North Vietnamese Class Genocide

The attempt to minimize or explain away the mass murder in North Vietnam that accompanied "land reform" in the 1950s constitutes one of the most shameful chapters in the sorry history of the American intellectual left. "Land reform" was a euphemism for campaigns by communist governments seeking to subordinate the majorities in peasant societies to tiny cliques of unchecked and corrupt party functionaries. Communist leaders such as Lenin, Stalin, Mao, Ho Chi Minh, and Fidel Castro tended to come from affluent or middle-class families (even Stalin came from the lower middle class of Georgia). As a rule, they despised the "backward" values of the peasant majorities in the countries in which they seized power. Marx, an unemployed professor whose bills were paid by his rich friend Engels, sneered at "the idiocy of rural life." Lenin, the heir of an aristocratic family, informed H. G. Wells of the importance of "defeating the Russian peasant en masse." In 1930, Stalin complained of the peasant farmer's "slavish attachment to his little plot of land." Communist leaders, ignorant of genuine economics, tended to assume that a big farm was inherently more productive than a small farm, and that people motivated by ideology (or, if that failed, by terror), would work as hard as those motivated by a desire for personal and family profit. When Marxist ideology collided with expertise, it was the nineteenth-century European pseudoscience that won. "Who should manage a farm?" Fidel Castro asked, then answered: "A revolutionary. What are his prerequisites? That he be a revolutionary."[25]

Communist agriculture could not produce good harvests—but it repeatedly produced bumper crops of the dead. In the Soviet Union, 6.5 million are thought to have died as a result of collectivization; an additional 8 million died of famine in Ukraine and Kazakhstan. With astonishing candor, Stalin told Churchill that collectivization had been worse than World War II.[26] During collectivization in the areas of China under communist rule between 1946 and 1957, the death tolls have been estimated at anywhere between 250,000 to 5 million. Most historians now agree that 25 to 30 million Chinese starved to death during the famine caused by Mao's Great Leap Forward of 1958–61.[27]

The North Vietnamese land reform of the 1950s was an atrocity comparable to those in the Soviet Union and China, if not quite as disastrous as Pol Pot's collectivization campaign in Cambodia in the 1970s.

Collectivization began on March 2, 1953, with the promulgation of a "Population Classification Decree" that divided the subjects of the Hanoi dictatorship into five categories, from "landlord" to "agricultural worker." Somewhere between 10,000 and 100,000 Vietnamese were summarily executed for being of the wrong class category; many more were imprisoned in the Vietnamese gulag. In North Vietnam, as earlier in the Soviet Union and China, the mass terror that accompanied collectivization promoted popular unrest. On August 17, 1956, Ho Chi Minh, in the Orwellian language he had learned from his mentors and role models Stalin and Mao, declared: "Errors have been committed in the implementation of unity in the countryside. . . . Those who have been wrongly classified as landlords and rich peasants will be correctly reclassified." The backtracking by the dictatorship came too late to prevent a popular rebellion. On November 2, 1956, when desperate villagers in Nghe-An, begging to be taken to South Vietnam, thrust petitions at Canadian observers, communist soldiers intervened and fighting broke out. According to the French journalist Bernard Fall, "Hanoi no longer had any choice; it responded in exactly the same way as the colonial power had, sending the whole 325th Division to crush the rebels. It did so with typical VPA thoroughness; allegedly, close to 6,000 farmers were deported or executed." Fall points out that the crushing of the Hungarian uprising by another Soviet satellite regime at the same time diverted attention from the brutal repression of the North Vietnamese people by Ho Chi Minh's dictatorship. "[N]o U.N. member—neither of the always touchy Bandung bloc so concerned about the fate of its brothers in colonial shackles, nor of the habitually anti-Communist nations—mustered sufficient courage (or marshalled sufficient facts) to present the Nghe-An case to the conscience of the world." Ho Chi Minh—portrayed as gentle, caring "Uncle Ho" in the propaganda of the communist bloc and the western left—responded as Stalin and Mao had when their schemes had backfired. He made his subordinates scapegoats, launched a "Campaign for Rectification of Errors," and dismissed the mass murder with the callous observation: "One cannot waken the dead."[28]

The intellectual integrity of Fall, a left-of-center critic of the Vietnam War who told the truth about Ho Chi Minh's Stalinist tyranny, made him unusual among the writers of the western left in the Vietnam era. The antiwar radicals Tom Hayden and Staughton Lynd, in their account of their Potemkin village tour of North Vietnam, *The Other Side* (1967), noted that estimates of the number of those killed during collectivization in North Vietnam were as high as 50 to 100,000. "To my knowledge," a North Vietnamese official told them, "no one was killed." What resistance there was to collectivization, Hayden and Lynd were told, resulted from the plotting of sinister Catholics. "Reactionary Catholic leaders took advantage of Catholic people to protest." Hayden and Lynd concluded, "We suggest that this episode should be viewed as an extension of the war against the French, and the violence involved should be assessed in the same context as the terror of the Resistance itself."[29] Far from having "originated in wartime in response to the needs of the rural poor," as the two American leftists claimed, the rural terror in North Vietnam was carried out in peacetime by a Communist party intent on terrorizing the rural poor into submission to its authority. Accepting the communist line that North Vietnamese peasants who rebelled against communist state terror were members of a pro-French Catholic reactionary plot was the equivalent of believing Stalin's claim that Ukrainian peasants were part of an international Trotskyist conspiracy, or Hitler's allegation that poor Jews in Polish ghettos belonged to a worldwide conspiracy against the Aryan race.

Most of the leading historians of the Indochina conflict on the American left treated the North Vietnamese land reform campaign as a worthwhile effort to improve the lives of North Vietnamese peasants that was marred by certain excesses. For example, in her 1991 book *The Vietnam Wars, 1945–1990*, Marilyn B. Young wrote: "Careful Party guidelines distinguished between productive and unproductive landlords, patriotic and traitorous rich peasants, but these distinctions were increasingly ignored as the campaign gained a radical momentum of its own." The "careful Party guidelines" to which Young refers were the pseudoscientific class categories dreamed up by Lenin that Ho derived from Stalin by way of Mao. Their absurdity is illustrated by the fact that land ownership in North Vietnam was far less concentrated than in South Vietnam. Even a Soviet study of September 1957 conceded that before the North Vietnamese land reform the average landlord in North Vietnam owned 0.65 hectares of rice land, or less than two acres. For the crime of owning such tiny holdings, thousands of North Vietnamese villagers were denounced and shot.[30]

Dismissing Bernard Fall along with Richard Nixon as "western propagandists," Young cites the "most careful historian of the land reform,

Edwin Moise" to the effect that at most "fifteen thousand people were executed during the land reform campaign."[31] Moise, in his *Land Reform in China and North Vietnam* (1983), admits: "In Vietnam there were more punishments [than in communist China] for imaginary crimes." As an example, Moise writes: "The Party definitely made the number of despots denounced for their crimes at mass struggle meetings in each *xa* much more uniform than the actual distribution of brutal and oppressive landlords would have justified." Translated from Stalinese into English, this means that communist officials persisted in condemning and executing villagers until they filled the quotas assigned by Hanoi. Moise argues in extenuation of the dictatorship's war on the rural population of North Vietnam: "There were valid reasons for the exaggeration of classism. . . . But this extreme view of the class nature of rural affairs sometimes went beyond the real interests of the revolution, and it often went beyond the bounds of objective truth." Moise makes it clear that he sympathizes with the "real interests of the [communist] revolution" in North Vietnam's model, the Soviet Union, as well. Regretfully, according to Moise, the fact that Russian peasants in 1917 took the initiative in expropriating the land they worked meant that the "Bolsheviks therefore did not get full credit from the peasants for the land reform."[32]

Historical studies like these illustrate the different standards applied by the western left to communist and noncommunist dictatorships. If any noncommunist regime had summarily executed fifteen thousand of its citizens in a few months during peacetime because they had been assigned to certain socioeconomic categories, the western left would have denounced the atrocity. The antiseptic and mostly favorable accounts of North Vietnamese collectivization by the two American leftist academics can be contrasted with an account published in 1995 by Bui Tin, formerly a colonel in the North Vietnamese army and one of Hanoi's leading journalists. "Land reform occurred after we had heard hundreds of Chinese advisers introduce the process on the basis of their experience in their own country," Tin explains. Of the party officials in charge of land reform, the former North Vietnamese official writes: "In their hands the power of life and death was absolute. . . . There were no lawyers, and in fact there was no law. Sentences were carried out by a rifle section selected from local guerrillas who were landless peasants with no relatives among the middle peasantry or landlords." Tin blames the murder of "more than ten thousand people" by Ho's dictatorship on the influence of Chinese communism: "Most of [the victims] were Party members or patriots who had supported the Revolution but nonetheless were reasonably well off. They were shot having been condemned by what amounted to kangaroo courts, although they were called people's tribunals. This was the result of the mechanistic application of Chinese experience imposed by their advisers."

Tin describes the fate of a plantation owner named Mrs. Nguyen Thi Nam, whose sons were high-ranking Communist party officials. "But the Chinese adviser concluded that she was a cruel landowner who had to be eliminated." The local peasants defended Mrs. Nam, and an official named Hoang Quoc Viet hurried to Hanoi to ask Ho Chi Minh to intercede on the woman's behalf. Ho promised to speak to Truong Chinh, the fervent admirer of Mao who led the collectivization program—but he did not. As a result, "Mrs. Nam was quickly condemned to death on the advice of Mao Tse-tung's representative who accused her of deceitfully entering the ranks of the revolution to destroy it from within."

Bui Tin concludes:

> Years later, I asked Hoang Quoc Viet what he thought about that case and he told me, "When I spoke to Uncle Ho, he knew it was not right, but he dared not tell them." By "them" he meant the sons of heaven, the representatives of Mao Tse-tung. . . . By remaining silent and failing to intervene in the case of Mrs. Nam, he showed a lack of responsibility not only towards her but also towards all the other people who were victimised and killed during the land reform programme. He allowed his country and his Party to be usurped by foreigners.[33]

The term "genocide," if it is to be meaningful, must be limited to cases in which people are singled out and killed on the basis of their identity—defined in terms of race, ethnicity, religion, sexual orientation, or socioeconomic class—rather than on the basis of their decision to actively resist a government. The systematic execution, in village after village of North Vietnam, of at least ten or fifteen thousand individuals who had committed no crime or act of political resistance but had been assigned to economic categories borrowed from Stalin's Soviet Union and Mao's China constituted genocide on the basis of class identity, even if it took place on a smaller scale than the comparable Marxist-Leninist class genocides in the Soviet Union, China, and Cambodia. Like members of the far right who question the existence or scale of the Nazi ethnic genocide in Europe, members of the western left who minimized or made excuses for the North Vietnamese land reform terror were apologists for state-sponsored genocide.

The Myth of the Diem-Ho Rapprochement

One myth about the Vietnam War that has become popular in recent years is the claim that the assassination of South Vietnam's dictator Ngo Dinh Diem in 1963 aborted a potential reconciliation between Diem and Ho that might have led to a peaceful reunification of Vietnam. This myth arose from the fact that both Diem and his brother Nhu, during the time when the Kennedy administration was in contact with generals plotting their overthrow, speculated in public about asking the United States to withdraw its troops. On May 12, 1963, Nhu told the *Washington Post* that "South Vietnam would like to see half of the 12,000 to 13,000 American military stationed here to leave the country." They also made gestures toward rapprochement with Ho using the good offices of a Polish communist diplomat in Saigon, Mieczyslaw Maneli.

Arthur M. Schlesinger, Jr., has suggested that "a Diem-Ho deal could have been the means of an American exit from Vietnam in 1963. . . . An opportunity of some sort was perhaps missed in the autumn of 1963."[34] The journalist Stanley Karnow and the historian George C. Herring have also speculated that the negotiations between North and South represented a chance for peace that was aborted by the murder of Diem.[35] Even Henry Kissinger has written: "In light of what followed the coup, it would have been easier for America to disengage by letting Diem collapse of his own inadequacies or, at a minimum, by not standing in the way of the negotiations he was suspected of planning with Hanoi."[36] Unfortunately for those looking for easy exits to roads not taken, it is almost certain that Diem and Nhu were using the threat of rapprochement with North Vietnam as a tactic to force the Kennedy administration to reduce its pressure on them. In similar circumstances, for similar purposes, both Nationalist China's Chiang Kai-shek and South Vietnam's Park used remarkably similar tactics.

As Diem would do later in South Vietnam, Chiang during the 1940s tried to make himself indispensable by means of a rule-or-ruin policy of making the entire government of Nationalist China dependent on him. Nevertheless, in a striking parallel with the situation in South Vietnam a decade and a half later, there was considerable discussion in Washington about finding a replacement for Chiang who would better be able to unite China against Mao's communist insurgency. Secretary of State George Marshall admitted that "there was constant pressure to eliminate Chiang Kai-shek, but no one ever suggested anyone [who] could take his place."[37] Aware that the United States was contemplating his ouster, Chiang had his government declare in November 1947 that while it would appreciate the dispatch of U.S. personnel it insisted on controlling "the employment of these personnel." Two months earlier, Chiang had told the Kuomintang Central Executive Committee that China, while maintaining its alliance with the United States, should strengthen its ties with the Soviet Union. The U.S. ambassador to China told Secretary of State Marshall on September 20, 1947, that Chiang made this statement "primarily for its effect on the United States." Indeed, "it has been suggested to the Ambassador that the Soviet Ambassador to China . . . might be asked to mediate the civil war and that he would be glad to accept." The historian Tang Tsou observes that Chiang "felt confident enough [in the certainty of the U.S. commitment] to threaten to go it alone in his fight against the Communists and to come to an understanding with the Soviet Union when he hoped to exert pressure on the United States." Tang notes that "the threats of Chiang and other Nationalist officials [to extend peace feelers toward the communist bloc] failed to achieve their primary objective, which was to draw the United States into the Chinese civil war or, at least, to obtain large-scale economic aid and military assistance from the United States."[38]

Another suggestive parallel to the contacts between Diem and Ho in the early 1960s can be found in Korea a decade later. In the spring of 1972, South Korean president Park Chung Hee, a dictator who had come to power in a military coup in 1961, sent the number two official in his regime, Korean CIA head Lee Hu Rak, on a secret mission to North Korea to meet with its communist dictator, Kim Il Sung. Following other contacts, the two regimes issued a joint statement on July 4, 1972, declaring that the unification of the Korean peninsula would "be achieved through independent efforts without being subject to external imposition or interference" and that "a great national unity, as a homogeneous people, shall be sought first, transcending differences in ideas, ideologies, and systems." In 1979, President Park was assassinated by the then director of the KCIA, Kim Jae Kyu. If Park had been assassinated in 1972 or 1973, soon after his negotiations with Kim, there might have grown up a myth that the tragic murder of the South Korean dictator had aborted the imminent reunification of North and South Korea. Evidence for the alleged North-South reconciliation might have been found in notes of conversations between KCIA director Lee and North Korean dictator Kim. Lee: "I'd like to tell that President Park is a person who detests foreign interference most." Kim: "Big powers and imperialism prefer to divide a nation into several nations."

In fact, neither side in Korea was serious about peaceful reunification. The communist regime in the North explained to the Politburo of the East German communist party that the purpose of its peace offensive was to accelerate the withdrawal of U.S. troops from South Korea. The policy "undermined the attempts of the U.S. imperialism to retain its troops in Korea, as well as the attempts of the Japanese imperialists. . . . The Park Chung Hee clique will capitulate to this peace offensive." One of Park's aides explained later that the South Korean dictator, for his part, saw the communications as nothing more than a tactic in an ongoing struggle. Park reportedly said, "As long as you can touch an opponent with at least one hand, you can tell whether he will attack."[39]

The most plausible explanation of the tactics of Diem and Nhu in publicizing the feelers they extended to Hanoi, then, is that they were trying to frighten the Kennedy administration into abandoning its collaboration with the Ngo family's enemies among South Vietnam's discontented generals. Diem, like Chiang earlier and Park later, wanted American military and economic aid without strings attached—and without a noose attached.

The Myth of the Coalition Government

Throughout the Vietnam War, many American leftists and liberals claimed that the goal of the National Liberation Front, the political wing of the Viet Cong, was a neutral South Vietnam with a multiparty government representing all elements in South Vietnamese society. In their influential antiwar polemic *The United States in Vietnam* (1967), George McTurnan Kahin and John W. Lewis wrote: "Providing for minority representation in the post-election government, [the NLF] asserts, will ensure an ultimate 'national concord' consistent with the pluralistic nature of South Vietnamese society."[40] This article of communist propaganda was taken at face value by many liberal critics of American participation in the war—among them, former attorney general Robert F. Kennedy. On March 2, 1967, Kennedy, then a senator from New York, proposed that multinational forces, replacing U.S. troops, would supervise elections including all political factions in South Vietnam. Kennedy, opportunistically trying to appeal to antiwar Democrats in advance of his run for the presidency, did not explain why multiparty elections would not also be required in North Vietnam, where Ho Chi Minh's regime had never held a free election and had murdered, exiled, or imprisoned the political opposition.[41]

Earlier, in an April 21, 1965, memorandum opposing the escalation of the U.S. military involvement in Vietnam, Johnson administration adviser George Ball had proven himself equally naïve or disingenuous. Ball suggested that Hanoi might be satisfied with a compromise that included an end to hostilities, international supervision of a cease-fire, and a fixed date for internationally supervised elections in which the NLF would participate. "What those who have praised Ball's 'realism' have failed to point out," writes historian R. B. Smith, "is that almost exactly the same terms as he proposed in 1965 were actually offered to Hanoi by President Nixon in May 1969; and that they were rejected even then, at a time when Communist forces in the South were in a relatively much weaker position than had been the case four years earlier."[42]

Even after the fall of Saigon, anti–Cold War liberals such as James C. Thomson continued to argue that Johnson had missed an alleged opportunity to turn over South Vietnam to a neutral coalition government: "Had he been more confident in foreign affairs, had he been deeply informed on Vietnam and Southeast Asia, and had he raised some hard questions that unanimity had submerged, this president could have used the largest electoral mandate in history to deescalate in Vietnam, in the clear expectation that at the worst a neutralist government would come to power in Saigon and politely invite us out."[43] In reality, such an option never existed. Communist-bloc archives have now made it clear that the Vietnamese communists were lying when they claimed that a neutral South Vietnam was their goal. Discussing the issue of a coalition government with Zhou Enlai in Beijing on September 17, 1970, Pham Van

Dong admitted: "For us and for Nixon, diplomacy is a play of words. Neither we nor he has any illusion about diplomacy." The North Vietnamese leader explained that the cynical proposals of the NLF and the North Vietnamese government for a coalition government and the unconditional withdrawal of U.S. troops served a strategic purpose: "First, we have to win the sympathy of the people in South Vietnam, especially the ones in the urban areas. Furthermore, we have to influence the antiwar public opinion in the US that includes not only the people at large but also the political, business, academic, and clerical circles to ensure a stronger support for them."[44]

The claim that Hanoi would be satisfied by the inclusion of South Vietnamese communists in a coalition government was another bit of propaganda recycled from apologists for Mao's Chinese communist insurgents. In November 1944 the American diplomat John Paton Davies told Washington: "A coalition Chinese Government in which the Communists find a satisfactory place is the solution of this impasse [the Chinese civil war] most desirable to us. It provides our greatest assurance of a strong, united, democratic and friendly China." Earlier in September 1944 John Stewart Service had claimed that Mao's communists would be content to share power with Chiang's Nationalists in a coalition government for an indefinite period: "They have no illusions that China can hope to build a proletarian state in anything like the near future."[45] During the Chinese civil war, as in the Vietnamese civil war, talk of a coalition government including communists was a ruse designed to fool western liberals.

The conquest of South Vietnam by the North Vietnamese military in 1975 proved that the promise of a neutral coalition government had been a hoax all along—even if some dissidents in the South had believed it. Claims that the North did not intend to impose Marxism-Leninism on the South by force "had been discarded like trash within months of victory," former Viet Cong minister of justice Truong Nhu Tang wrote in 1985. "By then it was clear that there was no further need for subterfuge—either toward the Western media or antiwar movements, or toward the Southern revolution itself."[46]

During the 1972 U.S. presidential campaign, Democratic nominee George McGovern invited Ngo Cong Duc, a member of the National Socialist party in South Vietnam and an opponent of the Thieu regime, to join him in a tour of the United States denouncing the war. After the communist conquest, Ngo Cong Duc coedited the only private newspaper in Vietnam, which was shut down by the regime in 1980. The communist government rewarded the leader of the National Socialist party, Tran Van Tuyen, for his earlier opposition to the Thieu dictatorship by throwing him in prison, where he died.[47]

The Myth of the Irrepressible Sino-Vietnamese Rivalry

One of the most frequently repeated assertions in the anti–Vietnam War literature is that the depth of historic Vietnamese hostility to China meant that U.S. leaders could have expected a falling-out between the Chinese and Vietnamese communists. If this were indeed true, then Vietnam would be an exception to the rule that international alignments usually result from the short-term calculations of the elites who control states, rather than from popular prejudices against or in favor of other nations. Countries with a history of mutual enmity are often reconciled when geopolitical conditions or regimes undergo change. Germany and France, archenemies for a century and a half, are partners today in the European Union. Following the end of the Cold War, the government of Mexico, for strategic reasons, sought a closer relationship with the now unchecked United States, despite the distrust and resentment of the United States shared by many Mexicans.

The record shows that Sino-Vietnamese relations have been influenced more by ideological and strategic factors than by alleged national hatreds dating to the Middle Ages. Opponents of the Vietnam War were fond of quoting Ho Chi Minh's statement to his comrades in 1946, "Better to sniff French shit for a while than eat Chinese shit for the rest of our lives." But as Nguyen Vu Tung of the Vietnamese Ministry of Foreign Affairs conceded in 1998, "Ho was, of course, referring to China under Jiang Jieshi's [Chiang Kai-shek's] Guomindang [Kuomintang]."[48] From the moment Mao's communists triumphed in China in 1949 until the early 1970s, the Chinese and Vietnamese communists, despite occasional differences, were closely allied. Indeed, as I observed above, Ho and his colleagues modeled their regime on Mao's, going so far as to invite Chinese communist advisers who sometimes helped Vietnamese communist cadres to decide which Vietnamese landlords and peasants should be executed during the Maoist "land reform" terror of the 1950s. The important pro-Chinese faction in the Vietnamese communist elite included

Truong Chinh, whose adopted name is a Vietnamese translation of "Long March," one of the episodes in the Chinese communist revolution. Hoang Van Hoan, a member of the Politburo, defected to China at the time of the Sino-Vietnamese War; he wrote a book to counter the minimization of China's contribution to the Vietnam War in Hanoi's official histories.[49] The Sino-Vietnamese War of 1979 itself reflected, not ancient Sino-Vietnamese hatreds, but the split between the Soviet Union, which by then was Vietnam's sole protector, and China, allied with the Cambodian Khmer Rouge. Nor can the Sino-Soviet split be interpreted as the result of ancient Sino-Russian hatreds, for there were pro-Soviet Chinese communists such as Lin Piao who lost their struggle with Mao in the 1960s. The problem with explanations of a country's foreign policy in terms of traditions of national enmity is obvious: It can explain episodes of hostility, but not periods of cooperation and solidarity.

Even if ancient and irrepressible Vietnamese Sinophobia had made an alliance of the Vietnamese and Chinese communists unsustainable, it does not follow that the United States inevitably would have benefited from Sino-Vietnamese divorce. As long as the Soviet Union existed, the Vietnamese communists could gain both legitimacy and protection by belonging to the Soviet bloc. An alliance with the United States or uneasy neutrality would have been less attractive to the communist rulers in Hanoi. Only after the Soviet Union collapsed and Marxism-Leninism was discredited worldwide did the Vietnamese dictatorship cautiously seek a rapprochement with the United States.

Today the argument that the Vietnamese communists were anti-Chinese nationalists all along serves the purposes of two groups—the communist leaders in Hanoi, who seek to minimize the record of Sino-Vietnamese cooperation in the early Cold War in order to gain American support against China, and western leftists, liberals, and realists still defending the simplistic claim of the sixties antiwar movement that the Vietnam War was essentially an anticolonial struggle rather than a proxy war in the Cold War like the wars in Korea and Afghanistan.

Robert McNamara and "Missed Opportunities"

The most sustained, if unconvincing, attempt to argue that there were a number of missed opportunities for peace and good relations between the United States and North Vietnam was published in 1999 by former Secretary of Defense Robert McNamara in collaboration with four American academic historians, James G. Blight, Robert K. Brigham, Thomas J. Biersteker, and Herbert Y. Chandler. In *Argument Without End: In Search of Answers to the Vietnam Tragedy*, McNamara and his fellow authors list half a dozen alleged "missed opportunities" for cooperation between the United States and Ho Chi Minh's regime between 1945 and 1968. Most of the missed opportunities that they cite are familiar from the left-liberal orthodoxy of the 1960s–1990s, including the alleged mistake of the Truman administration in supporting France in Indochina rather than befriending the Vietnamese communists and the alleged missed opportunity in the early 1960s for a neutral coalition government in South Vietnam. The authors claim that new revelations from Vietnamese government officials and archives prove that these various missed opportunities had been real. If this were true, then our understanding of the Vietnam War would be revolutionized. On close examination, however, the alleged revelations dissolve into word games or assertions resting on flimsy or nonexistent evidence.

McNamara and his fellow authors caricature the positions of those whom they oppose, then carefully qualify their own. For example, in the section entitled "Enemies: Washington's and Hanoi's Mindsets at the Beginning of the Kennedy Administration," they describe the "Received Wisdom in the West" as follows: "By January 1961, Vietnamese communists constituted a unified movement, directed and controlled from Moscow and Beijing, whose objective was undermining U.S. security interests, that is, knocking over the dominoes in Southeast Asia."[50] As a sentence in a left-isolationist polemic, this might pass muster; as a description of the actual views of members of the Kennedy and Johnson administrations in which McNamara served, it is a grotesque caricature. No American policymakers believed that Moscow or Beijing literally dictated the policies of Hanoi, or failed to recognize the rivalry between the Soviet Union and China. At the same time, communist elites in all three countries, for reasons of national interest as well as of ideological solidarity, collaborated in the effort to help communist insurgents in Indochina defeat the clients of the United States. By the standards of McNamara and his fellow authors, the Axis alliance against the United States and its allies must have been an illusion, inasmuch as there were conflicts of interest between Nazi Germany, Fascist Italy, and Imperial Japan.

In presenting their own proposed emendations to the historical record, the authors of *Argument Without End* parse their words as carefully as lawyers or the authors of a diplomatic communiqué:

> A Washington-Hanoi confrontation need not have occurred if the Kennedy administration had understood Vietnamese nationalism and the Hanoi leadership had understood U.S. motives in Southeast Asia. . . .
>
> The confrontation, leading to war, between Washington and Hanoi need not have occurred if each had correctly understood the other's perception of the evolution of the Cold War in Asia and the other's role in that evolution. . . .
>
> A neutral solution in Saigon, with a coalition government in place, was possible at any point between 1961 and 1964, if only Washington and Hanoi had understood the concerns and objectives of the other. . . .
>
> Escalation from confrontation to war between Hanoi and Washington was not inevitable, if only each had accurately understood the capabilities, intentions, and decisionmaking process of the other.[51]

The other assertions are similar.

The banality of the language should not be permitted to obscure the breathtaking boldness of the claim. Taken at face value, the statements imply that the genuine interests of both North Vietnam and the United States consistently were misconceived by their governments for a quarter century—even though both the true North Vietnamese communist interest and the true American interest are obvious, in retrospect, to a retired and repentant former U.S. secretary of defense and four American professors.

The major participants in the Vietnam War—not just the United States and North Vietnam, but also the regimes of South Vietnam, the Soviet Union, and China, which the authors ignore—were not perfectly informed, but they were adequately informed. Some of the strategies and tactics used by one or another participant might have been different, had this or that elite possessed better knowledge of another. North Vietnam and China underestimated the willingness of the United States to go to war to rescue South Vietnam; the United States underestimated the willingness of the North Vietnamese communists to impose horrendous costs on their unfree subjects in order to achieve their goals. Even so, the participants in the Vietnam War correctly perceived both the goals of the other major players and their incompatibility. The war began and was prolonged and widened by the intervention of the United States, China, and the Soviet Union not because the rivals misunderstood one another's goals, but because they understood perfectly well that their goals could be realized only if the efforts of their adversaries were thwarted. Ho Chi Minh, a communist and a nationalist, hoped to win a victory for Marxism-Leninism as well as to achieve national unity by annexing South Vietnam. The United States understood that this outcome was incompatible with its own goal of demonstrating its credibility as the leader of the global anticommunist alliance by protecting its noncommunist South Vietnamese client state from subversion or invasion. By helping the North Vietnamese, the Chinese and the Soviets hoped to win prestige in the communist world and among antiwestern forces in the Third World at the expense of the United States and its allies. A Soviet victory in this competition would hurt Mao's regime, just as a rise in the prestige of China as a sponsor of revolutions would be a defeat for Moscow. If elites in Washington, Moscow, Beijing, Hanoi, and Saigon did not believe their interests were compatible, this is not evidence that they were obtuse; rather, it is proof that they had gauged their own interests and those of their enemies and allies correctly.

In addition to making the implausible argument that Hanoi and Washington somehow overlooked the true harmony of Vietnamese communist and American interests for thirty years, McNamara and the four historians assert that Hanoi would have permitted a neutral, noncommunist coalition government in South Vietnam to exist indefinitely. On close examination, this radical assertion is not proved by the evidence that the authors adduce in its support. The evidence consists of claims made by functionaries of the Vietnamese communist dictatorship at a staged meeting in Hanoi with former U.S. officials and scholars in February 1998. McNamara admits that "the Vietnamese government had established limits to the candor of its participants."[52] Nevertheless, McNamara asserts that some of the Vietnamese participants could be trusted because they volunteered information in private conversations. He does not explain why the statements of academics and other officials of a totalitarian state, subject no doubt to close surveillance by internal security forces, should be taken at face value. Indeed, McNamara carefully qualifies his claim about the missed opportunity for a coalition government:

Particularly fascinating was the implication—maybe more than an implication—at the February 1998 conference that it was entirely possible that South Vietnam might *never* be reunified with the North and that this was understood by at least some in Hanoi.

"[T]he implication—maybe more than an implication . . . it was entirely possible . . . might . . . at least some. . . ."[53] Such tentative phrasing is evidence of a lack of confidence in the assertion being made.

Why would McNamara lend his name to a book as dubious as *Argument Without End*? In his introduction, McNamara claims that his larger purpose in arguing that the Vietnam War was a mistake based on mutual misunderstanding is to persuade his fellow Americans to abandon the logic of power-political realism in the twenty-first century and to work for a utopian world order based on interdependence and idealism. According to the former Cold War hard-liner, "the United Nations charter offers a far more appropriate framework for international relations in the future than does the doctrine of power politics."[54] Inasmuch as the UN can function only on the rare occasions when the great powers of the Security Council, for selfish power-political reasons of their own, agree to support a particular policy, this proposal is not very helpful. In the 1980s, McNamara called on the United States to renounce the option of unilateral military action abroad; in the 1990s, he testified against going to war with Iraq and opposed the war with Serbia.

In addition to his stated political purpose, McNamara may have been motivated by personal factors comparable to those that have driven McNamara's colleague, former attorney general Ramsay Clark, to assume the role of a perpetual critic of U.S. "war crimes" from a position on the extreme left. Throughout his post-Vietnam career, McNamara has sought to ingratiate himself not only with those who reviled him on the liberal and radical left at home but also with communist adversaries of the United States. McNamara made a pilgrimage to Moscow in 1986 to meet with Mikhail Gorbachev and met with Fidel Castro in Havana in 1992. *Argument Without End* is the latest episode in this campaign. McNamara's wish to believe that the Vietnam War might have been averted, if only American leaders and the totalitarians of Vietnam had understood and befriended one another, says more about McNamara than about the Vietnam War. In words that might apply to McNamara's newfound belief in the existence of numerous missed opportunities in U.S.-Vietnamese communist relations, his biographer Deborah Shapley writes skeptically that McNamara's "sincere belief that Kennedy would have gotten out of Vietnam was something that he arrived at later when the war had become tragic and traumatic for him and the nation."[55]

Cambodia: Myth and Reality

Most of the radical left's myths about the Vietnam War and Vietnamese communism, then, were updated versions of old propaganda themes: the missed opportunity, the pro-American communists, the coalition government. To these traditional motifs, the radical left in the 1970s and 1980s added an original myth of their own, when they blamed the Maoist class genocide carried out by Pol Pot's Khmer Rouge in Cambodia on the United States in general and on President Richard Nixon in particular.

During the Vietnam War, many American leftists and liberals shared the favorable view of the Khmer Rouge expressed by *New York Times* reporter Harrison Salisbury in 1973: "Of course, after Liberation, it would not be Sihanouk who would be the real master of Cambodia. It would be the Khmer Rouge. But they planned to let Cambodia remain a kingdom, with themselves in a cabinet that included non-Communist members."[56] As news of the emptying of the cities, summary executions, and mass starvation in Cambodia that followed the Khmer Rouge takeover leaked to the outside world, the first impulse of many western leftists was to deny that the horror was occurring. According to George McTurnan Kahin, one of the most prominent academic critics of the Vietnam War, writing in 1976, the forced evacuations of Cambodian cities "were not, then, applications of some irrational ideology, but reflected pragmatic solutions by leaders who had to rely exclusively on Cambodia's own food resources and who lacked facilities for its internal transport."[57] In 1975, Kahin had testified before the U.S. Senate in opposition to further U.S. support for the Lon Nol government, dismissing the possibility of a bloodbath in Cambodia if the Khmer Rouge took over.[58] Gareth Porter of the leftist Institute for Policy Studies told a House Committee in May 1977: "There is no reason to doubt that some violence took place. But there is reason to believe that was not the intention of the government."

Porter also justified the emptying of hospitals by the Khmer Rouge: "And I do indeed think that one can argue that it was a reasonable alternative to move the patients as fast as possible to locations outside the cities where there were in fact other medical facilities, not good medical facilities, but, in the circumstances which existed in Phnom Penh at the end of the war, probably better than what existed there."[59] In 1967, Tom Hayden and Staughton Lynd had used similar reasoning to excuse the mass murder accompanying the Maoist land reform program in North Vietnam in the mid-1950s, claiming that it "appears to have originated in wartime in response to the needs of the rural poor."[60]

Once it was no longer possible to deny the reality or magnitude of the horror in Cambodia, western leftists tended to respond with one of three arguments. In order of increasing absurdity, the triumph of the Khmer Rouge was blamed on the U.S.-backed overthrow of Prince Norodom Sihanouk by the Cambodian general Lon Nol; the actions of the Khmer Rouge were blamed on racist nationalism, rather than on communist ideology; and the actions of the Khmer Rouge were blamed on U.S. bombing, which allegedly inspired a genocidal frenzy among Cambodian peasants.

The Overthrow of Sihanouk. Todd Gitlin, a former president of Students for a Democratic Society (SDS), a radical left organization of the 1960s, recently restated one historical myth of the antiwar left about Cambodia: "All civilized people who are revolted by Khmer Rouge mass atrocities should also remember that it was the Nixon administration, not the [antiwar] movement, that encouraged the overthrow of Prince Sihanouk and weakened opposition to this regime of mass murderers."[61]

Throughout the 1960s, Sihanouk's government, in return for bribes from Hanoi, had allowed the North Vietnamese army to move men and supplies across Cambodian territory along the Ho Chi Minh Trail. Soviet and Chinese supplies also flowed through Cambodia from the port of Sihanoukville. Sihanouk explained in 1964, "To understand what I'm trying to achieve, just remember this: All of Southeast Asia is destined to become Communist. . . . When it happens in Cambodia, I want it to happen without breakage."[62] By 1970, North Vietnam had in effect annexed eastern Cambodia, to the extent of restricting the access of Cambodian officials and taxing and drafting Cambodian peasants. Meanwhile, Sihanouk—Southeast Asia's answer to Nero or Caligula—devoted his energies to making feature films starring himself and officials of his regime and their mistresses (some are available in the United States in video format). Under pressure from frustrated Cambodians to do something about the North Vietnamese invaders, Sihanouk tacitly approved the "secret" bombing of Vietnamese bases on Cambodian territory in 1969. This did not save him from being overthrown on March 18, 1970, by General Lon Nol, whose regime, which was as corrupt, but not as weird, as Sihanouk's, invited the support of the United States in expelling the North Vietnamese army from Cambodia and defeating the Khmer Rouge.

Sihanouk immediately allied himself with the Khmer Rouge. Meanwhile, the United States and South Vietnam invaded the North Vietnamese–controlled area of Cambodia. In a second incursion into Cambodia in 1971, South Vietnamese troops backed by U.S. airpower suffered heavy losses in battles with North Vietnamese regulars. In 1973, after the Khmer Rouge–led coalition refused to enter peace talks following the Paris Agreements, the United States prevented the Khmer Rouge from taking over Cambodia by dropping 250,000 tons of bombs over the country. Although the radical left cites far higher numbers, the most realistic estimates are that between thirty thousand and a quarter of a million Cambodians were killed.[63] The banning by the U.S. Congress of further U.S. air support for the Lon Nol regime ensured victory for Pol Pot and his followers.

Until the final stages of the war, the Khmer Rouge was a dependency of Hanoi. "[Pol Pot] himself was a creature of an earlier Vietnamese conflict, eased along inside the subsidiary Cambodian movement," writes David P. Chandler in *Brother Number One: A Political Biography of Pol Pot* (1992). "Until the end of 1972, his troops were armed, trained, and often led by the Vietnamese. The defeats suffered by Lon Nol in 1970–1971 had been at the hands of Vietnamese regular forces."[64] Although they later broke with the Vietnamese communists, the Khmer Rouge owed their victory in Cambodia to the North Vietnamese military.

And what of Sihanouk, who somehow was going to restrain his Khmer Rouge allies? A few years after the Khmer Rouge came to power, Sihanouk was in exile and between an eighth and a quarter of the Cambodian nation—including numerous members of Sihanouk's family—had been executed or starved to death by the communists. The outcome probably would have been similar had the North Vietnamese–sponsored Khmer Rouge coalition triumphed with Sihanouk as a figurehead in 1970 or 1972. Other than the wishful thinking of the western left, there appears to be no basis for the idea that Sihanouk could have led a "third force" capable both of defeating the Lon Nol regime and marginalizing the Khmer Rouge without relying on the North Vietnamese army. Indeed, in 1981 Sihanouk himself declared, "Today I pay homage to his grave. John Foster Dulles was right. There is no nonalignment."[65]

As it happens, in the course of the 1970s an influential faction of the western left quietly changed its story about the sequence of cause and effect in Cambodia. After the Khmer Rouge seized power, many western leftists blamed their rise on the destruction of a possible "third force" in Cambodia by the U.S.-backed Lon Nol regime and on the alienation of the peasantry by U.S. bombing. However, before the Khmer Rouge came to power, the Committee of Concerned Asian Scholars, a group including Noam Chomsky, Edwin Moise, John Dower, and Earl C. Ravenal that was formed in 1968 "to protest against American imperialism in Asia," had told a quite different tale. In *The Indochina Story* (1970), this is what the CCAS had to say about the Khmer Rouge, following the Lon Nol coup: "Strong support for Sihanouk among the peasantry, and the armed aid of the clandestine Khmer Rouge ('Red Khmer'), a rebel group which had patiently been biding its time since a brief period of armed struggle in 1967, would certainly have toppled the government [in the absence of U.S. support]—had it not tipped over of its own accord."[66] In 1970, the CCAS complained that the U.S. military effort was *preventing* the Khmer Rouge, with Sihanouk as a figurehead, from coming to power; after 1974–75, most on the left floated a new story—the U.S. military effort had *caused* the Khmer Rouge to come to power.

Were the Khmer Rouge Fascists, not Communists? A number of western leftists have sought to minimize the embarrassing resemblance of the Cambodian class genocide to the campaigns of state terror that accompanied rural collectivization in other communist countries, including North Vietnam. This line of argument has been made most forcefully by Ben Kiernan, a leftist Australian academic and former apologist for the Khmer Rouge. In 1977, Kiernan declared, "There is ample evidence in Cambodian and other sources that the Khmer Rouge is not the monster that the press have recently made it out to be." After renouncing this view, Kiernan was appointed director of the Cambodian Genocide Program, a taxpayer-funded institute located at Yale University (it is as though a former Nazi sympathizer and Holocaust denier had been appointed to direct Washington's Holocaust museum).[67]

In *The Pol Pot Regime* (1996), Kiernan claimed that "Khmer Rouge conceptions of race overshadowed those of class." The left was quick to disseminate a theory that exculpated communism. In 1997, the British leftist writer Tom Nairn, relying on Kiernan, announced with relief: "The Cambodian Hell was more truly an aberration of nationalist development than of socialism."[68] In *The Nation* in 1998, John Pilger wrote, "The [U.S.] invasion [of Cambodia] provided a small group of extreme nationalists with Maoist pretensions, the Khmer Rouge, with a catalyst for a revolution that had no popular base among the Cambodian people."[69] In reality, although the Khmer Rouge persecuted many ethnic minorities in Cambodia, most of its victims were political and class enemies. As Ross H. Munro, a leading American Asia expert, has pointed out, Kiernan "is out to prove that the Khmer Rouge weren't leftists or communists at all, despite their literally red name and the neo-Maoist ideology they so fervently professed."[70]

Notwithstanding the attempt of Kiernan and others to turn the Red (communist) Khmer into the Brown (fascist) Khmer, the origins of Khmer Rouge policies are easily traced to the Marxist ideology of the Chinese Cultural Revolution in the mid-1960s. Pol Pot visited China in 1966 at the height of Mao's enthusiasm for the Cultural Revolution and people's war.[71] Haing Ngor, the Cambodian doctor who gave an Oscar-winning performance in *The Killing Fields*, wrote that almost "everything about the Khmer Rouge was alien, from China. They had borrowed their ideology from Mao . . . like the concept of the Great Leap Forward. Sending the intellectuals to the countryside to learn from the peasants was an idea of the Chinese Cultural Revolution." Unfortunately for the Cambodian people, Pol Pot "did not realise that Mao's Cultural Revolution was already a disaster and that Stalin's attempts had set the Soviet economy back by decades."[72]

If one examines only executions by regimes, rather than mass starvation produced by socialist agricultural policies, then Pol Pot's Cambodia looks much less like Hitler's Germany than like Ho Chi Minh's North Vietnam. Indeed, most of the deaths in Cambodia were unintended by-products of socialist economic policies, like the earlier famine deaths in the Soviet Union and communist China. The number of Cambodians executed without trial during the reign of the Khmer Rouge is estimated to have been around one hundred thousand.[73] In the mid-1950s, Ho's government, following the counsel of advisers from Mao's China, presided over the systematic murder of between ten and one hundred thousand class enemies (mostly farmers) during the Mao-inspired collectivization campaign, and deported perhaps one hundred thousand to forced labor camps.[74] Even if only ten thousand North Vietnamese villagers were executed in the 1950s, they were executed for the same reason that many ordinary Cambodians were. They were classified as class enemies in a nightmarish purge carried out by a communist dictatorship that, like Pol Pot's Khmer Rouge regime later, modeled itself on Mao's China.

Did Nixon's Bombing Drive Cambodians Insane?   The most grotesque fiction in the mythology of the anti–Vietnam War left is the claim that President Nixon, by bombing the North Vietnamese and their allies in Cambodia, turned the Cambodian people into homicidal maniacs. This explanation was spread in the late 1970s by leftists such as Gareth Porter and George Hildebrand, who declared that the Cambodian bloodbath "should mainly be attributed to the American bombing."[75] The journalist William Shawcross disseminated this canard in his polemic *Sideshow: Kissinger, Nixon and the Destruction of Cambodia* (1979).

The U.S. bombing of Cambodia may well have helped the Khmer Rouge recruit Cambodian peasants to their cause. But the argument that the massacres and famines in Cambodia under Khmer Rouge rule were to be blamed, not on Marxist-Leninist ideology, but on the frenzy that U.S. bombing allegedly triggered in Cambodian peasants, was nonsense. Laos, not Cambodia, was the most heavily bombed country during the Vietnam War. The single greatest bombing campaign during the war took place in South Vietnam, following the Tet offensive, when 1.2 million bombs were dropped, a far greater amount than fell on Cambodia.[76]

The most elaborate attempt to minimize the Cambodian horror and to blame it on the United States was penned by Noam Chomsky in collaboration with Edward Herman. In extenuation of the Khmer Rouge, Chomsky and Herman wrote in 1988 that "when poor peasants are driven into the jungle from villages destroyed by bombing, they may seek revenge."[77] The attempt of Chomsky and Herman to portray

Khmer Rouge policies as spontaneous acts of revenge on the part of un-controlled mobs is similar to the argument of Staughton Lynd and Tom Hayden, noted in the previous chapter, that the systematic mass murder of North Vietnamese peasants in peacetime by Ho Chi Minh's dictator-ship in the mid-1950s, under the influence of Mao's China, had been nothing more than spontaneous lynchings of pro-French traitors.

Most of those who blamed Nixon for the atrocities of Pol Pot argued that Nixon had *inadvertently* turned the Cambodian peasants into homici-dal psychopaths by bombing their country. Chomsky and Herman, how-ever, promoted a conspiracy theory worthy of Oliver Stone. They found "quite plausible" the suggestion of another leftist, Michael Vickery, that "when it became clear [to U.S. leaders] that they could not win in Cambo-dia, they preferred to do everything possible to insure that the post-war revolutionary government be extremely brutal, doctrinaire, and frighten-ing to its neighbors, rather than a moderate socialism to which the Thai, for example, might look with envy."[78] Chomsky and Herman later restated the thesis that the atrocities were a "direct and understandable response to the still more concentrated and extreme savagery of a U.S. assault that may in part have been designed to evoke this very response."[79]

The historical record makes it clear that the American bombing of Cambodia, however objectionable it may have been on strategic or hu-manitarian grounds, did not turn the "moderate socialism" of the Khmer Rouge into something "brutal, doctrinaire, and frightening," either inad-vertently or as a result of a secret design by Nixon and Kissinger. Pol Pot's Stalinist/Maoist policies, including collectivization of agriculture, forced population movements, and the imposition of a standard peasant uniform, were first tried on a large scale in the territories that the Khmer Rouge controlled at the beginning of 1973. Pol Pot's rule in "liberated" Cambodia was so horrifying that more than twenty thousand Cambodi-ans fled to noncommunist South Vietnam, seeking asylum.[80] Cambodian refugees told of a radical effort to transform society, using mass terror-ism, population transfers, and utopian economic schemes.[81]

Indeed, one of the arguments that the Nixon and Ford administra-tions made in appealing to Congress to help the embattled Lon Nol regime in Cambodia was the need to prevent the Khmer Rouge from taking power and presiding over a bloodbath. On March 6, 1975, Philip Habib, assistant secretary of state for East Asian and Pacific affairs, gave the House Foreign Affairs Committee a chillingly accurate prediction of what would happen if Pol Pot's forces came to power: "If the present government falls, I think the impact within Cambodia . . . would be an unbelievable transformation of that society against the wishes of its general population and through the use of great force. I think that there certainly would be what people call the bloodbath, but in any event great cruelty."[82] On March 11, one of the leading left-liberal Democrats in the House, Donald Fraser of Minnesota, told Congress that it should vote for aid to Cambodia only on the condition that the Cambodian government surrender to the Khmer Rouge: "It ought to be a negotiated end— you might call it a negotiated surrender, if you will, but an orderly transfer of power." A few days later, during a committee hearing, Representative Fraser repeated this demand to Acting Secretary of State Robert Ingersoll. Ingersoll responded: "You are asking for a surrender, then, Mr. Fraser?" Fraser replied, "Yes; under controlled circumstances to minimize the loss of life. . . . If you are not prepared to move in that direction, then I am not prepared to vote any more money."[83]

Richard Nixon was guilty of a number of crimes; causing the communist atrocities in Cambodia was not one of them. If any Americans deserve a share of the blame for the Khmer Rouge massacres and famines, it is antiwar members of Congress such as Donald Fraser who sought to hasten a Khmer Rouge victory by denying U.S. military aid and air support for America's Cambodian allies.[84]

The Myth of the Disturbed Vietnam Veteran

Most of the men of the baby boom generation who belong to the American media elite today avoided service in the Vietnam War, often by means of college deferments. The eminent American journalist James Fallows is the only prominent member of this cohort who has written honestly about how the antiwar movement "exhibited contempt for the white proles" who fought the war. He describes the use by affluent leftists and liberals "of the phrase 'pig' for the blue-collar, lower-class people who were doing the job they thought they were supposed to do. They had been the 'pigs' holding down the black people in Mississippi, the children of the 'pigs' were being sent off to die in Vietnam, and now 'pigs' were clubbing our chosen people, the demonstrators, in Chicago."[85]

After the war ended, the condescension of members of the American overclass who avoided it for the working-class and middle-class Americans who fought it found a new expression in the myth that an immoral, insane war had turned American soldiers into emotional wrecks. In 1975, *New York Times* columnist Tom Wicker claimed that "hundreds of thousands of Vietnam veterans" were suffering from severe war-induced psychological difficulties.[86] The syndrome now labeled Post-Traumatic Stress Disorder (PTSD) was known in earlier generations as "shell shock" or "combat fatigue." This disorder, or rather group of disorders, is genuine. However, the most careful studies suggest that Vietnam veterans do not suffer from PTSD in greater proportions than veterans of World War II.[87] Indeed, psychiatric casualties in Vietnam itself were very low (12 per thousand) compared with those in Korea (37 per thousand) and World War II (28–101 per thousand).[88] This is the case even though the average Vietnam combat veteran spent more time in the combat zone than did his counterpart in World War II.[89] Vietnam veterans compare favorably not only to veterans of previous wars but to the civilian population as a whole. Every year since 1974, Vietnam veterans have had a lower unemployment rate than the national average.[90] The divorce rate of Vietnam veterans is no higher than that of the rest of the population.[91] Tom Wicker claimed that in 1975 five hundred thousand Vietnam veterans had attempted suicide. The number was completely bogus; Wicker had obtained it from *Penthouse* magazine.[92] In reality, the suicide rate among Vietnam veterans is similar to that of nonveterans.[93] Many veterans apparently did suffer from exposure to the defoliant Agent Orange, and drug abuse was a problem in Vietnam (although its rate increased only when more than 90 percent of those who served had already left).[94]

Most Vietnam veterans feel neither guilty nor bitter about their roles in America's failed campaign against the totalitarians in Indochina. Seventy-one percent of Vietnam veterans polled in 1980 agreed with the statement, "Looking back, I am glad I served my country."[95] Far from being pacifists disillusioned by their military experience, Vietnam veterans show greater support for U.S. military intervention abroad than do other Americans. Shortly before the Persian Gulf War, according to one survey, 58 percent of Vietnam veterans approved of waging war with Iraq if it failed to withdraw from Kuwait—compared to only 39 percent of the general population. While 18 percent of the American public thought that the United States should abandon the Persian Gulf, only 8 percent of the Vietnam veterans endorsed a U.S. retreat.

The continuing bias of the media was on display in 1998, when CNN publicized the false claim in a special report by Peter Arnett that American soldiers had used deadly nerve gas to kill American defectors in Vietnam (in the incident in question, tear gas had been used, and no American defectors were present). The dissemination of falsehoods about the effect of Vietnam and other wars on American soldiers serves the purposes of the antimilitary left. As the historian Eric T. Dean, Jr., has observed, "The portrayal of the Vietnam vet as well-adjusted and untroubled by the war would have undermined [the] antiwar agenda, and hence evidence that Vietnam veterans were readjusting or had readjusted well to American society tended to be drowned out by excited and strident recriminations leveled against the U.S. government."[96]

Vietnam and the Historians

In 1988, the historian Robert Divine noted that "[v]irtually all contemporary historical analyses of the Vietnam War shared a strong distaste for American intervention."[97] For the past generation, most of the journalists and historians who have written about the Vietnam War and Vietnamese communism, with the exception of military specialists, have done so from the perspective of the procommunist or anti-anti-communist left. It is as though the history of the Pacific campaign in World War II had been written by isolationists who believed that Franklin Roosevelt, a tyrant and a war criminal, had deceived the American people into believing that there had been a serious Axis threat in order to reward American industry with military contracts.

The biases of the sixties-era liberal left are manifested most clearly in polemics written at the time of the Vietnam War by journalists such as Frances Fitzgerald and David Halberstam. Fitzgerald ended her Pulitzer Prize–winning tract *Fire in the Lake* with a hopeful vision of a time when "the narrow flame of revolution [would] cleanse the lake of Vietnamese society" and purge it of "'individualism' and its attendant corruption."[98] Similar undisguised admiration for the communists pervades David Halberstam's *Ho* (1971). Halberstam's book is perhaps the most sympathetic portrait of a Stalinist dictator ever penned by a reputable American journalist identified with the liberal rather than the radical left.

In *Ho*, Halberstam omits any mention of the repression or atrocities of Ho Chi Minh's regime. For example, Halberstam writes that in August 1945, "the Vietminh had in one quick stroke taken over the nationalism of the country, that Ho had achieved the legitimacy of power."[99] From reading Halberstam, one would never guess that in 1945–46 Ho's deputy Giap carried out a reign of terror in which thousands of the leading noncommunist nationalists in territory controlled by Ho's regime were assassinated, executed, imprisoned, or exiled. Halberstam condemns the repression carried out by the Saigon regime: "Diem and the Americans had blocked elections in 1956 and Diem had carried out massive arrests against all his political opponents, particularly anyone who had fought with the Vietminh."[100] Of the far more severe repression in North Vietnam, there is not a word in Halberstam's book. The Maoist-inspired terror of collectivization in the mid-fifties, in which at least ten-thousand North Vietnamese were summarily executed because they belonged to the wrong "class," is not mentioned. Nor is the anticommunist peasant rebellion that followed; nor the deployment of the North Vietnamese military to crush the peasants; nor the succeeding purge of North Vietnamese intellectuals; nor the fact that almost ten times as many Vietnamese, during the brief period of resettlement, fled from communist rule as left South Vietnam for the North. The equivalent of Halberstam's book would be a flattering biography of Stalin that praised his leadership during World War II while omitting any mention of the gulag, the purges, and the Ukrainian famine, or an admiring biography of Mao that failed to mention the Cultural Revolution or the starvation of tens of millions during the Great Leap Forward.

Halberstam is even less forthcoming when the subject is relations among North Vietnam, China, and the Soviet Union. He accurately describes Ho's background in the French Communist party and his residence in the Soviet Union in the 1930s. But Halberstam omits any mention of Soviet or Chinese support for North Vietnam after 1949. "No matter that the superpower America was aiding the South; [Ho] realized that the Saigon government had no base of popular support."[101] No mention is made of the fact that the Hanoi government was aided by the Soviet superpower and China, a great power. The fact that in 1950, responding to pressure from Ho, Stalin ordered Mao to support Ho's regime; the fact that the victory of North Vietnam against the French depended on military supplies and advice from the Sino-Soviet bloc; the fact that Ho's dictatorship modeled its structure and policies on Mao's

China and Stalin's Soviet Union; the fact that Soviet and Chinese deterrence forced the United States to fight in unfavorable conditions in Vietnam; the fact that hundreds of thousands of Chinese logistics troops, as well as Chinese and Soviet antiaircraft troops and Soviet fighter pilots, took part in the Vietnam War; the fact that North Vietnam would have been forced to abandon its effort to conquer South Vietnam, if not for massive Soviet and Chinese subsidies—all of these facts are omitted from Halberstam's *Ho*.

That these damning facts were omitted by design rather than by mistake becomes clear when one examines the sources that Halberstam lists in his bibliography. Halberstam's book leaves out everything critical written about Ho Chi Minh by the authors that Halberstam used as his sources. For example, one of Halberstam's authorities, Joseph Buttinger, described the repressiveness of Ho's government in great detail, and bitterly condemned it, in *Vietnam: A Dragon Embattled* (1967).[102] The major source for Halberstam's *Ho* appears to have been the book *Ho Chi Minh* published by the antiwar French journalist Jean Lacouture in 1968.[103]

In an interview in the late 1970s with a Milan newspaper, Lacouture, referring to the communist dictatorship in Cambodia, spoke of "my shame for having contributed to the installation of one of the most oppressive regimes history has ever known." He added:

> [W]ith regard to Vietnam, my behavior was sometimes more that of a militant than that of a journalist. I dissimulated certain defects of North Vietnam at war against the Americans, because I believed that the cause of the North Vietnamese was good and just enough so that I should not expose their errors. I believed it was not opportune to expose the Stalinist nature of the North Vietnamese regime. . . . If we re-examine the dossier, it is true that I did not tell all that I knew about Vietnam.[104]

Lacouture described pro-Hanoi journalists in the West like himself as "vehicles and intermediaries for a lying and criminal propaganda, ingenious spokesmen for tyranny in the name of liberty." In light of this confession, the fact that Halberstam is even less critical of Ho than his source Lacouture, then a supporter of Hanoi, raises serious questions. Halberstam ends his book with a sentimental tribute to Stalin's Vietnamese disciple: "In his lifetime Ho had not only liberated his own country and changed the course of colonial rule in both Africa and Asia, he had done something even more remarkable; he had touched the culture and soul of his enemy. . . . [I]t had been a full life."[105]

American academic histories of the Vietnam War tend to show the same biases that are evident in the work of journalists such as Fitzgerald and Halberstam. The historian Gabriel Kolko even ended his book *Anatomy of a War: Vietnam, the United States, and the Modern Historical Experience* (1994) by calling on Vietnam's leaders to revitalize communism rather than to abandon it: "If Vietnamese Communism is to play a creative role in the future, it must adapt to the radically new conditions throughout the world and abandon its authoritarian legacies."[106] (The *Christian Science Monitor* described this procommunist tract as "One of the best written general histories of this conflict yet published.") Few journalistic or academic historians, however, are this blatantly enthusiastic about Marxism-Leninism. The typical history of the Indochina wars written in the style of late Cold War leftist revisionism attempts to strengthen the claim that the Vietnam War was an "anticolonial" war rather than a Cold War proxy war by devoting much attention to the French role from 1945 to 1954 while carefully minimizing the critical Soviet and Chinese roles in Indochina between the 1940s and the 1990s. For example, the journalist Stanley Karnow's *Vietnam: A History* (1983), which purports to be a comprehensive history of the conflict, mentions Soviet-Vietnamese relations only on twenty pages and relations between communist China and North Vietnam on a mere twenty-two pages—out of 684 pages in the text. One of the most breathtaking recent attempts to rewrite history to remove the Cold War from the Vietnam War appeared on June 22, 1997, in the Week in Review section of the *New York Times.* In an article entitled "How the War Goes On (And On) in Cambodia," Barbara Crossette describes Ho Chi Minh's communists as "the leftist-nationalist movement." (It seems that even in the 1990s, the word "communism" cannot be used to describe Indochinese Stalinists in the *Times.*) Crossette describes Indochinese history from the nineteenth century until the 1990s without once mentioning the Soviet Union, Ho Chi Minh's home for a decade, the chief model for his regime, and the major protector, sponsor, and supplier of North Vietnam from the mid-1960s until the beginning of the 1990s.

The most peculiar aspect of revisionist history on the left is the tendency for anti–Cold War historians to describe the accurate perceptions of American Cold War policymakers as though they had been illusions. In his book *Presidents' Secret Wars* (1990), the historian John Prados, after describing how the Soviet Union airlifted weapons and ferried twenty-five to thirty thousand Cuban troops to help out Soviet clients in Angola, writes: "The Soviet bloc aid *seemed to make* Angola a cold war battlefield *in Washington's eyes*" (emphasis added).[107] The large-scale Soviet bloc intervention *did* make Angola a Cold War battlefield. For an equivalent of Prados's formulation, one must imagine a historian who writes "Hitler's invasion of Greece to help Mussolini appeared to antifascist policymakers in London and Washington to confirm the existence of an 'international fascist conspiracy' including the so-called Axis powers." In his study *Masters of War: Military Dissent and Politics in the Vietnam Era* (1996), Robert Buzzanco refers to "the liberation of Saigon in 1975" and writes of "southern Vietnam" in order not to "convey the status of nationhood where it is not established" (by this theory, neither West Germany nor South Korea were legitimate states).[108]

Secondary school textbooks as well as college texts have displayed the semantic bias of the radical and liberal left. Martin F. Herz, examining six leading high school textbooks in 1978, discovered that most of them used euphemisms like "popular nationalist" and "pro-communist" for "communist." According to Herz, "It is also noteworthy that while all the textbooks describe Diem's regime as 'repressive,' not one of them considers it necessary to make any similar remark about the regime in North Vietnam, which, being totalitarian, was far more repressive."[109]

The fashion of anti–Cold War revisionism in leftist-dominated American history and political science departments in the second half of the Cold War recalled an earlier wave of revisionism. After World War I, most American historians were either Wilsonians or isolationists whose revulsion against military intervention abroad characterized their treatment of American policy in Europe, Latin America, and Asia. In the *Yale Review* of June 1951, Dexter Perkins, describing mainstream U.S. diplomatic historians of the interwar generation, noted that they tended to conclude "that the foreign policy of the United States has been almost uniformly inept; that every war in which this country has been engaged was really quite unnecessary or immoral or both, and that it behooves us in the future to pursue policies very different from those pursued in the past."[110] But in the years following Pearl Harbor, according to historian Jerald A. Combs in a survey of American diplomatic history, most American historians "tended to study isolationism as a kind of pathology." Then, in the aftermath of the Vietnam War, "hard-line realism that emphasized the unavoidability of conflict" went out of fashion among American academic historians. In the final quarter of the twentieth century, the dominant schools were a minimal, antiinterventionist realism and left liberal isolationist revisionism. "Almost all orthodox historians leaned toward the Kennan-Lippmann critique of America's Cold War policy and accepted the idea that the United States had been partially responsible for escalating and rigidifying the Cold War, if not for initiating it."

In 1983, Combs concluded his survey by writing "I believe we are still in the Age of Vietnam." Short of a dramatic change in the political culture of American academic historians, "most historians probably will continue to use their influence against intervention and in favor of restraint."[111] Fortunately the new wave of post- and antirevisionist history written in recent years by scholars unsympathetic to totalitarianism of the left and sympathetic to America's goals in the Cold War suggests that it is only a matter of time before the pendulum swings back toward a more rational and balanced approach to U.S. foreign policy.[112] In his 1989 presidential address to the Organization of American Historians, David Brion Davis observed that "now we can see the absurdity of the recently fashionable view that for two centuries the United States has been struggling to preserve a sclerotic Present and fight off the Future, as represented by a regenerative revolutionary world."[113]

Vietnam and the Tragedy of Liberal Perfectionism

In an address of April 4, 1967, to the antiwar group Clergy and Laity Concerned About Vietnam, the great civil rights leader Martin Luther King, Jr., reprised almost all of the themes of the leftist myth of the Vietnam War. There was the myth that Ho Chi Minh's communists saw the United States as a model: "Even though they quoted the American Declaration of Independence in their own document of freedom, we refused to recognize them." There was the myth that the Vietminh in 1945 were "clearly indigenous forces that included some communists," rather than a front group for Stalinists subordinate to Moscow who murdered, imprisoned, and exiled the nationalists whom they did not control. "For the peasants," declared King, "this new government meant real land reform, one of the most important needs of their lives." In reality, as we have seen, for the peasants of North Vietnam, most of whom were small land-holders, "this new government" meant the murder of at least ten thousand villagers on the basis of their "class," and the suppression, by North Vietnamese army units, of other peasants who dared to rebel against Ho Chi Minh's new ruling elite. Silent about the repression in North Vietnam, King described South Vietnam's Diem as "one of the most vicious modern dictators." King claimed falsely that North Vietnam "did not begin to send in any large number of supplies or men until American forces had moved into the tens of thousands." King described the National Liberation Front as "that strangely anonymous group we call VC or Communists." The NLF, as we have seen, was created and controlled by Hanoi. King claimed that the United States had already killed a million Vietnamese—"mostly children." The number was false; the source was communist propaganda.[114] Indeed, most of the statements of fact that King made about Vietnamese history or the Vietnam War were either false or misleading. Most despicable of all was King's comparison of the United States to Nazi Germany: "What do they think as we test our latest weapons on them, just as the Germans tested out new medicine and new tortures in the concentration camps of Europe?" The analogy between the United States and Nazi Germany was one of the standard themes of the propaganda of communist bloc regimes.

King was a liberal, not a radical leftist. And yet, like many other prominent American liberals of his time, he accepted, without question, the account of the Vietnam War disseminated by communist regimes and their apologists in the West. This is puzzling. After all, it was possible for American liberals to oppose the Vietnam War on strategic or humanitarian grounds, while denouncing Marxist-Leninist totalitarianism in Vietnam and elsewhere. A small number of anticommunist liberals and social democrats did so. All too many liberals, however, like King simply repeated the lies and half-truths spread by the communist enemies of the United States.

The solution to this mystery is found in the history of American liberalism. Throughout the twentieth century, American politicians and thinkers in the progressive-liberal tradition were divided between realists and perfectionists. Progressives and liberals in both schools tended to share the same goals in domestic policy, including government regulation of the market economy, in order to provide economic security for citizens and to promote a greater degree of economic equality, the dismantling of the American system of racial apartheid, and the elimination of discrimination against American citizens on the basis of gender and (in recent decades) sexual orientation. When it came to the role of the United States in the world, however, the two groups disagreed. Liberal realists did not believe that America's traditions of liberalism and democracy required the United States to adopt a "liberal" or "democratic" foreign policy different in kind from that of other great military and economic powers. The primary goal of United States foreign policy was to promote a world order in which hostile great powers did not control the resources of Europe and East Asia, the two centers of world power outside of North America. In order to succeed in this essentially negative goal, the United States had to strengthen its executive branch, build up its military and intelligence agencies, wage hot wars and cold war, and engage in alliances with foreign despots, including two of the most murderous tyrants of the century, Stalin (during World War II) and Mao (in the 1970s). Such activities did not represent a betrayal of liberal democracy, because liberal democracy is merely a form of domestic political organization. The United States could and did promote liberal democratic government abroad, notably in occupied Japan and West Germany after 1945. But the democratization of foreign countries was always incidental to America's policy of preventing global military hegemony by antiliberal and antidemocratic superpowers such as Nazi Germany and the Soviet Union. It was difficult enough to persuade Americans to sacrifice their lives and their income in the interest of defeating the fascist and communist powers; the American public showed no enthusiasm for crusades to bring good government to foreigners.

Unlike liberal realists, liberal perfectionists in the twentieth-century United States believed that the American democracy had to have a foreign policy whose ends and means were different in kind from those of nonliberal and nondemocratic great powers. Liberal perfectionists paid little attention to exploring the internal contradictions of a "liberal" and "democratic" foreign policy; they had little to say, for example, about whether self-determination should trump liberal democracy in cases in which national liberation movements were led by antiliberal and antidemocratic forces. Nor did liberal perfectionists devote much effort to devising institutions and strategies that, unlike traditional military and intelligence agencies and alliance strategies, would meet their exacting standards of national morality; they came closest in their misguided enthusiasm for transferring responsibility for world order to unworkable international institutions, such as the League of Nations and the United Nations. Vague about what the United States should do, and how it should do it, liberal perfectionists tended to have a clear idea about what the United States could *not* do. The United States could not ally itself with colonial empires or dictatorships (two categories which accounted for most regimes during the twentieth century). Nor could the United States engage in "un-American" power politics; it was all right to go to war to make the world safe for democracy, but not merely to make the world safe for the United States and its allies. Liberal perfectionists also alleged that it was "un-American" to employ methods of statecraft such as espionage and covert action. Needless to say, the conditions that liberal perfectionists sought to impose upon United States foreign policy would have ruled out any grand strategy other than isolationism. It was, and remains, impossible for the United States to pursue its national security and world order interests without allying itself with nondemocratic regimes, or engaging in espionage and covert action.

In addition to tending toward isolationism, liberal perfectionists were vulnerable to the propaganda of dictatorships of the totalitarian left and their agents and apologists in the United States. As we have seen, the radical left in the United States perfected a story or script that was used throughout the Cold War by critics of United States policy toward a number of Marxist-Leninist regimes, including the Soviet Union, China, North Vietnam, Cuba, and Nicaragua. The names of the countries and leaders changed, but the elements of the story remained the same, decade after decade: the communists who were "really" agrarians or nationalists; the alleged independence of the communists in this or that country from the rest of the communist bloc; the "missed opportunities" that resulted from blind American anticommunism; the contrast between the benevolence of the communists and the wickedness of the anticommunist governments that they sought to overthrow; the immorality of the means used by the United States in helping anticommunist dictatorships battle communist insurgencies. The point to be borne in mind is that this particular metaphorical script was composed, and used repeatedly on different occasions, in order to influence American liberal perfectionists. In trying to appeal to centrist liberals, American apologists for communist regimes and movements deliberately downplayed the aspects of Marxism-Leninism that liberals found repugnant—one-party dictatorship, class genocide, censorship, and the repression of intellectual and religious dissent. Instead, the procommunist left emphasized truths, and untruths, that would appeal to American liberal values. Thus liberal opposition to European imperialism was enlisted in the service of Soviet and Chinese imperialism; liberal rejection of authoritarian dictatorship was enlisted in the service of totalitarian dictatorship; and liberal loathing of the horrors of war and conscription was enlisted in the service of the most militarized and regimented societies in the world. The tragedy of liberal perfectionism lay in the ease with which all too many sincere liberals were deceived and manipulated by a totalitarian left whose ultimate goal was the eradication of liberalism both as a philosophy and as a way of life.

CHAPTER 6

CREDIBILITY GAP

The Myth of the Presidential War

While the antiwar movement's myths about communism in Indochina recycled old themes of twentieth-century American Marxists and liberal fellow travelers, the movement's claims about the constitutional aspects of the Vietnam War drew chiefly on a different tradition—the progressive isolationist tradition of the northern United States. The influence of Greater New England isolationism on the anti–Vietnam War movement is particularly evident in arguments that the war was unconstitutional.

For decades, critics of the Vietnam War have made two contradictory claims about its constitutionality. One school of thought holds that the Southeast Asia Resolution of 1964 did not authorize Johnson and then Nixon to wage war in Indochina. According to this theory, the Vietnam War was an undeclared presidential war, undertaken without congressional authorization. A rival interpretation holds that the Southeast Asia Resolution *did* authorize the Vietnam War, from the time the resolution was passed in 1964 until it was repealed in 1971; however, because the Johnson administration had lied to Congress about the details of the clashes between American and Vietnamese naval units in the Gulf of Tonkin in 1964, many if not most of the members of Congress had been tricked into voting for the resolution. Needless to say, these two theories are incommensurable. If the Southeast Asia Resolution was not a declaration of war, then whether Johnson and his aides lied about the Gulf of Tonkin incidents is irrelevant to the question of the war's constitutionality. In any event, both of these familiar arguments are wrong. The Vietnam War was not an undeclared war, because the Southeast Asia Resolution was a legitimate conditional declaration of war. Nor was any senator or representative tricked into voting for it, because everyone knew that the purpose of the resolution was to enable the president to increase U.S. military efforts to prevent the forcible incorporation of South Vietnam, Laos, and Cambodia into the communist bloc—not to retaliate for North Vietnamese attacks on U.S. vessels.

Under the U.S. Constitution, a congressional declaration of war can take one of two forms. It can be either a simple declaration of war or a conditional declaration of war. A conditional declaration is an ultimatum permitting, but not requiring, the president to use military force in certain circumstances. To date there have been eleven declarations of general war in American history, and twelve conditional declarations of war.[1] Conditional declarations of war, an instrument of American imperial expansion in the western hemisphere in the nineteenth century, were revived by the Eisenhower administration as an instrument of American Cold War grand strategy. In January 1956, as communist Chinese troops attacked islands held by the Nationalist government on Taiwan (also known as Formosa), Eisenhower submitted the Formosa Resolution, which sought to "make clear the unified and serious intentions of our government, our Congress and our people."[2] The resolution gave the president authority to go to war to defend Taiwan against conquest by Mao's communist regime. What followed was a rehearsal for the dissent of Senate doves during the Vietnam War. Senator Wayne Morse of Oregon, who with Ernest Gruening of Alaska was one of only two senators to vote against the Southeast Asia Resolution in 1964, claimed that the Formosa Resolution "was a preventive war resolution and we knew the Eisenhower Administration wasn't being honest with the American people." Morse arranged for General Matthew Ridgway, an opponent of most U.S. Cold War efforts in Asia, to testify against the Formosa Resolution. Even so, the resolution passed. Faced with a credible threat of war with the United States, China backed down.[3]

The success of the Formosa Resolution inspired the Eisenhower administration to ask Congress for an even broader conditional declaration of war in the following year. The Middle East Resolution committed the United States to defend the Middle East "from any country controlled by international communism." Senator J. William Fulbright of Arkansas, soon to be an important critic of the Cold War in Asia and elsewhere, opposed the resolution, calling it "a blank check for the administration to do as it pleased with our soldiers and our money." Once again, Senator Morse led the antiinterventionists in the Senate, asking Secretary of State John Foster Dulles whether "the power vested in the Congress to declare war carries with it the power to rescind any act of the President that may lead to war." Morse attempted to kill the Middle East Resolution by adding an amendment that required the president to give Congress a justification for the use of force, in advance or as soon as possible after troops were committed. The Morse amendment, a precursor of the 1973 War Powers Act, was defeated in a vote of 64–28; Senate Majority Leader Lyndon Johnson and Senator John F. Kennedy were among those who voted against it. Eisenhower signed the resolution into law on March 9, 1957.[4]

The Formosa Resolution was the model that Walt Rostow, deputy to National Security Adviser McGeorge Bundy, suggested to President Johnson in 1964 as a way to equip the president with "discretionary authority to conduct war in Asia."[5] By any reasonable reading, all of the Johnson and Nixon administration's military campaigns and covert operations in South and North Vietnam, Laos, and Cambodia were authorized by the Southeast Asia Resolution and did not require separate and specific approval of Congress.

It is less clear whether the war was legally terminated by congressional repeal of the Southeast Asia Resolution in 1971. The Nixon administration's argument that executive prerogative permitted Nixon to continue waging the war in Indochina was extremely dubious. On the other hand, a case can be made that the authors of the Constitution believed that wars would be ended by peace treaties negotiated by the president and ratified by the Senate—a process in which the House played no role. Although Johnson administration officials argued that the Southeast Asia Resolution was helpful but not necessary to authorize Johnson's actions, Johnson himself appears to have believed that Congress, which had authorized the war in Vietnam by passing the Southeast Asia Resolution, had the power to end the war at any time simply by repealing it.[6] He told Senator Fulbright: "If you want me to get out of Vietnam, then you . . . can repeal [the Southeast Asia Resolution] tomorrow. You can tell the troops to come home."[7]

Critiques of the constitutionality of the Vietnam War are vulnerable to an obvious question: If the Southeast Asia Resolution was *not* a conditional declaration of war, then what exactly was it? Did it authorize bombing, but not ground troops? Did it authorize five hundred ground troops, but not five thousand? Once hostilities were underway, at what point should Johnson have returned for a general declaration of war? If the resolution did not give Johnson the power to back up his threats to Hanoi, then what was the point of passing it at all? How much deterrent effect could there have been in a resolution that told the North Vietnamese dictatorship: "Cease your effort to overthrow the government of our ally South Vietnam or we will *almost* go to war"?

Even the legal scholar John Hart Ely, a harsh critic of the Vietnam War, admits: "Thus Congress did authorize the war in Vietnam—at least in its public aspects, at least as the law of authorization stood at the time."[8] What about the claim that the members of Congress were tricked into voting for the resolution? It is true that the Johnson administration misled Congress about the details of the Gulf of Tonkin incidents, which occurred in the context of U.S. covert operations against North Vietnam. The decision to use an incident as a pretext was a political mistake by the Johnson administration. (It was not unprecedented; during the Cuban missile crisis, Attorney General Robert Kennedy had speculated about arranging an incident as a pretext for a U.S. invasion of Cuba: "[we] should also think of . . . whether there is some other way we can get involved in this through . . . Guantanamo Bay, or something . . . or whether there's some ship that, you know, sink the *Maine* or something.")[9]

In any event, the details of the pretextual Tonkin Gulf incidents were irrelevant, because nobody thought that the resolution was about the defense of U.S. vessels in international waters. Section 1 of the resolution, which referred to the incidents, was merely a pretext; section 2, citing the commitment of the U.S. alliance to the Southeast Asian Treaty Organization (SEATO), clearly states the reason for the Vietnam War. "The President needed the authority," Florida Representative Dante Fascell later recalled. "Who cared about the facts of the so-called incident that would trigger this authority?"[10]

After the war had become unpopular, Senator Fulbright, who as chairman of the Senate Foreign Relations Committee had steered the Southeast Asia Resolution to enactment, declared, "I confess I was hoodwinked and taken in by the President of the United States, the Secretary of State, and the Chief of Staff and the Secretary of Defense who told us about certain alleged events that I do not believe occurred." Fulbright concluded, "Insofar as the consent of this body is said to derive from the Gulf of Tonkin Resolution, it can only be said that the resolution, like any other contract based on misrepresentation, in my opinion, is null and void."[11] However, in the Senate hearings about the Southeast Asia Resolution in 1964, Chairman Fulbright, asked by Senator Daniel Brewster whether the resolution "would authorize or recommend or approve the landing of large American armies in Vietnam or in China," replied that "the language of the resolution would not prevent it. It would authorize whatever the Commander in Chief feels is necessary."[12] According to Fulbright in 1964, then, the resolution authorized President Johnson not only to dispatch hundreds of thousands of U.S. troops to Vietnam, but to go to war with China without further permission from Congress. Granting the president such power seems excessive, to say the least, if the purpose had been merely the protection of the American fleet in the Gulf of Tonkin.

Inasmuch as the Southeast Asia Resolution authorized the United States to go to war with China, if necessary, it permitted the Johnson and Nixon administrations to wage war against North Vietnamese forces and their allies in Laos and Cambodia without additional grants of authority from Congress. The claim that Nixon violated the Constitution by his "secret war" in Cambodia is absurd; so is the argument that Nixon "enlarged the war." It was North Vietnamese units that had enlarged the war, by crossing borders and seizing territory in Laos and Cambodia. Indeed, by allowing the North Vietnamese military to construct the Ho Chi Minh trail on Cambodian soil, and permitting the resupply of the Vietnamese communists by Soviet and Chinese materiel entering Cambodia through the port of Sihanoukville, Cambodia's ruler Prince Norodom Sihanouk became a cobelligerent in the Vietnam War in the mid-1960s.

The Vietnam War, then, was not "Johnson's War" or "Nixon's War"; it was Congress's war. Only two of the major wars fought by the United States have been waged in violation of the U.S. Constitution. In 1950, the Truman administration claimed that the authorization of the "police action" in Korea by the United Nations Security Council made a declaration of war by the U.S. Congress unnecessary. This argument was unsound, because the United States had ratified the UN treaty only after the insertion of a clause stating that each member state reserved the right to decide according to its own constitutional processes whether to take part in UN efforts.

Like Harry Truman, and unlike Lyndon Johnson and George Bush, Bill Clinton involved the United States in a major war without seeking authorization from Congress in advance. Afraid that Russia and China would use the vetoes they possessed as permanent members of the Security Council to thwart U.S. policy toward Yugoslavia in the crisis over Kosovo, the Clinton administration cited the authority of NATO in launching its air war against the Milosevic regime in March 1999. The authority of NATO to dismember a sovereign state outside the territory of its members was questionable. Even if the NATO effort was legal under a broad interpretation of international law, the endorsement of a war by NATO did not eliminate the need for congressional authorization of U.S. participation in the war in the Balkans, any more than did endorsement by the UN of earlier U.S. military efforts. Before beginning the bombing, Clinton should have asked Congress to ratify the NATO decision, as Bush asked Congress to ratify the UN resolutions concerning Iraq in advance of hostilities in the Persian Gulf. When the House of Representatives, on April 28, 1999, did vote on a bill that would have authorized the president to conduct an air war against Yugoslavia, the bill failed on a tie vote of 213 to 213; even worse, the House voted 249 to 180 to withhold funds for U.S. ground forces in the Balkans unless Congress authorized their deployment. By failing to follow the examples of Johnson and Bush in obtaining general congressional endorsements of the war in advance, Clinton rendered his Balkan military policlty vulnerable to questions about its constitutional legitimacy and vulnerable as well to efforts by Congress to reassert its authority at a later time by approving or disapproving of particular campaigns in the war.

The Korean War and the Kosovo War were unconstitutional; the Vietnam War, like the Gulf War, was not. The only two presidents to have waged major wars in defiance of the U.S. Constitution have been Harry Truman and Bill Clinton.

Did Johnson Trick the Voters and His Advisers?

The myth that President Johnson deceived members of Congress who did not realize what they were voting for when they approved the Southeast Asia Resolution in the summer of 1964 was combined, in the folklore of the antiwar left, with the claim that the wily, sinister Johnson tricked the public in the election in the fall of that year. This myth appeared to be strengthened by the publication seven years later of summaries of, and excerpts from, the Pentagon Papers by the *New York Times*.

The Pentagon Papers—a Department of Defense study of the history of the U.S. involvement in Indochina—were secretly copied by Daniel Ellsberg, a former government official working at the RAND corporation, and delivered to Neil Sheehan, a *New York Times* journalist who was an outspoken critic of the war. President Nixon's rage at the theft of the documents led him to authorize a secret "plumbers" group that burglarized the office of Ellsberg's psychiatrist in a search for incriminating information; the revelation that this had occurred later led a judge to dismiss the government's case against Ellsberg. After the Nixon administration tried to prevent publication of the study by the *Times* and the *Washington Post* in June 1971, the Supreme Court ruled that the government had no right to do so.

In his history of the Pentagon Papers case, David Rudenstine, a supporter of the Supreme Court's decision, admits that the logic of the First Amendment did not force the Supreme Court to arrive at its holding: "Indeed, the Supreme Court could have decided the Pentagon Papers case either way—for the press or for the government—without straying beyond the parameters defined by prior case law." In addition, Rudenstine writes, "It now appears that the Pentagon Papers did contain some information that could have inflicted some injury—at least to a degree that makes the concerns of national security officials understandable—if disclosed, which it was not."[13]

The questionable behavior of the *New York Times* went beyond publishing the stolen government documents. The *Times* assigned four reporters—Neil Sheehan, Hedrick Smith, E. W. Kenworthy, and Fox Butterfield—to write stories based on the purloined study. As Edward Jay Epstein points out, "In comparing the *Times* reports with the actual text of the Pentagon study, however, it becomes clear that the *Times* version is something more than a simple paraphrasing of the secret history, or even an abridged 'rendering.' Substantial revisions in the history were made on major points."[14] Epstein notes that the *New York Times* team began its warping of history with the headline: VIETNAM ARCHIVE: A CONSENSUS TO BOMB DEVELOPED BEFORE '64 ELECTIONS, STUDY SAYS. According to the *Times*:

The Johnson administration reached a "general consensus" at a White House strategy meeting on Sept. 7, 1964, that air attacks against North Vietnam would probably have to be launched. . . . The administration consensus on bombing came at the height of the Presidential election between President Johnson and Senator Barry Goldwater, whose advocacy of full-scale air attacks on North Vietnam had become an issue.[15]

Epstein observes, "None of the actions recommended by the 'consensus' at the September 7 meeting involved American bombing of North Vietnam."[16] Indeed, on September 10, 1964, the Johnson administration explicitly ruled out any bombing of North Vietnam, either by the United States or South Vietnam.

The *New York Times* reporters misinformed the public about other events as well. In its June 14, 1971, story, the *Times* declared: "The last round of detailed planning of various political and military strategies for a bombing campaign began 'in earnest,' the study says, on November 3d, the day that Mr. Johnson was elected President in his own right." Here is what the Pentagon Papers study actually says about the November 3 meeting: "The President was not ready to approve a program of air strikes against North Vietnam, at least until the available alternatives could be carefully and thoroughly re-examined."[17] Leslie Gelb, one of the compilers of the Pentagon Papers, wrote: "The one disservice of the *New York Times* in its original expose of the Pentagon Papers was in implying that the decision to bomb North Vietnam was made in September 1964 and concealed to avoid jeopardizing Johnson's reelection."[18]

Gelb to the contrary, the *New York Times* was guilty of other "disservices" to the truth. An equally influential myth inspired by the tendentiously edited *Times* version of the Pentagon Papers turned on a controversial cable of July 17, 1965. The significance of this requires an explanation. Between July 21 and July 27, President Johnson held intense discussions with his advisers, before announcing, on July 28, his decision to commit combat troops to Vietnam. According to the *Times* commentary on the Pentagon Papers, however, Johnson had already made up his mind to commit combat troops by July 17. The alleged evidence for this was a cable that Defense Secretary Robert McNamara, in Vietnam on a fact-finding mission, received from Washington, D.C., on that date. In the words of the *Times*, "While he was in Saigon, he received a cable from

Deputy Secretary of Defense Cyrus Vance informing him that the President had decided to go ahead with the plan to deploy all 34 U.S. battalions." The *Times* reporters went on to infer that "Vance's cable to McNamara on the 17th of July indicated that the President had approved the 34 battalion deployment."

If President Johnson had made up his mind by July 17 to deploy troops, then why did he go through the motions of a debate with his advisers? The historian David M. Barrett complains that many historians and journalists "make a deduction consistent with the [*New York Times* interpretation of] the *Pentagon Papers'* account: that Johnson staged the tortuous discussions and debates of July 21-27 *not* to help him arrive at a decision but in order to fool the public, Congress, other government leaders and nongovernmental elites, and presumably history itself into believing that he prudently engaged in wide-ranging discussions of his alternatives in Vietnam before making up his mind."[19] The *New York Times* interpretation of the July 17 cable became the basis of the erroneous claim by historian Larry Berman that the debate over sending troops "never occurred."[20] This falsehood was spread to a wider audience by journalist Stanley Karnow, who in his book *Vietnam: A History* (1983) wrote that Johnson only "went through the motions" of asking his advisers for their views.[21] In the 1970s and 1980s, it became fashionable among American historians to blame the Vietnam disaster on Johnson's allegedly pathological inability to listen to advice.

The mystery of the July 17TH cable was resolved when the cable was declassified in 1988. In the cable, Vance tells McNamara of the president's "current intention" both to proceed with the thirty-four-battalion plan and to call up the reserves. Insofar as Johnson did not call up the reserves, his "current intention" as of July 17 clearly was not fixed.[22] Indeed, acording to Vance, Johnson had not made up his mind; rather, "there was continuing uncertainty about his final decision, which would have to await Secretary McNamara's recommendation and the views of congressional leaders, particularly the view of Senator [Richard] Russell."[23] By the time the issue was clarified in 1988, however, the July 17 cable had long since become a proof text for those such as Berman and Karnow who falsely portrayed Johnson as a sinister figure intent on hiding his determination to escalate the Vietnam War not only from the public but from his own advisers.

Edward Jay Epstein observes that it is not the Pentagon Papers study itself but "the revised version of history, organized along the lines of the duplicity [of Lyndon Johnson] theme, which *The New York Times* and other journals have made available to the public."[24] William Bundy, an official in the State Department under Presidents Kennedy and Johnson, agrees: "The first of these lead stories, by Neil Sheehan, a veteran reporter of the Vietnam War, to whom the Papers had been given, focused on the early summer of 1964, prior to the Gulf of Tonkin incident. It put the document in a harsh light, suggesting a high degree of deception, which quickly became the keynote of comment about the Papers as a whole."[25]

Did Johnson Reverse Kennedy's Course in Vietnam?

In addition to being accused of having tricked Congress into approving the Vietnam War, of having tricked the voters into reelecting him as the peace candidate in 1964, and of having tricked his own advisers into participating in a make-believe debate over U.S. policy in Indochina, Lyndon Johnson was accused of having reversed a secret plan by John F. Kennedy for U.S. disengagement from Indochina. After the Vietnam War had become unpopular, a number of individuals, including Kennedy aide Kenneth O'Donnell and antiinterventionist senator Mike Mansfield, in several remarkable cases of recovered memory syndrome, claimed to remember that Kennedy had told them of his intention to abandon Indochina after the election of 1964. Former secretary of defense Robert McNamara, who admits that Kennedy never told him this, speculates that Kennedy would have abandoned America's Indochinese allies after being reelected.[26] McNamara's biographer, Deborah Shapley, writes skeptically that his "sincere belief that Kennedy would have gotten out of Vietnam was something that he arrived at later when the war had become tragic and traumatic for him and the nation."[27]

Academic historians as well as Kennedy allies have succumbed to this kind of wishful thinking. Robert Dallek writes: "Nevertheless, judging from Kennedy's temperament and record, it is reasonable to assume that, if he had expanded U.S. military involvement in Vietnam, it would have been a restrained escalation that left open the possibility of withdrawal without the appearance of defeat."[28] Not even a politician as skilled as Kennedy could have avoided "the appearance of defeat" if a U.S. withdrawal from Indochina had led to communist takeovers in South Vietnam, Laos, and Cambodia, followed by the execution or imprisonment of many of America's former partners, the construction of gulags, the eradication of all political and intellectual dissent, the flight of hundreds of thousands of refugees into neighboring countries, and large-scale economic collapse and famine. What is more, Kennedy's role in encouraging the coup against Diem (which he later regretted) would have become an issue in American politics. Having inadvertently encouraged the murder of an American ally, Kennedy would have presided over the greatest U.S. foreign policy defeat since the fall of China to Stalin's allies in 1949. If Kennedy had lived and abandoned South Vietnam, his record in foreign policy would have been one of unmitigated failure in Cuba, Berlin, and Southeast Asia.

The myth of the secret withdrawal plan permitted Kennedy partisans to absolve their hero of responsibility for the Vietnam War, which could be blamed solely on his despised successor from Texas. As the years passed, an ever more intricate mythology grew up around the alleged Kennedy plan. The writer Seymour Hersh, piling speculation on speculation, suggested that "Ngo Dinh Diem was killed because he wanted to do something in 1963—get the Americans out of Vietnam—that Kennedy wanted to do only after the election."[29] Even more absurd was Oliver Stone's thesis, expressed in his movie *JFK*, that unidentified forces in the U.S. government arranged for the assassination of Kennedy in order to replace him with Lyndon Johnson, who would carry out their plan to escalate the war in Vietnam.

There is no doubt that Kennedy would have liked to have been able to withdraw U.S. troops from Indochina as soon as the communist threats to South Vietnam, Laos, and Cambodia had diminished. This, after all, was the goal of both Johnson and Nixon, who hoped to foster the development of a self-reliant South Vietnamese state that would bear the primary responsibility for its own defense, perhaps backed up by a U.S. commitment like that extended to South Korea. The only question is whether Kennedy ever contemplated withdrawing U.S. troops if the immediate consequence of doing so was a series of communist takeovers in Indochina and perhaps elsewhere in Southeast Asia. The historical record on this point is clear. "I don't agree with those who say we should withdraw," Kennedy told Walter Cronkite in September 1963. "That would be a great mistake." A few days later, on September 9, David

Brinkley asked Kennedy in a TV interview whether he doubted the domino theory. "No, I believe it. . . . What I am concerned about is that Americans will get impatient and say because they don't like events in Southeast Asia or they don't like the government in Saigon, that we should withdraw. . . . I think we should stay."[30] On September 12, Kennedy stated: "What helps to win the war, we support, what interferes with the war effort we oppose. . . . [W]e want the war to be won, the communists to be contained, and the Americans to come home." On the day of his assassination, Kennedy gave a speech in Fort Worth in which he said: "Without the United States, South Vietnam would collapse." In the speech that he was scheduled to give in Dallas, he described the threat posed by "the ambitions of international communism" and warned that the United States had to undertake missions that were "painful, risky, and costly, as is true in Southeast Asia today. But we dare not weary of the task."[31] This was a peculiar way to prepare the public for the abandonment of Indochina.

If President Kennedy had a secret plan for withdrawing without victory from Vietnam, it was so secret that he did not tell his brother Robert, the attorney general. As late as May 1965, Robert Kennedy denounced the very idea of a withdrawal from Indochina without victory as "a repudiation of a commitment undertaken and confirmed by three administrations." He warned that the abandonment of South Vietnam by the United States would "gravely—perhaps irreparably—weaken the democratic position in Asia." In his 1964 oral history, Robert Kennedy explained that his brother had got rid of Diem to get "somebody that can win the war."[32]

Was the Vietnam War the Result of Lyndon Johnson's Personality?

Many liberal and leftist scholars have sought the origins of the Vietnam War in the personalities of the presidents who conducted it, rather than in the incompatible geopolitical ambitions of the United States, the Soviet Union, China, North Vietnam, and South Vietnam. "Perhaps Presidents Kennedy and Johnson stayed the course in Vietnam because the place was a proving ground for their (rather different) senses of manhood," speculates Andrew J. Rotter, the chair of the department of history at Colgate University. "Kennedy's desire to prove his toughness was linked not only to a string of perceived policy failures in 1961 but to a deeper psychological need to avoid appearing effete or effeminate—a need particularly acute in men who had come of age politically during the Red and Lavender scares of the early 1950s. The slight, smooth-skinned men, and the women of the NLF challenged Lyndon Johnson's manhood simply by resisting him."[33] An equally far-fetched example of armchair psychoanalysis is provided by Blema Steinberg, a Canadian political scientist and psychoanalyst. According to Steinberg, the Vietnam War came about because, unlike President Dwight Eisenhower, who had refrained from direct military intervention in Indochina, "Lyndon Johnson and Richard Nixon were two highly narcissistic individuals who suffered from painful feelings of shame and humiliation." As Steinberg herself acknowledges, however, as Senate Majority Leader Johnson had opposed U.S. intervention in the first Indochina war in 1954—while ex-President Eisenhower urged Johnson to escalate the war in 1965. Steinberg concedes, "On the surface, this suggests that Eisenhower was no different from Johnson and Nixon in his willingness to use force." She tries to escape the contradiction by claiming that Eisenhower was not motivated by narcissism in his decision to endorse escalation.[34]

A more subtle but no more convincing example of this kind of psychological reductionism is found in the historian Robert Dallek's biography *Flawed Giant: Lyndon Johnson and His Times, 1961–1973*. Dallek accepts without question the left-liberal orthodoxy that holds that Johnson should have abandoned Indochina to the communist bloc in order to pursue an agenda of liberal reform at home. According to Dallek, "Plaguing Johnson as well was an irrational conviction that his domestic opponents were subversives or the dupes of subversives intent on undermining national institutions." Dallek concludes that "Johnson's paranoia raises questions about his judgment and capacity to make rational life and death decisions. I do not raise this matter casually."[35]

Any discussion of the alleged "paranoia" of Lyndon Johnson or for that matter of his successor Richard Nixon must take into account the fact that these two quite different statesmen were in charge of American national security at a moment when much of the American intelligentsia was romanticizing totalitarian dictatorships; when the *New York Review of Books* published a diagram of a Molotov cocktail on its cover; when the *New York Times* and the *Washington Post* published stolen, classified government documents relating to a war still in progress; and when members of the Communist Party USA, which was wholly controlled and showered with millions of dollars by the Soviet government, were playing a major role in the U.S. antiwar movement. Johnson knew, by means of wiretaps, that Nixon had plotted with the Thieu regime in South Vietnam during the election of 1968; Johnson went to his grave, however, without ever learning that then attorney general Robert Kennedy, in 1963–64, by means of an unauthorized back channel to the Soviet leadership, is alleged to have denigrated Johnson and encouraged the Soviet elite to patiently await the more sympathetic policy of a second President Kennedy. As Henry Kissinger once observed, even paranoids can have real enemies.

According to Dallek, Johnson's alleged paranoia led him to exaggerate the likely domestic and geopolitical consequences of a U.S. abandonment of Indochina to Soviet proxies:

> None of Johnson's fears have come to pass despite U.S. defeat in Vietnam. The dominoes in Southeast Asia never toppled; Russia and China took no greater risks in the Cold War, which could have heightened the likelihood of an East-West confrontation; conservative critics made no direct political gains from the outcome in Vietnam; and Communist victory in the war did nothing to prop up socialism in Russia, Eastern Europe, or even China.[36]

Dallek's argument that "Communist victory in the war did nothing to prop up socialism in Russia, Eastern Europe, or even China" is irrelevant; no supporter of the defense of Indochina ever suggested that it would. It is true that, as Dallek writes, "The dominoes in Southeast Asia never toppled" outside of Indochina proper—but the Kennedy, Johnson, and Nixon administrations were more concerned about U.S. global prestige than about domino effects confined to a few countries. Dallek is demonstrably mistaken when he writes that, as a result of the fall of Saigon, "Russia [more properly, the Soviet Union] and China took no greater risks in the Cold War, which could have heightened the likelihood of an East-West confrontation." On the contrary, the Soviet Union *did* take greater risks in the Cold War, the result of which *was* an East-West confrontation. Scholarly students of Soviet foreign policy agree that, in the words of William Curti Wohlforth, "The key event that sparked optimism [in Moscow] about the competition for influence in the Third World was the war in Vietnam."[37] Did the Vietnam-inspired wave of Soviet empire-building in the Third World "heighten" the "likelihood of an East-West confrontation"? According to Wohlforth, "The result [of the Soviet bloc's post–Vietnam expansion] was the lowest ebb in relations since the Berlin and Cuban missile crises, almost two decades earlier."[38]

Dallek's judgment about the effect of the American failure in Vietnam on U.S. domestic politics is equally unconvincing: "[C]onservative critics made no direct political gains from the outcome in Vietnam." To the contrary, one of the chief reasons for the Republican "lock" on the presidency in the aftermath of the Vietnam War between 1968 and 1992 was the conviction of Democratic swing voters that the victorious anti–Vietnam War faction of their own party could not be entrusted with responsibility for U.S. national security as long as the Cold War lasted. In short, Johnson's allegedly "paranoid" fears that the loss of Indochina might lead both to dangerously increased assertiveness by the Soviet empire or China and to a right-wing Republican backlash in national politics were vindicated by the events of the 1970s and 1980s.[39]

Vietnam and American Tradition

Some leftist and liberal scholars and journalists have blamed the Vietnam War not on Johnson's allegedly pathological personality, but on his Texan roots. Historians and journalists who would never dream of referring to FDR's "Knickerbocker craftiness" or to JFK's "Irish gift for blarney" do not hesitate to invest Johnson's occasional references to the famous defense of the Alamo by the Texan rebels in 1836 with great significance. For example, the British expatriate journalist and editor Harry Evans, in *The American Century* (1998), writes of Johnson's "Texassized fudging" and says that in escalating Kennedy's war in Vietnam Johnson "had climbed the red-mud parapets of the Alamo."[40] As Senate Majority Leader during the Dien Bien Phu crisis, Johnson opposed U.S. military intervention in Indochina. Had he forgotten the Alamo in 1954—only to remember it in 1965?

There *is* a highly martial southern culture, and there *are* militarist southern politicians—but Johnson was not one. The greatest cultural influences on Johnson were Highland South populism, which has often been accompanied by suspicion of foreign wars, and the progressive political legacy of the German-American majority in Johnson's native Texas Hill Country, a subculture whose members opposed the southern right and tended to support Republican progressive isolationists such as Robert M. La Follette in the twentieth century. Recently released tapes have proven that Johnson, caricatured during his lifetime as a ruthless hawk, was far more dovish than his major advisers; he agonized over the thought of sending American soldiers to die in Indochina, in a manner quite unlike that of his self-consciously tough-minded predecessor. Johnson's references to the Alamo, therefore, far from being clues to some psychological mystery, are best understood as being what they appeared to be—illustrations of the need for determination. It was in this context that Representative Henry Hyde of Illinois defended the unpopular impeachment of President Bill Clinton by comparing the effort to the vigils at Valley Forge and the Alamo.[41]

Not all of the cultural-determinist explanations of the Vietnam War focused on Johnson's Texan heritage. Some leftist thinkers claimed that an American culture of imperialism had led to Vietnam. The historian William Appleman Williams, the central figure of the left-isolationist Wisconsin School of diplomatic history, claimed to discern a tradition of commerce-driven American expansionism that began with the administration of George Washington (the United States took a wrong turn, according to Williams, when it replaced the Articles of Confederation with the federal Constitution).[42] A similar explanation of the Vietnam War in terms of American culture was provided by the journalist Garry Wills. In 1959 Wills wrote in *National Review*:

> Our dealings with our allies reflect the frivolous attitude that war is impossible. . . . We are told to avoid committing ourselves, and not to exact the commitments of honorable men from those who would stand with us. . . . Only such terrified sway over the mind can explain the complete inability to see in Chiang Kai-shek's little garrison a desperate romance of courage. . . . This brave little band, living on the very skirts of the giant and refusing to submit, is the stuff of epic.[43]

In his book *Inventing America* (1978), written a decade after he abandoned the anticommunist right for the New Left, Wills wrote that the rhetoric of Abraham Lincoln had inspired John F. Kennedy's 1960 declaration that Americans were "the watchmen on the walls of freedom." The Lincoln-Kennedy doctrine, according to Wills, made "us willing to throw communist devils out of Russia, China, Cuba, or Vietnam. . . . The virtue of our aims sanctified the means—so we could indulge in a Hiroshima or two, in napalm and saturation bombing, or a Chile putsch. Lincoln spoke of shed American blood as expiatory and cleansing, as a washing in the blood of the lamb; and if we shed even our own blood, might we not shed that of others for their salvation?"[44] (Wills omitted any discussion of this extraordinary theory in *Lincoln at Gettysburg* (1992), a bland book that might not have won the Pulitzer Prize if its author had explained his opinion that Abraham Lincoln had inspired an unjustified crusade against communist totalitarianism.)

Another leftist writer, Noam Chomsky, went even further than Williams and Wills, and traced American imperialism back beyond Washington and Lincoln to Columbus. Chomsky adopted the eccentric habit of dating world history, seen as a history of Euro-American conquest, from 1492. (Chomsky has never explained why Muslim imperialism, beginning in the eighth century A.D., was less objectionable than the expansion of European Christendom.)[45] The problem with the explanations of the Cold War in terms of American culture provided by leftists such as Williams, Wills, and Chomsky is obvious. The United States led a global alliance against the Soviet Union. Britain, France, West Germany, and other NATO allies, along with Japan and, toward the end of the Cold War, communist China, joined the American-led effort, not because they were influenced by American traditions of capitalism, racism, or imperialism, but because they perceived the Soviet bloc as a genuine threat.

Vietnam and the New Deal

A superficially more plausible critique of the Vietnam War blames it not on Lyndon Johnson's personality or the political culture of Texas or the United States, but on the ideology of New Deal Democrats. "Vietnam was a liberal war," writes conservative historian Walter McDougall.[46] According to McDougall, the Kennedy and Johnson administrations were motivated by what he calls "global meliorism." As examples of global meliorism he cites the foreign aid efforts of Herbert Hoover, the postwar planning of Franklin D. Roosevelt's administration, the Marshall Plan, and Harry Truman's Point Four foreign aid program, as well as the Vietnam War and the foreign policies of the Carter and Clinton administrations. McDougall's contrast of global meliorism, of which he disapproves, with containment, of which he approves, is unconvincing, inasmuch as most U.S. policymakers during the Cold War saw foreign aid as a complement to a military-diplomatic strategy of containment, not as a substitute for it.

As this suggests, it is in the context of Cold War competition with the Soviet and Chinese communists that Johnson's much-derided reference to a TVA [Tennessee Valley Authority] on the Mekong River delta must be understood. In a speech at Johns Hopkins University in March 1965, Johnson offered to allow Ho Chi Minh's regime to participate in a regional development plan, if it abandoned its attack on South Vietnam. In addition to promising medical and educational aid, Johnson declared: "The vast Mekong River can provide food and water and power on a scale to dwarf even our TVA."[47]

In proposing a Mekong River TVA, Johnson was within the mainstream of Cold War liberal foreign policy. David Lilienthal, the mastermind of the TVA, describes Harry Truman using a map to demonstrate potential demonstration sites for his Point Four program of foreign aid:

"Now here is the finest opportunity for development in the world" [pointing to the valleys of the Tigris and Euphrates.] "They have to know how to do things. We can show them that. Then here" [northern India] "and here" [the Parana, in South America, and the great plateaus of Brazil] "and here" [the Belgian Congo]. And so on and on . . .

Lilienthal and Truman also envisioned a TVA on the Yangtze River in China.[48]

There was nothing absurd about the idea of the United States sponsoring TVA-style development projects in Third World countries. In terms of narrowly Machiavellian realpolitik, it made excellent sense for the United States to compete with the Soviet Union in this area, as it did when it offered to help Egypt build the Aswan Dam. What is more, U.S. offers of money and assistance in rural infrastructure projects could be made to dictators as well as to democrats—something that was an advantage, given the fact that most of America's allies in the Cold War, like most regimes in the world at the time, were nondemocratic.

The Cold War, which in one dimension was a great power struggle, in another dimension was a rivalry between political creeds, each of which claimed that it could offer more to the desperately poor majorities in Asia, Africa, Latin America, and the Middle East. On the basis of the New Deal's success in promoting state-sponsored industrial capitalism in capital-starved regions of the American South and West by means of hydroelectric projects such as the TVA and the Lower Colorado River Authority (LCRA), the New Deal/ColdWar liberals believed that they could offer developing countries an economic model that was superior both to Marxism-Leninism and to discredited laissez-faire capitalism. Since the 1970s, environmentalists have drawn attention to the ecological costs of large-scale hydroelectric projects in the United States and elsewhere. Even so, the New Deal model of capitalism, in which governments finance the development of infrastructure in poor regions within a country, or poor countries as a whole, where private capital is scarce, was plausible during the Cold War—and remains plausible today. Indeed, the Truman/Johnson program of exporting New Deal capitalism to the Third World did not suffer from the defects of later United States approaches to foreign aid. Following the Cold War, conservatives favored the deregulation of capital markets and the opening up of all Third World economies to the short-term "hot" money of foreign private investors—a policy that resulted in mafia capitalism and economic disaster in Asia and post–Soviet Russia. The attempt to export democracy by the Clinton administration, like the human rights policy of the Carter administration, needlessly antagonized American allies without seriously threatening American enemies. The foreign aid policies of the Rooseveltian liberals did not require U.S. allies to subject their economies to Wall Street brokers, nor did they require nondemocratic American allies to overthrow themselves. (Johnson, it should be remembered, opposed the Kennedy administration's support for the overthrow of Diem.)

In April 1999, President Bill Clinton proposed a "Marshall Plan" for the Balkans to follow a conclusion of the war between the NATO alliance and Serbia. The original Marshall Plan provided cash that helped to restart the industrial economies of Western Europe, devastated by World War II. The poor and undeveloped Balkans today, like Indochina in the 1960s, need to develop new industries and infrastructure, not just to revive existing industrial systems. The New Deal model of developmental capitalism would have been more appropriate than any program inspired by the Marshall Plan.

Nor can efforts at "nation-building" in South Vietnam be dismissed as the foolish utopianism of liberal do-gooders with heads as soft as their hearts. Although the U.S. government's efforts in this area included much that was wrong and even silly, U.S. aid to the Saigon regime in rebuilding its sovereignty and legitimacy had to be an integral part of any coherent program for defeating the communist insurgency in South Vietnam. The counterinsurgency doctrine, with its emphasis on nation-building, was inspired by the experience of the United States and its allies in small wars in Greece, the Philippines, Malaya, and the Caribbean and Central America. Advocates of nation-building in Vietnam included Sir Robert Thompson, a British expert with experience in Malaya, Colonel John Paul Vann, one of the most insightful U.S. military officers in Vietnam, and Marine General Victor H. "Brute" Krulak.[49] None of these soldiers was a naïve Great Society liberal seeking to remake Vietnam in America's image.

Conservatives are mistaken, then, in arguing that the Vietnam War was lost because of Great Society or New Deal liberalism. Nor is there any substance to the left's claim that the Great Society was sacrificed to the Vietnam War. Johnson's window of opportunity for social reform closed, not as a result of the war, but as a result of the conservative backlash that was first manifested in the 1966 congressional elections. The claim that the Vietnam War turned the American people against the federal government is just as groundless. Today the very people who were most opposed to the Vietnam War—left-liberals and leftists—have the greatest faith in the federal government as an instrument of social reform, while conservatives, who were least opposed to the war, are the very people who trust the federal government in domestic policy the least.

Was the Vietnam War responsible for all of the economic troubles of the 1970s and 1980s? "Many scholars mistakenly remember the Vietnam War as the pivotal event in the history of inflation during the 1960s," the historian David Hackett Fischer writes. "In fact, the surge began only a few years earlier, in another part of the world." The war only "reinforced an existing trend and increased its momentum."[50] The costs of the Vietnam War may have hastened the collapse of the Bretton Woods system of fixed exchange rates—but that system was probably doomed to collapse anyway around the same time, as the result of the accumulation of dollars held overseas. "The dollar would have come under international pressure by the late 1960s even without Vietnam," the historian R. B. Smith observes, adding, "Vietnam was thus only one of several factors in a highly complicated financial and monetary situation."[51] Nor is it accurate to blame Johnson for not raising taxes to finance the war; he repeatedly tried, but failed, to persuade Congress to raise taxes. As it was, the Johnson administration was the last until the Clinton presidency to submit a balanced budget to Congress.

The Vietnam War, then, was not the result of a simple-minded effort to universalize the New Deal and Great Society, as many conservatives have claimed; nor, despite the wishful thinking of many liberals, did the waging of the war abort a possible extension of the New Deal and Great Society at home in the United States.

Was the United States in Danger of Becoming a Garrison State under Johnson and Nixon?

In *Achieving Our Country* (1998), an insightful book in which many other fallacies of the radical left are subjected to criticism, the distinguished American philosopher Richard Rorty writes that the radical movement of the 1960s and early 1970s "ended the Vietnam War. It may have saved our country from becoming a garrison state."[52]

Is this true? Was the United States on the verge of becoming a garrison state under Johnson and Nixon? The historical record shows that the U.S. government has actually grown less repressive over the course of the twentieth century. During World War I, German-Americans were persecuted; the socialist candidate for president, Eugene V. Debs, was tossed into prison for his antiwar statements; and teams of "Minute Men" were dispersed to public gatherings by the government's propaganda agency. The domestic repression during World War II was, if anything, even more intense. More than 120,000 Japanese nationals and Japanese-Americans were interned in concentration camps and many isolationists and conservatives were harassed in the "brown scare." Four times as many draft resisters as in World War I, a total of six thousand, were jailed. One historian calculates that ten times as many Americans faced official federal government prosecution or harassment in World War II as in World War I.[53] Government repression of radicals during the McCarthy era and later in the Cold War was mild by comparison.

Both Johnson and Nixon ordered the CIA to investigate communist-bloc influence on the antiwar movement. In doing so, they were following the example of Franklin Roosevelt, who had ordered the FBI to determine whether the Nazis were behind the antiinterventionist movement in the late 1930s. In the latter case as in the former the investigators concluded the movement was homegrown, but the precaution was reasonable, given the prominent role in the antiwar movement played by members of the Moscow-controlled and -funded Communist Party USA. What is more, a number of American radicals who were not agents of Moscow (in the sense that all CPUSA officials were by definition) plotted strategy with other American radicals in Vietnam, Cuba, Eastern Europe, and the Soviet Union. Tom Hayden confessed to *Rolling Stone* in November 1972:

> Rennie [Davis] and I had been in Vietnam with several other people in October and November, just before the idea of Chicago seized us and we started talking about it. Then I was in Cuba for three or four weeks in January with David Dellinger, and there we had already decided upon some plan for Chicago and being there in Cuba made it really clear that the demonstrations should have an international effect—not simply aimed at domestic things, but it should have the effect of making the U.S. government stand exposed as starting to lose domestic support in the eyes of the people of the world.[54]

Nixon abused his power by enlisting national security agencies in campaigns against his political enemies. And many if not most of the abuses committed by J. Edgar Hoover's FBI and other government agencies that investigated and infiltrated the antiwar movement along with the civil rights movement could not be justified by the interests of U.S. national security. Even so, Presidents Johnson and Nixon would have been derelict in their duties as commanders-in-chief and chief law enforcement officers of the United States if they had not investigated the activities of procommunist agitators such as Hayden in the middle of a shooting war with a Soviet satellite state. Indeed, Hayden's career did not suffer; a few years after plotting in North Vietnam and Cuba to humiliate the United States and wreck the Democratic party, Tom Hayden was given a White House Freedom Award by President Jimmy Carter.

The claim that Harry Truman created a repressive "national security state" in a departure from the irenic policy of Franklin Roosevelt was another myth created by leftists and liberal isolationists who tried to enlist Roosevelt's prestige for their cause after his death. Roosevelt dumped his vice president, Henry Wallace, because he was too pro-Soviet; threw the head of the Communist party USA, Earl Browder, into prison (and later released him, as a favor to Browder's master, Stalin); ordered FBI director J. Edgar Hoover to investigate antiwar rallies and to open the mail and tap the telephones of isolationist members of Congress such as Montana's Senator Burton Wheeler; issued an order to members of his cabinet ordering the dismissal of any employee considered a national security risk; and signed the Hatch Act (1939), the Smith Act (1940), and the Voorhis Act (1940), all aimed at deterring and punishing subversion by procommunist or profascist American citizens.[55] (Notwithstanding FDR's measures, it is now known that the penetration of the U.S. government by Soviet spies reached its peak in the 1930s.) The Johnson administration moved only slowly and reluctantly to prosecute leaders of the movement to disrupt the draft; in contrast, Roosevelt used the Smith Act and the Espionage Act to convict dozens of Trotskyists and far-right conservatives opposed to his military policies and pro-British measures. One completely marginal American fascist, William Pelley, was sentenced to fifteen years in prison on the basis that the arguments in his publications *resembled* those of Axis propagandists.[56]

In 1940, FDR had an idea for how to deal with the campus leftists who led the stay-out-of-war movement at universities such as Columbia, Michigan, and Berkeley: "[T]he best thing for the moment is to call them shrimps publicly and privately."[57] Roosevelt's protégé Lyndon Johnson was far less hostile toward the protesters, remarking, after he retired, "I don't blame them. They didn't want to be killed in a war, and that's easy to understand."[58] Nixon, in one of the oddest moments in his career, walked over to the Washington Monument and conversed with student protesters who had camped out there. One cannot imagine a similar effort by Wilson, Roosevelt, or Truman.

The relative lenience of the U.S. government during the Vietnam War was particularly striking with respect to the treatment of American citizens who engaged in questionable activities in North Vietnam during the war. None was more prominent than the actress Jane Fonda, who made a series of broadcasts to American and South Vietnamese soldiers over North Vietnamese radio between July 14 and July 22, 1972. When released POWs described how they had been tortured to encourage them to participate in a propaganda appearance with her, Fonda claimed that they were lying: "I think many POWs said they were tortured in order to excuse their circumstances of capture or their statements and actions opposing the war."[59] At the time, many outraged American politicians and columnists demanded that Fonda be tried for treason.

Between 1943 and 1948, a number of American citizens were indicted for making wartime radio broadcasts for Germany, Italy, or Japan. In the case of *Chandler v. United States* (1948), the Supreme Court let stand a lower-court decision that radio propaganda for an enemy government at war with the United States fits the definition of an "overt act" of treason under the U.S. Constitution.[60] The lower court held that it was irrelevant whether the radio propaganda reached American listeners, or even whether the recordings were used; the mere act of making radio programs to be broadcast by the enemy during wartime was treason. The claim that a "higher patriotism" overrode the constitutional prohibition against treason was dismissed. A number of "radio traitors," including one of the six women who had broadcast for Japan as "Tokyo Rose" during World War II, were convicted and sent to prison. One of them, Mildred "Axis Sally" Gillars, was, like Fonda, an American actress, who persuaded American POWs in Nazi camps to make "Hello, Mom and Dad" recordings (Fonda returned from Hanoi with letters from POWs). Gillars was sentenced to a ten-thousand-dollar fine and ten to thirty years in prison.[61]

The claim that the Vietnam War was an "undeclared war" might have provided no defense, because the Southeast Asia Resolution was a conditional declaration of war. In any event, the federal judiciary ruled during the Korean War, an undeclared shooting war, that North Korea was covered by the phrase "the enemy" in the Constitution's definition of treason to the United States.[62] The prudence of the decision of the U.S. government not to prosecute any American citizens for treason on the basis of their activitites in North Vietnam in the midst of a shooting war can be debated. The fact that such activities were tolerated at all refutes the assertion that the United States was in danger of becoming a "garrison state" during the Vietnam years.

The Folklore of Greater New England Isolationism

If all of this is true, then what accounts for the fact that these myths are so widespread in American discourse? The answer is to be found in the regional culture of the northern United States. In every foreign war that the United States has fought, beginning with the Mexican War, Greater New England isolationists have claimed that a sinister president tricked Congress or the public into acquiescence in an unjust and unconstitutional presidential war.

The elements of the story were first combined by Whig opponents of the Mexican War, who claimed that President Polk had dragged the United States into war dishonestly and/or unconstitutionally:

> But it is apparent that Texas [has] claimed, and we fear it is equally apparent that the Executive has granted, the occupation of everything up to the Rio Grande, which occupation is nothing short . . . of an invasion of Mexico. It is offensive war, and not the necessary defense of Texas. And should it prove, as we think it will, that the President has gone this additional length, then the President will be MAKING WAR, in the full sense of the word, on his own authority, and beyond all plea of need, and even without any thought of asking legislative leave.[63]

The Whig claim that Polk provoked the Mexican War by sending U.S. troops south of the Nueces River in Texas to the Rio Grande was wrong on the facts. From the Texas revolution until the war broke out, the Mexican government had consistently claimed all of Texas right up to the Louisiana border. The assertion that Mexico was willing to cede Texas north of the Nueces was an invention of Whig propaganda that became part of American political mythology, for the simple reason that American history, until recently, has been been written chiefly by antimilitary and antiexpansionist northerners.[64]

Like Polk, later wartime presidents including McKinley, Wilson, and Roosevelt were caricatured by mostly northern antiwar activists as power-crazed despots willing to deceive the public, violate the Constitution, and turn the American republic into an autocratic empire. For example, in February 1941, the progressive isolationist Senator Gerald Nye of North Dakota claimed that the Lend-Lease law gave Franklin Roosevelt the powers "of a dictator" and "the power to take this country into war." Nye declared: "I am now more alarmed by the encroachments upon our constitutional state, . . . than about possible aggression against us by potential, but not necessarily probable, foreign foes." The California progressive Hiram Johnson claimed that Lend-Lease was "founded upon hypocrisy and put over by misrepresentation."[65]

The fascination of the American left with the Tonkin Gulf incidents echoed arguments in previous generations that McKinley had deliberately sunk the *Maine* to trigger the Spanish-American War and that Wilson had arranged the sinking of the *Lusitania*. The historian Charles Beard, who displayed the northern progressive's typical mix of liberal domestic views and isolationism, accused Franklin Roosevelt of having staged Pearl Harbor to drag the United States into World War II. In *President Roosevelt and the Coming of the War: A Study in Appearances and Realities* (1948), Beard's chapter headings sound like the titles of the misleading stories in the *New York Times* based on the Pentagon Papers: The Attack—Official Explanation; The Beginning of Revelations; The Official Thesis Challenged in Congress and the Press; Engineering the Official Thesis of Guilt; Secret War Decisions and Plans; Maneuvering the Japanese into Firing the First Shot. Sounding like a seventies liberal writing about the Johnson or Nixon administrations, Beard declared: "The discrepancies between official representations and official realities in the conduct of foreign affairs during the year 1941, until the coming of war, stand out starkly in documents already available." The obsession with the Gulf of Tonkin incidents on the part of a later generation of American progressives was foreshadowed by Beard's insistence that Roosevelt had known about the Japanese attack in advance; this was "the only inference that is permissible in view of all the evidence on the point brought to light by the Congressional Committee on Pearl Harbor." The myth that Johnson had tricked the voters in 1964 by running as the peace candidate was anticipated by Beard's claim that "President Roosevelt had to dissemble in order to be reelected in 1940 against Wendell Willkie, then the antiwar candidate of the Republicans on an antiwar platform." Like later isolationists who would lecture Harry Truman and Lyndon Johnson and Ronald Reagan on the folly of attempting to remake the world in the image of the United States, Beard claimed that by opposing Hitler and Hitler's allies Roosevelt was guilty of "imposing international morality on recalcitrant nations by American power." Employing the characteristic hyperbole of the disproportionately northern progressive isolationist tradition, Beard declared that as a result of Roosevelt's alleged abuses of presidential war powers "constitutional and democratic government in the United States is at the end of its career."[66]

Another folklore motif that was recycled by several generations of the American left was what might be called "the posthumous dove syndrome." After his death, Franklin Roosevelt, who tossed the leader of the Communist party USA into prison and replaced the pro-Soviet Henry Wallace with Harry Truman as his vice president, was remembered by progressive followers of Henry Wallace as someone who would have avoided the Cold War by appeasing Stalin and befriending Mao. The myth that Kennedy, if he had lived, would have pulled out of Vietnam rather than escalate the war, was recognizably a variant of this fable. For the anti–Cold War Democrats of the late 1960s and 1970s, John F. Kennedy was not the president who began the war in Vietnam and collaborated with the Mafia to kill Fidel Castro, but a dove who signed the nuclear test ban treaty, sponsored the Peace Corps, and allegedly realized after the Cuban missile crisis that the real threat to the future of humanity was not the imperialism of totalitarian states but weapons of mass destruction. When Roman emperors died, it was said that their spirits turned into eagles. When twentieth-century Democratic presidents of the United States died, they turned into doves.

Another parallel can be found in the similarities between the "Dump Johnson" movement organized by anti–Vietnam War northern liberals and their radical allies and a similar anti-Roosevelt movement in the 1930s. In 1935, FDR wrote Woodrow Wilson's Texan adviser Colonel Edward House that northern "progressive Republicans like La Follette, Cutting, Nye, etc." were "flirting with the idea of a third ticket anyway with the knowledge that it would defeat us, elect a conservative Republican and cause a complete swing far to the left in 1940."[67]

Further proof, if any was needed, that the anti–Vietnam War activists had been reading from a standard, inherited script, as it were, was provided during the Gulf War. Several members of Congress introduced a measure calling for the impeachment of Bush, who, like Johnson and Nixon, was falsely accused of violating the U.S. Constitution. Like Johnson, Bush was accused of misleading the American people in order to wage an "aggressive" war. Leftist and isolationist conspiracy theories holding that FDR knew of Pearl Harbor in advance, that Johnson deceived the public into voting for him as the peace candidate in 1964, and that Nixon bombed Cambodia with the intent of discrediting socialism by provoking Khmer Rouge atrocities, were echoed in a wild assertion by Johnson's former attorney general, Ramsey Clark, a longtime radical critic of U.S. foreign policy: "As evidence proves beyond a reasonable doubt, the United States planned its assault on Iraq for years, and provoked Iraq to invade Kuwait to justify a U.S. reaction."[68] Just as Johnson and Nixon were accused of "war crimes"in a mock trial staged by radical leftists in Stockholm, so President Bush and the officials of his administration were found guilty in absentia of war crimes by an "International War Crimes Tribunal" that met in New York City and included John Jones and Key Martin, veterans of the anti–Vietnam War movement.[69] Just as the socialist philosopher Michael Walzer had compared the U.S. effort in Vietnam to "the Nazi conquests of Czechoslovakia, Poland, Denmark, Belgium, and Holland,"[70] so the novelist Kurt Vonnegut declared that "our leaders committed war crimes in the Gulf War no less surely than Nazis committed war crimes in World War II."[71]

Like Lyndon Johnson, George Bush was psychoanalyzed by journalists and scholars who snidely speculated that his decision to go to war with Iraq reflected personal pathology or Texan militarism. Writing in 1991 in *The New Yorker*, Elizabeth Drew speculated that Bush "was proving something to himself and the world—showing what a tough guy he is."[72] Just as critics complained of Johnson's alleged irrational obsession with the Vietnam War, so one anonymous congressman declared that "a good many people" were worried about Bush's "obsession" with Iraq.[73] In his book *How the South Finally Won the Civil War* (1995), Charles Potts drew an explicit parallel between the two Texan presidents and war leaders: "In 1964, LBJ was elected because he took a peace position in public, as Bush did, while he and his advisors prepared for war without informing the electorate."[74] For Potts, both the Vietnam War and the Gulf War were the result of Texan political culture: "Lyndon Johnson . . . was marching to the tune of the First Commandment of Texas, 'I'll neither surrender nor retreat,' enunciated by Colonel Buck Travis at his defense of the Alamo."[75] Even though Bush was a Yankee patrician by birth, according to Potts he "became a Texas Southerner" and "acquired the Texas disease of love of power for its own sake."[76] Potts, elaborating on what is only implied in the sneers at Johnson and Bush in the writings of other northern liberals, develops a conspiracy theory, with Texans (and South Carolinians) as the masterminds of American imperial expansion: "The siege mentality of the South Carolinians who had endeavored from their beginning in 1670 to recapitulate the English experience exactly, and of their spiritual kin the Texans from the Alamo, was confirmed as policy when the United States made a basket catch of the British Empire and became the world's foremost banana republic and an empire at (cold) perpetual war."[77]

The old canard that Texan politicians are irrational warmongers whose views in foreign policy are inspired by Alamo lore was revived yet again in the spring of 1999 in the pages of the *New York Times*. Describing Texas governor George W. Bush's comments on President Clinton's conduct of the war in Yugoslavia, Gail Collins wrote: "His only reservation, Mr. Bush added, was whether the bombing campaign was being done with enough 'ferocity.' He seemed to have been breathing deeply from that Alamo-enhanced air."[78] Inasmuch as Texas has joined California as one of the states that exports more than its share of presidents to Washington, it seems likely that future Texan presidents who send U.S. forces into combat will be defamed by northern isolationists and leftists in the same manner that Johnson and the two Bushes have been.

Defeat Is an Orphan

"Victory has many fathers, but defeat is an orphan," President Kennedy said in the aftermath of the Bay of Pigs debacle. In the aftermath of the far more disastrous Vietnam War, few were willing to rebut charges leveled against the presidents who waged it, no matter how preposterous those charges were.

Most of the libels that American progressives and American radical leftists flung at Presidents Johnson and Nixon earlier had been flung by progressives and leftists at Presidents Wilson, Roosevelt, Truman, and Eisenhower—and would be flung again, at Presidents Reagan and Bush. Those presidents or their successors won their wars, so the libels did not stick. The libels stuck to the Vietnam War, and to Johnson and Nixon, because the war was lost. If uncontrollable costs of the Korean War had forced the United States to abandon Korea in the mid-1950s, then Truman and Eisenhower probably would be condemned today by orthodox liberal and leftist historians for having waged an unconstitutional war, for having missed an opportunity to be friends with the North Korean dictator Kim Il Sung, for having failed to play the China card against the Soviet Union, or for having missed a chance to "exit" the Korean peninsula in the late 1940s, or in the early stages of the North Korean invasion in 1950.

The Vietnam War, like other American wars, uncovered, but did not create, deep divisions in the American body politic. After the United States abandoned Indochina, alliances of largely northern liberals and leftist radicals similar to the coalition that had opposed the Vietnam War opposed both the Second Cold War of the 1980s and the Gulf War, resurrecting the familiar clichés of the permanent American antiwar constituency. Following the U.S. bombing campaigns against Iraq, Afghanistan, and Sudan in 1998, a number of American leftist radicals, including veterans of the anti–Vietnam War movement such as Noam Chomsky and Barbara Ehrenreich, called for Clinton's impeachment for the alleged offenses of committing war crimes and violating the U.S. Constitution. Although some progressives supported the NATO campaign against Serbia, the war was opposed by most leftists, including the editors of *The Nation* and Tom Hayden.

Thus a prediction made by sixties radical Jerry Rubin was fulfilled: "If there had been no Vietnam war, we would have invented one. If the Vietnam war ends, we'll find another war."[79]

CHAPTER 7

WAS THE VIETNAM WAR UNJUST?

Was the Vietnam War an unjust war? Even when it is conceded that many of the arguments employed by the anti–Vietnam War movement were based on falsehoods, it is still possible to make a case against the justice of the American war in Indochina. The moral case against the Vietnam War can be divided into three different arguments:

- The Vietnam War was immoral because it was a war, and all wars are immoral.

- The Vietnam War was immoral because it was a campaign in the Cold War, and the Cold War as a whole was immoral.

- The Vietnam War in particular was immoral, even if other American Cold War campaigns such as the Korean War were not immoral.

Only the third of these arguments requires any discussion of the details of the Vietnam War. Obviously if all wars are unjust, or if the Cold War as a whole was unjust, then the Vietnam War was unjust by definition.

In this chapter and the chapter that follows, I will address these three arguments about the justice of the Vietnam War. Most of the discussion will be devoted to the third argument—the claim that the Vietnam War was an unjust campaign in an otherwise just Cold War struggle. Before that argument can be answered, however, it is necessary to address the moral case against war as such, and the moral case against the Cold War in general.

In analyzing the morality of the Vietnam War, I will not address either the Catholic just war theory or secular versions of it. The religious version of just war theory has no authority apart from Catholic Christianity. Secular attempts to discuss the justice of wars using the terminology of "just cause" and "proportionality" are doomed to fail, because outside of a rigorous and authoritative tradition the meanings of such terms can be manipulated to produce any desired conclusions. Instead, in this chapter I employ comparisons between the Vietnam War and comparable American military efforts, such as the Korean War and World War II, that most Americans consider to have been just and moral wars.

Whose Justice, Whose Morality?

Arguments about the justice of the Vietnam War, like most debates about justice in foreign policy, exhibit the traits of a certain class of moral arguments identified by the philosopher Alasdair MacIntyre—they can never be resolved, because the debaters belong to incompatible moral traditions and reason from different moral premises. In his book *After Virtue* (1981), MacIntyre provides rival views of justice in war as the first of his examples of "interminable" contemporary moral debates:

1. (a) A just war is one in which the good to be achieved outweighs the evils involved in waging the war and in which a clear distinction can be made between combatants—whose lives are at stake—and innocent noncombatants. But in a modern war calculation of future escalation is never reliable and no practically applicable distinctions between combatants and noncombatants can be made. Therefore no modern war can be a just war and we all now ought to be pacifists.

   (b) If you wish for peace, prepare for war. The only way to achieve peace is to deter potential aggressors. Therefore you must build up your armaments and make it clear that going to war on any particular scale is not necessarily ruled out by your policies. An inescapable part of making this clear is being prepared both to fight limited wars and to go not only to, but beyond, the nuclear brink on certain types of occasion. Otherwise you will not avoid war and you will be defeated.

(c) Wars between Great Powers are purely destructive; but wars waged to liberate oppressed groups, especially in the Third World, are a necessary and therefore justified means for destroying the exploitative domination which stands between mankind and happiness.[1]

For the sake of comprehensiveness, it is useful to add to MacIntyre's list what might be called the "militarist" or "fascist" argument:

(d) Social life, like biological life, consists of unceasing struggle for survival and domination. The most glorious human type is the warrior, and the only life worth living is one of armed combat against national or personal enemies. Peace is a contemptible state, tolerable only as an intermission between campaigns to conquer or avoid being conquered.

Adherents of these four views of morality in war have very little to say to one another, beyond stating their positions. "From our rival conclusions we can argue back to our rival premises," MacIntyre observes, "but when we do arrive at our premises argument ceases and the invocation of one premise against another becomes a matter of pure assertion and counter-assertion. Hence perhaps the slightly shrill tone of so much moral debate."[2]

The debate among these four moralities cannot be resolved here, if it can be resolved at all. It is my contention that the moral conception of war summarized by MacIntyre's position (b), the "realist" position, is correct, and that the other three positions—the pacifist, the Marxist, and the militarist—are based on false conceptions of morality.

The militarist view, along with the values that it justifies, is alien to the United States and similar societies, despite its appeal to historic communities such as those of the Vikings, Mongols, and twentieth-century fascists, and, perhaps, to a tiny minority within the liberal democracies. Of more political and social importance today are the pacifist and revolutionary leftist moralities—the former influenced by supernatural religion, particularly certain strains of Protestant and Catholic Christianity, the latter by denominations of the secular political religion of Marxism, in both its Leninist and non-Leninist forms.

Of these two "religious" arguments, the argument of the Marxist political religion is easy to refute. To the extent that the idea of emancipatory revolution in the Third World depends on the validity of the Marxist theory of history, it was never valid, because Marxism, with its mistaken interpretation of historical trends and its erroneous labor theory of value, was mistaken about society and politics from the very beginning. This is not to say that wars of national liberation against multinational empires (including the multinational empires of the Soviet Union and communist China and communist Vietnam after 1975) have not been justified in many instances, only that revolutions can only be justified on a case-by-case basis, not as examples of a global revolutionary transformation.

By contrast, it is all but impossible to engage in a reasoned refutation of Christian pacifism, which stands or falls, not only on belief in a particular alleged divine revelation, but on a particular interpretation of that supposed revelation. Secular pacifism, on the other hand, is easily dismissed. It is enough to demonstrate that all existing and historic polities have been established, and then maintained, as a direct or indirect result of armed conflict; that no state in the world, including the Vatican, lacks military forces, however feeble; and that no known community that has endured for any length of time has failed to honor those who fight on its behalf (this is true even of civilian societies in which soldiers are not assigned the highest status). Throughout history and across the world, men who refuse to take part in the military defense of their community are almost invariably treated as cowards and parasites. Only communities influenced by one or another variety of religious pacifism have shown any toleration of pacifists; and even that toleration has been limited and has tended to be withdrawn in crises. Pacifism requires supernatural sanction, because to the secular, commonsensical mind pacifists appear to be bad subjects or bad citizens, shirking their duties to the community or the state. (The two do not always coincide, of course; in a multinational empire or federation which includes two or more distinct ethnic communities, one's moral obligation to fight on behalf of one's ethnic nation may not translate into a moral obligation to fight on behalf of the state.)

From this follows the conclusion that there is nothing inherently "conservative" or "right-wing" about the "realist" position outlined in MacIntyre's position (b). Far from being a position of the political right, this should be the position of all secular thinkers and statesmen, on the left, right, and center, who reject both Marxist revolutionary romanticism and supernatural religious pacifism, and at the same time reject the militarist account of war (a false morality which has sometimes been justified by secular doctrines—for example, the Social Darwinism that influenced Nazi ideology). After all, in the twentieth century a democratic socialist America would have had as much reason to dread a world dominated by fascist or communist totalitarians as a democratic capitalist America.

The realist approach to world affairs then is, or should be, the approach shared by all secularists who are not war-glorifying militarists, as well as by religious believers who are not pacifists.

Is There a Realist Morality of War?

To adopt the realist view of world politics as an arena of frequent (though not perpetual) and legitimate armed conflict, it is not necessary to reject the attempt to apply moral reasoning to warfare. All too often this point is obscured by the familiar contrast between "realism" and "idealism." Properly understood, realism is a distinctive theory of political morality, not a theory that posits the incompatibility of politics and morality.

Indeed, realism is *more* moral than rival moralities, like bloodthirsty militarism or antiwar pacifism. For realists, war is like surgery—a painful and dangerous activity that is sometimes necessary. The art of war bears the same relation to the more comprehensive art of politics that the craft of surgery bears to the more comprehensive craft of medicine. One can oppose a particular instance of surgery as unnecessary—and conversely one can argue that surgery is required, to save a particular patient. But it is absurd, even insane, to be against surgery on principle, or in favor of surgery on principle. To be indiscriminately antiwar or indiscriminately prowar is morally confused in the same way. A pacifist is like a Christian Scientist who is against surgery even when the alternative is the crippling or death of the patient, while a militarist can be compared to a psychopath who derives a sadistic thrill from the very idea of amputation.

The analogy can be extended, to a comparison between soldiers and surgeons. Soldiers who kill in the line of duty are not "murderers," any more than surgeons who cut living people open are "torturers." Pacifists often claim that glorifying soldiers means approving of the evils of war. But honoring doctors has nothing to do with celebrating the diseases or accidents that unfortunately provide the occasion for doctors to demonstrate their expertise and their personal virtues. Indeed, the soldier who tries to provoke a war, like the doctor or nurse who murders patients, the policeman who is also an extortionist and the fireman who doubles as an arsonist, is a stock villain in popular fiction and drama.

To this comparison, the objection may be raised that "surgery" on behalf of the metaphorical body politic can and does result in damaging or destroying real human beings. This is true—but this is also true in the case of much public policy that has nothing to do with national defense and power projection. The price of domestic law enforcement is the death in armed combat, each year, of significant numbers of police officers as well as of criminals, along with a substantial degree of "collateral damage" to civilians in the form of accidental shootings and wrecks during car chases. Morality, properly understood, requires weighing the costs and benefits of law enforcement, but it does not require the abandonment of the effort to enforce the law on the grounds that any loss of innocent life is unacceptable.

Although realism is *a* morality, not *amorality*, the moral dimension of realist thought is relatively undeveloped. Indeed, the entire subject has been distorted by the influence of a particular kind of realism—"minimal realism." As we have seen in Chapter 2, minimal realists have been inclined to view the world wars of the twentieth century as a replay of the great-power struggles of the old European state system, whereas maximal realists have often thought of the world wars as international civil wars, if not quasi religious crusades.

The difference between the two schools is important, because much of the "moral" language of contemporary realism actually consists of the language of old-fashioned European diplomacy, elevated from the status of a contingent, historic set of regional customs to the status of eternal moral norms. The difference can be illustrated by minimal-realist and maximal-realist views of "national sovereignty." Minimal realists, wedded to the nineteenth-century conception of a world of sovereigns whose relations are highly regulated and limited to a few channels, are much more likely than maximal realists to treat "violations" of "national sovereignty" as a moral evil almost comparable to genocide or torture. Maximal realists in the liberal nations, by contrast, have understood the twentieth-century wars against the fascist totalitarians and the communist totalitarians as campaigns waged on many levels, by many means—ranging from embargoes and covert action to subsidies or military aid to prowestern parties to direct confrontations between the leading powers. If obeying old-fashioned European diplomatic conventions impeded the struggle, maximal realists were more willing to sacrifice the conventions than to forfeit battles to the likes of Hitler and Stalin and Mao. Maximal realists are therefore more likely than minimal realists to defend many of the covert activities that the United States engaged in during the Cold War, which included secret subsidies to pro-American politicians in Japan and Italy, and efforts to assassinate or overthrow Fidel Castro and other Soviet clients in key states. For their part, the Soviet and Chinese communists and their clients viewed notions of state sovereignty as "bourgeois" mystifications, to be overridden in the greater interests of the proletariat and humanity, as interpreted by Marxist-Leninist doctrine.

The Morality of Proxy Wars

Defending the morality of the Cold War today is as unnecessary as defending the morality of the anti-Axis effort in World War II. It is no longer possible to deny that Marxism-Leninism—responsible for the death, by execution, forced labor, or artificial famine, of as many as one hundred million people in the USSR, China, and the other countries of the communist bloc—was an ideology as evil as German National Socialism. Indeed, the communist and fascist versions of totalitarianism, despite their philosophical differences, justified regimes that were strikingly similar.

Some opponents of the Cold War argued that the Soviet Union, however evil, was never powerful enough to justify the anti-Soviet effort. The Cold War was therefore based on American paranoia. Those who make this argument must explain why paranoia about Soviet power was shared by Western European, Japanese, and communist Chinese leaders; if the Soviet threat was a hoax, it was a hoax that depended on the collaboration of vast numbers of quite different people on many continents for half a century.

What is more, the claim that the Cold War was unnecessary, because the Soviet Union was never capable of conquering the world, misstates the issue. At the height of their power, Nazi Germany and the Soviet Union were no more capable than the United States of physically conquering and occupying the world. The goal of the United States and its allies was to prevent either totalitarian state from attaining and consolidating the position of the world's preeminent military hegemon—a position that does not require a commensurate economic hegemony, only a sufficient economic base for a military capable of intimidating potential rivals into acquiescence. A world dominated by Nazi Germany or the Soviet Union would not have been a world in which all countries were fascist or communist (though the number of totalitarian states would have grown enormously, as a result of subversion or imitation). Instead, a Nazi or Soviet world would have been a world that reflected Nazi or Soviet preferences in the rules of world order—rules of war, diplomacy, trade, citizenship, and so on. Because the winner would write the rules for the world, for a generation or longer, World War II and the Cold War were not ordinary great-power conflicts, but hegemonic wars, in which the very character and future of world civilization were at stake.

To support the U.S. cause in the world wars against the totalitarians, then, it was not necessary to believe that a world in which the United States and its allies are militarily predominant resembles an ideal world; no honest American argues that. Nor was it necessary to favor the universalization of American institutions such as liberal democracy and liberal capitalism. It was only necessary to believe that American military hegemony was preferable to German or Soviet military hegemony, in an era in which those three outcomes were the only realistic alternatives. This leaves open the possibility that some other world order, based on some other superpower or alliance, might be preferable to an American-dominated world order in the distant future. What will always be impossible is a world order that does not rest, in the final analysis, on the military superiority of one or a few powerful states, however that military superiority may be disguised by international institutions.

The argument for the justice of the American cause in the world wars is not discredited by pointing to the fact that the motives of the Unites States were always selfish, although they were not *only* selfish. Even if the United States had fought Hitler and the communists solely on the basis of the self-interested calculations of ruling-class capitalists, this would not alter the conclusion that humanity was better off in a world order shaped by Washington than in one designed in Berlin or

Moscow. The case for U.S. foreign policy rests on the coincidence of the general interest of humanity and the particular interest of the United States, not on the claim that what is good for the world is good for America and vice versa in all circumstances. (The moral case for U.S. intervention in World War I is much more problematic, because the hegemony of Imperial Germany rather than the British Empire or the United States would not have been as obviously disastrous for civilization as the geopolitical triumph of National Socialism or Marxism-Leninism would have been.)

Many thoughtful people who admit the legitimacy and indeed moral necessity of the all-out war against Nazi Germany and its allies nevertheless question the legitimacy of the proxy wars waged by the United States and its allies against the communist great powers. It is often assumed that storming Omaha Beach was somehow less morally ambiguous than patroling South Vietnamese villages threatened by guerrillas supported by the communist great powers. Although it is widespread, this assumption is morally confused.

Our ability to understand the world conflicts of the twentieth century is handicapped by the near universal tendency to identify the first two conflicts with the periods of no-holds-barred general war among the great powers. Thus World War I is said to have lasted from 1914–18 and World War II from 1939–45. In each case, though, the general war followed, and resulted from, an earlier "cold war." World War I was preceded by a "cold war" between Imperial Germany and rival great powers such as Britain, France, and Russia that can began in the 1890s, if not earlier. The outbreak of general war in 1939 followed a six-year cold war between Nazi Germany and its rivals. Describing the Soviet-American rivalry as the third world war, then, is not entirely accurate, if by "world wars" one means the "hot wars" that began in 1914 and 1939. Rather, the Soviet-American Cold War of 1946–91 should be compared to the Anglo-German rivalry of the 1890s through 1914, as well as to the rivalry of the Axis powers and their enemies before 1939. Proxy wars between the communist bloc and the anticommunist alliance such as Korea, Vietnam, and Afghanistan were the geopolitical, though not the moral, equivalent of the Spanish Civil War—which was a proxy war between the fascist bloc and the Soviet Union.

The similarity between the Soviet-American Cold War and the earlier cold wars of the twentieth century was pointed out in 1959 by the

German historian Ludwig Dehio. Noting that the term "Dry War" was used by Germans before 1914 to describe the Anglo-German naval rivalry, Dehio wrote:

> What are the characteristics of such a "dry" or "cold" war? The ultimate ambition of those [like Imperial Germany and the Soviet Union] who wage it is to achieve their aims peacefully. But these aims are offensive and not defensive. The intention is to force the opponent out of his present position and rank, and achieve what can otherwise be achieved only by the use of arms. Arms, too, play their part; for in order to impose the desired course, whether by fear or by threats, the production of arms is accelerated—always in the hope that it will not be necessary to have recourse to them. The whole idea is that one's own arms should so increase the risk of war that one's opponent will not dare to break from the cold war forced upon him into a hot one, and that, exhausted, he will cede his position peacefully. . . . A peaceful offensive of this kind must itself also accept a risk of war, the only difference being that the decision to strike the first blow can, if necessary, be forced upon the other side. In this way the roles of aggressor and defender can, in the undesirable event of actual war, seem to have been completely reversed. In general terms the whole development that we have discussed always displays a blend of offensive and defensive elements and of peaceful and belligerent ones, but in such proportions that, in fact, the peaceful offensive ambitions of the rising power dominate the scene until the critical moment when the goaded opponent may risk the final step into war.[3]

Dehio provides the answer to a seemingly compelling argument of western opponents of the Cold War—if the Soviet Union was really the "aggressor," then why did the United States send troops to other countries more often, and in greater numbers, than the Soviet Union? (Until the Soviet invasion of Afghanistan, large-scale deployments of troops outside of Soviet territory had been limited to invasions of Eastern Europe to crush anticommunist revolutions before they spread from East Germany, Hungary, and Czechoslovakia.) During the Cold War, the United States was the defensive hegemonic power, and the Soviet Union was the rising challenger—roles played respectively by the British empire and Imperial Germany in the years preceding 1914. If

Dehio is correct, then in the circumstances of a cold war a defensive hegemon such as Britain or the United States might be justified—in moral as well as strategic terms—in providing a military response to a "peaceful offensive." The embattled defensive power might legitimately "strike the first blow," resorting to arms rather than consenting to being displaced from its position in the world power hierarchy by an enemy using methods other than direct attack—methods such as an intimidating arms buildup or sponsorship of subversion or revolution in critical countries and regions.

Indeed, it is a tribute to the success of American policy that the cold war with the Soviet Union ended without having escalated into a hot war, the way that the earlier cold wars involving Germany had. One of the reasons that the Cold War phase of the third world conflict never escalated into a hot war phase—the "World War III" that both sides wanted to avoid—was the balance of terror imposed by nuclear weapons. If one assumes that the great powers in the 1930s had possessed nuclear weapons, and if one also assumes (a big assumption) that Hitler would not have used them, for fear of the consequences for Germany, then the rivalry between the Axis powers, the Soviet Union, and the liberal democracies might have taken a form more like that of the post-1946 Cold War. Unable to invade one another's homelands, the rival blocs might have fought protracted, low-level proxy wars in places such as North Africa, the Middle East, Latin America, and Southeast Asia. The history of the second global conflict might have included episodes called "the Nicaraguan Civil War" and "the Manchurian Intervention." Indeed, it is not difficult to imagine a parallel universe in which the United States sent its troops to join those of its French allies in a proxy war in Indochina against the clients of Imperial Japan and the allies of the Third Reich, as part of an antifascist Cold War of, say, 1936–78.

The point is this: A global struggle against Nazi Germany and its allies, waged by means of arms races and proxy wars, would have been just as morally legitimate as the all-out general war that actually took place after 1939. Indeed, if it had been possible, it might have been morally preferable to bring down the Axis regimes over a longer period of time, by means that incurred fewer casualties around the world. Between thirty five and forty million died during World War II. Even counting the millions who died in the Korean, Vietnamese, and Afghan wars, the combat death toll of the Cold War was far lower.

Civil Wars as Proxy Wars

On humanitarian grounds, then, one should prefer world wars that take the form of limited proxy wars and arms races to those that erupt into all-out fighting among the great powers and end with the occupation of the homelands of one or more of the major combatants. But what about the hapless residents of countries and regions whose territories are chosen as arenas for tests of strength between rival superpowers and alliances? Is it not immoral for great powers to prolong civil wars by intervening in them—even if the goal of intervention is the ultimate and indirect defeat of a power like Nazi Germany or the Soviet Union?

If morality forbids the prolongation of civil wars by great powers that turn them into proxy wars, then the liberal great powers are deprived of one of the chief means—if not *the* chief means—of preventing antiliberal superpowers from achieving world domination by methods short of direct conquest. The most violent wars since 1945 have been the Korean War (1950–53), the Nigerian civil war (1967–70), the Third Indochina War in Cambodia, pitting the Vietnamese conquerors and their Cambodian allies against anti-Vietnamese Cambodians (1975–89), the Second Indochina or "Vietnam" War (1959–75), the Ethiopian War (1962–91), and the Afghan War (1979–89).[4] With the exception of the Nigerian civil war, all of these conflicts were not only civil wars but also proxy wars in which the United States and the Soviet Union and/or China were involved. Each of these conflicts was prolonged because one or more superpowers supplied one of the factions with arms and economic aid or sent its own troops to help with logistics or take part in combat.

"The Vietnam War dramatizes what had happened to the state system," the political scientist Charles Tilly writes of the mutation of international politics after 1945. "An increasing share of all major wars occurred within constituted states as one or more of the great powers intervened directly or indirectly on behalf of local parties to a civil war." Tilly notes that "the contest rarely concerned the territory to be occupied by a given state; instead, the combatants fought over what groups were to control the existing state within its established boundaries." Largely as a result of the substitution of proxy wars for direct wars between the great powers, the percentage of deaths in civil wars as opposed to interstate wars rose from 1948–58 to 15.9 percent; from 1959–69 to 59.4 percent; and from 1970–80 to 89.0 percent.[5]

The moral problem this poses should not be minimized. Most of the three million Koreans who died in the Korean War would have lived if the United States had chosen not to contest the Soviet- and Chinese-assisted North Korean conquest of South Korea. In the Afghan War, the last of the three major proxy wars in Asia between the United State and the Soviet bloc, an estimated 1.5 million Afghans died, beginning in 1979. If the United States is to be condemned for prolonging the Vietnam War by coming to the aid of the South Vietnamese government as well as U.S. allies in Laos and Cambodia, then consistency requires that the United States and its allies be condemned for prolonging the Afghan War by arming and subsidizing the Afghan resistance.

While world wars fought by proxy take the lives of millions of inhabitants of weak countries, world wars in which the great powers attack one another's homelands cause collateral death and destruction to peripheral nations on an even greater scale. In the Cold War, Koreans, Vietnamese, Afghans, and Cubans found themselves swept up in limited wars between the superpower blocs; but then in World War II Chinese, Egyptians, Norwegians, and Greeks were unable to escape being drawn into the maelstrom of general war among the great powers. Most of the tens of millions of victims of World War II (though not the victims of Hitler's Holocaust) would not have died if the United States and its allies had made peace with Nazi Germany and the other Axis powers in the early 1940s. If a bad peace is preferable to a just war because the loss of life is lower, then Nazi hegemony in Europe and the world would have been morally preferable to the prolongation of World War II that resulted from America's entry on the side of the British empire and the Soviet Union. Without minimizing the suffering of individuals or even whole nations, one may reasonably conclude that the goals of preventing Nazi or Soviet world domination were important enough to justify enormous human costs.

The U.S. and the Vietnamese Civil War—Intervention or Invasion?

In his influential book *Just and Unjust Wars* (1977), the philosopher Michael Walzer attempts to define a morality of international politics by translating conceptions from international law and diplomatic practice—chiefly, the quasi-sacred status of "sovereignty"—into the realm of morality, with little modification. The effort is misconceived, for two reasons—first, morality and law (to say nothing of diplomatic practice) are different things; and second, the conventions of old-fashioned international law and diplomacy to which Walzer looks for guidance were obsolete in a century of ideological warfare among superpower blocs (even if a certain amount of lip service was still paid to them after 1945).

According to Walzer, it is legitimate for a country to engage in "counterintervention" to help an ally that has been invaded—but it is not legitimate for a country to intervene to rescue an allied government from being overthrown from within. Under this theory, it was legitimate for the United States to go to war in Korea to rescue South Korea from a cross-border invasion by North Korea—but it was morally wrong for the United States to go to war to prevent the regime of South Vietnam from falling to a South Vietnamese insurgency: "The Korean War might look very different than it does if the Northerners had not marched in strength across the 38th parallel, but had made covert contact, instead, with a Southern rebellion." Walzer concludes with a comparison of the U.S. effort to defend noncommunist regimes in South Vietnam, Cambodia, and Laos against incorporation into the communist bloc and "the Nazi conquests of Czechoslovakia, Poland, Denmark, Belgium, and Holland."[6]

The influence of this general line of reasoning (if not of Walzer's shocking and vicious comparison of the United States to Nazi Germany) can be inferred from the fact that both supporters and opponents of the Vietnam War devoted so much effort to proving that the conflict was "really" an insurgency or "really" an invasion. The facts can be manipulated to support either side. Before the Tet offensive, the war in South Vietnam was predominantly an insurgency, and most of the Viet Cong were residents of the South, rather than infiltrees from the North. The war between 1965 and 1968, then, was "really" a southern insurgency, not an invasion.

Defenders of the war can reply that the insurgency in the South was controlled from the beginning by the North Vietnamese dictatorship. This was denied at the time by the western left. For example, in *The Indochina Story* (1970), the Committee of Concerned Asian Scholars had this to say:

From "somewhere in Nam Bo [Cochin China]" in December 1960, close to a hundred persons announced the creation of the "National

Liberation Front of South Vietnam." They called for a nation-wide uprising against the Saigon regime. Despite a certain reluctance, Hanoi had little choice but to sanction the southern initiative or lose whatever moral influence it had south of the Demilitarized Zone.[7]

In *The United States in Vietnam*, another book relied upon as a source of scholarly authority by the antiwar left, George McTurnan Kahin and John W. Lewis wrote: "In sum, the insurrection is Southern rooted; it arose at Southern initiative in response to Southern demands." According to these influential American academics, South Vietnamese dissidents "lost patience with the communist North and finally took matters into their own hands." Ho Chi Minh's regime only gradually and reluctantly came around to supporting the independent southern rebellion: "By September 1960, when the Northern government at last publicly sanctioned the insurrection in the South, the strength and potential of that insurgency had become so manifest that if Hanoi had not proclaimed its approval it might well have lost any influence over the future course of events below the 17th parallel." Kahin and Lewis write of "Hanoi's continued unwillingness to encourage armed resistance to Diem's regime" and conclude: "There is no evidence to assert, as does the U.S. 'White Paper' of 1965, that 'the Liberation Front for South Viet-Nam . . . was formed at Hanoi's order.'"[8]

In reality, the U.S. White Paper's assertion was completely correct: "The Liberation Front is Hanoi's creation; it is neither independent nor southern, and what it seeks is not liberation but subjugation of the South."[9] It is true that many southern members of the Viet Cong, unaware of Hanoi's control of the inner circle of the insurgency, sincerely believed that the NLF and its political branch, the Provisional Revolutionary Government, were independent southern organizations. During the war against the French, Ho Chi Minh had deceived the Vietnamese people by disguising the Communist party's control of the Vietminh patriotic front in exactly the same way. After the North Vietnamese *Anschluss* of South Vietnam in 1975, Nguyen Khac-Vien, an official party historian, confessed: "The Provisional Revolutionary Government was always simply a group emanating from the DRV [the Democratic Republic of Vietnam, the formal name of North Vietnam]. If we (the DRV) had pretended otherwise for such a long period, it was only because during the war we were not obliged to unveil our cards."[10]

An insurgency in one state, controlled by the government in another state, arguably has more in common with an invasion by the outside state than with a spontaneous and purely domestic insurgency. At any rate, the distinction between insurgency and invasion in Vietnam collapsed after 1968. Following the devastation of the Viet Cong during the battles of the Tet offensive, the Vietnam War primarily took the form of a conventional invasion of North Vietnam by South Vietnam. The failed North Vietnamese invasion of 1972, and the successful invasion of 1974–75, were no different in kind from the North Korean invasion of South Korea in the summer of 1950. If the United States was morally justified in going to war in response to the cross-border invasion of South Korea in 1950, then by the same logic the United States had every moral right to defend South Vietnam against a similar cross-border invasion—after 1968, if not earlier.

Indeed, in both Korea and Vietnam, a conventional invasion followed the failure of a communist insurgency in the southern, noncommunist section of a divided nation. The North Korean invasion of 1950 was preceded by a guerrilla war between 1945 and 1950 in which an estimated hundred thousand Koreans were killed.[11] The communist insurgency in South Korea between 1945 and 1950 never got as far as the Viet Cong insurgency did between 1959 and 1965. But suppose that it had? Suppose that in 1950 Syngman Rhee's regime in South Korea had been on the verge of losing to a largely Southern insurgency directed by Stalin's client and proxy Kim Il Sung? The Truman administration would have faced a situation similar to that which confronted the Johnson administration in 1965. The question is not as speculative as it may seem, because North Korea persisted in attempts at infiltration and terrorism in South Korea after 1953, and because South Korea, like South Vietnam, was repeatedly plunged into political turmoil by military coups.

The distinction between "invasion" and "civil war," then, cannot justify the Korean War while discrediting the Vietnam War. Both wars, in all of their phases, were civil wars and proxy wars at the same time. From the point of view of the capitals involved in the Vietnam War—Saigon, Hanoi, Washington, Moscow, and Beijing—insurgency and invasion were simply two instruments of a single North Vietnamese strategy. (Those members of South Vietnam's National Liberation Front, and their western leftist supporters, who believed otherwise were in for a shock in 1975.) The Cold War proxy wars in Indochina were different in detail, but not in kind, from major Cold War proxy wars in other regions such as the Korean peninsula, Afghanistan, and Greece.

The moral realist, then, must conclude that it is not inherently immoral to wage world wars by means of proxy wars, nor to fight proxy wars by means of intervention in civil wars; indeed, the moral imperative of preventing a totalitarian superpower or bloc from achieving military and diplomatic hegemony and using that hegemony to rewrite the rules of world order may require great-power intervention in particular civil wars. This is not to say that every proxy war waged in the service of a legitimate global strategy is necessarily justified. It is possible that the Cold War in general was moral, but that a particular campaign in the Cold War, such as the Vietnam War, was not. The morality of the Vietnam War in particular remains to be discussed.

Was It Immoral to Support the Saigon Dictatorship?

The case against the morality of the American war in Vietnam was not limited to the argument about the legitimacy of U.S. intervention in a civil war. Many critics of the war argued that the South Vietnamese regime that the United States was attempting to rescue was so evil that it did not deserve American support. The regime of President Ngo Dinh Diem was a repressive civilian dictatorship; after he was murdered by the South Vietnamese military, South Vietnam was ruled by generals.

Was it immoral for the United States to support a military dictatorship in South Vietnam? If it was, then it must have been immoral as well to support military dictators in South Korea, Taiwan, and Cambodia (under General Lon Nol). Between 1946 and 1991, the average state in the Third World was controlled for more than half of its history as an independent country by its military.[12] As late as the mid-1970s, only about two dozen of the 144 member states of the United Nations were democracies by any reasonable definition. During most of the twentieth century, any American foreign policy that went beyond the protection of North America and Western Europe required U.S. alliances with military dictators as well as with despots of other kinds (including communist despots such as Stalin during World War II and Mao in the 1970s).

The purpose of America's East Asia policy during the Cold War was not to bring liberal democracy to the nations of East Asia. It was to prevent the success of the Soviet geopolitical challenge to American world primacy by preventing either the Soviet Union or China from enlarging its Asian base at enormous cost to American power and prestige. Nevertheless, free elections did finally come about in South Korea and Taiwan, after decades of authoritarian rule, and partly in response to U.S. pressure. It is possible that if South Vietnam had survived, its government might have evolved in the direction of liberal democracy, like those of South Korea and Taiwan. However, as long as the Communist party remains in power democracy will be out of the question in Vietnam.

The antiwar movement denounced what Richard Falk called the "abhorrent policies and practices" of Saigon's military dictators.[13] Neither they nor their victim Diem were models of virtue or competence, by the standards of North Atlantic liberal democracies. But that is the wrong standard of comparison. Compared to America's other allies in East Asia, the Saigon elite does not appear to have been uniquely bad. And in retrospect they appear relatively enlightened, compared to most of America's allies in the Middle East.

The political history of South Korea was as marked by coup, riot, and repression as that of South Vietnam. The first leader, Syngman Rhee, was an anticommunist nationalist who, like Diem, had spent years in exile. The United States lost fifty six thousand troops in the war to restore Rhee to power. A student-led rebellion forced Rhee out in 1960; in 1961, the successor regime was ousted in a military coup led by Park Chung Hee, an officer trained by the Japanese. After eighteen years of increasingly despotic rule, Park was murdered in 1979 by the head of the Korean CIA. Among his other atrocities, Park had the leading dissident Kim Dae Jung kidnapped in Tokyo, and would have ordered his murder if the United States had not intervened. (Kim was elected president of South Korea in 1998.) After a period of turmoil following Park's assassination, power was consolidated by a general named Chun Doo Hwan. Chun imposed martial law and cracked down on dissent, arresting Kim Dae Jung among others. More than two hundred citizens were massacred by the military in its repression of a protest in Kwangju. Chun's designation of his handpicked successor, another general named Roh Tae Woo, as the ruling party's presidential candidate set off countrywide demonstrations. Because the liberal opposition split its vote, Roh won the presidency in a free election with only 36 percent of the popular vote in 1987, as the Cold War drew to a close.

The successive Korean dictatorships were as vicious as those in South Vietnam. The brutality of the South Vietnamese authorities who tortured dissidents and prisoners of war and confined them in the infamous "tiger cages" was matched in South Korea. At the hands of KCIA torturers under President Park, opponents of the regime were subjected to torture by immersion in water or strung up and spread-eagled over flame, a torture known as "Korean barbecue."[14]

If South Vietnam's dictators were no worse than South Korea's, they were not as bad as some of the despots in the Middle East whom the United States has aided in the service of its global grand strategy. Many of the Muslim mujahideen in Afghanistan, whom the United States helped in their struggle against the Soviet Union in the 1980s, are now taking part in a murderous jihad or holy war against America and the West. The regime of the anticommunist Taliban in Afghanistan makes South Vietnam look enlightened by comparison. In the Gulf War, the United States sent its armies into battle to restore a feudal monarch, the emir of Kuwait, to the throne of a country carved out of Iraq's Basra province in 1921 by Sir Percy Cox of the British Foreign Office. The *New York Times* described Kuwait as "less a country than a family-owned oil company with a flag."[15] Following the restoration of its rule by the United States and allied military forces, the emirate was accused of having engaged in summary executions, torture, deportation, and many other abuses.[16] Notwithstanding this, the *New York Times*, which had demanded that Diem be driven from office in Saigon and denounced the immorality of the American war in Indochina, declared that "if any war could be called 'just,' the gulf war qualified."[17]

Corruption and Repression, South and North

In retrospect, then, the South Vietnamese regime appears to have been no worse than other dictatorships and monarchies that the United States has supported as part of its foreign policy. The Saigon dictators look even better, when they are compared with the communist elites in North Vietnam and the united communist Vietnam founded in 1975–76.

Like most postcolonial regimes in the developing world, the South Vietnamese regime was extremely corrupt. In her Pulitzer Prize–winning antiwar polemic *Fire in the Lake* (1972), the journalist Frances Fitzgerald presented a caricature of South Vietnam as one great black market combined with a red light district for American GIs. She declared that only the "narrow flame of revolution" could purify a society so depraved. The "narrow flame of revolution" that Fitzgerald and other western leftists prayed for came in 1975. A former high-ranking Vietnamese official describes the result. The northern communist cadres "fought each other over houses, cars, prostitutes, and bribes. . . . It was as if the city [Saigon] had been invaded by a swarm of locusts."[18] Of the new communist ruling class, another former Vietnamese communist official, Bui Tin, writes: "Every day they become more like the Mafia, Red Capitalists who have emerged from the jungle in a way never before witnessed in our country's history."[19]

Following the practice of their counterparts in the Soviet Union, China, Cuba, and other communist dictatorships, the top Vietnamese communist leaders had their own special shops in Hanoi, where the families of elite officials could buy luxuries even when their subjects were going hungry. After the fall of Saigon in 1975, the most luxurious villas were assigned to party officials. The typical member of the Politburo had a private villa and a retinue worthy of a feudal lord, including a majordomo in charge of the house, a cook, servants, and sometimes personal photographers. Members of the party elite would commandeer helicopters and planes for their use on private vacations.[20]

The nepotism of Diem and other South Vietnamese rulers was notorious. The communist rulers of united Vietnam were just as guilty of abusing their power on behalf of their relatives. According to Bui Tin, a high-ranking Vietnamese defector, after unification the Politburo member Le Duc Tho arranged to have his sister manage the private shops of the party elite, while his brother Dinh Duc Thien was put in charge, in succession, of a steel factory, of military supplies, and of the oil and gas industry—despite the fact that he was unqualified for any of these posts. Another one of Le Duc Tho's brothers, with no experience of administration, became chairman of the Ho Chi Minh City People's Committee.[21] Just as America's affluent white overclass relied on college deferments and the National Guard to keep its college-educated sons from fighting in Southeast Asia during the Vietnam War, so the communist oligarchs of post-1975 Vietnam used their connections to ensure that their sons did not fight during the Vietnamese occupation of Cambodia. Almost all of the fifty two thousand who died in the Vietnamese conquest and occupation of Cambodia were children of the Vietnamese poor and working class.[22]

The Vietnamese communists, then, were at least as corrupt as Diem and the Saigon generals—and they were far more repressive. Following the North Vietnamese *Anschluss* of South Vietnam in 1975, the brutality of the Vietnamese version of Marxism-Leninism could no longer be denied. Between 1.5 and 2 million Vietnamese risked their lives trying to escape. Many of the "boat people" and "road people" were robbed and raped; enormous numbers drowned or were otherwise killed trying to escape from the vast prison camp that Vietnam had become. This should have come as no surprise, given the mass exodus from North Vietnam in the 1950s.

It was in the mid-1950s, not the mid-1970s, that the nature of the Vietnamese communists should have become apparent to everyone. The collectivization of agriculture in North Vietnam, or "land reform," made it apparent that Ho Chi Minh and his colleagues were cruel and doctrinaire disciples of Stalin and Mao. In its war against both communist and noncommunist opponents, the South Vietnamese regime committed many atrocities. And the South Vietnamese peasantry suffered terribly from repression and programs such as forced relocation. But nothing in the Saigon regime's bloody record compares in evil to the Hanoi regime's systematic and cold-blooded executions, in village after village of North Vietnam, of at least ten thousand individuals who had been assigned to arbitrary economic categories borrowed from the Soviet Union and China. The North Vietnamese mass murder, like its Soviet and Chinese equivalents, constituted genocide—genocide on the basis of "class" rather than of "race."

The distinction between "authoritarian" and "totalitarian" regimes, popularized by anticommunist U.S. conservatives and liberals in the 1970s and 1980s, does not necessarily correspond to the distinction between good and evil. An authoritarian regime such as Suharto's Indonesian dictatorship may engage in greater atrocities than a totalitarian regime such as Tito's communist Yugoslavia. Even so, the authoritarian/totalitarian distinction works well in explaining the political and moral differences between South Vietnam and North Vietnam, as well as the differences between South and North Korea, and Taiwan and mainland China. With respect to corruption and nepotism, the authoritarians of Saigon were no worse than the totalitarians of Hanoi. With respect to political repression, they were not as bad. Nor can it be argued that ordinary people in Vietnam were better off under communist rule. There can be no doubt that Vietnam, North and South, would have been much more prosperous under the rule of authoritarians, however corrupt and repressive, than under the rule of Marxist-Leninist ideologues. The Vietnamese civil war was not a battle between black and white; it was rather a clash between totalitarian black and authoritarian gray.

The argument that the Saigon regime was too evil to be supported collapses altogether when America's temporary alliances of expedience with the communist great powers are taken into account. It is difficult to imagine a theory of international morality that would permit the United States to ally itself with Stalin against Hitler, and later with Mao against the Soviet Union, and yet would forbid the United States to ally itself with France or South Vietnam at successive stages of the Cold War in Indochina. The United States subsidized France in the First Indochina War to check Soviet power, as it had earlier subsidized the Soviet Union to check the power of Nazi Germany; the Soviet empire was far more evil than the French empire. To be morally consistent, those who protested the U.S. alliance with the South Vietnamese dictatorship should have devoted most of the 1970s to mass demonstrations against the U.S. alliance with Mao, who directly or indirectly slaughtered more people than either Stalin or Hitler. The double standard of the western left during the Cold War was evident in the way that its members favored U.S. rapprochement with major communist tyrants such as Mao while criticizing U.S. alliances with minor anticommunist tyrants like Diem and Thieu.

On examination, then, the argument that the evil nature of the South Vietnamese regime rendered it unfit as an ally of the United States in the Cold War turns out to be a collection of debating points that do not add up to a coherent moral argument at all.

The Question of Nationalist Legitimacy

It is possible that the rulers of South Vietnam lacked national legitimacy in their country, even if they were to be preferred, on abstract moral grounds, to the Vietnamese communists, North and South. There is obviously a moral difference, as well as a practical difference, between an effort by an outside power such as the United States to shore up a minoritarian government with dubious legitimacy against a minoritarian insurgency with dubious legitimacy, on the one hand, and, on the other hand, an effort by an outside power to install a regime in the face of the hostility of a coherent national majority (like the installation, by France, of the Emperor Maximilian as ruler of Mexico in 1864). Many opponents of the Vietnam War claimed that the American effort fell into the second category, rather than the first. They claimed that the war was not a conflict between armed minorities, each supported by outside great powers, while a passive and frightened majority watched and attempted to survive. Rather, they argued that it was a struggle between Vietnamese patriots, whose only legitimate leader was Ho Chi Minh and his successors, against South Vietnamese leaders who lacked national legitimacy. In this view, the Vietnam War might be described as a proxy war that was *not* a civil war. The U.S. intervention in South Vietnam was less like a rescue of a struggling indigenous government than the installation of a puppet regime by a foreign great power.

This argument is made by Michael Walzer in *Just and Unjust Wars*. Even if the U.S. counterintervention in Vietnam had otherwise been legitimate, Walzer argues, the war was immoral because it was really a war between the United States and the Vietnamese communists (for the purposes of this argument, it does not matter whether the Viet Cong were controlled from Hanoi or independent). "We were far more vital to the government than they [the North Vietnamese] were to the insurgents. . . . And that fact must raise the most serious questions about the American defense: for counterintervention is morally possible only on behalf of a government (or a movement, party, or whatever) that has already passed the self-help test." Note the paradox inherent in Walzer's theory of intervention: only a government that is popular enough to survive without outside assistance is justified in requesting outside assistance.

In this view, the Vietnam War was not a war *in* Vietnam; rather, it was a war *on* Vietnam, an aggressive invasion of a helpless nation by a monstrous imperial superpower. The crumbling of the South Vietnamese regime in 1974–75, after the United States had abandoned it to invasion by a Soviet- and Chinese-equipped North Vietnamese conventional army, has been taken as evidence that the regime was completely lacking in popular support. If this is indeed the case, then the speed with which Syngman Rhee's regime in South Korea crumbled before the Soviet- and

Chinese-sponsored North Korean invasion in 1950 ought to lead to the conclusion that the South Korean regime was no more legitimate than the North Korean regime. This line of reasoning, in other words, leads to the conclusion that both the Korean and the Vietnam wars were illegitimate "invasions," or, to use Walzer's term, "aggressive wars" comparable to Nazi Germany's conquest of its neighbors. Even on the left, few have been willing to denounce *both* the Korean and Vietnam Wars.

But the comparison cannot be avoided. Walzer's contemptuous description of the Saigon regime applies with equal force to Syngman Rhee's South Korean dictatorship. Each of these noncommunist tyrannies "was so much an American creature that the U.S. government's claim to be committed to it and obligated to ensure its survival is hard to understand. It is as if our right hand were committed to our left. There is no independent moral or political agent on the other side of the bond and hence no genuine bond at all."[23]

The obvious rejoinder is that America's task in Indochina would have been much easier if its South Vietnamese allies really had been the mere lackeys depicted in the propaganda of the communist bloc and the western left. The Kennedy administration conspired in the overthrow of Diem precisely because he was reluctant to follow Washington's orders. The generals who succeeded him were more pliant, but still far from subservient—one need only think of the frustration of the Johnson and Nixon administrations with the obdurate President Thieu. The rulers of South Vietnam, like the rulers of North Vietnam, were the clients of great powers without being their puppets.

Nor can the failure of successive Saigon regimes to create a South Vietnamese "nation" be held against them. Naturally, there was no South Vietnamese community corresponding to the South Vietnamese state, because the community was the Vietnamese nation as a whole. Like South Korea and Taiwan and West Germany, South Vietnam was a fragmentary society, whose existence was the result of compromises among the Cold War superpowers.

The comparison with Korea is particularly apt. Korea was partitioned in December 1945 by the United States, the Soviet Union, and Britain, the way that Vietnam was partitioned at the 1954 Geneva Conference with the formal or tacit consent of the United States, the Soviet Union, Britain, France, and China. The claim that South Vietnam was doomed from the beginning, because the division of Vietnam was so artificial, is hard to square with the claim of the Korea expert Gregory Henderson that the partition of Korea made even less sense:

> No division of a nation in the present world is so astonishing in its origins as the division of Korea; none is so unrelated to conditions or sentiment within the nation itself at the time the division was effected; none is to this day so unexplained; in none does blunder and planning oversight appear to have played so large a role. Finally, there is no division for which the U.S. government bears so heavy a share of the responsibility as it bears for the division of Korea.[24]

If dependence on the U.S. military and American influence of much internal as well as foreign policy proved that a country was, to use Walzer's term, a mere "creature" of the United States, then West Germany and South Korea fit the bill as surely as did South Vietnam, which unlike those countries was not garrisoned by the United States on a large scale before 1965.

Many opponents of the Vietnam War alleged that Ho Chi Minh's communists were the only legitimate nationalists in Vietnam. The truth is somewhat more complex than this simple melodrama that pits Ho Chi Minh's patriots against the unpatriotic opportunists whom the United States inherited from the French.

It is true that none of the successive regimes in South Vietnam ever succeeded in establishing a solid base of legitimacy in the deeply divided population. It is also true that the communists were supported by a substantial part of the South Vietnamese population. These facts, however, are compatible with two interpretations of Vietnamese politics. One holds that a clear majority supported the communists. The other, more plausible interpretation holds that neither the Hanoi regime nor the Saigon regime had a clear majority mandate, in their own territories or among the Vietnamese people as a whole. In this view, the civil war in Vietnam, like many civil wars, was a contest between two minorities in which much of the population, interested in survival and local issues, watched to see which side would win. The ultimate success of the communists had less to do with their success in winning "the hearts and minds" of the Vietnamese people than with their superior organization and their more ruthless and efficient use of coercion. The Leninists in Hanoi were better able to crush dissent in their own territory, and to exploit division in South Vietnam because they were Leninists, not because they were patriots.

A dispassionate examination of the historical record supports this interpretation of the question of national legitimacy in Vietnam. At the end of World War II, a number of Vietnamese nationalist factions were independent of Ho's communist-controlled Viet Minh front group. In 1945, the communists executed, among others, the leader of the Constitutional party, Quang Chieu; the head of the Party for Independence, Vo Van Nga; and Ngo Dinh Koi, the brother of Ngo Dinh Diem, who later became the dictator of South Vietnam.[25] In the fall of 1945 Vietminh death squads murdered all the Trotskyists (left-wing rivals of the Stalinist communists) whom they could find. A French leftist, Daniel Guerin, asked Ho about the assassination of a prominent Vietnamese Trotskyist, Ta Thu Thau: "'Thau was a great patriot and we mourn him,' Ho Chi Minh told me with unfeigned emotion. But a moment later he added in a steady voice: 'All those who do not follow the line which I have laid down will be broken.'"[26]

Further murders and purges followed, when the first Viet Minh National Congress, controlled by the communists, convened in Hanoi. The congress delegated all of its powers to a communist-dominated National Resistance Committee, chaired by Giap. Having delegated sweeping power to Ho and Giap, the congress adjourned after only four hours; it met only one more time.[27] In the months that followed, Giap—left in charge while Ho traveled to France for negotiations—systematically eradicated or subordinated noncommunist Vietnamese nationalist parties such as the VNQDD, the Dai Viet, the Constitutionalists, the Independent party, and the Trotskyists. During the purges that began in March 1946 and peaked in the summer, thousands of potential leaders of noncommunist Vietnamese nationalism were murdered. In his biography of Giap, John Colvin writes: "Terrorists killed most of such leaders as existed; there were mass executions, death by harrow, some were buried alive, many after tortures of the vilest kind."[28] The "nationalist" Giap did not hesitate to use fifteen hundred Japanese troops and to collaborate with French authorities in eliminating the noncommunist nationalist resistance to Ho's Stalinist regime. Twenty-five thousand nationalists were thrown into labor camps, while six thousand managed to flee to China (then governed by Chiang Kai-shek's Nationalists).[29] All parties other than the Vietminh were banned or replaced by subservient fronts, and local governments that the communists did not control were purged.[30] To ensure that no new opposition appeared, Ho's dictatorship set up secret committees in every village to spy on the citizens. They also controlled the population by copying the Soviet system of internal passports for travel between regions.[31]

In May 1949, U.S. Secretary of State Dean Acheson approved a cable that rejected the argument that Ho should be considered a "nationalist" rather than a "communist":

> [The] Question [of] whether Ho [is] as much nationalist or Commie is irrelevant. All Stalinists in colonial areas are nationalists. With [the] achievement of national aims (i.e., independence), their objective necessarily becomes subordination [of the] state to Commie purposes and [the] ruthless extermination [of] not only opposition groups but all elements suspected [of] even [the] slightest deviation.[32]

By the mid-1950s in North Vietnam, everything had come to pass exactly as Acheson had predicted.

During the Vietnam War, many antiwar journalists, activists, and politicians in the United States parroted the communist line that the war was a continuation of the struggle against the French, and that the Saigon regime was dominated by French collaborators. In fact Diem was hostile to France and did his best to purge his military and government of French sympathizers. Perhaps the only leftist historian who has written honestly about this subject is Gabriel Kolko in *Anatomy of a War* (1994). "The pro-French and French-backed Vietnamese posed a greater immediate threat to the consolidation of Diem's power than the Communists," Kolko writes. With the backing of the United States, which wanted to replace French with American influence in Indochina, Diem in mid-1955 attacked "the Binh Xuyen, Cao Dai, and Hoa Hoa private armies, all of whom France had funded until early that year. In October he had Bao Dai dethroned; at the end of the year he broke off economic relations with France and left the French Union, proclaiming the creation of the 'Republic of Vietnam'. The formal vestiges of the French colonial order were gone." Diem then purged the military of former French loyalists and replaced them with graduates of new officer schools he established. As he consolidated his power, "Diem rounded up opponents without concern for ideology, *and pro-French Vietnamese were espe-*

cially vulnerable."[33] Diem and his supporters were anything but French puppets.

In the final analysis, the Vietnamese themselves are the only ones capable of judging the extent to which nationalism and communism in Vietnam were compatible. The former high-ranking member of the communist regime, Colonel Bui Tin, has recently lamented his nation's "blindness in going along with foreign ideology and worshipping it as the supreme truth." According to Tin:

After accepting Maoism, we also became subject to the influence of Stalin. His works which were printed and reprinted in Vietnamese long after he was discredited in the Soviet Union, became required reading for all middle- and high-ranking cadres. Then there were the pictures. Everywhere, in all offices and along the main roads, the faces of the world's leading communists looked down on us. But the people soon noticed that with the exception of Mao Tse-tung, all of them—Marx, Engels, Lenin, Stalin and Ho Chi Minh—had beards or in Stalin's case a big mustache. So in popular parlance, Communism became equated with 'ong rau,' the bearded gentlemen, and not always politely.[34]

Like North Korea's Kim Il Sung and Cambodia's Pol Pot, Ho Chi Minh saw no contradiction between Vietnamese nationalism and "proletarian internationalism." Guided by the universalist secular religion of Marxism-Leninism, Ho and his subordinates did their best to suppress both traditional and modern Vietnamese culture in order to replace them with crude copies of the official culture of the Soviet Union and China. A poem written by the Party poet To Huu on the death of Stalin in 1953 is an example of the kind of literature favored by the Hanoi regime:

Stalin, oh Stalin, alas He is gone!
Do Heaven and earth still exist?
Devotion to father, to mother, to husband,
Devotion to Him ten times more than to oneself.
Love for the children, for the country, for the race,
But so much more love for Him.
In the old days, we were so withered and desolate

With Him there is joy
In the old days, there was hunger and torment
With Him there is more than enough rice to fill the pot.[35]

Poets, novelists, and musicians who refused to tailor their work to the glorification of Vietnamese and foreign communism were persecuted and often imprisoned. The poet Nguyen Chi Thien, one of a number of North Vietnamese members of the dissident writers' movement of 1956 who was confined for decades to "reeducation camps," managed to smuggle a sheaf of handwritten poems entitled "Flowers from Hell" to British diplomats in Hanoi in 1980. In one the dissident poet wrote:

If Uncle and the Party, let's suppose,
Allowed free movements in and out,
Grandfather Marx's paradise
Would soon become the wilds where monkeys roam.[36]

There is abundant evidence, then, that Ho Chi Minh was never as widely admired in his own country as the western left claimed. Doan Van Toai, a South Vietnamese dissident who was imprisoned after the communist conquest of the South in 1975, recalled an incident in jail: "As we chime in with 'At Night I Dream I See Uncle Ho,' I realize that several voices in the choir are changing 'I see' to 'I kill.' No doubt the new version corresponds more closely to the reality of their dreams."[37]

The historical record, then, suggests that the failure of the Saigon regime to acquire solid popular legitimacy did not mean that the Hanoi regime succeeded at the same task. The fall of Saigon was the result of a North Vietnamese invasion, not of the southern insurgency, which was weaker after 1968 than it had been before. The conquest of South Vietnam by the Soviet-backed North, after it had been abandoned by the United States, cannot be interpreted as evidence of the South's utter lack of legitimacy, unless a similar conclusion is to be drawn about the legitimacy of the South Korean regime, which fell rapidly to a North Korean invasion in 1950, and survived after 1953 only under the protection of tens of thousands of U.S. troops.

That Ho Chi Minh's regime never monopolized Vietnamese nationalism is also suggested by the flight of much of the Vietnamese population from communist rule in the 1950s and again in the 1970s and 1980s, and by the fact that many patriotic South Vietnamese fought to prevent communist domination from being extended throughout their country. Indeed, the legitimacy of the Communist party in North Vietnam was evidently so weak from the beginning that Ho and his successors, to this day, have refused to permit free elections and have brutally snuffed out dissent. Both nonviolent and armed resistance to communist rule in Vietnam has continued since 1975, even though it has been ignored by the western media. Ho's regime was superior to the successive Saigon governments in the use of coercion in the service of internal repression, defense, subversion, and conquest. The Saigon regime was everything its opponents claimed it was—dictatorial, corrupt, incompetent. But it did not fall because it was a tyranny. It fell to a more brutal tyranny that was more effective, in part, *because* it was more brutal.

Was the Vietnam War Uniquely Savage?

In 1980, the sociologist Peter Berger, a former opponent of the Vietnam War, wrote an article in *Commentary* examining the moral case against the war. Berger admitted that the communist takeovers in Indochina were a "human catastrophe of monumental dimensions" and that as a result of the U.S. retreat from Southeast Asia "totalitarianism has grown stronger." Nevertheless, he wrote, "I continue to believe that the war was marked by a distinctive brutality which cannot be subsumed by some statement that 'all war is hell.'"[38] This perception that the Vietnam War was uniquely brutal is widely shared, even among Americans who were not opposed in general to the Cold War. But is it accurate?

The reputation of the Vietnam War as a uniquely horrible war is based primarily on the absence or censorship of horrifying visual images of the kind that was exercised in World War I, World War II, and Korea, and later in the Gulf War. The public in the United States and around the world never saw the charred corpses in Hiroshima or Dresden—or on the Iraqi "highway of death." As a result, gruesome images and nightmarish incidents, of a kind which occur in most wars, are associated, in the popular mind, with just one war—the Vietnam War.

For example, in 1966 the journalist Malcolm Browne published a book about the Vietnam conflict entitled *The New Face of War.* According to William Prochnau, "The cover photograph showed a bright-eyed

American GI thrusting forward the decapitated head of a Viet Cong guerrilla."[39] The image was horrifying—but it was hardly the *new* face of war. In October 1943, Chief of Staff General George C. Marshall cabled U.S. commanders in the Pacific, instructing them to discourage their soldiers' hobby of making necklaces from the teeth of dead Japanese and taking photographs showing the stages of removing flesh from a skull. On May 22, 1944, *Life* magazine, remarking that "the armed forces disapprove strongly of this sort of thing," published a photo of an Arizona woman gazing at a Japanese skull sent to her by her boyfriend with the inscription: "This is a good jap—a dead one picked up on the New Guinea beach."[40]

Individual acts of murder, rape, and looting have been committed by U.S. troops in every American war. The claim that the infamous massacre of hundreds of unarmed civilians on March 16, 1968, at My Lai indicated that American soldiers and units were more likely to engage in atrocities in Vietnam than American soldiers in previous wars was an illusion, produced by the relative absence of censorship during the Vietnam War. During World War II, the journalist Eric Sevareid complained that U.S. troops often shot German soldiers and Italian civilians to avoid having to provide for them. "As weeks went by and this experience was repeated many times," Sevareid wrote, "I ceased even to be surprised—only, I could never again bring myself to write or speak with indignation of the German's violations of the 'rules of warfare.'"[41] Notwithstanding such incidents, the journalist and historian Philip Knightley was "unable to find any report in the Allied press of a single atrocity committed by an Allied soldier" during World War II.[42] In the Vietnam War, by contrast, such atrocities were widely reported (but only after the public and elite had already turned against the war because of its cost). Even so, a *Time* magazine poll in May 1970 showed that a majority of Americans correctly believed that incidents such as My Lai took place in all wars.[43] Even Peter Arnett, the antiwar journalist who in 1998 falsely reported on CNN that U.S. soldiers had used nerve gas in Vietnam, admitted that during his time as a reporter during the war he never saw any U.S. soldiers murder civilians. "They didn't even think of it. Every unit I was with, [the GIs] went out of their way to be kind and decent with the people."[44]

The moral critique of U.S. military methods in Vietnam was not limited to criticism of crimes by individual soldiers. Many critics of the war claimed that the tactics used by the United States were unjust in themselves. Indeed, some American tactics can be plausibly criticized, on moral grounds. However, a dispassionate comparison of the methods used by the United States in Vietnam and comparable wars provides no support for the claim that the Vietnam War was a uniquely horrible atrocity.

The Air War in Vietnam

Operation Rolling Thunder, the campaign of bombing against North Vietnam that lasted from 1965 until 1968, focused carefully on military and industrial targets. Only eight of North Vietnam's ninety-one dikes were bombed—and these supported canals that transported military goods. Inevitably, others were hit accidentally. Almost all of the targets of U.S. bombing were remote from centers of population. One study notes that "the risks to population centers were low, Hanoi's propaganda again notwithstanding. Civilians actually became less vulnerable to attack as the war progressed."[45] The evacuation of the major cities and towns after 1965 minimized casualties.

The statistics about the amount of U.S. bombing, to be put into proper perspective, must be accompanied by mention of the the sophisticated air defense system that North Vietnam installed and operated with Soviet and Chinese help. With 250 interceptor aircraft, more than 8,000 antiaircraft guns, and 25 surface-to-air missile battalions, North Vietnam had an air defense network matched only by that of Nazi Germany in World War II.[46] Compared to North Vietnam, North Korea during the Korean War, Iraq during the Gulf War, and Serbia during the Kosovo War were practically defenseless against U.S. bombing.

More than fifty thousand North Vietnamese civilians are estimated to have died as a result of American bombing. As a percentage of population, the 0.3 percent of North Vietnam's 1965 population that was killed in the Rolling Thunder campaign was a fraction of the 3 percent of the Japanese population and the 1.6 percent of the German population killed in Allied bombing raids during World War II.

In bombing North Vietnam, the Johnson administration rejected the kind of large-scale terror bombing of civilians that had been U.S. policy not only in World War II but in the Korean War. In 1952, after interdiction bombing had failed to persuade the Chinese and North Koreans to agree to U.S./UN terms, emphasis shifted to attacks on civilian morale. In the spring and summer of 1952, the United States attacked civilian hydroelectric plants. On July 11 and 29, 1952, as part of an operation of incendiary bombing entitled "Pressure Pump," the U.S. air force dropped thousands of tons of napalm on alleged military targets. A planned operation labeled Strike, which was to have used incendiary and delayed-fuse bombs from B-52s to obliterate seventy-eight towns and villages, was halted after two towns had been incinerated because of objections from the State Department. Indeed, allies such as Britain and neutrals such as India criticized the U.S. bombing campaigns in Korea in 1952 and 1953.

New bombing aimed at civilian morale followed in May 1953, when the North Korean food supply was targeted by means of the destruction of dams. Major General Emmett O'Donnell of the Strategic Air Command wanted the United States to "go to work burning five major cities in North Korea to the ground, and to destroy completely every one of about 18 major targets." In the event, however, the United States did not carry out a policy of creating firestorms in Korean cities, as the Allies had in Japan and Germany during World War II.[47]

One of the most controversial episodes in the Vietnam War was Linebacker II—the bombing campaign against North Vietnam that Richard Nixon ordered in December 1972 to force the North Vietnamese to resume peace negotiations. Dubbed "the Christmas bombing" by antiwar journalists who sought to make it sound particularly inhumane, Linebacker II was denounced by many liberals in the press and Congress as an atrocity of Hitlerian proportions. On December 26, Tom Wicker announced that "we . . . have loosed the holocaust." On the same day, George McGovern told NBC: "It's a policy of mass murder that's being carried on in the name of the American people."[48] McGovern described Linebacker II as "the most murderous aerial bombardment in the history of the world" and "the most immoral action that this nation has ever committed in its national history."[49] Columnist Anthony Lewis claimed that Linebacker II was "a policy that many must know history will judge a crime against humanity." According to Lewis, the bombing of Hanoi was "the most terrible destruction in the history of man."[50]

Ironically, the North Vietnamese dictatorship was much more restrained in its response than American leftists and antiwar liberals. According to the Hanoi regime, 1,624 civilians died in two cities during the

Linebacker II campaign.[51] This is comparable to the upper range of the estimated Iraqi deaths that occurred during President Clinton's week-long bombing of Iraq in December 1998 (the U.S. government estimated that between six hundred and two thousand Iraqis had been killed). In contrast, almost eighty-four thousand people died in one night of U.S. bombing of Tokyo in March 1945. The contrast makes George McGovern's claim that Linebacker II was "the most murderous aerial bombardment in the history of the world" and Anthony Lewis's assertion that it was "the most terrible destruction in the history of man" seem peculiar, to say the least. Telford Taylor, a former prosecutor in the Nuremberg Trials and a critic of the Vietnam War, was present in Hanoi during the bombing. "Despite the enormous weight of bombs that were dropped," Taylor wrote, "I rapidly became convinced that we were making no effort to destroy Hanoi. The city remained largely intact and it seemed quite apparent that if there were an effort to destroy Hanoi it could have been done very readily in two or three nights."[52]

In both Operation Rolling Thunder and the Linebacker campaigns, the attempts of the United States to limit collateral damage were constrained by the technology available at the time. In the bombing of Germany and Japan, the average error ranged from thousands of feet to miles. During the Gulf War, 85 percent of the "smart bombs" landed within ten feet of their targets; the average error of laser-guided munitions was only one or two feet.[53] Thanks to this extraordinary degree of precision, the massive bombardment of Iraq during the Gulf War resulted in an estimated fifteen hundred to two thousand Iraqi civilian deaths.[54] The U.S.-led coalition shut down Iraq's oil refineries, reduced its electricity generation to 15 percent, and knocked out fifty Iraqi bridges with far fewer sorties and in far less time than had been required for similar tasks in Vietnam, Korea, and World War II.[55] Advances in both technology and tactics also permitted NATO to bomb Serbia into abandoning Kosovo. The North Vietnamese, by contrast, had state-of-the-art technology installed, and sometimes operated, by Soviet and Chinese soldiers; there were even Soviet fighter pilots who took part in the air war, shooting down American pilots. For these reasons, bombing missions against North Vietnam were far more hazardous than missions against Iraq or Serbia. During the Vietnam War, one U.S. plane was lost for every 25 sorties; during the Gulf War, the ratio was one plane for every 750 sorties.[56] The image of the "small, poor country" pounded into submission by the technological superpower is far more applicable to the Gulf War and the subsequent bombing campaigns against Iraq and Serbia by the Clinton administration than to the Vietnam War.

Pacification in South Vietnam

In South Vietnam itself, the United States and its South Vietnamese allies waged two wars—a conventional war of attrition against the Viet Cong guerrillas and their North Vietnamese allies, and what U.S. ambassador to South Vietnam Henry Cabot Lodge called "the other war" of pacification. The term "pacification" included a spectrum of activities, ranging from the provision of security to South Vietnamese villagers by U.S. and South Vietnamese military units to humanitarian and economic development activities undertaken by U.S. agencies such as USAID to U.S.-sponsored efforts to destroy the secret Viet Cong Infrastructure (VCI). The latter effort was necessary because the shadow government of the Viet Cong in the South included political as well as military cadres. The cadres recruited new troops, operated logistics networks, taxed villagers in areas that they controlled, and assassinated tens of thousands of South Vietnamese officials and ordinary citizens. Identifying and thwarting these Viet Cong cadres required a combination of intelligence and police work and military action. In May 1967, the Johnson administration united U.S. military and civilian pacification programs under the control of an agency, run by Robert W. Komer, named Civil Operations and Development Support (CORDS). CORDS supervised a CIA-sponsored program code-named "Phoenix," which had a South Vietnamese parallel, the Phung Hoan program.

The intelligence-gathering aspects of these programs were not controversial, but the "neutralization" of Viet Cong cadres was. *New York Times* reporter Tad Szulc claimed that "as many as 20,000 Viet Cong or suspected Viet Cong are believed to have been murdered under the aegis of Operation Phoenix. . . . Along with the My Lai massacre of Vietnamese civilians by American troops, Operation Phoenix unquestionably looms as one of the most degrading enterprises carried out by Americans in Vietnam."[57] The image of South Vietnamese forces assassinating great numbers of unarmed civilians is inaccurate. "To equate persons who belonged to NLF with true civilians was erroneous and discounted the violent and subversive purpose of the infrastructure," Richard A. Hunt writes in *Pacification: The American Struggle for Vietnam's Hearts and Minds* (1995). "Given the way that the [Vietnamese communist] party prosecuted the war, there was no bright, clear line differentiating the military and civilian."[58] Most of the Viet Cong infrastructure members who were killed were killed in combat. "Only in a few cases did the Allies have a realistic chance of neutralizing illegal cadres by methods not involving combat," writes historian Mark Moyar in the most thorough study of the Phoenix program. Attempts to capture armed Viet Cong cadres often turned into firefights.[59] Between January 1970 and March 1971, 9,000 of the 10,444 members of the Viet Cong infrastructure who were killed died in firefights with the military; only later were they identified. Less than 2 percent of the members of the VCI who were captured, rallied, or killed in the same period had been targeted for arrest.[60]

The fact that U.S. personnel were merely advisers to South Vietnamese military and police forces limited their ability to prevent them from engaging in murder, torture, and extortion.[61] Even so, U.S. advisers created incentives for pacification forces to capture Viet Cong personnel rather than to kill them.[62] It would be unreasonable to hold the Saigon regime to higher standards in a civil war than comparable Third World governments fighting insurgencies, such as Peru or Turkey. In the chaos of wartime, pacification efforts may not always have been discriminating enough, but they were far more discriminating than the attrition strategy that the United States and its South Vietnamese allies also employed. The war could not have been won without the identification and destruction of the secret Viet Cong political network. Indeed, after the war the communists admitted that the Phoenix program, along with military operations and the program to "rally" communists to the side of the Saigon regime, had sapped the strength of the southern insurgency and helped motivate Hanoi's switch to a conventional invasion strategy after 1968.

The War of Attrition in South Vietnam

In South Vietnam, as we have seen, the U.S. military under General Westmoreland dealt with a threat that had characteristics of both an insurgency and a conventional war by waging a predominantly conventional war of attrition between 1965 and 1968. Westmoreland's stated goal was to use massive firepower by the United States to kill Viet Cong and North Vietnamese infiltrees until a "crossover point" was reached at which deaths exceeded replacement. Claims that the attrition strategy represented genocide were nonsense; during the war, the South Vietnamese population grew twice as rapidly as the U.S. population. But the attrition approach did raise grave concerns in the minds of many observers who were by no means opposed to the Cold War in general or the Vietnam War in particular. Guenter Lewy, a friendly critic of the U.S. government, estimated that between 1965 and 1974 there were 1,160,600 civilian war casualties in South Vietnam, of which 301,000 resulted in deaths. Even conservative estimates hold that roughly half of these casualties were inflicted by U.S. and South Vietnamese units.[63]

The U.S. military used airpower as lavishly as though the war was purely conventional—and as though South Vietnam was the enemy's homeland, rather than the home of the people the United States was attempting to defend. At the peak of the war, the U.S. Air Force flew three hundred sorties a day—not against North Vietnam, but against targets in South Vietnam. There were also two hundred sorties a day by the marine air wings and a hundred by the South Vietnamese air force, not counting unplanned reaction sorties. In addition, between 1966 and 1972 helicopter gunships flew 3,592 attack sorties. A high degree of collateral damage to civilians and their property was made inevitable by the fact that air force pilots in most cases were ordered to bomb at no lower than 3,500 feet.[64] By the end of the war, the United States had dropped 13 million tons of bombs in South Vietnam itself, along with more than 400,000 tons of napalm and 11.2 million gallons of the carcinogenic herbicide Agent Orange, which is alleged to have caused significant numbers of birth defects in Vietnam as well as illnesses among many U.S. veterans. An estimated twenty-five million acres of farmland and twelve million acres of forest were destroyed. Denunciation of the attrition strategy that produced such results was not limited to the antiwar left. General Harold K. Johnson, the army chief of staff, complained that "[we] were indiscriminate in our use of firepower. . . . I think we sort of devastated the countryside."[65]

The attrition strategy was used in Korea as well as in Vietnam. During the Korean War, General James Van Fleet of the Eighth Army ordered his commanders to "expend steel and fire, not men. I want so many artillery holes that a man can step from one to the others."[66] A 1951 minority report on the Korean War by the Senate committees on armed services and foreign relations questioned the morality of such attrition tactics in Korea:

> The policy of the United States in Korea, as outlined in the testimony of the Secretary of State and the Secretary of Defense and others is that of destroying the effective core of the Communist Chinese armies by killing that government's trained soldiers, in the hope that someone will negotiate. We hold that such a policy is essentially immoral, not likely to produce either victory in Korea or an end to aggression. At the same time such a policy tends to destroy the moral stature of the United States as a leader in the family of nations.[67]

The use of attrition in the Korean and Vietnam wars was no more brutal than it had been in the various theaters of World War II. Colonel Lewis L. Millett, who fought in World War II, Korea, and Vietnam, told historian Mark Moyar that during the Second World War in Italy, "If we wanted to take a town, we'd blast it all to pieces first. . . . If there happened to be civilians there, tough."[68]

Even if the reliance on massive firepower was justified in the conventional Korean War, or in the Vietnam War after it turned into a predominantly conventional North Vietnamese invasion following the Tet offensive, it does not follow that the attrition strategy was justified in the campaign against the South Vietnamese insurgency between 1965 and 1968.

In a postwar critique, Colonel John M. Collins, chief of the Campaign Planning Group, Vietnam, in 1967–68, condemned the U.S. military for employing excessive violence against the Viet Cong guerrillas: "General Sir Gerald Templer, the British High Commissioner in Malaysia, used no air power to root out rebels in the jungles. Not one bomb was dropped. [Ramon] Magsaysay [in the Philippines] never massed artillery or napalm against hamlets held by [communist] Huks."[69] The incineration and cratering of much of the South Vietnamese countryside by airpower was effective in the narrow sense that it helped to prevent the fall of the Saigon government to the Hanoi-controlled insurgency between 1965 and 1968. But given the existence of methods of fighting an insurgency that were more humane and discriminating as well as more effective, a powerful argument can be made that the employment of such disproportionate firepower was not only counterproductive but also immoral.

Justice and the Proxy Wars in East Asia

What conclusions are to be drawn about the morality of the methods used by the United States in the Vietnam War? Johnson administration adviser John McNaughton, in a 1964 memo about U.S. Vietnam policy, stressed how important it was that the United States "emerge from the crisis without unacceptable taint from methods used."[70] A compelling case can be made that the United States was wrong for moral as well as for practical reasons to rely heavily on a strategy of attrition in South Vietnam between 1965 and 1968, when the war was a mixture of an insurgency and a conventional war. The attrition strategy was more defensible during the predominantly conventional stage of the Vietnam conflict from 1969–75.

The moral alternative to waging the Vietnam War by indiscriminate and disproportionate means, however, was waging it by more discriminate and proportionate means—not abandoning Indochina to Stalinism, to the detriment of both the peoples of Indochina and the U.S.-led alliance system. One can condemn many of the tactics used by the United States in Vietnam without condemning the war as a whole, just as one can condemn the terror bombing of civilians in Germany and Japan during World War II without arguing that the war against the Axis powers was unjust.

When the two Cold War proxy conflicts in East Asia are compared in their entirety, it is clear that the Korean War was more brutal than the Vietnam War. U.S. bombing in Korea was less discriminating. Although Soviet fighter pilots took part in combat in Korea, as they did later in Vietnam, North Korea lacked the effective air defense system that the Soviets and Chinese provided for North Vietnam. By the end of the Korean War, almost every city, town, and village in the Korean Peninsula had been damaged or destroyed. When casualties are compared, the Korean War looks even worse. An estimated three million people died in the Korean peninsula in only three years—most of them in a short time near the beginning of the conflict. By contrast, an estimated two million died in the Vietnam War during the space of a decade and a half. Seventy percent of those killed in the Korean War were civilians, compared to 45 percent in the Vietnam War.[71] The disparity between the Korean War and the Vietnam War appears even more pronounced when it is remembered that the Vietnam War was fought in three countries, while the Korean War was fought in only one.

The most concentrated, indiscriminate, hellish fighting between the two alliances in the Cold War took place, not in Indochina between 1959 and 1973, but in the Korean peninsula between 1950 and 1953. Either the American wars in both Korea and Vietnam were essentially, and not just incidentally, immoral—or neither was.

CHAPTER 8

THE GENUINE LESSONS OF
THE VIETNAM WAR

In the mid-1960s, the sound and ultimately successful Cold War grand strategy of global military containment of the communist bloc required Presidents Kennedy and Johnson to escalate the U.S. involvement in Vietnam rather than withdraw without a major effort. Any president in office at the time probably would have done so. On February 17, 1965, former president Dwight Eisenhower told President Johnson that "the U.S. has put its prestige onto the proposition of keeping SE Asia free. . . . We cannot let the Indo-Chinese peninsula go. [Eisenhower] hoped it would not be necessary to use the six to eight divisions mentioned, but if it should be necessary then so be it."[1] Similarly, any president in the 1960s probably would have led the United States to war if North Korea had invaded South Korea a second time, or if China had invaded Taiwan. In the circumstances of the Cold War, a president who abandoned any of the three fronts in Asia to the communist bloc without a major struggle would have been guilty of dereliction of his duties as commander-in-chief and leader of the worldwide American alliance system. To argue otherwise is ahistorical. If the United States today, a decade after the demise of the Soviet Union, is prepared to go to war on behalf of South Korea and possibly Taiwan as well, then it makes no sense to argue that it was irrational for the United States to defend its Indochinese protectorate at the height of the Third World War.

Once the Vietnam War is viewed in the context of the Cold War, it looks less like a tragic error than like a battle that could hardly be avoided. The Cold War was fought as a siege in Europe and as a series of duels elsewhere in the world—chiefly, in Korea and Indochina. Both the siege and the duels were necessary. Power in world politics is perceived power, and perceived power is a vector that results from perceived military capability and perceived political will. The U.S. forces stationed in West Germany and Japan demonstrated the capability of the United States to defend its most important allies. U.S. efforts on behalf of minor allies in peripheral regions such as South Korea and South Vietnam and Laos proved that the United States possessed the will to be a reliable ally. Had the United States repeatedly refused to take part in proxy-war duels with the Soviet Union, and with China during its anti-American phase, it seems likely that there would have been a dramatic pro-Soviet realignment in world politics, no matter how many missiles rusted in their silos in the American West and no matter how many U.S. troops remained stationed in West Germany.

Most of the major duels between the American bloc and the communist bloc took place in countries that were peripheral (so that proxy wars between the superpowers would be unlikely to escalate into all-out global war) and symbolic (because they were divided between communist and noncommunist states). Along with China, which was divided between the communist mainland and Nationalist Taiwan, and partitioned Korea, Vietnam was one of a handful of front-line countries. The argument that the United States should have "chosen its battles" more carefully and avoided peripheral regions in which its allies were at a disadvantage posits a false alternative. It would have been foolish for Moscow or Beijing to risk general war by attacking major U.S. allies, or to sponsor military challenges to the U.S. alliance system in places where the United States and its allies had a clear military and political advantage. The United States, then, was fated to forfeit the Cold War, or to fight in difficult conditions in battlefields that its enemies chose.

While the need to preserve a surplus of American credibility required the United States to escalate its involvement in Indochina by going to war, the need to preserve a surplus of American public support for the Cold War in its entirety required the U.S. government to avoid escalating the war in Indochina too much. Presidents Johnson and Nixon defended America's Cold War credibility, at the cost of eroding America's Cold War consensus. The high costs of the Vietnam War between 1965 and 1968 destroyed U.S. public support for an open-ended commitment to the defense of the noncommunist states of Indochina, while the additional costs of the prolonged withdrawal between 1968 and 1973 endangered public support for the Cold War on any front.

In the United States, the domestic result of the Vietnam War was a neoisolationist consensus in the 1970s. Disaffected moderate supporters of the Cold War teamed up with the permanent antiinterventionist made up of mostly northern progressive isolationists and Marx-influenced leftists. The neoisolationism of the U.S. Congress and the Carter administration in its first years permitted and encouraged the Soviet Union, with the assistance of its Vietnamese and Cuban auxiliaries, to engage in empire-building in the Third World without fear of American reprisal. The perception of rising Soviet power and American retreat inspired European appeasement of Moscow in the mid-seventies and also inspired bandwagoning with Moscow on the part of Third World states in the UN General Assembly. Only the Second Cold War of 1979–89, orchestrated in the face of significant leftist and neutralist opposition by Ronald Reagan, Margaret Thatcher, Helmut Kohl, François Mitterrand, and other western democratic leaders, reversed the pro-Soviet trend in world politics and drove the Soviet Union into bankruptcy by raising the costs of its bid for world military primacy. Far from having no affect in world politics, the U.S. defeat in Indochina inaugurated a period in which the relative power, influence, and ambition of the Soviet empire peaked.

What Should the U.S. Have Done in Indochina?

With this outline of the Vietnam War and its aftermath in mind, it is possible to speculate about an alternate American policy that might have mitigated the effects of the debacle in Indochina on both American external credibility and American internal consensus.

During the Eisenhower and Kennedy administrations, the U.S. military failed to adapt to the demands of low-intensity Cold War conflicts. The inability of the U.S. Army to deal adequately with insurgents was passed on to the South Vietnamese military, organized along American lines. "The failure and the ineffectiveness of the ARVN," marine colonel William R. Corson wrote in 1968, "is the failure of our own military establishment to understand and fashion a workable response to the challenge posed by a war of national liberation."[2] Further damage was done by the Kennedy administration's support for the coup against Diem, which gave the communists an unexpected opportunity by plunging the South Vietnamese government into chaos.

Inheriting the disastrous situation created by Eisenhower and Kennedy, Lyndon Johnson made the appropriate strategic decisions. He was right to reject withdrawal in 1964–65, because of the effects that a retreat at that moment would have had on America's global military and diplomatic reputation. He was also right to reject the phony alternative of neutralization. At the same time, Johnson was right to reject the strategic alternatives of an invasion of North Vietnam, which probably would have led to a Sino-American war, and an incursion into Laos and Cambodia, which could be deferred until the insurgency in South Vietnam was defeated. Although his basic strategic decisions were sound, Johnson, influenced by his own desire for a quick, decisive war rather than a long-term, low-intensity conflict, made a disastrous error in acceding to General Westmoreland's plan for a massive, high-tech war of attrition against the Hanoi-controlled insurgency in South Vietnam. By 1967, Johnson and his advisers belatedly began to emphasize pacification, but by then the human and financial costs of Westmoreland's conventional war tactics were spiraling out of control.

On the basis of the most persuasive critiques of U.S. military policy in Vietnam, it is possible to argue that the United States should have planned its military involvement in Vietnam in terms of three stages— inkblot, incursion, and attrition.[3] During the first stage, the United States should have concentrated on pacifying South Vietnam. The control of the Saigon regime over the country should have been extended according to the inkblot strategy, in which small U.S. and South Vietnamese units acted as a slowly expanding cordon cutting off the Viet Cong from an ever-growing number of the villages on which they depended for recruits and supplies. The big-unit war would have been limited to defending the pacification effort from large-scale Viet Cong attacks. A pacification-oriented strategy might have had the best chance for success if control over both American and South Vietnamese forces had been given to a single U.S. official in South Vietnam—preferably a Marine general experienced in low-intensity warfare, rather than an Army general such as William Westmoreland. It might have been worthwhile to try something along the lines of Marine Colonel William R. Corson's proposal in 1968 for "[m]erging and placing the [South Vietnamese] Regional and Popular forces under direct U.S. Command to form a massive

Combined Action Program with a U.S. contribution of approximately 60,000 troops."[4]

Cut off from the populous coastal region of South Vietnam, the Viet Cong and North Vietnamese infiltrators would have become more dependent on recruits and supplies from North Vietnam. In the second stage of the war, with the government in Saigon in control of most of South Vietnam's population (if not all of its territory), the United States and its allies could have afforded to launch an incursion to sever the Ho Chi Minh Trail in Laos and Cambodia and to create a demilitarized zone from the Vietnamese coast to the Thai border. With the South Vietnamese insurgents cut off from both their sources of supply, Hanoi would have had no choice but to abandon its policy or to launch a conventional invasion that would have been highly vulnerable to attrition by U.S. bombing.

If that in turn had succeeded, then, in the third stage, tens of thousands of U.S. troops had to be permanently stationed in South Vietnam, and possibly parts of Laos, Cambodia, and Thailand as well, in order to deter a conventional invasion of South Vietnam by North Vietnam. When the Johnson administration in 1965 correctly decided to escalate the U.S. military commitment to Indochina, its members should have realized that even success in the Vietnam War would have required that the United States garrison Indochina indefinitely in the way that it had garrisoned South Korea since 1953. This outcome might have required the construction, at some point, of a militarized frontier across Vietnam and the Laotian panhandle to the border of Thailand. The war to restore the control of the South Vietnamese government over its own territory therefore had to be seen as a prelude to a wider Indochinese war in which the Ho Chi Minh Trail would be severed and the North Vietnamese military sanctuaries in Laos and Cambodia would be annihilated. Any thought that the United States would be able to depart after restoring the status quo in South Vietnam in two or three years should have been dismissed as wishful thinking. This was a ten- or twenty-year project.

The United States had to do all of this within the limits of a budget in American resources and, more important, American lives. The United States needed to lose, at the most, far fewer than the fifty-six thousand soldiers it had lost in the Korean War, which had created a backlash in the United States against Cold War proxy wars for a decade—a backlash which contributed to the unwillingness of American leaders and the American public to intervene in Indochina in 1954, as well as in the early

1960s. If the three-stage approach discussed above had been followed, then most of the U.S. casualties could have been expected to occur in the second phase, in which U.S. forces based in a secured South Vietnam engaged in conventional warfare with units of North Vietnamese regulars in Cambodia and Laos. If the United States suffered too many losses in the first phase of counterinsurgency, then it would have been necessary to abandon the entire project rather than endanger public support for similar small wars on other Cold War fronts in the 1970s and 1980s. Because the United States had put up a fight on behalf of a dependent ally in a symbolic front-line state, withdrawal after failure in the first stage, although still humiliating, would have been less harmful to America's credibility than a panicked "bug-out" from Indochina in 1965 would have been. Having withdrawn, however, the United States would have needed to compensate for its defeat in the Indochina theater by increasing pressure on the Soviet empire on other fronts and in other dimensions of the superpower competition. Even as it was withdrawing from Vietnam, the United States should have launched an arms buildup, comparable to the one that began in the late Carter administration, in order to counter the growing military power of the Soviet Union. At the same time, the United States should have responded swiftly and forcefully by shows of force short of war to Soviet and Cuban intervention in Angola and Ethiopia, proving that the defeat in Indochina had not undermined America's resistance to Soviet bloc expansion elsewhere in the world. However, the ability of the United States to redouble its efforts in the Cold War in the aftermath of a reluctant forfeiture of Indochina would have depended on the existence of a reserve of public support for an anti-Soviet foreign policy—a reserve that too high an American body count in Indochina would have depleted.

The key variable in the strategic/political equation that the United States had to control was U.S. casualties. "The [South Vietnamese] people, however, were not the center of gravity of the war, as we had erroneously believed," Colonel Harry Summers has written. "The center of gravity was the North Vietnamese Army."[5] To the contrary, the center of gravity in the Vietnam War was neither the South Vietnamese population nor the North Vietnamese Army but American public opinion. The Johnson administration's major error was to acquiesce in General Westmoreland's attrition-oriented strategy, which led to greater losses in American life than an alternate strategy emphasizing pacification might have done.

And the major mistake of the Nixon administration was to pursue a prolonged withdrawal of U.S. combat forces from Vietnam that resulted in an additional twenty-one thousand American deaths in the war zone.

"For want of a nail, the shoe was lost; for want of a shoe, the horse was lost; for want of a horse, the rider was lost; for want of a rider, the battle was lost." The chain-reaction dynamic illustrated by this proverb is illustrated as well by the disastrous chain of events in U.S. domestic politics and foreign policy that followed from America's misconceived military strategy in Vietnam. The cause of the dangerous pro-Soviet bandwagoning in world politics in the 1970s was the impressive expansion of the Soviet bloc. The precondition for successful Soviet bloc expansion in the 1970s was the neoisolationist consensus in U.S. domestic politics. The neoisolationist consensus, in turn, was a response to the costs of the war in Vietnam. And the costs of the war in Vietnam were greater than they need have been because of General Westmoreland's misguided decision to wage an expensive war of attrition to defeat what before 1968 was primarily, though not exclusively, an externally controlled insurgency in South Vietnam. For want of appropriate military tactics, the First Cold War was forfeited by the United States.

Flexible Response Reconsidered: The Tactical Lesson of Vietnam

If this analysis is correct, then the chief lesson of the Vietnam War is this: Military tactics must be tailored to fit both a nation's overall geopolitical grand strategy and the nation's political culture—in particular, its willingness to accept losses in battle.

The fact that different military strategies suit different countries is illustrated by the Cold War. The major changes in the Cold War were brought about not by decisions on the battlefield but by the effects of the military competition on the domestic societies of the two superpowers. A country can be defeated by the degradation of its will or of its capability to fight. The United States forfeited the First Cold War in the late 1960s and early 1970s, even though its military and economic capability were intact and formidable, because of a collapse of political will caused by the high number of U.S. casualties in the Vietnam War. The Soviet Union forfeited the Second Cold War in the mid-1980s, despite its intact political system and the will to power of its leaders, because of a collapse of military and economic capability—a collapse exacerbated by the costs that the Second Cold War imposed on Moscow's attempts to hold its own in sieges such as the arms race in Europe and duels such as the Afghan War.

The strength of the United States was economic; its weakness was political and cultural. Its people were willing to spend treasure but not blood. The strength of the Soviet Union was political; its weakness was economic. The Leninist political system, based on the monopolization of all sources of power, wealth, and prestige by a single elite, was much stronger and more enduring than most political orders, but its socialist economy could not bear the strains of a high level of military competition with the American bloc. Each superpower achieved its greatest victory when it took advantage of its adversary's weakness. By enabling the North Vietnamese to bleed the United States in combat, the Soviet Union knocked the United States out of the First Cold War. The United States, in turn, knocked the Soviet Union out of the Second Cold War by using American and western industry in arms races and proxy wars to drive the Soviet economy into bankruptcy. If the United States had learned to wage proxy wars such as the Vietnam War with relatively low American casualty rates, then American public support for the Cold War might not have temporarily collapsed, whether or not the United States had ultimately succeeded or failed in Indochina. The United States would have possessed the means to defend most if not all of its weak allies and at the same time to blunt the initiatives of Soviet proxies in the Third World, while concentrating on America's strength—the large-scale industrial production of high-quality conventional and nuclear arms. Conversely, if the Soviet Union had abandoned its costly effort to match the United States in high-tech armaments and had concentrated on its own comparative advantage in aiding proxies engaged in low-intensity conflict, then the Soviet Union might have survived and even prevailed in the Second Cold War. The most cost-effective elements of Soviet foreign policy were its military and economic support to clients such as the Vietnamese and Cuban communists, who provided mercenaries for the empire. The least cost-effective Soviet military assets were nuclear missiles and Warsaw Pact tanks.

The lesson that aspiring challengers in the future, if they are relatively poor like the Soviet Union, should learn from the Soviet failure is that the expansion of influence by support for proxy wars in key peripheral regions makes more sense than the suicidal attempt to win arms races with rich industrial countries. In this respect, Mao and other theorists of "people's war" have been vindicated, and Brezhnev and his successors have been proven wrong. And the lesson of the American failure in Vietnam is that the United States, whether it is the hegemonic global power or merely one of several great powers, must learn how to help its allies prevail in low-intensity civil wars and interstate wars without testing the culturally imposed limits of American public tolerance for American casualties.

The United States needs small, well-trained, highly professional armed forces that are willing and able to police the violent frontiers of the American alliance system. Unfortunately, from the 1950s until the present, repeated efforts by reformers in and outside of the military have failed to shake the hold of orthodox conventional war doctrines on the armed services, with the partial exception of the marines. Although light-infantry formations are most appropriate for the kinds of low-intensity conflicts in which the United States is likely to take part in the near future, the United States Army today has even fewer light-infantry formations, compared to armored and mechanized divisions, than it did during the Cold War.[6] Instead of focusing on the strategies and weapons appropriate for low-intensity conflicts in the Somalias, Haitis, Bosnias, and Kosovos of tomorrow, all too many military thinkers and civilian national security analysts are devising high-tech gimmicks for the very kind of all-out conventional wars that are unlikely to be fought. As in the 1950s, when the U.S. Army fantasized about armored operations on postnuclear battlefields instead of studying counterinsurgency tactics, visions of large-scale conventional war in a science-fiction future created by the "Revolution in Military Affairs" (RMA) are driving out more realistic but less glamorous scenarios for conflict in Third World slums and countrysides.

Ironically, the RMA may transform conventional war while leaving unconventional warfare more or less the same. The development and spread of "smart" precision-guided munitions, which have proven their value in the Gulf War and in the Clinton administration's attacks against suspected terrorists in Afghanistan, may soon render crewed weapons platforms such as tanks and bombers vulnerable and therefore obsolete. The result of the interaction of high-tech deterrence and low-intensity conflict might be a pattern of conflict reminiscent of the Cold War, with its proxy wars, or perhaps of the chessboard wars of eighteenth-century Europe. While engaged in a high-tech standoff at sea, in the air and perhaps in space, the great military powers would fight limited proxy wars in countries shattered by civil war, injecting small, highly professional forces of volunteers or draftees and pulling them out when the costs grew too high. In contrast to the era of mass wars that began with Napoleon and culminated in World War II, neither the publics nor the economies of the major countries would need to be mobilized to support the small wars being fought in marginal regions of the globe (this fate would be denied the hapless denizens of the countries in which the great powers tested one another's strength and determination).

A world in which Orwellian blocs forever measure one another's determination in proxy wars is unappealing to American soldiers and the American public alike. Americans want "real" wars like World War II and the Gulf War, not limited wars like Korea and Vietnam. They want American soldiers to be sent into battle, if at all, to take territory, not to prop up weak and tyrannical regimes threatened by civil war, in order to signal American resolve in great-power showdowns. Americans prefer to fight in temperate countries, preferably countries with sanitary and familiar food and drink, or at least in deserts where they can see the enemy coming from a distance. They want world wars to end with the enemy capital in smoking ruins under U.S. military administration, not in a seismic shift of allegiances on the part of governments that leaves the world superficially looking much the same as it did before. Above all, Americans do not like quagmires like the half-century conflict in Indochina.

Unfortunately, if the characteristics of a quagmire are low-intensity conflict, political chaos, and moral ambiguity, then avoiding quagmires means avoiding intervention in most wars in which the world-order interests of the United States and its allies are likely to be at stake in the twenty-first century. And avoiding those wars means sooner or later ceding world leadership to a nation, liberal or (more likely) illiberal, whose political culture does not paralyze its military policy. If the United States is to continue to be the dominant world power, or even one of several great military powers, then American soldiers must learn to swim in quagmires.

The Strategic Lesson of Vietnam: A Favorable Imbalance of Power

In addition to vindicating the advocates of flexible response, history has vindicated the maximal realists of the Cold War era—and discredited the minimal realists who argued that the United States could safely retreat behind an imaginary line encircling North America, Western Europe, and Japan. In light of what we know now about the Cold War, many of the prescriptions for U.S. strategy by leading minimal realists such as George Kennan, Walter Lippmann, and George Ball appear to have been extremely unwise. It would have been disastrous if the U.S. government had followed Walter Lippmann's advice in the early Cold War to break Germany up into small states and neutralize Central Europe; or Kennan's advice in the 1970s to limit its military commitments to Western Europe and Japan; or George Ball's advice, also in the 1970s, that the United States could blithely ignore Soviet and Cuban efforts to bring allies to power in the Caribbean and Central America.

The end of the Cold War produced the outcome predicted by maximal realism—worldwide bandwagoning with the United States—not balancing against the United States, the outcome predicted by minimal realism. The victory of the United States in the Gulf War produced an equally striking example of bandwagoning, as the governments of the region, with the exceptions of Iraq, Iran, and Libya, bandwagoned with Washington out of a mixture of respect for American military might and fear of American wrath. When these examples of bandwagoning are considered along with the bandwagon effect that made Hitler master of Europe and almost master of the world, it is no longer possible to deny that maximal realism has been confirmed as a rough description of the way the world really works. Nor is it possible any longer to argue that U.S. Cold War policymakers were misled by "the Lesson of Munich." If that lesson is defined as the danger that adversaries will interpret restraint as a sign of lack of capability or will or both, then the Lesson of Munich receives much confirmation from the history of the Cold War. Stalin probably would not have authorized the North Korean invasion of South Korea if he had expected the United States to intervene; and Mao might not have encouraged and supported the subversion of South Vietnam by North Vietnam if he had not believed that the United States was bluffing about going to war in Vietnam. The concern of the "Munich" generation of U.S. policymakers that the appearance of weakness could encourage assertiveness by enemies and make war necessary in response was grounded in an understanding of world politics far superior to that of their minimal-realist critics in the professoriate and the press.

If minimal realism is discredited, then so are proposed grand strategies for the United States after the Cold War that are justified by minimal-realist logic. One such grand strategy is complete U.S. isolationism.

Another is a global balance-of-power strategy in which the United States would play the role of "offshore balancer," ending its military alliances with Europe and Japan and South Korea, while remaining determined to intervene to tip the balance should the equivalent of Hitler or Stalin threaten to achieve hegemony in Europe or Asia. Minimal realists who advocate this American strategy repeat the mistake made by their precursors in the "solvency school" and "world-order liberal" school of the 1970s, who wrongly predicted the emergence in the 1980s and 1990s of a multipolar world with a Japanese superpower and a militarily independent Western Europe. The mistake then and now has been to assume that the pattern of world politics must resemble an idealized version of the balance-of-power system that existed in Europe for only a brief time in historical terms.

The maximal realist understanding of world politics is much more accurate. In this view, the "typical" international order is a hierarchical order, in which the entire system is dominated by a single military power—a hegemon, empire, or bloc—and in which lesser states adapt by specializing in particular functions. The specialization of states in a hegemonic order works in favor of the hegemon, inasmuch as it ensures that not all potential challengers will actually undertake a bid for hegemony. The United States before 1945 did not plot to destroy the British position in the world, and present-day Germany and Japan are likely to continue to specialize as civilian commercial powers as long as they are confident of American military protection.

A hegemonic power can lose its position at the top of a regional or global hierarchy in one of two ways. The dominant state can be replaced gradually, as a result of the slow diffusion of military power and economic capability to another state or states, or it can be displaced abruptly against its will, by a hegemonic challenger. Germany, under the kaiser and Hitler, sought to forcibly displace Britain as the dominant world power; after the United States, with Britain's consent, replaced Britain, the Soviet Union sought to displace the United States.

History reveals that hegemonic displacers have been more common than hegemonic replacers. Among the most militarily powerful nations of history, the majority have been half-civilized, warlike peoples who specialized in borrowing the military technology of wealthier but weaker nations, in order to subjugate them or intimidate them into appeasement. Examples include the ancient Chinese state of Ch'in, the Mace-

donian monarchy, the Romans, the Arabs, the Ottoman Turks, the Spanish, and the Russians. Only a minority of leading powers have been both
economically advanced and powerful, such as the Athenians, the Vene-
tians, the Dutch, the British, the French, the Germans, and the Americans. In the generations to come, the premodern dichotomy between
large, poor, powerful, and militaristic empires and tiny, rich, weak city-
states may reemerge in the form of a dichotomy between huge and well-
armed but relatively poor countries, such as China and India, and
medium-sized or small rich nation-states, such as Japan and the countries of Europe, including postimperial Russia, which has only slightly
more people than Japan. The United States, with a population estimated
to grow to between three hundred and six hundred million in the next
century, will be the only advanced industrial democracy that also has a
continental scale and a population comparable to that of semi-developed
giant nations such as China and India.

The tendency toward bandwagoning in world politics means that it is
possible for a nation with only a fraction of the world's resources and
population to dominate the world. It is not necessary to be all-powerful
in order to be most powerful. It is necessary only to dominate one of the
world's industrial regions, while pitting the other industrial centers
against one another. And the nation that is best situated to dominate one
of the regional centers of the world economy is not necessarily the economic leader of that region, such as Japan in East Asia or Germany in
Europe. A well-armed, relatively poor nation such as China, India, or
Russia may be able to intimidate more advanced states from a secure location on the geographic periphery, facing only weak, backward neighbors on its other flanks.

In combining population and scale with moderate but not desperate
poverty, future hegemonic challengers may resemble the Soviet Union.
Future aspirants to global hegemony, however, are unlikely to repeat the
mistakes of the Soviet leadership. For one thing, their leaders are likely
to derive their legitimacy from nationalism, or from secular ideologies or
supernatural religions that do not commit them to a particular set of
economic arrangements that can be discredited by poor performance. In
addition to sacrificing their economy to their ideology, the Soviets were
remarkably maladroit when it came to alliance diplomacy. By the time of
the Second Cold War of 1979–89, the Soviet Union found itself without
any great power allies. A revisionist challenger with powerful allies might

present the United States and its allies with an even greater threat than the Soviet bloc did. Furthermore, a hegemonic challenger determined to avoid repeating Moscow's mistakes would be wise to avoid competing in the realm of high-tech armaments in which the United States has a comparative advantage. The Soviet empire was bankrupted by the arms race, not by overextension in the Third World, where Soviet efforts were cost-effective and frequently quite successful.

Finally, a future hegemonic rival would be wise to challenge American military primacy without threatening the global economic order over which the United States presides. The Soviet Union was unique in being both a revisionist great power, that is, one concerned with revising the global distribution of power and prestige in its favor, and a revolutionary great power, the holy land of a messianic political religion with adherents in many countries, including many of the states opposed to it such as the United States. In the foreseeable future, however, it seems likely that revision and revolution, which were united in Soviet imperialism, will have different addresses. A rival great-power, or great-power coalition, that seeks to displace the United States at the apex of the global power hierarchy in the twenty-first century might find the task much easier if its leaders promised to respect the values and institutions of the nations that now find shelter under the American security umbrella. For example, a moderate, authoritarian China that accepts the international economic order and respects the constitutions and borders of other countries would be more successful in challenging American primacy in the Asia-Pacific region and perhaps in the world than a neo-Maoist China frightening other countries with radical rhetoric. To minimize this danger, the United States should define its global role as the provision of public goods such as freedom of the seas and the lender of last resort in an integrated global economy (which can come in liberal as well as conservative versions). Beyond insisting on a minimum of legality and morality, the United States should not try to dictate the political or economic arrangements of other countries. American hegemony is more likely to be accepted by other nations if the United States acts as the global village's sheriff and not as its preacher.

The desire of a revisionist power to avoid sharing the spoils of victory should lead it to gain as many allies as necessary to win—and no more. The logic governing defense of a given international order by a hegemonic power such as the United States is quite different. "For obvious reasons," the political scientist Randall Schweller writes, "large, overpowering alliances best serve the purposes of deterrence and defense against would-be aggressors. The larger the alliance, the less likely the status quo will be challenged and the less cost to each member of balancing the threat."[7] This observation indicates the fallacy underlying the argument that there could never have been a genuine Soviet threat because the United States always had more allies than the Soviet Union. The United States, as the incumbent hegemon defending the international order, *needed* far more allies than the Soviet Union, the revisionist challenger.

American global military primacy will not last forever; for that matter, neither will the United States. But U.S. military hegemony might be prolonged for decades, if not generations, even if some other entity such as the European Union were to surpass the United States in overall economic leverage. The United States should pursue, not a balance-of-power policy, but an *imbalance-of-power* policy. Washington should seek to replace its outmoded Cold War alliance system with a new hegemonic "concert" or peacetime bloc. The more overwhelming the power controlled by the American-led concert, the more effectively potential challengers will be deterred from seeking to change the international status quo without the consent of the United States and its major allies. As we have seen, the assertion that such a policy will "inevitably" or "automatically" lead the states of the world to band together against American hegemony is based on a misreading of early modern European diplomatic history.

Even if the United States were a medium power like Britain or France or a minor power like Australia or Canada, it would need to be concerned about its military credibility in the interest of proving its *Bündnisfähigkeit* or "alliance-worthiness." As the hegemonic leader of a global concert, the United States must be especially concerned about its reputation for power plus determination. However, in a unipolar world centered on an American-led concert, U.S. credibility is not as important as it was in the bipolar world order of the Cold War. During the Cold War, every loss by the United States was the geopolitical gain of the Soviet Union, if only indirectly. In the absence of a challenger comparable to the Soviet Union, however, the United States can carry out retreats or suffer defeats in peripheral areas with consequences somewhat less severe than those that would have followed from similar setbacks between 1946 and 1991.

The Domestic Politics of American Foreign Policy

The military lesson of Vietnam, then, is the continuing importance of a military tailored for flexible response, while the strategic lesson of the Cold War as a whole is the desirability of an imbalance of power policy that preserves U.S. global military and diplomatic primacy and deters potential hegemonic challengers. If the Vietnam War holds a lesson for domestic politics, it is the importance of preserving American public support for both grand strategy and military tactics.

The difficulty of creating and maintaining a public consensus in favor of a grand strategy of U.S. global military primacy is exacerbated by the deep divisions over all things military in the American body politic. These divisions are less partisan or ideological than they are regional and cultural. The most important and most enduring is the regional division between the antimilitary, antiinterventionist old-stock whites of Greater New England and the promilitary, interventionist white southerners. The contrast between the abhorrence of the military by the former and the martial values of the latter is paralleled by the gap between northern and southern attitudes toward the death penalty, gun control, and the legitimacy of violence in response to insults.

Will the dichotomy of northern doves and southern hawks endure into the twenty-first century? There is no reason to believe that the regional divide in attitudes toward American foreign policy will diminish any time soon. The melting away of regional subcultures has been announced frequently, but it has not yet occurred, and it may not occur. The geographic mobility of Americans may actually reinforce regional subcultures by encouraging a voluntary partition, with liberal southerners moving to the North and conservative northerners fleeing Boston or New York for the more congenial environment of Atlanta or Dallas.

The division between socially liberal, antiinterventionist and antimilitary northerners and socially conservative, interventionist, and promilitary southerners is as old as the American republic. This divide manifested itself throughout the period of New Deal Democratic hegemony, when both camps had representatives in both parties. Since the 1960s, the two national parties in the United States have become more internally coherent and regionally polarized than at any time since the 1920s. For the foreseeable future, therefore, the pattern of the past generation will probably persist. The Republicans, with their new base in the South, will be identified with a strong military and an assertive U.S. defense policy; the Democrats, dominated by Greater New England, will be more likely to favor defense cutbacks and a minimal or isolationist foreign policy.

In the long run, demography may favor the southern coalition. The core constituencies of the Democrats in the white population—Greater New England Protestants and Jews—have low birth rates. Northeastern states lose congressional seats to the South and West with every census. Blacks, the most loyal Democratic voting bloc, will soon be outnumbered by Latinos, whose long-term loyalty to the northern Democratic coalition is far from certain. Indeed, it is possible that many if not most assimilated Mexican-Americans will find southern traditionalism more familiar and attractive than the values of the post-Puritan North.

The enduring regional divisions will be reflected in institutions as well as parties. The southerners who are disproportionately represented in the leadership of the U.S. military and the Republican party leadership will tend to have a radically different view of the proper goals and instruments of U.S. foreign policy than the antimilitary, isolationist northerners who are overrepresented in the prestige media and the universities and the Democratic party. The breakdown of the largely northeastern bipartisan foreign policy establishment in the 1960s and 1970s has led to the formation of rival Democratic and Republican foreign policy elites. If these rival elites, over time, recruit from different regional populations, then profound cultural and moral differences may come to separate southern and western hawks from northern and eastern doves. Such polarization is bad for the United States and its allies for several reasons. If changes in party control of the federal government can result in dramatically different foreign policies, then the reliability and stability of the United States as an ally will be thrown into question. And the capture of different branches of the U.S. government by parties with incompatible conceptions of the national interest is a recipe for paralysis.

Public policy can do little to alter the enduring regional subcultures in the United States, but a few institutional reforms might reduce the direct translation of regional differences into political rivalries. The overrepresentation of the radical and liberal left in the academic and media elite might be corrected by outreach efforts designed to ensure that Americans with centrist and conservative views are represented in substantial numbers among the editors and journalists of prestige publications and on the faculty of elite universities. A conscious effort by the Republicans and Democrats to represent all regions in their parties would benefit both the parties and the country as a whole. The adoption of proportional representation for House elections, by making it easier for northern conservatives and southern liberals to elect representatives, would weaken the solid conservative South and the solid liberal North and tend to detach ideological liberalism and conservatism from regional identity. The reinstatement of a draft, if necessary for other reasons, might have the added advantage of diluting the overrepresentation of southern conservative Republicans in the U.S. military. In Congress, the traditional division between the foreign relations committees (often dominated by northerners) and the armed services committees (usually dominated by southerners) might be overcome by merging these in a single "foreign policy" or "national security" committee in each House. In addition, the overrepresentation of antiinterventionist, antimilitary Greater New Englanders in the malapportioned U.S. Senate could be neutralized by merging House and Senate foreign policy committees in a single joint foreign policy committee—a reform that would also strengthen the leverage of Congress as a whole in its dealings with the presidency.

These reforms are not likely. In their absence, it seems almost certain that the next major U.S. national security crisis will once again pit hawks based in the military and Congress and the southern and southwestern states against doves who find their strongest institutional support in the media and the academy and their strongest geographic support in states such as Massachussetts, Wisconsin and Oregon.

Limited Wars and the Constitution

From the experience of the Vietnam War, the left and the right drew contradictory lessons about constitutional procedures for making U.S. foreign policy. The liberal lesson is that Congress should reduce the president's discretion to use force abroad. The conservative lesson is that once a war has begun, the president and his civilian advisers should not question the judgments of the military. Each of these "lessons of Vietnam" is based on a misreading of the history of the Vietnam War.

The President and Congress Liberal efforts to reduce the foreign policy discretion of the president, to the extent that they have been more than a reflection of northern isolationism, have been inspired by the myth that the Vietnam War was an unconstitutional, undeclared war. As I have demonstrated, Congress explicitly authorized the Vietnam War in 1964 with the Southeast Asia Resolution, a constitutional conditional declaration of war. An informed debate should focus on the relative merits of conditional declarations and general declarations of war. In most cases in which the United States is not under attack, a conditional declaration of war can provide a chance to avoid hostilities. A conditional declaration gives the president authority to wage war, without requiring him to do so if the enemy accedes to U.S. diplomatic demands. By contrast, a straightforward general declaration of war would be an embarrassment, if it were not followed by large-scale military operations.

Under a conditional declaration of war, the president should have discretion to initiate and end hostilities. This means rejecting the argument made by former defense secretary Robert McNamara, legal scholar John Hart Ely, and others that Presidents Johnson and Nixon should have returned to Congress for supplementary grants of authority for each major campaign in Vietnam, including the incursions into Laos and Cambodia. Was Franklin Roosevelt guilty of violating the Constitution because he did not obtain separate congressional authorization for the North Africa campaign, the Italian campaign, and the Normandy invasion during World War II? Would he have been guilty of an impeachable offense if he had bombed Nazi troops crossing neutral Sweden? Congress must retain the ability to end a war by repealing a conditional declaration or general declaration. But it cannot and should not insist on a separate vote for each military campaign in a single war.

To be effective in providing the president with leverage in negotiating from strength, a conditional declaration of war must not be undercut by the statements or actions of a majority in Congress. U.S. credibility will collapse in situations like the one in the 1970s, in which the president is more hawkish than Congress. In a "good cop, bad cop" routine, Congress should play the "bad cop" to the president's "good cop."

Since the Vietnam War, many conservatives have emphasized the need for general declarations of war, because they think that it was a political mistake to refrain from mobilizing the American population for the war in advance. This neglects the fact that a general declaration of war need not automatically lead to the mobilization of the reserves, the freezing of enemy assets, and other measures. At any rate, the avoidance of all-out mobilization during the Vietnam War *was not a mistake*. The Johnson administration had good reason to fear that stirring up war fever in the United States would make it far more difficult to keep the limited war for Indochina limited. Indeed, *the Vietnam War was not limited enough;* what the situation required was a long-term, low-cost, low-intensity war, which might have gone on for a decade or more before evolving into a conventional war, if it ever did. If such a low-level war is necessary, it would be disastrous to create a degree of popular tension that cannot be sustained and that provokes demands for premature escalation or premature exit.

Edward Luttwak has suggested a revival of the approach to war of eighteenth-century Europe, in which "most wars were fought for much less than imperative purposes that rarely evoked popular enthusiasm, with prudent strategies and tactics to conserve professional forces."[8] The customs of the era of mass armies between 1789 and 1989 are irrelevant. The soldiers of the future, whether they are professionals or conscripts, should be thought of as the equivalent of firemen. We have parades for firemen now and then, but we do not have a parade every time they put out a fire.

The Commander-in-Chief and the Military   The main "lesson" that conservatives have learned from the Vietnam debacle is that once a war begins civilian leaders should defer to the judgment of military commanders without question. This "lesson of Vietnam" is based upon the idea that the Vietnam War could have been won quickly and decisively if the Johnson administration had not imposed limits on the bombing of North Vietnam, ruled out early incursions into Laos and Cambodia, and ruled out an invasion of North Vietnam. As I demonstrated in Chapter 3, the constraints that the Johnson administration imposed did not cause the United States to lose the Vietnam War, while they might have prevented a far more disastrous Sino-American war. The problem was a strategy devised chiefly by the military that was inadequate to the challenge presented by the peculiar mixture of insurgency and conventional war in South Vietnam. Indeed, throughout the Cold War, civilian national security experts and dissidents within the military often showed a deeper understanding of strategic imperatives and even tactics than did orthodox military strategists focused on refighting World War II with the Red Army in Central Europe.

Presidents have a duty to overrule their military advisers in some cases. "Had Lincoln followed the advice of his senior military advisers there is a good chance that the Union would have fallen," Eliot A. Cohen has written. "Had Roosevelt deferred to General George C. Marshall and Admiral Ernest J. King there might well have been a gory debacle on the shores of France in 1943. Had Harry S. Truman heeded the advice of his theater commander in the Far East (and it should be remembered that the Joint Chiefs generally counseled support of the man on the spot) there might have been a third world war."[9] John F. Kennedy was right to question the judgment of top military officers who insisted that the United States had to consider using nuclear weapons if it chose to intervene in Laos. Lyndon Johnson was right to complain that more bombing appeared to be the military's preferred solution to every challenge.

Censorship and Treason　Conservatives are on stronger ground when they support wartime censorship of the media. According to radical libertarians, censorship of the press during wartime is impermissible. In the United States, however, cameras and reporters are not permitted into police interrogation rooms, jury rooms, many court rooms, and hospital operating rooms; why should they be permitted into war zones? News management and propaganda are an essential aspect of warfare, because each side seeks to maintain the morale of its people while demoralizing the enemy public. Secrecy is also important. Other governments will not trust the U.S. government if their leaders fear that their secrets will be publicized by sensationalistic, for-profit media conglomerates.

Nor does wartime censorship violate the ideals of American liberal democracy. The United States is a representative democracy, not a direct or plebiscitary democracy. The American people vote for representatives whom they trust to make decisions on their behalf—decisions that, in some cases, should be made secretly. The voters can judge their representatives on the basis of the results they achieve in foreign policy; they do not need to know the details of foreign policy, to which only a tiny and unrepresentative minority of the public pays attention in any case. As the economist Joseph Schumpeter once observed, "Normally, the great political questions take their place in the psychic economy of the typical citizen with those leisure-hour interests that have not attained the rank of hobbies and with the subjects of irresponsible conversation."[10]

In some cases, of course, too much secrecy can backfire. Senator

Daniel Patrick Moynihan has argued that the attempts of the federal government to hide the degree of Soviet espionage in the United States in the 1930s and 1940s only encouraged conspiracy theories and demagogues such as Senator Joe McCarthy.[11] A case can be made that the Johnson and Nixon administrations should have revealed the extent of Chinese and Soviet participation in the Vietnam War to discredit central claims of the antiwar movement. At the price of compromising FBI penetration of the Communist Party USA, the government might have revealed what it knew about Soviet control and funding of this major institution of the American radical left while the Cold War was still raging, rather than waiting until the conflict was over. But such decisions are, and should be, political judgments.

If the government is justified in imposing censorship in wartime and punishing the publication of classified material during and after a war, then it is certainly justified in prosecuting American citizens whose actions bring them under the constitutional prohibition of providing "aid and comfort to the enemy." An administration may decide for political reasons that prosecuting traitors whose actions do little or no harm would have no effect except to make the U.S. government look like a bully. On the other hand, ordinary people assume that if behavior is tolerated by law then it must not be very bad. If it is legitimate to jail an American citizen for refusing to answer questions before a grand jury, it is difficult to understand why the government should refrain from prosecuting an American citizen who, during wartime, collaborates with an enemy regime killing or torturing American soldiers. If the interests of the American republic are worth defending from enemies without, they are worth defending from enemies within.

In conclusion, then, the twenty-first century United States should reject the anachronistic balance-of-power panaceas of the minimal realists. Instead, the United States should pursue an imbalance-of-power strategy promoting American global military primacy by means of flexible response. To this end, the United States should improve its capabilities to engage in unconventional, low-intensity conflict in wars, including civil wars, in cases where the outcome is important for American global strategy. For the foreseeable future, political support for such a strategy of American global primacy will probably require reliance on southern and western representatives and senators in the U.S. Congress (in domestic policy, other alliances may be preferable).

Finally, a new modus vivendi needs to be worked out between Congress and the president, to avoid both congressionally mandated isolationism, like that of the 1930s and 1970s, and presidential warmaking like that of Harry Truman and Bill Clinton. Conditional declarations of war like the Southeast Asia Resolution and its predecessors, the Formosa and Middle East Resolutions, can give the president leverage in coercive diplomacy by authorizing him to wage war without requiring him to do so. The president must have the authority to commit U.S. advisers and troops to low-intensity conflicts for years without being pressured into hasty escalation or retreat by mobilization of the reserves and the economy. Properly understood, the Vietnam experience illustrates the danger not of presidential tyranny, but of a rigid military unable to adapt to the demands of American grand strategy, and of a Congress too easily panicked into isolationism.

Kosovo and the Lessons of Vietnam

The war against Serbia launched by the United States and its NATO allies in March 1999 demonstrated the failure of the Clinton administration to understand most of the genuine lessons of Vietnam. The tragedy was tinged with irony, because Clinton, who had denounced the Vietnam War, avoided the draft, and campaigned for the antiwar candidacy of George McGovern in 1972, found himself forced to choose between options almost as bad as those faced by his predecessors John F. Kennedy, Lyndon Johnson, and Richard Nixon.

The Yugoslav War could be justified as part of a post–Cold War American grand strategy of preserving an imbalance of power in favor of the United States and its allies. The Clinton administration's decision to expand NATO and then to employ it to impose a preferred order on a region outside the boundaries of the NATO countries might be defended as part of an effort to turn NATO from an anti-Soviet alliance into the nucleus of a great-power concert led by the United States. Objections to this strategy could be raised by those who believe that Russia, or China, or both, should participate in a hegemonic concert of great powers. Even so, the conversion of NATO into an instrument of indefinite U.S. military hegemony in Europe and the surrounding regions was one legitimate way that the United States could promote a favorable imbalance of power. What is more, it was reasonable to argue that the United States would lose much of its credibility, both as the hegemonic power of Europe and as the leading power in the world, if it refused to intervene in the wars of the Yugoslav succession in order to shape a Balkan order favorable to the interests of America's allies and clients in the region. The United States and its allies might have avoided giving Milosevic an ultimatum with respect to his treatment of Kosovo; but once the ultimatum had been delivered, the United States could not back down without a significant loss of credibility that would have affected its standing not only in Europe but around the world.

Although American military intervention in the Balkans could be justified in terms of post–Cold War U.S. grand strategy, the Clinton administration's policy in the Kosovo crisis reflected a failure to learn the tactical and political lessons of Vietnam—or rather, to learn the wrong lessons. With respect to tactics, the United States should have deployed ground troops to Serbia's borders in an effort to deter the Serbs from emptying Kosovo by ethnic cleansing or, if deterrence failed, to invade Kosovo to protect the ethnic Albanians. Instead President Clinton, in what may be the single greatest act of incompetence ever committed by an American commander-in-chief, publicly ruled out the use of ground troops not once but repeatedly. This permitted the Serbs to engage in the most brutal campaign of ethnic cleansing that Europe had seen since the aftermath of World War II. Even as NATO bombs and missiles rained with little effect on Yugoslavia, Serb military, police, and paramilitary forces used terror in the form of mass executions and mass rapes to force hundreds of thousands of Kosovar civilians to flee into neighboring countries. The mismatch between U.S. goals and U.S. military tactics was even greater in the Balkans than it had been in Vietnam. In both cases, a reluctance to commit U.S. ground troops who might be killed and wounded in large numbers led U.S. officials to hope that an air war would force an offending regime to submit to the demands of the United States and its regional allies.

Clinton's domestic political tactics were as misguided as the military tactics he approved. Unlike Johnson and Bush, Clinton did not seek congressional authorization of the war in advance. Instead, he followed the example of Harry Truman and claimed that authorization of the war by an international organization—in this case, NATO—made a congressional declaration of war unnecessary. The result was a humiliating defeat for the president, when a measure to endorse the war failed in the House of Representatives on April 28, 1999. By failing to mobilize congressional support Clinton created what, from the point of view of U.S. diplomacy, is the worst of all possible situations—as in the early 1970s—in which a hostile and reluctant Congress undercuts the prosecution of a war by a president. Fortunately, the capitulation of Serbia averted what might have been a disaster for the United States.

Clinton may have been correct, though, in fearing that the American public would not have supported a ground war in Yugoslavia in which significant numbers of American soldiers were killed. This fear of provoking a backlash by the voters in the United States and the other NATO countries produced a perverse and grotesque spectacle: While thousands, perhaps tens of thousands, of the people whom the United States was allegedly trying to protect were being murdered or were dying of sickness or starvation, the first priority of the United States and other NATO countries was the safety of their own soldiers. Arguably, Clinton and other American leaders have learned the wrong lesson about public attitudes from the Vietnam War. The right lesson is that there is a limit to the number of American casualties that the U.S. public will tolerate. It does not follow from this lesson that preserving public support for a war means ensuring that no Americans soldiers at all are killed in combat.

On the other hand, it is by no means clear that the United States is still capable of fighting wars more serious than the Gulf War, in which only 148 American military personnel died. Since the late 1970s, the U.S. public has tended to support extensive U.S. geopolitical commitments without being willing to pay a significant price in the lives of American soldiers—even professional soldiers. It seems unlikely, though, that a nation can maintain its position at the top of the world power hierarchy indefinitely merely by means of deterrent forces, subsidies to allies, peacekeeping deployments, and the occasional missile strike.

Perhaps the greatest weapon in the arsenal of American pacifists, leftists, and isolationists is the claim that a world-order strategy based on a system of American protectorates and alliances squanders the lives of American soldiers more than would a strategy limited to territorial defense. History proves that the reverse is the case. More Anglo-Americans died, as a percentage of the total population, in the colonial wars fought on North American soil than in the wars of the United States since 1776, including the Civil War. As a percentage of the total American population, the death toll in combat has diminished steadily as U.S. military power in North America and the world has increased.

If the Cold War is considered to have been the Third World War, fought by proxy, then the United States won with considerably fewer casualties a little more than a hundred thousand—than it suffered in the first two world wars. Indeed, the United States losses in the Korean and Vietnam wars—fifty-six thousand and fifty-eight thousand respectively—compare to U.S. losses in the bloodiest single battles in World Wars I and II. In forty-seven days in the fall of 1918, the U.S. Army suffered 26,667 dead as part of 120,000 casualties in the Meuse-Argonne campaign. In World War II, 23,000 American soldiers of the Twenty-eighth Infantry Division died between November 2 and 16, 1944, in a disastrous attempt to divert German forces from the Rhine River. The rate at which lives were lost in the American Civil War also dwarfs the rates in Vietnam and Korea. In the bloodiest battle, Antietam, on September 16, 1861, 4,700 men on both sides died in a day. On June 3, 1864, at Cold Harbor, 7,000 Federal troops were killed in half an hour.

The political scientist Charles Tilly has calculated that the average number of great-power battle deaths in the twentieth century per year works out to have been 290,000.[12] The United States won the Cold War and emerged as the predominant world power after losing roughly as many soldiers in combat over four decades as were lost in the Pacific theater in World War II alone in a mere four years. As a percentage of the ever-growing U.S. population, this was a fraction of the sacrifice in World War I and II. Relative to the population, significantly fewer American soldiers died in the Vietnam War than in the Korean War. The claim that "empire" and alliance lead to profligate bloodshed is therefore the reverse of the truth in the case of the United States. Wartime losses were far higher, in relative terms, when the United States was young and weak than they have been as the United States matured into a great military power with allies around the world.

Pacifists to the contrary, it is honorable and moral to fight on behalf of one's nation in a just cause—and that cause may take the form of a necessary war on behalf of the hegemonic credibility or alliance-worthiness of one's country. A consensus to the opposite effect in the United States will only prove that the accused Bosnian war criminal Ratko Mladic was right when he sneered, "The Western countries have learned that they cannot recruit their own children to realize goals outside their homelands."[13] The leader of the Bosnian Serbs, Radovan Karadzic, admitted that "if the West put in 10,000 men to cut off our supply corridors, we Serbs would be finished." But another accused Serb war criminal, Vojislav Seslj, remarked: "The Americans would have to send tens of thousands of body bags. It would be a new Vietnam."[14] If American radical leftists, pacifists, and libertarian isolationists prevail in promoting a pacifist political culture in the United States, then it is only a matter of time before the world is dominated by a military superpower whose leaders have an ethos like that of today's Serb leaders.

The Verdict on Vietnam

In the House of Commons on April 4, 1940, Winston Churchill described the British retreat from Dunkirk: "We must be careful not to assign to this deliverance the attributes of a victory." Indochina was the Dunkirk of the American effort in the Cold War. The Vietnam War will never be understood as anything other than a horrible debacle. At the same time, it cannot be understood except as a failed campaign in a successful world war against imperial tyrannies that slaughtered and starved more of their own subjects than any regimes in history.

For the past generation, the Vietnam War has been considered not only a disastrous defeat (which it was), but an easily avoidable mistake (which it was not, any more than was the Korean War) and a uniquely horrible conflict (more Americans were killed in three months in the trenches in World War I than in a decade in Vietnam). The anti–Vietnam War orthodoxy is so exaggerated, and so implausible, that it is certain to change as younger historians uninfluenced by the partisan battles of the Vietnam era write a more accurate and dispassionate history.

In the long run, the greatest danger is that the Vietnam War will be treated by mainstream historians as an inexplicable mistake. It is only a slight exaggeration to say that academic historians are paid to explain why what happened had to happen more or less as it did happen. Historians tend to applaud success and to condemn failure without considering that a successful policy may have been a mistake and that a failed policy might have been worth attempting. (This kind of retroactive determinism is applied to Cold War conflicts other than Vietnam; most American historians take it for granted that the United States could and should have done nothing to prevent the Chinese communist victory in 1949 and the consolidation of power by the Castro regime in Cuba.)

It should be obvious, though, that neither the United States nor any other great military power can wage a world war without losing any battles. It should be equally obvious that tremendous failures in foreign policy have something to do with world conditions and cannot always be ascribed to the incompetence of individual foreign policymakers. Truman and Eisenhower, early in the Cold War, like Reagan and Bush, in the conflict's final stages, held much stronger cards than the presidents in office in the middle of the Cold War. Kennedy, Johnson, and Nixon had to face a Soviet Union that had recovered from the devastation of World War II, that was growing in military power and diplomatic prestige, and that was far from being bankrupted by military competition with the West. To make matters worse, Kennedy and Johnson had to deal with Mao at a time when he was engaged in a last spasm of revolutionary radicalism. Harry Truman is remembered today as a great president only because Eisenhower managed to end the Korean War in a stalemate. Nixon failed to achieve a similar stalemate in Indochina, and thereby doomed Johnson's reputation as a commander-in-chief along with his own (Nixon's historical reputation would have been ruined anyway by his criminal abuses of power for partisan ends). It should not be forgotten that a critical factor in the American success in Korea (if an expensive half-century siege can be called a success) was the fact that Eisenhower, equiped with nuclear and conventional superiority over the Soviet bloc as a result of the Truman-era rearmament, had a degree of military and diplomatic leverage that Nixon in the 1970s simply lacked.

The rehabilitation of the reputation of the once unpopular Harry Truman in the 1970s and 1980s shows that provisional historical judgments are not stable. Indeed, the American public's retrospective view of individual wars has often fluctuated wildly, usually in response to later events in world politics. History shows a tendency for wars that were later considered to have been "good" or "just" wars to have been extremely unpopular in the decade or generation that followed them. For example, in January 1937 64 percent of those in one poll believed that the United States made a mistake in entering World War I; only 28 percent thought that United States participation had been a good idea. In December 1941, after Pearl Harbor, the percentage of those who thought that World War I had been a mistake plunged to 21 percent, and 61 percent now thought that America had been right to enter the First World War. For many years after it ended the Korean War was as unpopular as World War I had been—and as the Vietnam War would be in the generation that followed it. Only in 1956 did a majority agree that South Korea had been worth fighting for. By 1967, however, only 16 percent of the public agreed with the statement that the United States had made a mistake in fighting in Korea.[15]

How will the Vietnam War be considered a generation or two from now? It seems likely that historians free from the biases of Marxist leftism, liberal isolationism, and minimal realism will consider the Korean and Vietnam Wars to have been comparable Cold War proxy battles between the United States and the Soviet Union and China. It will be taken for granted that the United States was able to bring about a stalemate in the Korean War in large part because the enemy was vulnerable to American conventional forces backed by nuclear threats. The United States won a Pyrrhic victory in Indochina and withdrew because the U.S. military's misguided conventional-war approach to combating what, in the early years, was predominantly an insurgency piled up American casualties too quickly and destroyed American public support, first for the U.S. commitment to Indochina and then, temporarily, for the Cold War in general. Disinterested historians of the twenty-first century will also take it for granted that similar coalitions of progressive isolationists, Marxist radicals, and pacifists opposed U.S. intervention in World War I, World War II, the major and minor conflicts of the Cold War, the Gulf War, and no doubt wars yet to come. The continuities in the ethnic and regional influences on isolationists and interventionists in the American population will be understood just as well.

Here, then, is a provisional verdict. The Vietnam War was a just, constitutional and necessary proxy war in the Third World War that was waged by methods that were often counterproductive and sometimes arguably immoral. The war had to be fought in order to preserve the military and diplomatic credibility of the United States in the Cold War, but when its costs grew excessive the war had to be forfeited in order to preserve the political consensus within the United States in favor of the Cold War.

The Vietnam War was neither a mistake nor a betrayal nor a crime. It was a military defeat.

Notes

Chapter 1. The Indochina Theater

This chapter relies on standard historical works about the Vietnam War, including Harry Summers and Stanley Karnow, *Historical Atlas of the Vietnam War* (Boston: Houghton Mifflin, 1996), Guenter Lewy, *America in Vietnam* (New York: Oxford University Press, 1978), D. J. Sagar, *Major Political Events in Indochina 1945–1990* (New York: Facts on File, 1991), Bernard C. Nalty, ed., *The Vietnam War: The History of America's Conflict in Southeast Asia* (New York: Smithmark, 1996), Ronald J. Cima, ed., *Vietnam: A Country Study*, Area Handbook Series (Washington, D.C.: U.S. Government Printing Office, 1989), and others. Sources are cited only for facts found in specialized studies which are not in most general histories of the subject.

1. Martin Malia, *The Soviet Tragedy: A History of Socialism in Russia, 1917–1991* (New York: The Free Press, 1994), p. 504.

2. Sergei N. Goncharov, John W. Lewis, and Xue Litai, *Uncertain Partners: Stalin, Mao, and the Korean War* (Stanford: Stanford University Press, 1993), pp. 84–87 (emphasis added).

3. Stephen T. Hosmer and Thomas W. Wolfe, *Soviet Policy and Practice Toward Third World Countries* (Lexington, MA: Lexington, 1983), pp. 3–4.

4. Ruth T. McVey, "The Southeast Asian Insurrectionary Movements" in Cyril E. Black and Thomas P. Thornton, eds., *Communism and Revolution: The Strategic Uses of Political Violence* (Princeton: Princeton University Press, 1964), pp. 177–78.

5. General Oleg Sarin and Colonel Lev Dvoretsky, *Alien Wars: The Soviet Union's Aggressions Against the World, 1919 to 1989* (Novato, CA: Presidio, 1996), p. 52.

6. Chen Jian, "China and the First Indo-China War, 1950–54," *China Quarterly*, 133 (1993), pp. 85–110.

7. Chen Jian, "China's Involvement in the Vietnam War, 1964–69," *China Quarterly*, 142 (1995), p. 359.

8. Qiang Zhai, "Beijing and the Vietnam Conflict, 1964–1965: New Chinese Evidence," *Cold War International History Project 6–7*, (Winter 1995/96), pp. 234–35.

See also Chen Jian, "China's Involvement in the Vietnam War, 1964–69," *China Quarterly* 142 (1995), p. 362.

9. Chen Jian, "China's Involvement" p. 359–60.

10. William Duiker, *Sacred War: Nationalism and Revolution in a Divided Vietnam* (New York: McGraw Hill, 1995), pp. 164–65.

11. Milton Osborne, *Sihanouk: Prince of Light, Prince of Darkness* (Honolulu: University of Hawaii Press, 1994), pp. 162–63, 172.

12. Chen Jian, "China's Involvement," pp. 360, 364–65.

13. Quoted in John Mueller, *Retreat From Doomsday: The Obsolescence of Major War* (New York: Basic Books, 1989), p. 171.

14. Martin Walker, *The Cold War* (New York: Henry Holt, 1993), p. 191.

15. W. W. Rostow, *The United States and the Regional Organization of Asia and the Pacific, 1965–1985* (Austin, TX: University of Texas Press, 1986), p. 5.

16. Chen Jian, "China's Involvement," pp. 372–73, 380.

17. Ilya V. Gaiduk, *The Soviet Union and Vietnam* (Chicago: Ivan R. Dee, 1996), p. 109.

18. Gaiduk, p. 111.

19. Ramesh Thakur and Carlyle A. Thayer, *Soviet Relations with India and Vietnam* (London: Macmillan, 1992), p. 117.

20. Thakur and Thayer, p. 117.

21. Sarin and Dvoretsky, *Alien Wars*, p. 94.

22. Sarin and Dvoretsky, pp. 96, 108.

23. Gaiduk, p. 139.

24. Gaiduk, p. 4.

25. Thakur and Thayer, p. 119.

26. Melvin Croan, "A New Afrika Korps?" *The Washington Quarterly*, Vol. 3, No. 1 (Winter 1980), p. 31.

27. Steven R. David, "Soviet Involvement in Third World Coups," *International Security*, Vol. 11, No. 1 (Summer 1986), pp. 8–9.

28. Martin Walker, p. 214.

29. Thakur and Thayer, p. 121.

30. Thakur and Thayer, p. 123.

31. Douglas Pike, *People's Army of Vietnam* (Washington D.C.: Brassey's, 1986), pp. 1–2.

Chapter 2. Why Indochina Mattered

1. William R. Corson, *The Betrayal* (New York: W. W. Norton, 1968), p. 81.

2. Rusk told a French diplomat that if the United States did not protect South Vietnam, American "guarantees with regard to Berlin would lose their credibility" because the conflicts in Asia and Europe were "all part of the same struggle." Memorandum of conversation, Rusk and French ambassador, July 1, 1964, Declassified Documents Reference System (75)105A, cited in George C. Herring, *America's Longest War: The United States and Vietnam, 1950-1975* (New York: McGraw-Hill, 1996), p. 129.

3. Quoted in Ross Gregory, "The Domino Theory," in Alexander DeConde, ed., *Encyclopedia of American Foreign Policy*, Vol. 1 (New York: Scribner's, 1978), p. 275.

4. Public Papers: Kennedy, 1961, p. 241.

5. George McTurnan Kahin and John W. Lewis, *The United States in Vietnam* (New York: Dial Press, 1969), p. 305.

6. W. W. Rostow, "Vietnam and Asia," *Diplomatic History*, Vol. 20, No. 3 (Summer 1996), pp. 467–71.

7. Quoted by David Fromkin and James Chace, "What Are the Lessons of Vietnam?" *Foreign Affairs* (Spring 1985), p. 743.

8. Mark N. Katz, *Revolutions and Revolutionary Waves* (New York: St. Martin's Press, 1997), p. 92.

9. Thucydides, *The Peloponnesian War* (New York: Modern Library, 1951), pp. 79–80.

10. Department of State Bulletin, 72 (April 14, 1975), p. 462.

11. Quoted in Robert Jervis, "Domino Beliefs and Strategic Behavior," in Robert Jervis and Jack Snyder, eds., *Dominoes and Bandwagons* (New York: Oxford University Press, 1991), p. 34.

12. John McNaughton, "Proposed Course of Action Re Vietnam," March 24, 1965, in George C. Herring, ed., *The Pentagon Papers*, Abridged Ed. (New York: McGraw-Hill, 1993), pp. 115–18.

13. James C. Thomson, "How Could Vietnam Happen? An Autopsy," in Eugene R. Wittkopf, *The Domestic Sources of American Foreign Policy* (New York: St. Martin's Press, 1994), p. 264.

14. Robert Cohen, *When the Old Left Was Young: Student Radicals and America's First Mass Student Movement, 1929–1941* (New York: Oxford University Press, 1993) p. 518, n. 130.

15. Yuen Foong Khong, *Analogies at War: Korea, Munich, Dien Bien Phu, and the Vietnam Decisions of 1965* (Princeton: Princeton University Press, 1992), p. 59.

16. Quoted in John Henry and William Espinosa, "The Tragedy of Dean Rusk," *Foreign Policy* 8 (Fall 1972), p. 187.

17. John Harvey, ed., *The Diplomatic Diaries of Oliver Harvey, 1937–1940* (New York: St. Martin's, 1970), p. 425.

18. Stalin is quoted in Sergei N. Goncharov, John W. Lewis, and Xue Litai, *Uncertain Partners: Stalin, Mao and the Korean War* (Stanford, CA: Stanford University Press, 1993). Douglas J. Macdonald, "Communist Bloc Expansion in the Early Cold War: Challenging Realism, Refuting Revisionism," *International Security*, Vol. 20, No. 3 (Winter 1995/96), p. 178. Macdonald's reference is to Ted Hopf, "Soviet Inferences from Their Victories in the Periphery: Visions of Resistance or Cumulating Gains?" in Robert Jervis and Jack Snyder, eds., *Dominoes and Bandwagons: Strategic Beliefs and Great Power Competition in the Eurasian Rimland* (New York: Oxford University Press, 1991), p. 147.

19. "Record of Conversation Between Comrade I. V. Stalin and Zhou Enlai, 20 August 1952," reprinted in *Cold War International History Project Bulletin*, Issues 6–7 (Washington, D.C.: Woodrow Wilson International Center for Scholars, Winter 1995/1996), p. 12.

20. Telegram from Ribbentrop to Ott, August 25, 1941, *Documents on German Foreign Policy*, Series D, vol. 13, 375–76 (Washington, D.C.: United States Government Printing Office, 1956), quoted in Randall L. Schweller, *Deadly Imbalances: Tripolarity and Hitler's Strategy of World Conquest* (New York: Columbia University Press, 1998), p. 170.

21. "Mao Zedong's Handling of the Taiwan Straits Crisis of 1958," *Cold War International History Project Bulletin*, Issues 6–7 (Washington, D.C.: Woodrow Wilson International Center for Scholars, Winter 1995/96), pp. 209–10 (emphasis added).

22. "Mao Zedong and Pham Van Dong, Hoang Van Hoan, Beijing, 5 October 1964," in Odd Arne Westad, Chen Jian, Stein Tonnesson, Nguyen Vu Tung, and James G. Herschberg, *77 Conversations Between Chinese and Foreign Leaders on the Wars in Indochina, 1964–1977*, *Cold War International History Project*, Working Paper No. 22 (Washington, D.C.: Woodrow Wilson International Center for Scholars, May 1998), p. 74, n. 117; p. 75.

23. "Mao Zedong and Pham Van Dong, Beijing, 17 November 1968," in *77 Conversations*, p. 145.

24. Bill Moyers, "Flashback," *Newsweek*, February 10, 1975.

25. "Mao Zedong and Pham Van Dong, Beijing, 17 November 1968," p. 141.

26. "Mao Zedong and Le Duan, Beijing, the Great Hall of the People, 6:45–8:15 p.m., 11 May 1970," in *77 Conversations*, p. 165 (emphasis added).

27. Ilya V. Gaiduk, *The Soviet Union and the Vietnam War* (Chicago: Ivan R. Dee, 1996), p. 250.

28. William Curti Wohlforth, *The Elusive Balance: Power and Perception During the Cold War* (Ithaca: Cornell University Press, 1993), pp. 204–5.

29. Lyndon Johnson, "We Will Stand in Vietnam," in *Department of State Bulletin* (August 16, 1965) p. 262.

30. See John Lewis Gaddis, *Strategies of Containment* (New York: Oxford University Press, 1982). The term "bandwagoning" apparently originated with Arnold Wolfers. See Arnold Wolfers, "The Balance of Power in Theory and Practice," in Wolfers, *Discord and Collaboration: Essays on International Politics* (Baltimore: The Johns Hopkins University Press, 1962), p. 124. The term was popularized by Kenneth N. Waltz, in *Theory of International Politics* (Reading, MA: Addison-Wesley, 1979).

31. Stephen M. Walt, "The Case for Finite Containment: Analyzing U.S. Grand Strategy," *International Security* Vol. 14, No. 1, (Summer 1989) p. 35. For statements of the minimal realist theory, see George F. Kennan, *Realities of American Foreign Policy* (Princeton: Princeton University Press, 1954); Walter Lippmann, *U.S. Foreign Policy: Shield of the Republic* (Boston: Little, Brown, 1943); Hans J. Morgenthau, *In Defense of the National Interest* (Lanham, MD: University Press of America, 1982 (reprint of 1951 ed.).

32. Wohlforth, p. 24. For a critique of minimal realism, described as "defensive realism," see Fareed Zakaria, *From Wealth to Power: The Unusual Origins of America's World Role* (Princeton: Princeton University Press, 1998). For a defense of minimal realism, see Christopher Layne, "Less Is More: Minimal Realism in East Asia," *National Interest*, No. 43 (Spring 1996).

33. George Kennan, *Memoirs, 1925–1950* (New York: Pantheon Books, 1967), pp. 129–30.

34. Quoted in Robert Jervis, "Domino Beliefs and Strategic Behavior," in Jervis and Snyder, p. 33.

35. George Kennan, in Martin F. Herz, ed., *Decline of the West? George Kennan and His Critics* (Washington, D.C.: Ethics and Public Policy Center, 1978), p. 87.

36. Quoted in Roger Slusser, *The Berlin Crisis of 1961* (Baltimore: Johns Hopkins University Press, 1973), p. 112.

37. Daniel Patrick Moynihan, with Suzanne Weaver, *A Dangerous Place* (Boston: Little, Brown, 1978), pp. 31, 53.

38. Stephen M. Walt, *The Origins of Alliances* (Ithaca, NY: Cornell University Press, 1987), p. 29.

39. Willy Brandt, *People and Politics: The Years 1960–1975*, trans. Maxwell Brownjohn (Boston: Little, Brown, 1976), p. 20.

40. Bahr is quoted by Dana H. Allin, *Cold War Illusions: America, Europe and Soviet Power, 1969–1989* (New York: St. Martin's Press, 1995), Chapter 2, footnote 41.

41. John Orme, "The Unexpected Origins of Peace: Three Case Studies," *Political Science Quarterly*, Vol. 111, No. 1 (Spring 1996), p. 116.

42. Quoted in Mark Mason, *American Multinationals and Japan* (Cambridge, MA: Council on East Asian Studies, Harvard University, 1992), p. 183.

43. Chalmers Johnson, "La Serenissima of the East," *Asian and African Studies*, Vol. 18, No. 1 (March 1984), p. 59.

44. George Ball, *Diplomacy for a Crowded World*, (Boston: Little, Brown, 1976), pp. 49–50, 305.

45. Ball, p. 66.

46. Quoted in Herz, ed., *Decline of the West?* p. 124.

47. "From Containment to . . . Self-Containment," in Herz, ed., p. 13.

48. Edward N. Luttwak, in Martin F. Herz, ed., p. 111.

49. Charles A. Beard, *President Roosevelt and the Coming of the War, 1941: A Study in Appearances and Realities* (New Haven: Yale University Press, 1948), p. 587.

50. James McGregor Burns, *Roosevelt: The Soldier of Freedom* (New York: Harcourt Brace Jovanovich, 1970), p. 158.

51. Stephen M. Walt, "The Case for Finite Containment: Analyzing U.S. Grand Strategy," *International Security*, Vol. 14, No. 1, (Summer 1989) p. 35.

52. Dean Acheson, *Present at the Creation: My Years in the State Department* (New York: Norton, 1969), p. 376.

53. Martin Wight, *International Theory: The Three Traditions* (New York: Holmes & Meier, 1992), p. 224.

54. Bertrand Russell, *The Practice and Theory of Bolshevism* (London: Allen and Unwin, 1920), pp. 5, 114.

55. Nikita Khrushchev, *Khrushchev Remembers*, Edward Crankshaw and Strobe Talbott, eds. (Boston: Little, Brown, 1970), p. 370.

56. "Zhou Enlai with Le Duan and Pham Van Dong, Hanoi, 7 March 1971," in *77 Conversations*.

57. Douglas Jehl, "Holier Than Thou: Behind the Iranian-Afghan Rift," *New York Times*, September 7, 1998, p. A3.

58. "Zhou Enlai and Nguyen Van Hieu, Nguyen Thi Binh, Beijing (The Great Hall of the People), 16 May 1965," in *77 Conversations*, p. 86.

59. George Kennan, "Containment of the Kremlin," *Washington Post*, Feb. 16, 1976, p. A15.

60. Foreign Relations of the United States 1950 (7), pp. 623–4, memorandum by Kennan, August 21, 1950 (emphasis added).

61. David DiLeo, George Ball, *Vietnam, and the Rethinking of Containment* (Chapel Hill: University of North Carolina Press, 1991), p. 28.

62. Arthur M. Schlesinger, Jr., "The Roots of Misconceptions," in Richard M. Pfeffer, ed., *No More Vietnams? The War and the Future of American Foreign Policy* (New York: Harper and Row, 1968), pp. 8–9.

63. Quoted in William Conrad Gibbons, *U.S. Government and the Vietnam War*, Pt. II (Princeton: Princeton University Press, 1986), p. 41.

64. "Zhou Enlai with Le Duan and Pham Van Dong, Hanoi, 7 March 1971," in *77 Conversations*, pp. 179–80.

65. "Mao Zedong and Le Duan, Beijing, the Great Hall of the People, 6:45–8:15 p.m., 11 May 1970," in *77 Conversations*, p. 168.

66. Ralph G. Hawtrey, *Economic Aspects of Sovereignty* (London: Longmans, Green, 1952), pp. 64–65.

67. Thomas Etzold and John Lewis Gaddis, eds., *Containment: Documents on American Foreign Policy and Strategy, 1946–1950* (New York: Columbia University Press, 1978), pp. 71–83.

68. Harry S Truman, *Years of Trial and Hope, 1946–1952* (New York: Doubleday, 1956), p. 337.

69. Robert A. Pape, *Bombing to Win* (Ithaca, NY: Cornell University Press, 1996), p. 142.

70. *ABC This Week*, April 4, 1999.

71. Senate Committee on Foreign Relations, Prepared Statement of Madeleine K. Albright, April 20, 1999.

72. House Committee on Appropriations Defense Subcommittee, *Hearing: Supplemental Appropriations for Military Operation in Kosovo*, April 21, 1999.

73. *ABC This Week*, April 11, 1999.

74. Quoted in "The National Interest," *Weekly Standard*, April 26, 1999, p. 8.

75. Quoted in George W. Grayson, "How to Wreck NATO," *Christian Science Monitor*, April 28, 1999.

76. Senator John McCain, *McCain Speech to the National Association of Broadcasters Convention*, Congressional Press Releases, Washington, D.C., April 20, 1999.

Chapter 3. Inflexible Response

1. John McNaughton draft, January 4, 1965, "Observations re. South Vietnam," in Gravel, ed., *Pentagon Papers*, 3:683–4.

2. William C. Westmoreland, *A Soldier Reports* (Garden City, NY: Doubleday, 1976); Ulysses S. Grant Sharp, *Strategy for Defeat* (San Rafael, CA: Presidio Press, 1978).

3. Harry G. Summers, *On Strategy: A Critical Analysis of the Vietnam War* (Washington, D.C.: Government Printing Office, 1981).

4. Westmoreland, p. 425.

5. Hanson W. Baldwin, Foreword to U.S. Grant Sharp, p. xiii.

6. *Washington Post*, February 21, 1981, p. 2.

7. Eliot A. Cohen, "Enough Blame to Go Round," *The National Interest*, No. 51 (Spring 1998), p. 104.

8. William R. Corson, *The Betrayal* (New York: W. W. Norton, 1968), p. 286.

9. Veterans Administration, *Myths and Realities: A Study of Attitudes Toward Vietnam Era Veterans* (Washington, D.C.: Government Printing Office, 1980), p. 62.

10. Summers, p. 142.

11. Sharp, p. 4.

12. Westmoreland, p. 411.

13. Dave R. Palmer, *Summons of the Trumpet* (San Rafael, CA: Presidio, 1978), p. 62.

14. Summers, Jr., pp. 93–94.

15. Zhou Enlai and Nguyen Van Hieu, Nguyen Thi Binh, May 16, 1965, in Odd Arne Westad, Chen Jian, Stein Tonnesson, Nguyen Vu Tung, and James G. Hershberg, *77 Conversations between Chinese and Foreign Leaders on the Wars in Indochina, 1964–1977*, Cold War International History Project Working Paper No. 22 (Washington: Woodrow Wilson International Center for Scholars, May 1998), p. 86.

16. Chen Jian, "China's Involvement in The Vietnam War, 1964–69," *China Quarterly*, No. 142 (June 1995), pp. 366–69.

17. Qiang Zhai, "Beijing and the Vietnam Conflict, 1964–1965: New Chinese Evidence," in *The Cold War in Asia, Cold War International History Project Bulletin*, Issues 6–7 (Washington, D.C.: Woodrow Wilson International Center for Scholars, Winter 1996), p. 243.

18. Chen Jian, "China's Involvement," p. 378.

19. Zhai, p. 237.

20. SDS, "National Vietnam Examination," 1966, cited in Tom Wells, *The War Within: America's Battle Over Vietnam* (New York: Henry Holt, 1994), p. 82.

21. "Mao Zedong and Ho Chi Minh, Changsha (Hunan), 16 May 1965," in *77 Conversations*, p. 87 (emphasis added).

22. "Zhou Enlai, Deng Xiaoping, Kang Sheng and Le Duan, Nguyen Duy Trinh, Beijing, 13 April 1965," in *77 Conversations*, p. 96.

23. "Mao Zedong and Pham Van Dong, Beijing, 23 September 1970," in *77 Conversations*, p. 177. One of China's motives for limiting its contribution to logistics troops, in the absence of a U.S. invasion of North Vietnam, was the fear that if it sent "volunteer" combat troops then it would inspire the rival Soviet Union and its clients to do the same. On August 23, 1966, Zhou Enlai told Pham Van Dong: "If it is said that China has volunteer troops in North Vietnam, then Cuba, Algeria, and the Soviet Union, etc., may ask to have their volunteers in Vietnam." "Zhou Enlai and Pham Van Dong, Hoang Tung, Beijing, 23 August 1966," in *77 Conversations*, p. 99.

24. Quoted in Ilya V. Gaiduk, *The Soviet Union and the Vietnam War* (Chicago: Ivan R. Dee, 1996), p. 217.

25. General Oleg Sarin and Colonel Lev Dvoretsky, *Alien Wars: The Soviet Union's Aggressions Against the World, 1919 to 1989* (Novato, CA: Presidio Press, 1996), p. 98.

26. Sarin and Dvoretsky, p. 107.

27. Gaiduk, p. 62.

28. *People's Daily* and Xinhua News Agency, *On the Vietnamese Foreign Ministry's White Book Concerning Viet Nam–China Relations* (Beijing: Foreign Languages Press, 1979); Hoang Van Hoan, "Distortion of Facts About Militant Friendship Between Viet Nam and China is Impermissible," *Beijing Review*, No. 49 (December 7, 1979), pp. 16–17; Hoang Van Hoan, *A Drop in the Ocean* (Beijing Foreign Languages Press, 1988). Cited in Douglas J. Macdonald, "Communist Bloc Expansion in the Early Cold War: Challenging Realism, Refuting Revisionism," *International Security*, Vol. 20, No. 3 (Winter 1995/96), p. 183.

29. Westmoreland, p. 410.

30. Sharp, pp. 3–4, p. 268.

31. Thomas H. Moorer (Adm., ret.), "Lessons Learned in the Air War Over Vietnam," *Proceedings —U.S. Naval Institute*, August 6, 1987.

32. "Zhou Enlai and Pham Van Dong, Beijing, 10 April 1967," in *77 Conversations*, p. 101.

33. Robert A. Pape, *Bombing to Win: Air Power and Coercion in War* (Ithaca, NY: Cornell University Press, 1996), pp. 189–91.

34. Pape, pp. 186–87.

35. Quoted in Mike Cauzzo, "Once a Hawk," *San Jose Mercury News*, April 3, 1991, p. E12.

36. John Prados, *The Hidden History of the Vietnam War* (Chicago: Ivan R. Dee, 1995), pp. 187–88.

37. Quoted in David Halberstam, *The Best and the Brightest* (Greenwich, CT: Fawcett Crest, 1972), pp. 683–84.

38. "Telegram from the President to the Ambassador in Vietnam (Taylor)," December 30, 1964, FRUS (1964-68), 1:1058–1059, cited in Christopher M. Gacek, *The Logic of Force: The Dilemma of Limited War in American Foreign Policy*, (New York: Columbia University Press, 1992), p. 192.

39. Bruce Palmer, Jr., *The Twenty-Five Year War: America's Military Role in Vietnam* (New York: Simon and Schuster, 1984), p. 178.

40. James R. Ward, "Vietnam: Insurgency or War?" *Military Review* 69 (January 1989), p. 17.

41. Eliot A. Cohen, "Constraints on America's Conduct of Small Wars," *International Security* Vol. 9, No. 2 (Fall 1984), p. 162.

42. Andrew Krepinevich, *The Army and Vietnam* (Baltimore: Johns Hopkins, 1988), p. 188.

43. Mark Clodfelter, *The Limits of Air Power: The American Bombing of North Vietnam* (New York: Free Press, 1989), p. 134.

44. James R. Ward, pp. 18, 20.

45. Ward, pp. 22–23.

46. Quoted in Dave R. Palmer, *Summons of the Trumpet* (San Rafael, CA: Presidio, 1978), p. 148.

47. Lieutenant Colonel Carl Bernard, *The War in Vietnam: Observations and Reflections of a Province Senior Adviser*, student paper, U.S. Army Command and General Staff College, Fort Leavenworth, Kansas; cited in Chaplain (Colonel) Cecil B. Currey, "Preparing for the Past," *Military Review* Vol. 69, No. 1 (January 1989).

48. Andrew F. Krepinevich, Jr., *The Army in Vietnam* (Baltimore: Johns Hopkins University Press, 1986).

49. Lewis W. Walt, *Strange War, Strange Strategy: A General's Report on Vietnam* (New York: Funk and Wagnall's, 1970), p. 29.

50. William Colby, *Lost Victory* (Chicago: Contemporary Books, 1989), p. 365.

51. Michael E. Peterson, *The Combined Actions Platoons: The U.S. Marines' Other War in Vietnam* (New York: Praeger, 1989).

52. Robert W. Komer, *Bureaucracy at War*, (Boulder, CO: Westview Press, 1986), p. 116.

53. Summers, p. 88.

54. Summers, p. 120.

55. D. Michael Shafer, *Deadly Paradigms: The Failure of U.S. Counterinsurgency Policy* (Princeton: Princeton University Press, 1988).

56. James J. Wirtz, review of Shafer, *Deadly Paradigms*, in *International Security* (Summer 1989), p. 191.

57. Corson, p. 97.

58. Nathan Leites and Charles Wolf, Jr., *Rebellion and Authority: An Analytic Essay on Insurgent Conflict* (Chicago: Markham, 1970), p. 150.

59. Richard A. Hunt, *Pacification: The American Struggle for Vietnam's Hearts and Minds* (Boulder: Westview Press, 1995), p. 279.

60. Andrew F. Krepinevich, Jr., *The Army and Vietnam* (Baltimore: Johns Hopkins University Press, 1986), p. 232.

61. Edward N. Luttwak, *The Pentagon and the Art of War* (New York: Simon and Schuster, 1985), p. 32.

62. Russell F. Weigley, *History of the United States Army*, quoted in Palmer, p. 156.

63. Robert W. Komer, *Bureaucracy Does Its Thing: Institutional Constraints on U.S.-G.V.N. Performance in Vietnam* (Santa Monica: RAND, 1973), p. 150.

64. Anthony Verrier, "Strategically Mobile Forces—U.S. Theory and British Practice," *Journal of the Royal United Services Institute*, No. 624 (November 1961), pp. 479–85.

65. Reprinted in Donald Robinson, ed., *The Dirty Wars: Guerrilla Actions and Other Forms of Unconventional Warfare* (New York: Delacorte Press, 1968), p. 813.

66. Quotations in Col. John D. Waghelstein, "Post-Vietnam Counterinsurgency Doctrine," *Military Review* (May 1985), pp. 45–46.

67. John A. Nagl, "Learning to Eat Soup with a Knife: British and American Army Counterinsurgency Learning During the Malayan Emergency and the Vietnam War," *World Affairs* Vol. 161, No. 4 (Spring 1999), p. 193.

68. Quoted in Brian M. Jenkins, *The Unchangeable War* (Santa Monica, CA: RAND, 1972), p. 3.

69. H. R. McMaster, *Dereliction of Duty* (New York: HarperCollins, 1997), p. 7.

70. John Foster Dulles memorandum of conversation with Eisenhower, May 25, 1954, White House Memorandum series, "Meetings with the President 1954 (3)," Dulles Papers, Seeley G. Mudd Library, Princeton University; quoted in Gacek, p. 122.

71. Robert J. Dallek, *Lyndon Johnson and His Times, 1961–1973* (New York: Oxford University Press, 1998), p. 259.

72. Westmoreland, p. 193.

73. Westmoreland, p. 425.

Chapter 4. The Fall of Washington

1. Leslie H. Gelb with Richard K. Betts, *The Irony of Vietnam: The System Worked* (Washington, D.C.: Brookings Institution, 1979), p. 332.

2. Hans Schmidt, *The United States Occupation of Haiti, 1915–1934* (New Brunswick, NJ: Rutgers University Press, 1995); Brenda Gayle Plummer, *Rising Wind: Black Americans and U.S. Foreign Affairs, 1935–60* (Chapel Hill: University of North Carolina Press, 1996).

3. James E. Westheider, *Fighting on Two Fronts: African Americans and the Vietnam War* (New York: New York University Press, 1997), p. 15.

4. Quoted in Jervis Anderson, *A. Philip Randolph: A Biographical Portrait* (New York: Harcourt Brace Jovanovich, 1973), p. 275.

5. Plummer, p. 74–75.

6. Paul Buhle, "Themes in American Jewish Radicalism," in Paul Buhle and Dan Georgakas, eds., *The Immigrant Left in the United States* (Albany: State University of New York Press, 1996), p. 95.

7. Paul Berman, *A Tale of Two Utopias: The Political Journey of the Generation of 1968* (New York: W. W. Norton, 1996), p. 44.

8. Alexander W. Astin, "Personal and Environmental Determinants of Student Activism," *Measurement and Evaluation in Guidance* 1 (Fall 1968), pp. 149–62.

9. Maurice Isserman, "You Don't Need a Weatherman but a Postman Can Be Helpful," in Melvin Small and William D. Hoover, eds., *Give Peace a Chance: Exploring the Vietnam Antiwar Movement* (Syracuse, NY: Syracuse University Press, 1992), p. 23.

10. John E. Mueller, *War, Presidents, and Public Opinion* (New York: John Wiley & Sons, 1973), p. 166.

11. Mueller, Table 5.5., "Support for the Wars by Religion, Race, Sex."

12. B. G. Burkett and Glenna Whitley, *Stolen Valor: How the Vietnam Generation Was Robbed of Its Heroes and Its History* (Dallas, TX: Verity Press, 1998), p. 57.

13. John E. Haynes, *Red Scare or Red Menace? American Communism and Anticommunism in the Cold War Era* (Chicago: Ivan R. Dee, 1996), p. 92.

14. Michael Kazin, *The Populist Persuasion* (New York: Basic Books, 1995), p. 130.

15. James F. Dunnigan and Albert A. Nofi, *Dirty Little Secrets of the Vietnam War* (New York: St. Martin's Press, 1999) p. 7.

16. David Hackett Fischer, *Albion's Seed: Four British Folkways in America* (New York: Oxford University Press, 1989), p. 834.

17. Harry L. Coles, *The War of 1812* (Chicago: University of Chicago Press, 1965), p. 33.

18. David Herbert Donald, *Charles Sumner* (New York: Da Capo Press, 1996), pp. 108–10.

19. Robert W. Johannsen, *To the Halls of the Montezumas* (New York: Oxford University Press, 1985), pp. 275–76.

20. Samuel P. Huntington, *The Soldier and the State* (Cambridge: Harvard University Press, 1957), pp. 211, 213.

21. Richard F. Bensel, *Sectionalism and American Political Development* (Madison: University of Wisconsin Press, 1984), p. 90.

22. Fischer, p. 866.

23. John Milton Cooper, *The Vanity of Power: American Isolationism and the First World War, 1914–1917* (Westport, CT: Greenwood, 1969), pp. 220–22.

24. Peter Trubowitz, *Defining the National Interest: Conflict and Change in American Foreign Policy* (Chicago: University of Chicago Press, 1998), p. 281.

25. Thomas N. Guinsberg, *The Pursuit of Isolationism in the United States Senate from Versailles to Pearl Harbor* (New York: Garland, 1982), p. 17.

26. Justus D. Doenecke, *The Battle Against Interventionism, 1939–1941* (Malabar, FL: Krieger Publishing, 1997), p. 6.

27. Alfred O. Hero, Jr., *The Southerner and World Affairs* (Baton Rouge: Louisiana State University Press, 1965), p. 85.

28. Wayne S. Cole, *Roosevelt and the Isolationists, 1932–45* (Lincoln: University of Nebraska Press, 1983), p. 381.

29. Trubowitz, p. 163.

30. Cole, p. 261.

31. Cole, p. 441.

32. Cole, p. 454.

33. Lady Bird Johnson, *White House Diary* (New York: Holt, Rinehart and Winston, 1970), p. 185.

34. Terry Dietz, *Republicans and Vietnam, 1961–1968* (New York: Greenwood Press, 1986), p. 91.

35. Quoted in Dietz, p. 121.

36. P. Edward Haley, *Congress and the Fall of South Vietnam and Cambodia* (East Brunswick, NJ: Associated University Presses, 1982), p. 135. See also Nicol C. Rae, *The Decline and Fall of the Liberal Republicans: From 1952 to the Present* (New York: Oxford University Press, 1994); Robert W. Speel, *Changing Patterns of Voting in the Northern United States: Electoral Realignment, 1952–1996* (University Park, PA: Pennsylvania State University Press, 1998).

37. Walter A. McDougall, *Promised Land, Crusader State* (Boston: Houghton Mifflin, 1997), p. 195.

38. John Kenneth White, *Still Seeing Red: How the Cold War Shapes the New American Politics* (Boulder: Westview Press, 1997), pp. 133–34.

39. Martin F. Herz, *The Prestige Press and the Christmas Bombing, 1972* (Washington, D.C.: Ethics and Public Policy Center, 1980), p. 41.

40. Trubowitz, p. 183.

41. Douglas C. Waller, *Congress and the Nuclear Freeze* (Amherst: University of Massachusetts Press, 1987), p. 165.

42. U.S. House of Representatives, final vote results for roll calls 102 and 103, April 29, 1999.

43. Samuel Lubell, *The Future of American Politics* (Garden City, NY: Doubleday, 1956), pp. 137–43.

44. Trubowitz, pp. 134–37.

45. Michael Paul Rogin, *The Intellectuals and McCarthy: The Radical Specter* (Cambridge, MA: MIT Press, 1967), p. 267.

46. Wilbur Zelinsky, *The Cultural Geography of the United States* (Englewood Cliffs, N.J.: Prentice-Hall, 1973), pp. 13–14.

47. John Porter, quoted in Jack P. Green and J. R. Pole, eds., *Colonial British America: Essays in the New History of the Early Modern Era* (Baltimore: Johns Hopkins University Press, 1984), p. 205.

48. Benjamin Schwarz, "The Idea of the South," *The Atlantic Monthly* (December 1997), p. 121.

49. Bertram Wyatt-Brown, *Southern Honor: Ethics and Behavior in the Old South* (New York: Oxford University Press, 1982), p. 366.

50. Alexis de Tocqueville, *Democracy in America*, George Lawrence, trans. (Garden City, NY: University of Chicago Press, 1969 [1835]), p. 379.

51. Richard E. Nisbet and Dov Cohen, *Culture of Honor: The Psychology of Violence in the South* (Boulder: Westview Press, 1996), pp. 18, 63.

52. Nisbet and Cohen, pp. 38, 90–91, 103.

53. Henry Adams, *History of the United States of America during the Administrations of Thomas Jefferson* (New York: Viking Press, 1986), p. 121.

54. Henry Adams to Samuel Tilden, January 24, 1883, *The Letters of Henry Adams* (Cambridge, MA: Belknap Press, 1982–1988), Vol. 2, p. 491.

55. For the "national honor" thesis, see Norman K. Risjord, "Conservatism, War Hawks, and the Nation's Honor," *William and Mary Quarterly*, 3d ser., XVIII (1961), pp. 196–210.

56. Fischer, p. 843.

57. Russell Jacoby, *The Last Intellectuals* (New York: Basic Books, 1987), p. 10.

58. Allen Ginsberg, *Collected Poems, 1947–1980* (New York: Harper & Row, 1984), p. 478.

59. Quoted in Joseph Epstein, "Mistah Lowell—He Dead," *The Hudson Review* (Summer 1996), p. 192.

60. Daniel Patrick Moynihan, with Suzanne Weaver, *A Dangerous Place* (Boston: Little, Brown, 1978), p. 52, 64.

61. Mary McCarthy, *Hanoi* (New York: Harcourt, Brace and World, 1968), p. 3–4.

62. Quoted in Sandy Vogelgesang, *The Long Dark Night of the Soul* (New York: Harper & Row, 1974), p. 38.

63. Robb Ross, quoted in Stanley Rothman and S. Robert Lichter, *Roots of Radicalism: Jews, Christians and the New Left* (New Brunswick, NJ: Transaction, 1996).

64. Cited in Douglas Brinkley, "The Other Vietnam Generation," *New York Times Book Review*, February 28, 1999, p. 27.

65. Richard Nixon, *RN: The Memoirs of Richard Nixon* (New York: Warner Books, 1978), p. 345.

66. Ilya V. Gaiduk, *The Soviet Union and the Vietnam War* (Chicago: Ivan R. Dee, 1996), p. 4. Gaiduk's evidence is Pham Van Dong's conversation with Shcherbakov on October 14, 1970.

67. Gaiduk, p. 197.

68. Truong Nhu Tang, *A Viet Cong Memoir*, with David Chanoff and Doan Van Toai (New York: Random House, 1985), pp. 143–44.

69. "Zhou Enlai and Pham Van Dong, Beijing, 17 September 1970," in Odd Arne Westad, Chen Jian, Stein Tonnesson, Nguyen Vu Tung and James G. Herschberg, eds., *77 Conversations Between Chinese and Foreign Leaders on the Wars in Indochina, 1964–1977*, Cold War International History Project Working Paper No. 22 (Washington, D.C.: Woodrow Wilson International Center for Scholars, May 1998), p. 174, emphasis added.

70. "Mao Zedong and Kaysone Phomvihane, Beijing, The Great Hall of the People, 3–4 p.m., 7 July 1970," in *77 Conversations*, p. 172.

71. Aleksandr Fursenko and Timothy Naftali, *"One Hell of a Gamble": Khrushchev, Castro, and Kennedy, 1958–1964* (New York: W. W. Norton, 1997), pp. 345–46.

72. Fursenko and Naftali, p. 347.

73. Fursenko and Naftali also learned that during a 1955 trip to the Soviet Union accompanying Supreme Court Justice William O. Douglas, Robert Kennedy asked his Soviet Intourist guide to "send a woman of loose morals" to his hotel room—making himself subject to possible Soviet blackmail, the way that his brother John had made himself vulnerable to blackmail by sleeping with a Nazi spy in the 1940s and allegedly sleeping with an East German spy while in the White House. See Fursenko and Naftali, pp. 114–15.

74. George Kennan, Testimony to Senate Foreign Relations Committee, February 10, 1966, quoted in R. B. Smith, *An International History of the Vietnam War*, Vol. III, *The Making of a Limited War, 1965–66* (New York: St. Martin's Press, 1991).

75. John E. Mueller, *War, Presidents, and Public Opinion* (New York: John Wiley & Sons, 1973), pp. 164, 173.

76. W.W. Rostow, *The Diffusion of Power* (New York: Macmillan, 1972), p. 498.

77. Mueller, p. 167.

78. W. W. Rostow, p. 167.

79. John E. Reilly, ed., *American Public Opinion and U.S. Foreign Policy, 1975* (Chicago: Chicago Council on Foreign Relations, 1975), p. 18, p. 26.

80. Ronald Radosh, *Divided They Fell: The Demise of the Democratic Party, 1964–1996* (New York: The Free Press, 1996), pp. 168–69.

81. Marine colonel William R. Corson in 1968 provided his own taxonomy of the American "aviary": "Beyond the usual 'hawks' and 'doves' who visit Vietnam there are 'vultures,' 'parrots,' 'woodpeckers,' 'magpies,' 'do-dos,' 'owls,' 'falcons,' 'hummingbirds,' and 'peacocks,' to name but a few." William R. Corson, *The Betrayal* (New York: W. W. Norton, 1968), p. 245.

Chapter 5. Disinformation

1. Quoted in Walter Lippmann, *U.S. Foreign Policy: Shield of the Republic* (Boston: Little, Brown, 1943), pp. 141–42.

2. Barbara Tuchman, "If Mao Had Come to Washington in 1945," in *Notes From China* (New York: Macmillan, 1972), p. 112.

3. Louis A. Fanning, *Betrayal in Vietnam* (New Rochelle, NY: Arlington, 1976), pp. 245–47.

4. David Halberstam, *The Best and the Brightest* (New York: Random House, 1992), pp. 110–11.

5. "From 1945 to 1949 the Soviets strategically directed and physically facilitated the move of some 400,000 Chinese communist troops and 20,000 cadres into the key region of Manchuria in late 1945 and early 1946 in violation of agreements they had made with the United States and the Nationalist Government; supplied the CCP [Chinese Communist Party] with bloc-manufactured and -captured Japanese military equipment in sufficient amounts to equip 600,000 men; provided tanks and heavy artillery that proved critical in the communists' battles with the Nationalists; helped the Chinese communists build munitions factories in the Soviet-controlled areas of Manchuria that were crucial to the defeat of the Nationalists; and provided economic and political guidance, which was, especially after 1947, largely followed by Mao and the CCP leadership." Douglas J. Macdonald, "Communist Bloc Expansion in the Early Cold War: Challenging Realism, Refuting Revisionism," *International Security*, Vol. 20, No. 3 (Winter 1995/1996), pp. 172–73.

6. Halberstam, pp. 110–11.

7. David Halberstam, *The Powers That Be* (New York: Alfred A. Knopf, 1979), p. 452.

8. Quoted in Tang Tsou, *America's Failure in China, 1941–50* (University of Chicago Press, 1963), pp. 202–204.

9. Michael M. Sheng, *Battling Western Imperialism: Mao, Stalin, and the United States* (Princeton: Princeton University Press, 1997), p. 77.

10. Halberstam, p. 339.

11. Quoted in Tang Tsou, p. 224.

12. Quoted in Richard L. Walker, "China Studies in McCarthy's Shadow: A Personal Memoir," *The National Interest* (Fall 1998), p. 101.

13. "Symposium: Rethinking the Lost Chance in China," *Diplomatic History*, Vol. 1, No. 1 (Winter 1997).

14. Warren I. Cohen, Dean Rusk, *American Secretaries of State and Their Diplomacy*, Vol. 19, Robert H. Ferrell, ed. (Totowa, N.J.: Cooper Square, 1980), p. 330.

15. Walker, ibid.

16. Martin Wight, *International Theory: The Three Traditions* (New York: Holmes & Meier, 1992), pp. 147–48.

17. Archimedes Patti, *Why Viet Nam? Prelude to America's Albatross* (Berkeley, CA: University of California Press, 1980).

18. Tang Tsou, p. 89.

19. Frank Gibney, "Syngman Rhee: The Free Man's Burden," *Harper's* (April 1954); quoted in Frank Gibney, *Korea's Quiet Revolution: From Garrison State to Democracy* (New York: Walker, 1992), p. 174.

20. Ramesh Thakur, *Peacekeeping in Vietnam: Canada, India, Poland, and the International Commission* (Edmonton: University of Alberta Press, 1984), p. 169.

21. U.S. State Department, "The Legality of United States Participation in the Defense of Viet-Nam," in Richard Falk, *The Vietnam War and International Law* (Princeton: Princeton University Press, 1968), pp. 595–96. See also John Norton Moore, *Law and the Indo-China War*, (Princeton: Princeton University Press, 1972).

22. Truong Nhu Tang, *A Viet Cong Memoir* (New York: Random House, 1985), p. 169.

23. Thakur, p. 134.

24. Kennan to George C. Marshall, March 15, 1948, FRUS/1948, III, pp. 848–849, cited in Eduard Mark, "Mr. 'X' Is Inconsistent and Wrong," in Martin F. Herz, ed., *Decline of the West? George Kennan and His Critics* (Washington, D.C.: Ethics and Public Policy Center, 1978), p. 161.

25. Frederic L. Pryor, *The Red and the Green: The Rise and Fall of Collectivized Agriculture in Marxist Regimes* (Princeton: Princeton University Press, 1992), pp. 51, 220.

26. Winston S. Churchill, *The Hinge of Fate* (Boston: Houghton Mifflin, 1950), p. 498.

27. See also Robert Conquest, *Harvest of Sorrow* (New York: Oxford University Press, 1987); Judith Banister, *China's Changing Population* (Stanford: Stanford University Press, 1987); Jasper Becker, *Hungry Ghosts* (New York: The Free Press, 1997).

28. Bernard Fall, *The Two Vietnams* (New York: Praeger, 1963), pp. 155–57.

29. Tom Hayden and Staughton Lynd, *The Other Side* (New York: New American Library, 19867), pp. 205–7.

30. The Soviet study is cited in Bernard B. Fall, *Last Reflections on a War* (Garden City, NY: Doubleday, 1964), p. 94.

31. Marilyn B. Young, *The Vietnam Wars, 1945–1990* (New York: HarperCollins, 1991), p. 50.

32. Edwin E. Moise, *Land Reform in China and North Vietnam: Consolidating the Revolution at the Village Level* (Chapel Hill: University of North Carolina Press, 1983), pp. 5, 221, 274.

33. Bui Tin, *Following Ho Chi Minh: The Memoirs of a North Vietnamese Colonel*, trans. Judy Stowe and Do Van (Honolulu: University of Hawaii Press, 1995), pp. 26–29.

34. Arthur M. Schlesinger, Jr., *Robert Kennedy and His Times*, (Boston: Houghton Mifflin, 1978), pp. 717–18.

35. Stanley Karnow, "Lost Chance in Vietnam," pp. 17–19; George C. Herring, *America's Longest War: The United States and Vietnam, 1950–1975* (New York: Wiley, 1979), p. 101.

36. Henry A. Kissinger, *Diplomacy* (New York: Simon & Schuster, 1994) pp. 656–57.

37. Tang Tsou, p. 387.

38. Tang Tsou, pp. 388, 390, 392 (emphasis added).

39. Don Oberdorfer, *The Two Koreas* (Reading, MA: Addison-Wesley, 1997).

40. George McTurnan Kahin and John W. Lewis, *The United States in Vietnam* (rev. ed.), (New York: Dial Press, 1969), p. 397.

41. Schlesinger, pp. 769–74.

42. R. B. Smith, *An International History of the Vietnam War*, Vol. III, *The Making of a Limited War, 1965–66* (New York: St. Martin's Press, 1991), p. 104.

43. James C. Thomson, Jr., "How Could Vietnam Happen? An Autopsy," in Eugene R. Wittkopf, ed., *The Domestic Sources of American Foreign Policy*, 2nd ed. (New York: St. Martin's Press, 1994), pp. 263–64.

44. "Zhou Enlai and Pham Van Dong, Beijing, 17 September 1970," in Odd Arne Westad, Chen Jian, Stein Tonnesson, Nguyen Vu Tung, and James G. Hershberg, *77 Conversations between Chinese and Foreign Leaders on the Wars in Indochina, 1964–1977, Cold War International History Project* Working Paper No. 22 (Washington: Woodrow Wilson International Center for Scholars, May 1998), p. 174.

45. Quoted in Tang Tsou, pp. 201, 208.

46. Truong Nhu Tang, with David Chanoff and Doan Van Toai, *A Viet Cong Memoir* (New York: Random House, 1985), p. 284.

47. Truong Nhu Tang, p. 216.

48. Nguyen Vu Tung, "Interpreting Beijing and Hanoi: A View of Sino-Vietnamese Relations, 1965–1970," in *77 Conversations*, p. 47.

49. Hoang Van Hoan, *A Drop in the Ocean* (Beijing: Foreign Languages Press, 1979), cited in Douglas J. Macdonald, "Communist Bloc Expansion in the Early Cold War: Challenging Realism, Refuting Revisionism," *International Security*, Vol. 20, No. 3 (Winter 1995/96), pp. 182–83.

50. Robert S. McNamara, James Blight, Thomas Biersteker, and Col. Herbert Schandler, *Argument Without End: In Search of Answers to the Vietnam Tragedy* (New York: Public Affairs Press, 1999), p. 400.

51. McNamara et al., pp. 401–5.

52. McNamara et al., p. 13.

53. McNamara et al., p. 148.

54. McNamara et al., p. 4.

55. Deborah Shapley, *Promise and Power: The Life and Times of Robert McNamara* (Boston: Little Brown, 1993), p. 263.

56. Harrison Salisbury, *To Peking—And Beyond* (London: Hutchison & Co., 1973), p. 183.

57. George McTurnan Kahin, introduction to George Hildebrand and Gareth Porter, *Cambodia: Starvation and Revolution* (New York: Monthly Review Press, 1976), p. 8.

58. Testimony of George McTurnan Kahin, "Supplemental Assistance to Cambodia," Hearings Before the Subcommittee on Foreign Assistance and Economic Policy of the Committee on Foreign Relations, United States Senate, 94th Cong., 1st sess., February 24 and March 6, 1975. Cited in Stephen J. Morris, "Ho Chi Minh, Pol Pot, and Cornell," *The National Interest* (Summer 1989).

59. Quoted in Stephen J. Morris, "Ho Chi Minh."

60. Hayden and Lynd, p. 212.

61. Todd Gitlin, "Seizing History: What We Won and Lost at Home," *Mother Jones*, November 1983, reprinted in Grace Sevy, ed., *The American Experience in Vietnam* (Norman: University of Oklahoma Press, 1989), pp. 190–91.

62. Quoted in Henry Kamm, "A Broken Country," *New York Times Magazine*, Sept. 19, 1987, p. 96.

63. David P. Chandler, *Brother Number One: A Political Biography of Pol Pot* (Boulder: Westview Press, 1992), p. 101.

64. Chandler, p. 98.

65. Quoted in the *New York Times*, September 5, 1981.

66. Committee of Concerned Asian Scholars, *The Indochina Story* (New York: Random House, 1970), p. 59.

67. Eyal Press, "Unforgiven: The Director of the Cambodian Genocide Program Rekindles Cold War Animosities," *Lingua Franca* (April/May 1997), pp. 67–75.

68. Tom Nairn, *Faces of Nationalism: Janus Revisited* (London: Verso, 1997), p. 92.

69. John Pilger, "The Friends of Pol Pot," *The Nation*, May 11, 1998.

70. Quoted in Press, p. 74.

71. Chandler, pp. 75–77.

72. Haing S. Ngor with Roger Warner, *Surviving the Killing Fields* (London; Chatto & Windus, 1988), p. 401.

73. Chandler, p. 168.

74. Fall, p. 157.

75. Gareth Porter and George Hildebrand, *Cambodia: Starvation and Revolution* (New York: Monthly Review Press, 1976), pp. 33–38.

76. Timothy J. Lomperis, *From People's War to People's Rule* (Chapel Hill: University of North Carolina Press, 1996), p. 260.

77. Noam Chomsky and Edward Herman, *Manufacturing Consent: The Political Economy of the Mass Media* (New York: Pantheon Books, 1988), p. 287.

78. Chomsky and Herman, p. 219.

79. Chomsky and Herman, p. 291.

80. Chandler, p. 100.

81. Kenneth M. Quinn, "Political Change in Wartime: The Khmer Krahom Revolution in Southern Cambodia, 1970–1974," *Naval War College Review* (Spring 1976).

82. U.S. Congress, House Committee on Foreign Affairs and its Special Subcommittee on Investigations, The Vietnam-Cambodia Emergency, 1975, Part II: The Vietnam-Cambodia Debate, p. 281.

83. P. Edward Haley, *Congress and the Fall of South Vietnam and Cambodia* (East Brunswick, NJ: Associated University Presses, 1982), p. 73, 201, n. 69.

84. Even today, the discredited canards of the 1970s Left continue to be repeated in the prestige press. Writing in the *New York Times Book Review* on August 16, 1998, Arnold R. Isaacs, who covered Indochina for the *Baltimore Sun* in the 1970s, has this to say: "From 1970 to 1975, American aid and bombs prolonged Lon Nol's hopeless war against the Communists. . . . Later, after failing to lift a finger to stop the Khmer Rouge bloodbath, the United States gave diplomatic support to the ousted torturers after Vietnamese invaders drove them from Phnom Penh in early 1979." Note how Isaacs first condemns the United States for trying to prevent the Khmer Rouge from coming to power—and then condemns the United States for failing to stop the Khmer Rouge once they were in power! (The U.S. aid to the Khmer Rouge was an incidental part of an alliance backed by the United States, China, and Thailand against the Soviet-sponsored Vietnamese occupation of Cambodia; Isaacs disingenuously makes it sound as though the United States goal was the restoration of the Khmer Rouge.)

In recent years, former Kennedy-Johnson adviser William Bundy and others have argued that an earlier U.S. abandonment of Indochina would have allowed the Vietnamese to administer Cambodia, freezing out the Khmer Rouge. However, there is no evidence that the Vietnamese communists had any plans to prevent the Khmer Rouge from governing Cambodia in the early 1970s. See William Bundy, *A Tangled Web: The Making of Foreign Policy in the Nixon Presidency* (New York: Hill and Wang, 1998).

85. James Fallows, "What Did You Do in the Class War, Daddy?" *Washington Monthly* (October 1975), reprinted in Grace Sevy, ed., *The American Experience in Vietnam* (Norman: University of Oklahoma Press, 1989), p. 222.

86. Tom Wicker, "The Vietnam Disease," *New York Times*, May 27, 1975.

87. Eric T. Dean, Jr. *Shook Over Hell: Post-Traumatic Stress, Vietnam, and the Civil War* (Cambridge, MA: Harvard University Press, 1997), p. 15.

88. Dean, Jr., p. 40.

89. B. G. Burkett, "Telling It Like It Is," Interview, *Vietnam* (February 1997), p. 32.

90. Burkett, pp. 28–29.

91. Burkett, p. 29.

92. B. G. Burkett and Glenna Whitley, *Stolen Valor* (Dallas: Verity Press, 1998), p. 149.

93. Dean, Jr., p. 18.

94. Burkett, p. 30.

95. Cited in Dean, Jr., p. 182.

96. Dean, Jr., p. 183.

97. Robert A. Divine, "Historiography: Vietnam Reconsidered," *Diplomatic History* (Winter 1998), reprinted Walter Capps, *The Vietnam Reader* (New York: Routledge, 1991), p. 100.

98. Frances Fitzgerald, *Fire in the Lake: The Vietnamese and the Americans in Vietnam* (Boston: Little, Brown, 1972), p. 442.

99. David Halberstam, *Ho* (New York: Random House, 1971), p. 82.

100. Halberstam, p. 108.

101. Halberstam, p. 109.

102. Joseph Buttinger, *Vietnam: A Dragon Embattled*, Vols. 1 and 2 (New York: Praeger, 1967).

103. Jean Lacouture, *Ho Chi Minh* (New York: Random House, 1968).

104. Quoted in Guenter Lewy, "Is American Guilt Justified?" in Sevy, ed., pp. 261–62.

105. Halberstam, p. 118. Halberstam's eulogy for Ho might be compared to Stanley Karnow's tribute to the murderous Mao Zedong in *Mao and China: From Revolution to Revolution* (New York: Viking, 1972): "More than any individual in modern times, Mao led [the Chinese people] to the rediscovery of their grandeur by inculcating them with a spirit of national identity, a sense of purpose, and a dedication to self-reliance. . . . A lesser man would have died satisfied with his accomplishment. The depth of his disappointment, then, reflected the dimensions of his unfulfilled dream." (p. 516). Earlier, Karnow writes that during the Great Leap Forward, in which as many as thirty million Chinese starved, "Widespread famine, which had so often afflicted China in the past, when the death toll during lean years ran into the millions, did not occur" (p. 104).

106. Gabriel Kolko, *Anatomy of a War: Vietnam, the United States, and the Modern Historical Experience* (New York: The New Press, 1994), p. 602.

107. John Prados, *Presidents' Secret Wars* (Chicago: Ivan R. Dee, 1996), p. 339.

108. Robert Buzzanco, *Masters of War: Military Dissent and Politics in the Vietnam Era* (Cambridge, MA: Cambridge University Press, 1996), pp. 8–9.

109. Martin F. Herz, *How the Cold War is Taught: Six American History Textbooks Examined* (Washington, D.C.: Ethics and Public Policy Center, 1978), p. 62.

110. Dexter Perkins, "American Wars and Critical Historians," *Yale Review* (June 1951), p. 686.

111. Jerald A. Combs, *American Diplomatic History: Two Centuries of Changing Interpretations* (Berkeley: University of California Press, 1983), pp. 212–13, 334, 347, 387.

112. See, for example, John Lewis Gaddis, *We Now Know: Rethinking Cold War History* (Oxford: Clarendon Press, 1997).

113. David Brion Davis, "American Equality and Foreign Revolutions," *Journal of American History* 76 (December, 1989), pp. 730–31.

114. Guenter Lewy, *America in Vietnam* (New York: Oxford University Press, 1978), pp 444–45.

Chapter 6. Credibility Gap

1. The general declarations have been against Britain (1812), Mexico (1846), Spain (1898), Germany (1917), Austria-Hungary (1917), Japan (1941), Germany and Italy (1941), and Bulgaria, Hungary, and Rumania (1942). The conditional declarations of war have been congressional authorization of the president to seize East Florida if a foreign government (Britain) tried to occupy it (1811) and to use force to prevent Britain from seizing a disputed section of Maine (1839); conditional declarations of war arising from naval conflicts with Paraguay (1858) and Venezuela (1871, 1890); authorization of the president to use force to persuade Spain to indemnify American nationals for property losses in the war between Spain and Cuba (1895), and to use force if Spain did not withdraw from Cuba (April 20, 1898). The result was the Spanish-American War, which Congress ratified by a general declaration of war against Spain on April 20, 1895. The other

conditional declarations of war have been the Formosa Resolution (1956), the Middle East Resolution (1957), the Southeast Asia Resolution (1964), and the vote authorizing President Bush to use military force to enforce UN resolutions against Iraq (1990).

2. Quoted in Philip J. Briggs, *Making American Foreign Policy: President-Congress Relations from the Second World War to Vietnam* (Lanham, MD: University Press of America, 1991), p. 99.

3. Briggs, pp. 100–1.

4. Briggs, pp. 28–29.

5. Quoted in Briggs, p. 197.

6. "July 25, 1967—Senate Committee Chairman," Folder, July 1967–May 1968, Tom Johnson's notes, box 1, LBJ Library.

7. "July 25, 1967—Senate Committee Chairman," Folder, July 1967–May 1968, Tom Johnson's notes, box 1, LBJ Library. For the Johnson administration's claim that the president could act in Vietnam without congressional authorization, see Gordon Silverstein, *Imbalance of Powers: Constitutional Interpretation and the Making of American Foreign Policy* (New York: Oxford University Press, 1997), p. 85.

8. John Hart Ely, *War and Responsibility: Constitutional Lessons of Vietnam and Its Aftermath* (Princeton: Princeton University Press, 1993), p. 47.

9. Quoted in Aleksandr Fursenko and Timothy Naftali, *"One Hell of a Gamble": Krushchev, Castro, and Kennedy, 1958–1964* (New York: W. W. Norton, 1997), p. 226.

10. William Conrad Gibbons, "The U.S. Government and the Vietnam War: Executive and Legislative Roles and Relationships," prepared for the Committee on Foreign Relations, U.S. Senate, April 1984, II, p. 308.

11. Quoted in Ely, p. 19.

12. 110 Cong. Rec. 18, 403 (1964).

13. David Rudenstine, *The Day the Presses Stopped: A History of the Pentagon Papers Case* (Berkeley: University of California Press, 1996), pp. 9–10.

14. Edward Jay Epstein, *Between Fact and Fiction: The Problem of Journalism* (New York: Vintage, 1975), p. 82.

15. Cited in Epstein, p. 82.

16. Epstein, p. 85.

17. Cited in Epstein, p. 88.

18. Leslie H. Gelb and Richard K. Betts, *The Irony of Vietnam*, (Washington D.C.: Brookings Institution, 1979), p. 108.

19. David M. Barrett, *Uncertain Warriors: Lyndon Johnson and His Vietnam Advisors* (Lawrence, Kansas: University Press of Kansas, 1993), p. 42.

20. Larry Berman, *Planning a Tragedy* (New York: Norton, 1982), pp. 99–100.

21. Stanley Karnow, *Vietnam: A History* (New York: Viking Press, 1983), p. 425.

22. Barrett, p. 43.

23. Correspondence between Cyrus Vance and Fred I. Greenstein, March 10, 1988, cited in John P. Burke and Fred I. Greenstein, *How Presidents Test Reality: Decisions on Vietnam, 1954 and 1965* (New York: Russell Sage Foundation, 1989), p. 215, n. 30.

24. Epstein, p. 100.

25. William Bundy, *A Tangled Web: The Making of Foreign Policy in the Nixon Presidency* (New York: Hill and Wang, 1998), p. 233.

26. Robert S. McNamara and Brian VanDeMark, *In Retrospect: The Tragedy and Lessons of Vietnam* (New York: Times Books, 1995), pp. 95–96.

27. Deborah, Shapley, *Promise and Power, The Life and Times of Robert McNamara* (Boston: Little, Brown, 1993), p. 263.

28. Robert Dallek, *Flawed Giant: Lyndon Johnson and His Times, 1961–1973* (New York: Oxford University Press, 1998), p. 99.

29. Seymour M. Hersh, *The Dark Side of Camelot* (Boston: Little, Brown, 1997), p. 430.

30. Quoted in Noam Chomsky, *Rethinking Camelot: JFK, The Vietnam War, and U.S. Political Culture* (Boston, MA: South End Press, 1993), pp. 73–83.

31. Chomsky, ibid.

32. Quoted in Chomsky, p. 107.

33. Andrew J. Rotter, "Operation Exculpation," review of Robert Buzzanco, *Masters of War*, in *Diplomatic History*, Vol. 21, No. 4 (Fall 1997), p. 660.

34. Blema Steinberg, *Shame and Humiliation: Presidential Decision Making in Vietnam* (Pittsburgh: University of Pittsburgh Press, 1996), pp. 6, 110–11.

35. Dallek, p. 627.

36. Dallek, ibid.

37. William Curti Wohlforth, *The Elusive Balance: Power and Perceptions During the Cold War* (Ithaca, NY: Cornell University Press, 1993), p. 205.

38. Wohlforth, p. 248.

39. The bibliography of Dallek's biography of Johnson contains no references to the growing scholarly literature that draws on post–Cold War revelations from the Soviet Union, China, and Vietnam. Instead, Dallek cites only books—some of them decades old—by left-of-center American critics of the Vietnam War and the Cold War such as Noam Chomsky, David Halberstam, Lloyd C. Gardner, Stanley Karnow, Neil Sheehan, and Tom Wicker.

40. Harry Evans, *The American Century* (New York: Alfred A. Knopf, 1998), pp. 520, 529.

41. As a fifth-generation Texan and the author of a narrative poem entitled "The Alamo" (1997), I shall no doubt be accused of being a bloodthirsty Texan war-monger. For what it is worth, I disapprove of the War of 1812, the Philippine War, and the invasion of Panama, notwithstanding my admiration for the courage of the defenders (and the stormers) of the Alamo.

42. William Appleman Williams, *The Tragedy of American Diplomacy* (Cleveland: World Publishing, 1959).

43. Garry Wills, "Principles and Heresies: Nero in our Camp," *National Review*, September 12, 1959.

44. Garry Wills, *Inventing America: Jefferson's Declaration of Independence* (Garden City, NY: Doubleday, 1978), p. xx.

45. See Noam Chomsky, *Year 501: The Conquest Continues* (Boston: South End Press, 1993).

46. Walter A. McDougall, *Promised Land, Crusader State: America's Encounter with the World Since 1776* (Boston: Houghton Mifflin, 1997), p. 172.

47. Johnson speech, cite. PPP: LBJ, 1965, I, 394–99.

48. David E. Lilienthal, *Journals: The Atomic Energy Years 1945–1950* (New York: Harper & Row, 1964), pp. 525–26, 593–94.

49. See Robert G. K. Thompson, *Defeating Communist Insurgency* (New York: Praeger, 1966); Thompson, *No Exit from Vietnam* (New York: David McKay, 1969).

50. David Hackett Fischer, *The Great Wave: Price Revolutions and the Rhythm of History* (New York: Oxford University Press, 1996), p. 204.

51. R. B. Smith, *An International History of the Vietnam War*, Vol. III, *The Making of a Limited War, 1965–66* (New York: St. Martin's Press, 1991).

52. Richard Rorty, *Achieving Our Country: Leftist Thought in Twentieth-Century America* (Cambridge, MA: Harvard University Press, 1998), p. 67.

53. Bruce D. Porter, *War and the Rise of the State: The Military Foundations of Modern Politics* (New York: Free Press, 1994), p. 284.

54. Porter, ibid.

55. John E. Haynes, *Red Scare or Red Menace? American Communism and Anticommunism in the Cold War Era* (Chicago: Ivan R. Dee, 1996), pp. 28–35.

56. Haynes, p. 29.

57. Franklin D. Roosevelt to Roger B. Merriman, May 20, 1940, in Elliott

Roosevelt, ed., *Franklin D. Roosevelt: His Personal Papers*, Vol. II (New York: Duell, Sloan and Pearce, 1947–1950), p. 1028.

58. Quoted in Melvin Small, *Johnson, Nixon and the Doves* (New Brunswick, NJ: Rutgers University Press, 1988), p. 152.

59. Quoted in Christopher Andersen, *Citizen Jane*, (New York: Henry Holt, 1990): *The Turbulent Life of Jane Ford*, pp. 252–60.

60. *Chandler v. United States* (171 F. (2d) 921 (C.C.A. 1st 1948), affirming 72 F. Supp. 231 (D. Mass. 1947); certiorari denied, 336 U.S. 918 (1949); rehearing denied, 336 U.S. 947 (1949).

61. Nathaniel Weyl, *Treason: The Story of Disloyalty and Betrayal in American History* (Washington, D.C.: Public Affairs Press, 1950), p. 381. See also James Willard Hurst, *The Law of Treason in the United States: Collected Essays* (Westport, CT: Greenwood Press, 1971 [1945]).

62. *Martin v. Young*, 134 F. Supp. 204, 207, 208 (N.D. Cal. 1955); *Thompson v. Whittier*, 185 F. Supp. 306, 314, 315 (Dist. Ct. D.C. 1960). See Loane, "Treason and Aiding the Enemy," *Military Law Review* 43, 62 (1965), and Ruddy, "Permissible Dissent and Treason," 4 *Criminal Law Bulletin* 145, 151–153 (1968).

63. Quoted in John Edward Weems, *To Conquer a Peace: The War Between the United States and Mexico* (Garden City, NY: Doubleday, 1974), p. 71.

64. Weems, pp. 71–72.

65. Quoted in Wayne S. Cole, *Roosevelt and the Isolationists, 1932–45* (Lincoln: University of Nebraska Press, 1983), pp. 420–21.

66. Charles A. Beard, *President Roosevelt and the Coming of the War, 1941: A Study in Appearances and Realities* (New Haven: Yale University Press, 1948), pp. iii–iv, 551, 573, 574, 591, 595.

67. Quoted in Wayne S. Cole, *Roosevelt and the Isolationists, 1932–1945* (Lincoln: University of Nebraska Press, 1983), p. 193.

68. Ramsey Clark, *The Fire This Time: U.S. War Crimes in the Gulf* (Emeryville, CA: Thunder's Mouth Press), p. 199.

69. Clark, pp. 270–71.

70. Michael Walzer, *Just and Unjust Wars: A Moral Argument with Historical Illustrations* (New York: Basic Books, 1977), pp. 100, 292.

71. Kurt Vonnegut, comment for Clark.

72. Elizabeth Drew, "Letter from Washington," *The New Yorker*, Feb. 4, 1991, p. 83.

73. Drew, pp. 82–83.

74. Charles Potts, *How the South Finally Won the Civil War and Controls the Political Future of the United States* (Walla Walla, WA: Tsunami Press, 1995), p. 307.

75. Potts, p. 252.

76. Potts, p. 295.

77. Potts, p. 14.

78. Gail Collins, "Who's Afraid of the Big Bad Balkan Quagmire?" *New York Times*, April 19, 1999, p. A26.

79. Quoted in Paul Hollander, *Political Pilgrims: Travels of Western Intellectuals to the Soviet Union, China, and Cuba, 1928–1978* (New York: Oxford University Press, 1981), p. 198.

Chapter 7. Was the Vietnam War Unjust?

1. Alasdair MacIntyre, *After Virtue: A Study in Moral Theory* (Notre Dame: University of Notre Dame Press, 1981, p. 6.

2. MacIntyre, p. 8, n. 1.

3. Ludwig Dehio, *Germany and World Politics in the Twentieth Century* (New York: W. W. Norton, 1959), pp. 76–77.

4. Dan Smith, *The State of War and Peace Atlas* (New York: Penguin, 1997), pp. 24–25.

5. Charles Tilly, *Coercion, Capital, and European States, A.D. 990–1992* (Cambridge, MA: Blackwell, 1992), pp. 180, 201.

6. Michael Walzer, *Just and Unjust Wars: A Moral Argument with Historical Illustrations* (New York: Basic Books, 1977), pp. 100, 292.

7. Committee of Concerned Asian Scholars, *The Indochina Story* (New York: Random House, 1970), p. 35.

8. George McTurnan and John W. Lewis, *The United States in Vietnam* (New York: Dial Press, 1967), pp. 108, 119.

9. U.S. Department of State, "Aggression from the North: The Record of North Viet-Nam's Campaign to Conquer South Viet-Nam" (Washington, D.C.: U.S. Government Printing Office, 1965), p. 20.

10. Nguyen Khac-Vien, interview from Vietnam Press, Foreign Language Publishing House (Hanoi, 1978); quoted in Truong Nhu Tang, *A Viet Cong Memoir* (New York: Random House, 1985), p. 20.

11. Frank Gibney, *Korea's Quiet Revolution: From Garrison State to Democracy* (New York: Waller, 1992), p. 28.

12. Tilly, p. 213.

13. "American Guilt: An Interview with Richard Falk," in Grace Sevy, ed., *The American Experience in Vietnam* (Norman: University of Oklahoma Press, 1989), p. 244.

14. Don Oberdorfer, *The Two Koreas: A Contemporary History* (Reading, MA: Addison-Wesley, 1997), p. 41.

15. "News of the Week in Review," *New York Times*, Aug. 5, 1990.

16. *New York Newsday*, Mar. 29, 1991.

17. "For Veterans, A Prouder Time," *New York Times*, Nov. 11, 1991.

18. Truong Nhu Tang, p. 289.

19. Bui Tin, *Following Ho Chi Minh: The Memoirs of a North Vietnamese Colonel* (Honolulu: University of Hawaii Press, 1995) p. 192.

20. Bui Tin, pp. 106–7.

21. Bui Tin, p. 99.

22. Bui Tin, p. xiii.

23. Walzer, p. 99.

24. Quoted in Oberdorfer, p. 1.

25. Joseph Buttinger, *Vietnam: A Dragon Embattled*, vol. 1. (New York: Praeger, 1967).

26. Quoted in Loren Goldner, "The Anti-Colonial Movement in Vietnam," *New Politics* (Summer 1997), p. 141.

27. Joseph Buttinger, *Vietnam: A Political History* (New York: Praeger, 1965), pp. 256–60.

28. John Colvin, *Giap: Volcano Under Snow* (New York: Soho Press, 1996), pp. 50–51.

29. Cecil B. Currey, *Victory At Any Cost* (Washington: Brassey's, 1997), p. 126.

30. Colvin, p. 51.

31. Currey, p. 119.

32. "Pentagon Papers," U.S. Department of Defense, United States-Vietnamese Relations, 1945–1967 (Washington, D.C.: U.S. Government Printing Office, 1971), vol. I, pt. IC, C-5.

33. Gabriel Kolko, *Anatomy of a War: Vietnam, the United States, and the Modern Historical Experience* (New York: The New Press, 1994), p. 87–89 (emphasis added).

34. Bui Tin, pp. 37–38.

35. Quoted in Bui Tin, p. 18.

36. Quoted in Neil L. Jamieson, *Understanding Vietnam* (Berkeley: University of California Press, 1993), p. 372.

37. Doan Van Toai with David Chanoff, *The Vietnamese Gulag* (New York: Simon and Schuster, 1986), p. 234.

38. Peter L. Berger, "Indo-China and the American Conscience," *Commentary* (February 1980), pp. 29–39.

39. William Prochnau, *Once Upon a Distant War* (New York: Random House, 1995), p. 26.

40. George H. Roeder, Jr., *The Censored War: American Visual Experience During World War Two* (New Haven: Yale University Press, 1993), p. 134.

41. Eric Sevareid, *Not So Wild a Dream* (New York: Atheneum, 1976), pp. 388–89.

42. Philip Knightley, *The First Casualty* (New York: Harcourt Brace Jovanovich, 1975), p. 294.

43. Richard Hammer, *One Morning in the War* (New York: Coward-McCann, 1970), p. 176.

44. Quoted in B. G. Burkett and Glenna Whitley, *Stolen Valor: How the Vietnam Generation was Robbed of its Heroes and its History* (Dallas: Verity Press, 1998), p. 117.

45. Robert A. Pape, *Bombing to Win: Air Power and Coercion in War* (Ithaca, NY: Cornell University Press, 1996), p. 190.

46. John Prados, *The Hidden History of the Vietnam War* (Chicago: Ivan R. Dee, 1995), p. 190.

47. Pape, pp. 145, 160–63, 347.

48. Quoted in Martin F. Herz, *The Prestige Press and the Christmas Bombing, 1972: Image and Reality in Vietnam* (Washington, D.C.: Ethics and Public Policy Center, 1980), p. 41.

49. Quoted in Al Hemingway, "Into the Teeth of the Tiger," *VFW*, December 1997, p. 28.

50. Cited in Herz, p. 47.

51. Hemingway, p. 28.

52. Telford Taylor, quoted in John Morocco, *Rain of Fire: Air War, 1969–1973: The Vietnam Experience* (Boston: Boston Publishing, 1985), p. 157.

53. John Orme, "The Utility of Force in a World of Scarcity," *International Security* (Winter 1997/98), pp. 146–47, 152.

54. Orme, p. 147.

55. Orme, p. 152.

56. Jeffrey Record, *Hollow Victory* (McLean, VA: Brassey's, 1993), p. 84.

57. Tad Szulc, *The Illusion of Peace: Foreign Policy in the Nixon Years* (New York: Viking Press, 1978), pp. 46–47.

58. Richard A. Hunt, *Pacification: The American Struggle for Vietnam's Hearts and Minds* (Boulder: Westview Press, 1995), p. 240.

59. Mark Moyar, *Phoenix and the Birds of Prey: The CIA's Secret Campaign to Destroy the Viet Cong* (Annapolis: Naval Institute Press, 1997), pp. 226–27.

60. Hunt, pp. 240–41.

61. On the South Vietnamese side, responsibility for pacification and population security was divided among the Army of the Republic of Vietnam (ARVN), the Regional and Popular Forces (RF and PF), Civilian Irregular Defense Groups (CIDG), Armed Combat Youth (ACY), and the National Police.

62. Mark Moyar, *Phoenix and the Birds of Prey* (Annapolis, MD: Naval Institute Press, 1997), pp. 228–29.

63. Guenter Lewy, *America in Vietnam* (New York: Oxford University Press, 1978), pp. 301, 446–47, 451.

64. Edward Luttwak, *The Pentagon and the Art of War: The Question of Military Reform* (New York: Simon and Schuster, 1985), p. 37.

65. Quoted in Robert Buzzanco, *Masters of War* (New York: Cambridge University Press, 1996), p. 346.

66. Quoted in Andrew F. Krepinevich, Jr., "Past as Prologue: Counterinsurgency and the U.S. Army's Vietnam Experience in Force Strategy and Doctrine," in George

K. Osborn, Asa A. Clark IV, Daniel J. Kaufman, and Douglas E. Lute, *Democracy, Strategy, and Vietnam: Implications for American Policymaking* (Lexington, MA: Lexington Books, 1987), p. 270.

67. 82nd Congress, 1st sess., Military Situation in the Far East, Part 5, p. 3598; cited in Harry G. Summers, Jr., *On Strategy* (Novato, CA: Presidio, 1982), pp. 37–38.

68. Quoted in Mark Moyar, *Phoenix and the Birds of Prey: The CIA's Secret Campaign to Destroy the Viet Cong* (Annapolis, MD: Naval Institute Press, 1997), p. 291.

69. John M. Collins, "Vietnam Postmortem: A Senseless Strategy," *Parameters*, Vol. III, No. 1, p. 9.

70. John T. McNaughton, "Plan of Action for South Vietnam," March 24, 1965, in George C. Herring, ed., *The Pentagon Papers*, abridged ed. (New York: McGraw-Hill, 1993), pp. 115–18.

71. Lewy, pp. 450–53.

Chapter 8. The Genuine Lessons of the Vietnam War

1. Papers of Lyndon Baines Johnson, Meeting Notes File, Box 1, meeting with General Eisenhower and Others on February 17, 1965, p. 13; quoted in Christopher M. Gacek, *The Logic of Force: The Dilemma of Limited War in American Foreign Policy* (New York: Columbia University Press, 1994), p. 200.

2. William R. Corson, *The Betrayal* (New York: W.W. Norton, 1968), p. 95.

3. The argument made here is influenced by James R. Ward, "Vietnam: Insurgency or War?" in *Military History Review* 69 (January 1989), and Andrew F. Krepinevich, Jr., *The Army and Vietnam* (Baltimore: Johns Hopkins, 1988). Lewis Sorley argues that General Creighton Abrams, who replaced General Westmoreland as the top U.S. commander in Vietnam, achieved superior results beginning in 1968 by replacing Westmoreland's attrition strategy with a "one war" strategy that emphasized pacification and population security. See Lewis Sorley, *A Better War: The Unexamined Victories and Final Tragedy of America's Last Years in Vietnam* (New York: Harcourt, Brace, 1999).

4. Corson, p. 276.

5. Col. Harry G. Summers, Jr., Foreword to Mark Moyar, *Phoenix and the Birds of Prey: The CIA's Secret Campaign to Destroy the Viet Cong* (Annapolis: Naval Institute Press, 1997), p. xi.

6. John A. Nagl, "Learning to Eat Soup with a Knife: British and American Army Counterinsurgency Learning During the Malayan Emergency and the Vietnam War," *World Affairs* Vol. 161, No.4 (Spring 1999), p. 199, n. 41.

7. Randall L. Schweller, *Deadly Imbalances: Tripolarity and Hitler's Strategy of World Conquest* (New York: Columbia University Press, 1998), p. 197.

8. Edward Luttwak, "Toward Post-Heroic Warfare," *Foreign Affairs* (May/June 1995), p. 110.

9. Eliot A. Cohen, "Civil-Military Relations," *Orbis*, Vol. 41, No. 2 (Spring 1997), p. 186.

10. Joseph Schumpeter, *Capitalism, Socialism and Democracy* (London: George Allen & Unwin, 1976 [1942]), p. 261.

11. Daniel Patrick Moynihan, *Secrecy: The American Experience* (New Haven: Yale University Press, 1998).

12. Charles Tilly, *Coercion, Capital, and European States*, A.D. 990–1992 (Cambridge, MA: Blackwell, 1992), p. 74.

13. Quoted in Arthur M. Schlesinger, Jr., "America and the World: Isolationism Resurgent?" *Ethics and International Affairs*, No. 10 (1996), p. 161.

14. Quoted in Yadya Sadowski, "Ethnic Conflict," *Foreign Policy* (Summer 1998), pp. 20–21.

15. John E. Mueller, *War, Presidents and Public Opinion* (New York: John Wiley and Sons, 1973), pp. 169, 171.

Index

Acheson, Dean, 21, 63, 242
Adams, Henry, 125
Adenauer, Konrad, 56
Afghanistan, 4, 27–28, 37, 48, 49, 55, 59, 66, 79*n*, 88, 138, 225, 227, 228, 234
Agent Orange, 175, 252
Aiken, George, 117
Albania, 70
Albright, Madeleine K., 73
Ali, Muhammad, 108
Angola, 28, 37, 38, 48, 49, 119, 138, 180, 261
Antiwar movement, xvii, 20, 21, 109, 113, 207–208, 277
  folklore of, 140–285
Ap Bac, 14
Arab-Israeli War, 26
Arnett, Peter, 176, 246
Asia hands, myth of, 143–146
Association of Southeast Asian Nations (ASEAN), 37

Bahr, Egon, 57
Balance-of-power theory, 55, 58–60, 267. *See also* Maximal realism; Minimal realism
Baldwin, Hanson W., 81
Ball, George, 17, 31, 60, 61, 68, 78–79, 159, 266
Bandwagon effect, 49–55, 58–60, 70, 266, 268. *See also* Maximal realism; Minimal realism
Bao Dai, 11, 148, 242

Barrett, David M., 194
Bartlett, Charles, 132, 134
Barton, Joe, 120
Bay of Pigs invasion, 13, 214
Beard, Charles, 211–212
Bell, Daniel, 127
Bensel, Richard Franklin, 113
Berger, Peter, 245
Berlin crisis of 1961, 5, 13, 42, 56, 66, 80, 88, 200
Berlin Wall, 70
Berman, Larry, 194
Berman, Paul, 109
Bernard, Carl, 97
Berrigan brothers, 110
Betts, Richard, 107
Biersteker, Thomas J., 163–165
Binh Xuyen, 11, 242
Bismarck, Otto von, 63
Black Americans, 107–108, 272
Blair, Tony, xiv
Blight, James G., 163–165
Bolshevism, 62, 63, 110, 142
Borah, William E., 114, 118, 126
Bradford, M.E., 129
Brandt, Willy, 56–57
Bretton Woods system, 26, 205–206
Brewster, Daniel, 190
Brezhnev, Leonid, 23, 48, 89, 131, 264
Brigham, Robert K., 163–165
Brinkley, David, 196–197
Brooks, Preston S., 112
Browder, Earl, 208